MONITORING THE OUTCOMES OF ECONOMIC DEVELOPMENT PROGRAMS

Harry P. Hatry
Mark Fall
Thomas O. Singer
E. Blaine Liner

MONITORING THE OUTCOMES OF ECONOMIC DEVELOPMENT PROGRAMS: A Manual

THE URBAN INSTITUTE PRESS
Washington, D.C.

THE URBAN INSTITUTE PRESS
2100 M Street, N.W.
Washington, D.C. 20037

Library of Congress Cataloging in Publication Data

Monitoring the Outcomes of Economic Development Programs:
A Manual / Harry P. Hatry . . . [et al.]

1. Economic development projects--Maryland--Evaluation. 2. Industrial promotion--Maryland--Evaluation. 3. Economic development projects--Minnesota--Evaluation. 4. Industrial Promotion--Minnesota--Evaluation. 5. Economic development projects--United States--Evaluation. 6. Industrial promotion--United States--Evaluation. I. Hatry, Harry P.

HC107.M33E446 1990 90-12733
338.975'0068--dc20 CIP

ISBN 0-87766-488-9 (alk. paper)

Urban Institute books are printed on acid-free paper whenever possible.

Printed in the United States of America.

9 8 7 6 5 4 3 2 1
Distributed by:

University Press of America

4720 Boston Way
Lanham, MD 20706

3 Henrietta Street
London WC2E 8LU ENGLAND

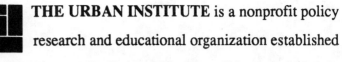

THE URBAN INSTITUTE is a nonprofit policy research and educational organization established in Washington, D.C., in 1968. Its staff investigates the social and economic problems confronting the nation and government policies and programs designed to alleviate such problems. The Institute disseminates significant findings of its research through the publications program of its Press. The Institute has two goals for work in each of its research areas: to help shape thinking about societal problems and efforts to solve them, and to improve government decisions and performance by providing better information and analytic tools.

Through work that ranges from broad conceptual studies to administrative and technical assistance, Institute researchers contribute to the stock of knowledge available to public officials and private individuals and groups concerned with formulating and implementing more efficient and effective government policy.

Conclusions or opinions expressed in Institute publications are those of the authors and do not necessarily reflect the views of other staff members, officers or trustees of the Institute, advisory groups, or any organizations that provide financial support to the Institute.

ACKNOWLEDGMENTS

Our work would not have been possible without the participation of the two pilot states, Maryland and Minnesota. In Maryland, J. Randall Evans, Secretary of Economic and Employment Development, and Deputy Secretary Michael S. Lofton provided the leadership and resources needed to make the project successful. In Minnesota, this leadership was provided by David J. Speer, Commissioner of the Department of Trade and Economic Development and Jayne Khalifa, Chief of Staff.

Within the Maryland Department of Economic and Employment Development, Robert G. Schult, Director of the Office of Program Analysis and Audit, provided overall coordination for the project, including managing the efforts of working groups of department managers and staff in each of four program areas. The tourism working group was headed by Daniel McCleod, Director of the Office of Tourism Development, with the assistance of Peter Chambliss. John Fitzpatrick, Association Director of the Maryland Industrial Development Financing Authority (MIDFA), facilitated the efforts of the Finance Program working group, with the support of Benjamin Hackerman, Executive Director of MIDFA, and Stanley Tucker, Executive Director of the Maryland Small Business Development Financing Authority. Harold Zassenhaus, Executive Director of the Office of International Trade, headed the international trade working group with the assistance of Andrew Gordon. The working group was facilitated by Herbert Thweatt with the assistance of Campbell Johnson, then Chief of the Marketing Resources section of the Division of Business Development, and with the support of James Peiffer, Division Director. Robert Schoeplein, Director of the Office of Research, participated in several aspects of the overall project.

Within the Minnesota Department of Trade and Economic Development, Lee Munnich, Assistant Commissioner of the Policy Analysis, Science and Technology Division, and Dan Quillin, Director of the Office of Information Services for that division, provided overall coordination for the project, including overseeing the efforts of four program working groups. The Business Promotion Division, under the leadership of Bob de la Vega, had two working groups headed by office directors. The Star Cities and Economic Development Technical Program working group was headed by Harry Rosefelt, Director of the Development Resources Office. Charles Schaffer, Director of the Department's Small Business Assistance Office, headed the second working group. The Minnesota Trade Office had one working group covering all its programs. Both P. Richard Bohr, Executive Director of the Minnesota Trade Office, and James Jarvis, Assistant Commissioner, provided valuable leadership and support to this working group. In the Community Development Division, Bob Benner, Deputy Director, and Mike Auger, Director of the Small Cities Development Program, headed the efforts of the working group on the state's Economic Development Grant Program. In addition, Hank Todd, Director of the Minnesota Office of Tourism, and Linda Limback, Manager of the Office's Information Services Unit, provided helpful suggestions.

Major participants in the Minnesota pilot were Dr. Robert Kudrle and Cynthia Kite of the University of Minnesota. Both played major parts, especially on the development of the procedures for minority export promotion programs.

We are also grateful to Nancy Belden of Belden Associates in Washington, D.C. and Arsen Darnay, a Minnesota private consultant, who were facilitators for the client focus groups in Maryland and Minnesota, respectively.

A special note of thanks is due the many employees of both the Maryland and Minnesota Departments who helped immeasurably in each of the working groups, as well as those who provided the analytic and data processing support that made the project a success.

A number of individuals helped shape our research and findings. We would like to acknowledge the members of the national advisory committee to the project: Henry Blekicki, New Jersey Department of Commerce and Economic Development; R. Scott Fosler, Committee for Economic Development; Larry Ledebur, University of South Carolina; Dan Pilcher, National Conference of State Legislatures; and Ralph Widner, Fairfax House International. Our project officer at the Economic Development Administration, Richard Hage, provided invaluable guidance and encouragement, and Ken Voytek, of the Michigan Department of Commerce, contributed significantly to the concept and the methodology while he was an Urban Institute staff member.

Finally, we are very grateful to the U.S. Department of Commerce's Economic Development Administration, the Aetna Life and Casualty Foundation, J. Howard Pew Freedom Trust, and Northwest Area Foundation for their financial support for this work.

CONTENTS

List of Exhibits

ABSTRACT

State and local governments have increased their focus on investments in economic development in recent years. With increased effort comes increased desire to determine the quality and results of that effort. Managers need to be able to regularly identify the strengths and weaknesses of individual programs. Yet, effective means for assessment of program quality and outcomes are lacking.

The Urban Institute and the States of Maryland and Minnesota undertook the task of designing a performance monitoring system for selected, major economic development programs. The performance monitoring procedures presented here are aimed at helping economic development offices improve their programs and increase their accountability. Maryland and Minnesota served as the test states. The techniques prepared for and with these two states are condensed and presented so that other states or local governments can adapt these procedures to their own needs.

Performance indicators and associated data collection procedures were developed for the following economic development programs: a) business attraction/marketing; b) business assistance; c) export promotion; d) business financing; e) community economic development; and f) tourism promotion. The primary data sources recommended,in addition to agency records, are surveys of clients of the programs and the state's unemployment insurance information data base.

The manual includes material designed to help economic development managers understand the methodology, cost, and implementation of the suggested procedures. Recommended questionnaires and report formats are included for each of the six programs. Recommendations are also provided about the analysis and presentation of the outcome information, uses for regular outcome information, roles of the various economic development organizational levels, and steps for starting up a performance monitoring process.

1

INTRODUCTION

■

PURPOSE

The need for procedures to monitor the quality and outcomes of economic development programs has been apparent for many years. Critics often question claims of jobs created or of other benefits of state and local efforts to attract new plants or expand existing companies. Legislators perennially call for audits of economic development expenditures to ensure that their budget allocations are spent effectively. Development administrators worry over chronic questions about displacement of existing jobs as a result of their efforts, or the sometimes thin connection between cause and effect in their work. Yet, effective performance monitoring systems have not been developed and used by most economic development agencies.

Between 1982 and 1988 there was a 400 percent increase in state economic development budgets, with the average state outlay increasing from $4,700,000 in 1982 to about $20,000,000 in 1988. It is almost axiomatic that along with these elevated expenditures has come a stronger desire on the part of legislators, budget analysts, and administrators to determine the outcome of this spending. State and local economic development program managers need to be able to identify the strengths and weaknesses of individual economic development programs as a first step to improving program quality. But assessment of economic outcomes is not a simple task, given the complexity of the economic environment and the lack both of generally accepted performance monitoring procedures and of generally accepted outcome measures.

Many states have experimented in a limited fashion with performance monitoring. Efforts include ad hoc projections of future employment made by businesses receiving state assistance, accounts of program results and service quality obtained through surveys of clients, and informal, anecdotal information. Such efforts have usually been sporadic, insufficiently comprehensive, unsystematic, or unreliable. We believe that recent advances in data processing and the emergence of low-cost survey techniques now enable states to make practical and useful advances in regular monitoring of the outcomes of their economic development programs.

The performance monitoring procedures presented in this manual offer a set of standard performance indicators tailored to each of the major economic development program areas. They incorporate periodic client surveys that provide detailed primary data about program use and impact. The measurement procedures are relatively easy to implement and are designed to be institutionalized, to provide regular ongoing monitoring information at regular intervals throughout the year, and permit year to year comparisons.

This manual presents procedures for monitoring most traditional economic development initiatives of state and local governments, such as business attraction, export promotion, tourism, community development, and other programs widely used to enhance or promote state and local economies. Sample survey questionnaires and reporting formats are included. Although the manual was developed for state governments and with direct involvement of state personnel, most of the suggested procedures seem equally applicable to local government economic development programs. The procedures are based on a series of pilot tests undertaken by the states of Maryland and Minnesota, and The Urban Institute.

This manual focuses on indicators of program quality and outcomes. The indicators are measures of the outcomes a program seeks to bring about, or of the quality of the services provided. To be useful, these performance indicators should be readily understandable and relevant.

The manual presents performance indicators and appropriate monitoring procedures for the following major state economic development programs:

1. Business attraction
2. Assistance to existing businesses
3. Financial assistance
4. Tourism promotion
5. Export promotion
6. Community economic development assistance

The intent of these procedures is to provide information that allows program managers (and their staffs), higher-level development administrators, governors, and legislators to assess regularly the performance of governmental programs for economic development. These procedures help to provide more valid and more accurate information on program quality and outcomes than is usually available to public officials. Most important, the data can assist economic development managers to improve their programs by providing a fuller picture of the results of their economic development expenditures, as well as supportable evidence relating to the quality and timeliness of services.

■

APPROACH

The monitoring procedures outlined here depart from tradition in three basic ways. First, the procedures rely, to a considerable extent, on information provided by agency clients. As such, many of the procedures can be viewed as providing a client-based assessment of performance. Second, the procedures are designed to be incorporated into the normal operations of the development agency, so as to provide regular, periodic reports that, over time, can be used to identify trends in performance. Third, the suggested performance indicators include both "intermediate" and "end" outcomes. From a program management point of view, information on intermediate outcomes is important and can be acted on even though information on end outcomes, like jobs, may not be available. The intermediate indicators highlight *actions taken by clients* that are accepted as being significant steps toward achievement of the longer-term end results, such as increased jobs. Many program actions will not necessarily lead to the end results for many months. But program managers and other agency officials need to be able to track significant intermediate progress. For example, administrators are interested in knowing if a state agency's seminar on export trade convinced a firm to begin seeking foreign markets for its products.

The procedures were developed through an approach that included:

- Advice from a panel of a number of nationally recognized experts in economic development;
- A review and analysis of the performance monitoring or auditing methods used in the past for economic development programs by state executive and legislative offices;
- Nine focus groups with clients of economic development programs to identify the attributes clients believe should be considered as indicators of the quality and outcomes of economic development services;
- Extensive interviews and discussions with program managers in Maryland and Minnesota to identify what they considered to be proper and palatable outcomes of their activities;
- Work by eight teams of state program officers for a period of about one year in Maryland and Minnesota. The teams helped select the indicators and data gathering procedures. Each team focused on a different agency program; and
- Testing of data gathering procedures for each of the eight pilot programs by the two states.

■

COVERAGE

The system was designed to provide regular feedback on service *outcomes* and service *quality*. It does *not* include measurements of:

- Activity levels, such as the number of trade shows conducted, loans processed, or newsletters mailed;
- Actual expenditures (perhaps as compared to budgeted amounts for each program); or
- Efficiency and productivity measures--that is, information that relates inputs (such as staff and appropriations) to outputs (such as jobs created). A fully comprehensive performance monitoring system would incorporate these measures to provide a balanced and total picture of departmental operations. This effort, however, concentrated on service quality and outcomes.

■

BASIC CHARACTERISTICS OF THE PROCEDURES

An analysis of current performance monitoring among the states, supplemented by focus group discussions and deliberations with program managers, resulted in the adoption of 12 key characteristics as criteria for the development of the measurement procedures.

1. *The performance monitoring system should focus on service outcomes and quality.* The major gap in information available to executive and legislative branch leadership is quantitative evidence on service outcomes and quality. Public economic development agencies seek to provide services in a timely, informed, and helpful manner (service quality), and to achieve their principal functional objectives of improving the jurisdiction's economy or client competitiveness, as measured by basic indicators like increases in numbers of jobs. Thus, the performance measurement procedures described in this manual focus on indicators of service quality and outcomes.

2. *The performance monitoring system should focus on helping program managers improve their operations.* Managers and administrators need relevant, detailed information to help guide them in making program improvements. In addition, however, the procedures should permit top officials and policymakers to obtain summary data needed for policymaking and accountability purposes.

3. *The procedures should provide frequent and timely performance information.* To be of maximum utility to program managers, the procedures should be designed to measure performance as soon as possible after service delivery but not before enough time has elapsed for at least some major results to occur. Different intervals are appropriate for different programs. Feedback as infrequent as once yearly was deemed too long a wait to be useful to operating managers.

4. *The performance monitoring procedures for individual programs should focus on the outcomes accruing to clients of program services (businesses and communities).* Economic development agencies serve only a small percentage of the state's businesses in a given year. (It is doubtful that more than 1 percent of businesses receive economic development agency assistance in any year.) Therefore, the performance monitoring procedures should focus on gathering data on those businesses or communities for which the agency provided services. This contrasts with traditional reliance upon secondary employment and wage data for all firms in a jurisdiction or data that measure "business climate" or "economic conditions."

An exception to this principle is the need in some cases to obtain information from nonusers of program services to ascertain reasons for nonuse of the services, which can be of considerable importance to agency managers.

5. *Multiple performance indicators are needed to assess service quality and outcomes.* Numerous aspects of service quality and outcomes are relevant to program managers and their clients. Single performance indicators will seldom, if ever, be adequate and are more likely to be misleading than informative. The performance indicators offered for each program in this manual are

expected to cover aspects of program quality and outcomes that are of most interest to economic development officials. However, we recognize the possibility that additional indicators tailored to the circumstances of a particular state may be needed. Managers should review their program's goals and objectives, as outlined in the program's enabling legislation, statements by the governor and agency director, program mission statements, budget documents, and so on, to ensure that all important aspects of program quality and outcomes are being monitored.

6. *Nontraditional data sources, such as client surveys and unemployment insurance data, are needed, and should be used to help assess service quality and outcomes.* Program records normally maintained by economic development agencies seldom include information on service quality and outcomes. At best, program managers are usually limited to informal and anecdotal indications of service quality and secondary data for indications of outcomes. The sources and unsystematic nature of this information are of dubious validity and are accepted only reluctantly by most policymakers.

7. *Performance indicators should include both "intermediate" and "end" outcomes.* Although increased numbers of jobs, sales, and wages are usually accepted as the major end objectives of economic development agencies, these outcomes are often slow to materialize, and even more slowly recorded. Program managers should have access to information on actions taken by their clients as a result of program services that represent significant performance *toward* increases in jobs, sales, and wages. Such indicators in this report are labeled "intermediate" outcome indicators. For example, if the work of the export promotion program encourages businesses to establish overseas market contacts, these actions by the businesses can be considered as progress and can be counted as intermediate outcomes.

The intermediate outcome indicators offered for each program were derived from reviews of previous monitoring efforts, interviews with program managers, focus groups with program clients, and project team members' own professional judgment. (Data gathered by the performance monitoring system can, in the future, be used to test their correlation with end outcomes, providing an empirical basis for the validity and reliability of specific intermediate outcome indicators.)

8. *The procedures should include indicators that attempt to show the extent of the contribution of agency assistance to the outcome(s) reported by clients.* A continuing problem in most, if not all, program evaluations and performance measurement systems is that of determining the extent to which a program's service *caused* successful outcomes. Causality has been, and will continue to be, a difficult issue in economic development. For example, controlled experiments are seldom feasible. The performance monitoring procedures in this manual take a step toward assessing causality by obtaining feedback from clients on the extent to which they believed the agency's services contributed to reported outcomes. Although not conclusive, this feedback can be considered relevant and instructive. Agencies adopting the performance monitoring procedures will be able to use the data collected over time to undertake special statistical analyses to obtain more conclusive evidence of association.

9. *The system should provide breakouts that array service quality and outcome indica-*

tors by client characteristics. Program managers need service quality data and outcome information broken out by key client characteristics, such as region or county, industry group (SIC, standard industrial classification), size of firm, and other characteristics. These breakouts will vary from program to program. For example, export promotion program managers may want to see service quality and outcomes broken out by the types of services received (counseling, catalog shows, trade missions, etc.) and tabulated against other characteristics of the firms (region, size of firm, industry group, etc.). This enhanced level of information allows program managers to assess the extent to which they are successfully serving different categories of clients, so that they can improve services as necessary to specific categories.

10. *The system should provide comparisons of performance for previous years, for target levels, and across categories of clients.* The ability to compare performance over time or across categories of clients, and to judge progress toward targets or goals, will allow program managers to gauge whether their efforts are closing on goals or whether they are falling behind the desired level of performance. This feature is particularly valuable in monitoring specific program targets, such as distressed areas or particular industrial sectors. Comparisons with other states or local governments, however, will be possible only if the other states (or local governments) have compatible performance monitoring procedures.

11. *The system should include explanatory factors as well as performance data.* Performance data are subject to misinterpretation and misuse. To enhance understanding, data on explanatory factors frequently should be added to the system. Two procedures can be included to achieve these purposes:

a. Program manager review *before* performance data are reported by the program. This enables managers to append explanatory information, rationales, or recommendations for corrective or clarifying steps; and

b. Inclusion of explanatory data along with performance indicator information. For example, a currency exchange rate index reported along with export promotion performance indicators should enhance interpretation.

12. *The data collection and management procedures should be designed to be as inexpensive as possible and to keep demands on personnel time to a minimum.* If the performance monitoring procedures are viewed as onerous or cumbersome by agency personnel, the system will not achieve its objective. The data collection procedures have been designed to be low cost. (We estimate that an operational system will require the equivalent of approximately two full-time, mostly clerical, personnel.)

■

LIMITATIONS OF THESE PERFORMANCE MEASUREMENT PROCEDURES

The information that economic development agencies can obtain from the measurement procedures presented in this manual has the following important limitations. These should be recognized by agencies implementing such procedures, to avoid overexpectations and subsequent disappointment.

1. The information provides outcome information but does *not* provide in-depth evaluations of program activities. It does not provide definitive information on the extent to which the program itself has caused the outcomes identified by the procedures. (The procedures, however, provide some clues, such as ratings of clients on the extent of the contribution of the program to successful outcomes.)

2. Similarly, the information obtained does not identify the causes of increased, or decreased, outcomes. The information obtained provides clues, such as client responses to open-ended questions about reasons for low outcomes. However, more in-depth program evaluation will be needed both to determine causes and to estimate the extent of the program's own contribution (see #1 above).

3. With one exception, the procedures do not address the overall impact of the jurisdiction's programs on the jurisdiction's overall economy. Many agencies, policies, and programs outside the economic development agency will affect the jurisdiction's overall jobs and income situation. Most of the procedures described here are aimed at assessing the quality and outcomes of individual economic development programs. (The exception is Section 8, "Global Indicators," which provides suggestions on reporting statewide performance information.)

4. This manual does not provide procedures for translating outcomes into indicators of productivity, that is, for relating outcomes to the amount of input (such as the number of jobs created per dollar of expenditures). The data from the procedures, however, should provide more valid information for subsequently making such calculations.

■

STRUCTURE OF THIS MANUAL

Performance monitoring procedures for the major programs of economic development agencies are presented in the following six sections of this manual. Each section presents candidate performance indicators, a discussion of recommended data collection procedures, examples of data collection instruments (questionnaires) that agencies can use as starting points for their own procedures (based on pilot tests in Maryland and Minnesota), and suggested reporting formats. Procedures are presented for six major program areas: business attraction (Section 2), business assistance (Section 3), financial assistance (Section 4), tourism promotion (Section 5), export promotion (Section 6), and community development assistance (Section 7).

Subsequent sections of the manual address other important measurement issues, including: jurisdiction-wide "global" performance indicators (Section 8), client survey procedures (Section 9), procedures for obtaining performance indicator information from the unemployment insurance database (Section 10), suggested ways to analyze and present the outcome information (Section 11), the roles and responsibilities for an ongoing performance measurement system (Section 12), and a discussion of the various uses of outcome information (Section 13). The manual concludes with suggestions on how to start up a performance monitoring program in an agency (Section 14).

Program personnel should read not only the section relevant to their own program but also the relevant sections on client surveys and/or unemployment insurance data procedures, analysis and reporting, and uses of outcome information.

2

BUSINESS ATTRACTION PROGRAMS

■

SCOPE

Business attraction programs are designed to identify and attract new businesses interested in locating in a state or substate jurisdiction. These programs undertake such activities as: providing interested firms with information, including details on the jurisdiction economic and social conditions; identification of particular sites in the jurisdiction suitable to the client's needs; providing details on local labor supply and information about quality-of-life characteristics, such as the quality of local educational institutions and available housing; and serving as a liaison with other departments to solve problems, such as those related to government regulations. Often, these programs work with economic development officials at other governmental levels to assist a firm in locating in that jurisdiction.

These programs may focus on attracting new manufacturing or high-technology companies, or other types of firms a jurisdiction feels are particularly valuable (because of their likelihood to rapidly increase in size and profitability, or because they match well with the resources available in the jurisdiction). A program may try to attract firms that have similar resource needs to firms already in the state, or companies that will utilize the products of the state's existing manufacturers to produce a new value-added product. Programs may also target certain regions in the state for development or particular categories of workers, such as minorities or those displaced by structural changes in the economy (e.g., automobile workers or steelworkers).

These programs also link firms with other state or local financial assistance programs that can provide incentives to attract new firms. These incentives might include loans, loan guarantees, bonds, tax abatements, or job training funds provided to induce a firm to locate in the jurisdiction. This manual discusses these incentives in Section 4, "Financial Assistance Programs."

Business attraction can be aimed at firms from other states or from other countries. The latter is usually handled by a separate program, sometimes as part of an international trade program, and has a number of special considerations. This section focuses on attracting businesses coming from within the United States. At the end of this section, however, we discuss special considerations for monitoring programs aimed at attracting business investments from other countries.

The objectives of these programs are to: (1) increase the number and quality of jobs by attracting new firms to the state or local community; (2) increase revenues through taxes generated from greater economic activity resulting from new firm locations; and (3) improve the state's image as a place to conduct business.

There are some concerns that the agency should consider when evaluating performance, but these are not included here as part of regular performance monitoring. These include: (1) the amount of displacement of existing workers resulting from attracting new firms in competing industries; (2) effects on air, water, and noise pollution from new facilities; (3) possible congestion effects in the location chosen by the firm; (4) the extent to which the new jobs are held by persons from outside the jurisdiction and (5) the quality of the jobs brought to the state and the extent to which they upgrade employment opportunities. These elements should also be assessed periodically, but the assessments probably need to be done by special studies rather than through performance monitoring procedures.

■

PERFORMANCE INDICATORS FOR BUSINESS ATTRACTION AND MARKETING PROGRAMS

The candidate performance indicators for business attraction and marketing activities are listed in Exhibit 2.1. The indicators are separated into three groupings: indicators of service quality, intermediate outcomes, and end outcomes. The exhibit also indicates the potential sources of data for each indicator. Each indicator is described next.

Indicators of Service Quality

Service quality indicators provide program managers with client assessments of various characteristics of program services. To add detail to these service quality ratings, the program should include open-ended questions in its survey of businesses, asking for reasons why services were rated as fair or poor.

The primary source for this information and many of the remaining indicators is a periodic survey of businesses that have been assisted. A sample questionnaire is presented in Exhibit 2.2.

PI-1,[1] the percentage of clients who rated the timeliness of each service they received as excellent or good, rather than fair or poor, provides an estimate of the responsiveness of the program's services from the client's perspective. This is particularly crucial for services providing information that may determine whether a client will further consider a potential site. If the program cannot provide timely information, it may be out of the running regardless of the attractiveness of a location.

PI-2, the percentage of clients who rated the overall helpfulness of each service they received as excellent or good, provides a way for the program to gauge how helpful its services are in meeting the needs of its clients, as perceived by the clients themselves. This information will be particularly helpful when broken out by such elements as region from which the request for information has come. Low ratings for certain services, for example, might indicate problems with the way a certain service is provided. Low overall ratings for helpfulness may indicate that necessary services are not being provided, or that, relative to other states or other local agencies, the services are not being provided in a way useful to the client.

The agency might also want to ask clients about other specific characteristics of the services, such as the courteousness (or professionalism) of program staff and the accuracy of the information they received from the program. These can be addressed by adding columns to question 2 of the sample questionnaire (Exhibit 2.2).

In addition to the preceding data, the agency should ask clients giving the fair or poor ratings for reasons why. These responses should be subsequently compiled and examined by program personnel to identify problems and give clues on specific improvements that may be needed.

Intermediate Outcome Indicators

Intermediate outcome indicators are indicators of actions taken by clients that are important steps toward desired outcomes. If they represent significant progress, such intermediate outcomes should be included in the performance monitoring process.

PI-3 is the number of assisted firms that visited the state to assess it as a possible location for a facility. A visit is one necessary step on the path to actually locating a facility. This suggests (but does not guarantee) that the firm was seriously considering locating in the state. If the services provided by the program led to a firm's visit, this would indicate progress. However, it is possible that the agency's assistance had nothing to do with the firm's decision to visit. For example, they may have already decided to visit before the service was received. Thus, this indicator should probably be considered a weak measure.

PI-4, the number of responses to advertising or direct mail solicitations, indicates the initial success of these marketing programs. Advertising or direct mail campaigns are often used to develop leads on potential prospects. These range from advertising in magazines to letters directed to senior officials in a firm. Both usually contain a return response card, telephone number, or other mechanism that will allow the recipient to seek additional information. Tabulating the number of responses to these campaigns provides a partial measure of the success of the program's outreach function, since it gives a count of respondents. However, not all who request information will become prospects.

PI-5, the number of jobs *projected* by assisted businesses at the time of the announcement of their decision to locate in the state, is frequently reported by economic development agencies. These projections have often been used as primary outcome indicators for business attraction programs. Economic development programs obtain estimates of the number of jobs added by firms that received assistance. Programs can obtain these estimates directly from the firms at the time they make their location decision. (Some programs have also obtained the estimate from other levels of government or even the press.) One problem here is that the program may not be obtaining this information in a systematic manner, and the data may not be complete.

Of greater concern, however, is that the number of jobs actually created is likely to differ considerably from the number estimated. However, so long as this indicator is clearly labeled as a projection, not as actual jobs added, it can be justifiably used as an intermediate outcome indicator for the program.

End (Long-term) Outcome Indicators

The long-term outcome indicators for this program include measures relating to jobs added and new capital investment. Indicators are more valid to the extent they consider which program services contributed at what level to their location decision.

PI-6, the number and percentage of assisted firms that subsequently located in the state, and PI-9, the percentage of firms that felt that such assistance had contributed to their location decision, represent the program's "success rate." PI-6 is sometimes referred to as the "conversion rate." However, the assistance provided by the program may not have had a significant effect on the firm's decision to locate. For example, some businesses may have made an inquiry to the program *after* making a location decision. Other firms may have made their decision based almost solely on factors independent of the assistance provided by the economic development agency.

PI-9 attempts to avoid this problem, or at least reduce it, by counting as successes only those firms that, when surveyed, report that the assistance provided did contribute at least somewhat to their location decision. Asking firms to assess whether the services received contributed to their location decision helps to identify those firms for which the assistance was an important factor in their decision to locate.

How accurately respondents can answer a question regarding contribution months later is unclear. (See question 4b in the sample questionnaire (Exhibit 2.2) for an example.) However, respondents to such a question in a recent state of Maryland client survey appeared willing to provide such a rating and to make distinctions as to the level of the state's contribution. Thus, although the information obtained is by no means likely to be 100 percent accurate, the data for this indicator (PI-9) appear to provide more accurate, more valid, information of program performance than in PI-6 (based only on the firm's locational decision).

PI-7 is the number of actual jobs added by assisted firms (a) 12 months and (b) 24 months after their initial contact with the program. PI-10 is the number of jobs added by those firms that also felt that the assistance had contributed to their location decision. Again, not all firms that added the jobs counted by PI-7 will feel that the agency's services were important to their decision to locate. PI-10 indicates the number of jobs added by those firms that report that the assistance contributed to their decision.

State unemployment insurance (UI) programs are also a potentially good source of data for PI-7 and PI-10. UI can provide approximate firm-specific total employment for each month. These data are collected quarterly by states as a federal requirement. There are problems with the lag time for reporting of data and other definitional complexities. For example, data are generally not available to economic development agencies until five to six months after the end of the reporting period, and identifying firms by their names may be difficult. These problems, other considerations, and procedures for use of the database are discussed in Section 10, which covers ui data. (Several state economic development agencies currently have been accessing UI data and experimenting with their application. Whether local governments can also access these data is not clear. However, because the database includes county codes, the data could potentially be useful to local governments as well.)

PI-8, dollars of capital investment made by assisted firms 12 months after the announcement of their location decision, and PI-11, the capital investment dollars spent by assisted firms that felt the assistance they received contributed to their location decision, provide information on investment by new firms. Capital investment is important, in part, because it represents increased property value and tax returns to the state and local governments. Most often, economic development programs have used projections as to the dollar value of investment the firm estimates it will make. (Governmental agencies often ask firms to estimate their capital investment in future years at the time they announce a location decision, usually based on the point when the facility will be at full capacity or at one-, three-, or five-year intervals.) However, PI-8 and PI-11 are intended to provide estimates of the actual amount of investment at a later time, say 12 months afterward, as a more valid indicator of what actually occurred. These data probably need to be collected directly from the client.

PI-12, the percentage of clients locating elsewhere for reasons over which the department had some influence, provides information on firms that did not locate within the jurisdiction. There will be some reasons over which the program has little or no control. However, focusing on reasons that are, at least partially, controllable by the state or local government can provide important information about performance. Responses such as "did not receive sufficient information about the state or locality," or "felt the attitude of program staff was negative" are reasons controllable by the program and can be corrected. On the other hand, the state tax rate or the amount of government regulation are factors not controllable by the program (but can be affected by other parts of state or local government). Information about these reasons can provide the program with valuable policy information.

This information can be obtained directly from firms through client surveys. Question 5b in Exhibit 2.2 illustrates the type of question that clients can be asked. It includes a list of reasons for not locating, about which respondents can be individually asked. There is some question about the ability and willingness of the firms to make candid judgments as to their reasons, but it appears likely that the response will be at least roughly accurate. In addition, substantial changes from year-to-year in the percentage of clients giving particular reasons are likely to warrant program attention.

■

DISAGGREGATIONS OF INDICATOR DATA

Breaking out the data on individual performance indicators by key client or service characteristics will likely add considerably to the usefulness of the outcome information, especially for program managers. The principal disaggregations typically useful for business attraction programs are (1) region of the country from which the firm originated; (2) region of the state (or local government) in which the firm located; (3) size of firm; and (4) industry category (e.g., standard industrial classification (SIC) code.

The region from which the firm originated can be based on states (or counties). Regions should be selected that are of greatest use to program managers, and if certain areas are of special interest, these can be reported individually, with multistate regions used for those areas from which few firms are likely to come.

The size of firms should be based on the number of employees of the company receiving assistance, at the time the assistance was provided, not the employment level of the new facility built in the jurisdiction. The industry category should refer to the primary product to be manufactured at the new facility. In each case the breakouts should be into relatively broad categories so that each category contains more than just a few clients.

Some requests for assistance may come from agents of firms rather than the firms themselves. In those situations where the agents do not provide information on their clients, these agents become another client category of the program. The program may choose not to ask agents to complete the follow-up questionnaire, or, preferably, the questionnaire may be modified to apply to agents rather to the locating businesses.

■

SOURCES FOR PERFORMANCE DATA

There are three sources of data for these indicators (as indicated in Exhibit 2.1): program records, client surveys, and UI data.

Program Records

Program records are needed to provide information for tracking clients (both for client surveys and for use of UI data). Program records also serve as a source of information on client characteristics needed for the disaggregations discussed previously, and for some of the performance indicators (particularly the intermediate outcome indicators). Good management dictates that programs should maintain accurate information on their clients. This should include firm size; industry category; state of origin; services provided; date when firm first received assistance; and basic information such as the firm's name, telephone number, address, and primary contact person. If a firm has located in the jurisdiction, the program should obtain the new address and official name for the new facility. Incorporating this information into the records makes it easier to contact firms for client surveys and to locate firms in the UI database.

Client Surveys

Regular surveys of each of the program's clients are needed for many of the performance indicators as described here and listed in Exhibit 2.1. After a specified time period, such as 12 months from the time a firm begins to receive assistance, the program should survey the firm. For most business attraction programs in the United States, the number of firms that receive assistance is likely to be small enough so that all can be surveyed, rather than having to draw samples.

Information from program records will be needed to conduct the survey: the firm's name, address, telephone number, and the contact person. Additional information from program records is highly desirable to later break out the performance data by various client categories: employment size, industry category, state of origin, a status code (located in the jurisdiction, located elsewhere, no decision yet), where in the jurisdiction the client located (if the client came to the jurisdiction), and an indication of the services received by the client. (Question 2 of Exhibit 2.2 provides an example of service categories.) The program should set the ground rules as to how much assistance justifies inclusion in the survey. A firm that contacted program personnel by telephone only once probably would not have received enough assistance to be included in the survey.

Clients should be surveyed approximately one year after they begin receiving services. This time interval strikes a balance between respondent memory problems and the likelihood that the firm will have had enough time to generate significant outcomes. One year, however, will probably not be sufficient time for firms that located in the jurisdiction to have built up their employment to full levels. UI data can be used to obtain longer-term levels of employment.

The sample questionnaire in Exhibit 2.2 provides an example of the survey questionnaire. However, the questionnaire (especially questions 2a-2h) should be tailored to fit the specific services provided by the particular program. The form should be sent to the primary contact person in the client firm, with a cover letter from a high-level official such as the government's chief executive or department head. Some form of (nonmonetary) incentive, if possible, should also be offered to respondents for completing the questionnaire, such as an appropriate agency publication. (Some economic development agencies have magazines, special periodicals, or "handouts" that might be offered to firms that return the completed questionnaire.)

Section 9, "Client Surveys," provides details on survey procedures and suggestions for increasing response rates. The agency should at least send a second mailing to nonrespondents to achieve an appropriate response rate. Follow-up telephone calls probably should be made if the response rate still does not reach 50 percent.

Regular client surveys can also be used by the program to obtain timely information on other issues of interest. The agency can set aside a small portion of the questionnaire (approximately one to three questions) that can be varied periodically. For example, the program might have recently issued a new publication and want feedback on its impact. A small number of questions could be added to a subsequent questionnaire to seek this information.

State Unemployment Insurance Data

State unemployment insurance data can provide information on the size of employment of firms that located in the state. The program will need to maintain information on the status of clients, to determine which firms should be searched for in the UI database. To find employment data in the UI system, the program should provide the firm's correct name, industry category (SIC code), the county in which the facility is located, and, preferably, the firm's federal or state identification number. Given that information, it should be possible to determine the actual employment of each locating firm for every month since the firm hired its first employees at the facility. The program may choose to track employment for one or more years. To assess the accuracy of these projections, this information can also be compared to employment projections made by firms at the time they make their location decision. If the program also uses client surveys, the information on employment from the surveys can be checked against the UI data. (See Section 10 for further information on unemployment insurance data.)

■

EXPLANATORY DATA

Information that helps explain performance on the indicators might also be included along with the performance information in reports to higher-level officials. Such information typically will address national or international trends that affect the economy generally and are likely to have consequences for the performance of business attraction programs.

National indicators that programs might use to help interpret performance include: the gross national product, prime lending rate, national unemployment rate, corporate profits, personal income, new housing starts, the consumer price index, and manufacturers' shipments and orders for durable goods. These indicators can be reported regularly with the program's performance indicators. Unexpected events that influence the performance of business attraction programs, such as a major catastrophe in the state that could deter efforts to attract industry, should also be reported by the program in its discussion of the results of the performance indicators for a particular time period.

■

REPORTING THE RESULTS

Illustrative report formats for this program are presented in Exhibits 2.3 and 2.4. Exhibit 2.3 displays a table format containing disaggregation for an individual indicator in a "multiple cross-tab" format. Exhibit 2.4 is an example of a *summary* table format containing the major performance indicators and providing comparison information for each indicator. This table format provides comparisons of one time period to another and of actual performance to program targets. (See Section 11, "Analysis and Presentation of Performance Information," for more suggestions on presenting and analyzing the performance information.)

■

SPECIAL ISSUES IN MONITORING PROGRAMS AIMED AT ATTRACTING FOREIGN FIRMS

Many states have programs designed to attract firms from outside the United States. States, and some local governments, have offices in foreign countries, one of whose functions is to assist interested firms and to identify prospects.

These offices are usually staffed by government employees or consultants who are bilingual and familiar with the particular countries.

Most of the procedures described here also apply to programs attempting to attract foreign firms. The sample questionnaire (Exhibit 2.2) can readily be adapted for foreign use. Similarly, the same procedures that use unemployment insurance information to track employment growth for United States firms that locate in the state can be used for foreign firms that locate in the state. Some elements, however, should be treated differently, and include the following:

1. To facilitate a response, the survey questionnaires should be translated into the language of the client. This also makes interpretation and translation of any narrative responses necessary. Translation may complicate data entry and analysis.

2. Feedback response time will likely be longer because of overseas mail. Even if questionnaires are mailed by foreign office personnel, more time will be needed to work out the details and transmit responses to the office processing the returns.

3. The list of foreign firms to be contacted, and contact information, will likely originate from each foreign office. The accuracy of the findings will thus be dependent on the accuracy of the foreign offices in obtaining and recording the information.

4. Surveys of foreign firms are likely to achieve lower response rates than surveys of domestic businesses. This may be, in part, cultural. Certain cultures are less familiar with surveys and may be less willing to respond than American businesses. One partial solution is to survey only those foreign firms that actually locate in the state (or local jurisdiction) and send the questionnaire to the firm's facility in the jurisdiction. The questionnaire should focus on the quality of the service received and the extent of the services' contribution to the firms' decision to locate in the jurisdiction. Obviously, the program would not be able to obtain such information from firms that did not locate in the jurisdiction. This, of course, can introduce a bias into the results, since firms that locate in the jurisdiction are more likely to rate highly the services they received and to have experienced long-term outcomes desired by the program. This approach, however, eliminates the need for translation of the questionnaire and extra survey time.

5. Program personnel should be able to exempt certain firms from participation in the survey in those situations where there are ongoing sensitive negotiations. However, the staff person should provide a written justification for the exclusion. (Requiring written justification helps the program avoid possible later claims that the program manipulated the sample to obtain more favorable responses.)

6. When reporting the outcome information, the program should tabulate the

responses for each of its foreign offices and/or regions of origin, to determine how performance differs among them.

7. Explanatory information that might be provided along with the outcome information probably should include changes in trade regulations, to help explain why performance is different for different foreign offices or regions of the world.

Note, section 2

1. Throughout this manual, individual performance indicators are referenced with the letters PI (performance indicator) and the number of the indicator contained on the relevant exhibit.

EXHIBIT 2.1

PERFORMANCE INDICATORS FOR BUSINESS ATTRACTION AND MARKETING PROGRAMS[1]

Service Quality Indicators:

PI-1 **Percentage of clients who rated the timeliness of each service they received as excellent or good rather than fair or poor (Question 2a, Exhibit 2.2).**

PI-2 **Percentage of clients who rated the helpfulness of each service they received as excellent or good rather than fair or poor (Question 2b, Exhibit 2.2).**

Intermediate Outcome Indicators:

PI-3 **Number of assisted firms that visited the jurisdiction to assess it as a possible location for a facility (program records).**

PI-4 **Number of responses to advertising or direct mail solicitations (program records).**

PI-5 **Number of jobs projected by assisted businesses at the time of the announcement of their decision to locate in the jurisdiction (program records).**

End (Long-term) Outcome Indicators:

PI-6 **Number and percentage of assisted firms that subsequently located in the jurisdiction (program records or Question 3, Exhibit 2.2).**

PI-7 **Number of actual jobs added by assisted locating firms 12 months/24 months after their initial contact with the program (Question 4c of Exhibit 2.2, or unemployment insurance data).**

PI-8 **Dollars of capital investment made by assisted firms 12 months after the announcement of their location decision (Question 4d, Exhibit 2.2).**

PI-9 **Number and percentage of assisted firms that located in the jurisdiction and that felt the assistance contributed to their location decision (Question 4b, Exhibit 2.2).**

Exhibit 2.1 *(continued)*

PI-10 Number of actual jobs added by assisted locating firms 12 months/24 months after their initial contact with the program that felt that the assistance contributed to their location decision (Questions 4b and 4c of Exhibit 2.2, or UI data).

PI-11 Dollars of capital investment made by assisted firms 12 months after the announcement of their location decision that felt that the assistance contributed to their decision (Questions 4b and 4d, Exhibit 2.2).

PI-12 Percentage of clients locating elsewhere for reasons over which the department had some control (Question 5b, Exhibit 2.2).

1. The information in parentheses refers to the source of data for each indicator.

EXHIBIT 2.2

SAMPLE CLIENT QUESTIONNAIRE FOR BUSINESS ATTRACTION PROGRAMS

Our records indicate that your firm received assistance from the Economic Development Department to help you consider [name of jurisdiction] as a place to locate a facility.

1. What initially led your company to consider [jurisdiction] as a place to locate a facility? **(PLEASE CIRCLE ALL THAT APPLY.)**

   [jurisdiction] advertisement in publication.. 1

   Direct Mail advertisements from [jurisdiction].. 2

   Personal Contacts with staff of [jurisdiction's] Economic Development Department............ 3

   Company analysis that indicated [jurisdiction] should be a candidate.................................. 4

   Other (please specify): ____

2. Please rate each of the three following characteristics for *each* service you received from the Economic Development Department. **(PLEASE CIRCLE.)**

   RATING SCALE

1	=	Excellent	3	=	Fair
2	=	Good	4	=	Poor

(continued on next page)

Exhibit 2.2 *(continued)*

Service Received	A. Timeliness of Assistance	B. Overall Helpfulness of the Assistance
a. Information on [jurisdiction's] economic and social conditions..........	1 2 3 4	1 2 3 4
b. Information on buildings and sites in [jurisdiction]. .	1 2 3 4	1 2 3 4
c. Personal assistance with specific problems relevant to your project needs..........	1 2 3 4	1 2 3 4
d. Financial assistance or incentives..........	1 2 3 4	1 2 3 4
e. Job training/employee recruitment assistance..........	1 2 3 4	1 2 3 4
f. Assistance in coordinating with other [jurisdiction] agencies..........	1 2 3 4	1 2 3 4
g. Assistance in coordinating with other [jurisdiction] agencies..........	1 2 3 4	1 2 3 4
h. Other (please specify):	1 2 3 4	1 2 3 4

i. Overall, how would you rate the assistance you received from the Economic Development Department? **(PLEASE CIRCLE ONE.)**

Excellent.......... 1

Good.......... 2

Fair.......... 3

Poor.......... 4

Exhibit 2.2 *(continued)*

j. If you rated any of the above as Fair or Poor, would you please explain why?

3. What is the status of the project for which you received assistance? **(PLEASE CIRCLE ONE.)**

Located in [jurisdiction] .... 1 **(Go to Question 4)**

Located elsewhere .... 2 **(Skip to Question 5)**

Project still active but have not yet made a final decision .... 3 **(Skip to Question 6)**

Project is on hold .... 4 **(Skip to Question 6)**

No longer planning a move or expansion .... 5 **(Skip to Question 6)**

Don't know .... 6 **(Skip to Question 6)**

4. If your project is located in [jurisdiction]:

a. In what city or county did you locate? ____________________

b. Which of these responses is closest to your feeling of the extent to which the assistance you received from the [name of jurisdiction] Economic Development Department *contributed* to your decision to come?

It contributed significantly 1

It contributed somewhat 2

It contributed a little 3

It did not contribute at all 4

Exhibit 2.2 *(continued)*

c. Approximately how many, if any, jobs have you added--owing at least in part to the assistance your company received from [jurisdiction]? (Full-time equivalent employees, please)

0 1

1 to 4 2

5 to 9 3

10 to 19 4

20 to 49 5

50 to 99 6

100 to 249 7

250 to 499 8

500 to 999 9

1,000 and up 10

d. What do you estimate is the total capital investment your company has made at this location up to the current time?

0 1

Less than $99,000 2

$100,000 to $499,000 3

$500,000 to $999,000 4

Over $1,000,000 5

Exhibit 2.2 *(continued)*

e. Would you please tell us the *three major reasons* why you selected [name of jurisdiction]? **(PLEASE CIRCLE *NO MORE* THAN THE *THREE* MOST IMPORTANT.)**

Site was better than alternatives.. 1

Supply of labor better.. 2

Cost of labor less expensive.. 3

Proximity to markets.. 4

Physical environment more attractive than other options.. 5

Taxes lower than other options.. 6

Received more needed information on specific sites than from other jurisdictions. 7

The attitude or behavior of *business* people with whom you dealt.. 8

The attitude or behavior of *government* personnel with whom you dealt.. 9

Received more incentives (such as financial or training assistance).. 10

Could not obtain competitive private financing elsewhere.. 11

Quality of life (such as education, housing, cost of living, etc.) more attractive than other locations.. 12

Other (please specify): ______________________________

____

PLEASE SKIP TO QUESTION 6

Exhibit 2.2 *(continued)*

5. If your project is located elsewhere:

   a. In which jurisdiction did you locate? ________________________

   b. Please circle the *three major reasons* why you selected that jurisdiction. **(PLEASE CIRCLE *NO MORE* THAN THE *THREE* MOST IMPORTANT.)**

Could not find a suitable site in [jurisdiction].. 1

Supply of labor not as adequate as other options.. 2

Cost of labor was more expensive than other options.. 3

Not close enough to markets.. 4

Physical environment not as attractive as other options... 5

Taxes were higher than other options... 6

Did not received needed information on your jurisdiction or on specific sites........ 7

The attitude or behavior of *business* people in [jurisdiction] with whom you dealt 8

The attitude or behavior of *government* personnel in [jurisdiction] with whom you dealt.. 9

Received more incentives elsewhere (such as financial or training assistance)..... 10

Could not obtain competitive private financing in [jurisdiction].......................... 11

Quality of life (such as education, housing, cost of living, etc.) more attractive in other locations.. 12

Other (please specify): ________________________

Exhibit 2.2 *(continued)*

6. Do you have any other comments or suggestions on the services you received that might help the Economic Development Department improve its assistance to firms?

Thank You for Your Help!

EXHIBIT 2.3

EXAMPLE OF A DETAILED REPORT FORMAT FOR BUSINESS ATTRACTION

Performance Indicator PI-9: Percentage of assisted firms that located in the jurisdiction and that felt that the assistance contributed to their location decision.

	Number in Sample	Percentage			
		Significantly	Somewhat	Little	None
Total					
Region of Origin					
Region 1					
Region 2					
Region 3					
Region 4					
Region of Location					
Region 1					
Region 2					
Region 3					
Region 4					
Size					
0					
1-4					
5-9					
10-19					
20-49					
50-99					
100-249					
250-499					
500-999					
1,000 and up					
SIC					
20					
30					
40					
50					
60					

EXHIBIT 2.4

EXAMPLE OF SUMMARY REPORT FORMAT FOR BUSINESS ATTRACTION

Performance Indicators	Most Recent Period	Last Period	Year to Date	Year to Date Last Year	Target % for Current Year
Service Quality Indicators					
PI-1 Percentage of clients who rated each service they received as excellent, good, fair, or poor.					
PI-2 Percentage of clients who rated helpfulness of each service they received as excellent, good, fair, or poor.					
Intermediate Outcome Indicators					
PI-3 Number of assisted firms that visited [jurisdiction] to assess it as a possible location for a facility.					
PI-4 Number of responses to advertising or direct mail solicitations.					
PI-5 Number of jobs projected by assisted businesses at the time of the announcement of their decision to locate in [jurisdiction].					
Long-term Outcome Indicators					
PI-6 Number and Percentage of assisted firms that subsequently located in [jurisdiction].					

Exhibit 2.4 *(continued)*

Performance Indicators	Most Recent Period	Last Period	Year to Date	Year to Date Last Year	Target % for Current Year
PI-7 Number of actual jobs added by assisted locating firms 12 months/24 months after their initial contact with the program.					
PI-8 Dollars of capital investment made by assisted firms 12 months after the announcement of their location decision.					
PI-9 Number and percentage of assisted firms that located in the jurisdiction and that felt the assistance contributed to their location decision.					
PI-10 Number of actual jobs added by assisted locating firms 12 months/24 months after their initial contact with the program that felt that the assistance contributed to their location decision.					
PI-11 Dollars of capital investment made by assisted firms 12 months after the announcement of their location decision that felt that the assistance contributed to their decision.					
PI-12 Percentage of clients locating elsewhere for reasons over which the department had some control.					

3

BUSINESS ASSISTANCE (NONFINANCIAL) PROGRAMS

■

SCOPE

Many state and local governments provide technical assistance to businesses to help them function more effectively. Technical assistance can include seminars on regulations or other governance issues, individual counseling on business plans, marketing strategies, financial plans, and referral to other sources of assistance, often to financial assistance programs. Technical assistance programs may also provide services to individuals (such as attorneys and accountants) who, in turn, use the information to help their clients.

These programs frequently are focused on small businesses or firms in particular markets, such as high-technology manufacturers, telecommunications firms, or biotechnology firms that the agency feels need assistance to compete in the marketplace. Programs also may target firms that are in emerging markets to help them gain an advantage over competitors in other jurisdictions. Occasionally, special programs are designed to provide assistance to women and to minority-owned businesses.

Government programs that provide financial assistance are considered in Section 4, "Financial Assistance Programs." In addition, programs encouraging exporting are covered in Section 6, "Export Promotion Programs."

The objectives of business assistance programs generally are to: (1) help improve business operations and their viability; (2) help firms comply with state regulations that govern their operations; (3) refer firms to other programs, such as financial assistance or export promotion programs, and other sources of technical assistance to help them improve or expand operations; and (4) help persons wanting to launch a business make good start-up decisions. The long-term objectives of these programs include providing assistance that will help firms initiate operations, stay in business, increase sales, and expand their employment.

■

PERFORMANCE INDICATORS FOR BUSINESS ASSISTANCE PROGRAMS

Exhibit 3.1 presents a set of performance indicators that can be used for monitoring business assistance programs. These are grouped into three categories: indicators of service quality, intermediate outcome indicators, and long-term outcome indicators. The information generated for these performance indicators comes from agency records, surveys of business assistance clients, and in some instances, from the state unemployment insurance (UI) database. A sample questionnaire is included at the end of this section as Exhibit 3.2.

Indicators of Service Quality

Indicators of service quality can highlight specific aspects of service quality that need attention and improvement.

The *accuracy of information* (PI-1) provided to clients is particularly important for a technical assistance program. Firms come to the business assistance office for its expertise in an area, such as state regulation, and expect to receive accurate answers to their questions. Since the program's primary commodity is information, its accuracy, as found by the program's clients, is an important indicator of program performance.

Clients' perceptions of the *timeliness* (PI-2) of the services indicate the program's success in responding quickly to requests.

Some clients may not actually receive the services they sought from the program. The indicator showing the percentage who actually received the services they requested (PI-3) provides information on the actual receipt of desired services as perceived by clients. This indicator captures information that would be lost if the agency only sought information on the quality of services *received*, regardless of what was requested.

Ratings by clients of the *overall quality of the program's assistance* (PI-4) provide the program with a composite rating for service quality. This indicator in effect combines into one rating, the client's perspective on receipt of services, accuracy, timeliness, plus any other factors the client feels were important. The percentage of clients that indicate that they would recommend the program's services to other businesses (PI-5) is an indicator of overall client satisfaction and of the value of services. It has additional importance because clients often are a major source of program referrals. If clients are not satisfied with the assistance they receive, they are unlikely to recommend the services to others, thus decreasing the coverage of the program and possibly undermining long-term support for it.

Accuracy, timeliness, and overall quality should be queried for each individual service offered by the program, as illustrated in question 2 of the sample questionnaire (Exhibit 3.2). The questionnaire provides the opportunity to break out information on basic assistance services such as: publications, seminars and workshops, counseling, and referrals. This list can be modified to meet any agency's particular variety of business assistance programs.

Publications are usually the primary information tool provided to clients. Indeed, publications are often the only contact the program has with a client. Seminars or workshops are given on general or specific topics of interest to businesses. They may be attended by owners or employees of businesses, or by those who will use the information to assist their own clients to improve their businesses. Ratings of seminars and workshops provide the program with information on the quality of these activities. Individual counseling is a one-on-one service for businesses on specific issues, such as development of a business plan, a marketing strategy, or an operational problem. Ratings of this service provide information from those clients who received the in-person assistance. Referrals to other sources of assistance, whether a different department, a different level of government, or a private source, are a significant service if the program has limited technical services of its own or is not the appropriate source of certain types of assistance or information. Ratings of this service can help the program judge whether its referrals have been useful.

The survey questionnaire should ask respondents to give their reasons for poor ratings. The business assistance program can obtain valuable information from these reasons. As illustrated by questions 2f and 3a of Exhibit 3.2, the questionnaire requests respondents to explain any poor ratings. Such information should be compiled and subsequently analyzed by program staff to provide clues to problems with the program and how they might be corrected.

Intermediate Outcome Indicators

Intermediate outcome indicators are indicators that, although not measuring increased employment or sales, nevertheless represent actions taken by clients that can be considered important, positive steps toward these desired outcomes.

The percentage of clients that decided to start a business is an important intermediate outcome indicator for programs that provide technical assistance to start businesses (PI-6a). However, the list of indicators (Exhibit 3.1) does not include businesses that decide to defer or abandon forming a new business. Although the program's assistance may alert the clients about serious competitive weaknesses that result in postponement or abandonment of startups, such situations are likely to be secondary to the program's objectives and have not been included as a major performance indicator (although such data can be sought, as shown in question 4 of Exhibit 3.2). This information can be reported as individual outcome indicators or as one summary indicator, as shown in Exhibit 3.1.

Another important intermediate outcome for clients is alteration of their business or market strategy, based on the state service (PI-6b)--for example, a shift to a new product or market segment. Such outcomes indicate that the firm is adopting new long-term strategies to improve performance.

Solving operational problems (e.g., obtaining permits) or improving regular business operations or methods (e.g., working capital management) are also relevant outcomes (PI-6c and d). These outcomes tend to strengthen the firm's ability to stay in business and grow.

Only asking clients whether such outcomes occurred does not tell whether the business assistance program had any role in these outcomes. To address this issue, clients should also be queried about the extent to which the program's assistance contributed to these outcomes (question 5 of Exhibit 3.2). To calculate the values for PI-6, therefore, the agency will need to combine information from each client as to whether the intermediate outcomes occurred with the same client's rating of the extent of the business assistance program's contribution. This should be accomplished in the data processing step. The agency can also tabulate the answers to the question on the extent of contribution without directly linking the contribution to the specific outcome categories--as an added intermediate outcome indicator.

To what extent will respondents be able to answer accurately about the business assistance program's contribution to outcomes? This is a major technical issue for these procedures. The answer depends on the extent to which the respondent knows about, and can recall accurately, circumstances regarding the program's assistance and subsequent actions by the respondent's firm. Although 100 percent accuracy in the responses to these questions cannot be expected, asking key representatives of client firms for their perceptions appears to be the only practical way to obtain at least rough information on the extent of contribution. Note that while the *precision* of the indicators is in considerable doubt, they should be *accurate* enough to identify major differences over time and across different types of businesses.

End (Long-Term) Outcomes

End (long-term) outcome indicators (PI-7 and 8) assess the extent to which the business assistance program helped firms increase their sales and employment. These are generally the major long-term objectives of business assistance programs. PI-7, percentage of clients who actually start businesses or expand them and increase jobs and sales, is one of the long-term outcomes of a business assistance program. Jobs added by those actually starting or expanding a business, PI-8, is another, perhaps the single most important, outcome.

As with the intermediate outcomes, an indication by a firm that these results have occurred does not tell whether the program helped to bring them about. *The contribution of the service received by clients to end outcomes realized is a central concern of performance monitoring*. Only in instances where clients indicated that the services they received contributed to the outcomes they experienced can the program really take credit for these outcomes. As with the intermediate outcomes, the most practical way to obtain this information appears to be to ask clients about the extent of the business assistance program's contribution, as illustrated in question 5 of Exhibit 3.2. Issues and cautions regarding this procedure were discussed previously under "Intermediate Outcome Indicators."

The *number* of new jobs, PI-8, poses additional concerns about accuracy. Asking respondents for exact numbers is likely to create considerable difficulties for many respondents. To ease their burden and encourage responses to the question, clients might better be asked to check off ranges of results (0-4, 5-9, etc.). This procedure is illustrated in question 4a of accompanying sample questionnaire. An alternative procedure is to track changes in employment for clients through the state's UI database. This procedure should give reasonably accurate estimates of employment levels for each month. UI data will not, however, by themselves provide information as to the contribution of the program to the increases in jobs.

The matter of when to survey clients is an important issue. Clients should be surveyed approximately nine months to one year after they begin receiving services. This time interval balances potential client memory problems on the one hand with, on the other hand, the need to allow sufficient time to elapse for significant outcomes to occur.

■

DISAGGREGATIONS OF INDICATOR DATA

The performance indicator values should be broken out by key characteristics of the client firms, to make the indicators most useful to program managers. The disaggregations for these programs should include: (1) size of firm (as measured by number of employees); (2) standard industrial classification (SIC) code (two-digit codes should be sufficient--if the program focuses on a particular set of industries, the data should be presented for these industries); (3) area (county)--perhaps arranged to distinguish urban from rural areas; and, possibly, (4) minority status.

Firm size is important, particularly for programs that target small- and medium-sized firms. This breakout will show program differences in service to firms of different sizes. The industry category breakout will show how well the program is serving different industries in the state. It will be especially helpful if the program is targeting certain industries for assistance. Area disaggregations should allow the program to gauge how it is doing with firms in different parts of the jurisdiction. For state agencies, these regions could be aggregations of counties that the program finds to be similar, perhaps because of certain shared characteristics, or because these are the economic development regions used for other agency purposes. These counties can be grouped into regions based on geographic contiguity, although they could be based on other factors, such as metropolitan or nonmetropolitan. The minority status breakout will provide information on the program's success in reaching minority firms.

■

SOURCES FOR PERFORMANCE DATA

Program Records

Information from program records are needed to: (1) provide basic client information in order to contact clients with a survey questionnaire or to track employment through the UI database such as firm name, address, name and title of key contact person, telephone number, dates of service provided, and the firm's federal or state identification number (for determining a firm's growth in employment); and (2) obtain information on client characteristics needed for disaggregating performance indicators, such as firm size, industry, region, information about the services each client received, and minority status. The program's database on its clients should contain information on each firm that receives assistance. The program can obtain this information from each firm as part of its regular client information system at the time clients first seek assistance.

Client Surveys

Client surveys provide the major source of information on program quality and outcomes. Surveys generate data on clients' perception of service quality, on the outcomes they have experienced, and on the contribution of the program's services to the outcomes.

The program should consider surveying all those who received assistance from the program on a quarterly basis. If the number of quarterly clients is large, say over 200, and the data collection costs are a problem, the agency can survey a sample of clients in a manner to ensure that the findings are representative. The sample might be a random selection of all clients, or a stratified sample to achieve representation of all clients on different services received, size groups, industries, and location within the jurisdiction in order to later break out the performance data.

For performance monitoring purposes, the program should define reasonably precisely who is a client. To avoid excessive cost and little extra value, it should establish the amount of a service that needs to be provided for a firm to be classified as a client. For example, it might specify that the firm needs to receive a minimum of four hours of assistance before being categorized as a client. This amount could vary for each type of service. A firm requesting one business assistance program publication, for example, should not be included in the client survey.

Clients can be surveyed approximately nine months to one year after receiving assistance. If the survey is earlier, such as after three months, not enough time will have elapsed for many clients to have achieved long-term, or even intermediate outcomes. By the same token, if the survey is delayed much later, to more than one year, the individuals in the firms will likely have major problems remembering the assistance given them and/or the outcomes relating to the assistance. Also, at this later date, the relevance of the performance information is likely to lessen because of staff, program, and funding changes.

For each client to be surveyed, probably by mail, the program needs to provide the names of the primary contact persons, their address, and telephone number (for telephone reminders to firms not returning questionnaires). To disaggregate the survey data, the program should also collect and provide the SIC, size, location (county), and minority status of the firm.

The survey questionnaire should include questions on the quality of the services received, the outcomes experienced, and clients' estimation of the contribution of the services to these outcomes. The sample questionnaire in this section (Exhibit 3.2) illustrates how this can be done. A few open-ended questions should be included so that respondents can give reasons why they answered in certain ways, especially if they report poor ratings. (See, for example, questions 2f, 5a, and 7a in Exhibit 3.2.) Open-ended questions can also be included to ask for suggestions to improve the program's services. (See, for example, question 9 in Exhibit 3.2.)

Mailed questionnaires should be sent with a personalized cover letter signed by a top executive such as the government's chief executive or agency head. The letter should indicate the need for feedback to improve the program's services and should point out that information will be kept confidential and only reported in aggregate form. An incentive to respond is desirable. As an incentive to respond, an attractive professional publication or a report could be offered to those who return the questionnaires. Section 9, "Client Surveys," describes survey procedures in greater detail. A sample transmittal letter is included in that section.

State Unemployment Insurance Data

The state UI database can be used to determine the change in employment of assisted firms. Program personnel should be asked to request the identification number from clients as part of one of the initial contacts. (The UI database contains federal and state identification numbers for each firm that pays taxes on employees in the state.) If the program does not obtain an identification number, it may still be possible to find the firm in the UI database by using the firm's name and county code. Because of certain characteristics in the system (described more fully in Section 10), it may not be possible to find all firms using the company name and county code.

The UI database can be used to track the monthly employment of assisted firms. The system collects monthly employment figures from firms on a quarterly basis. The program could identify employment change in assisted firms for several quarters. The UI data are useful because they allow the program to track long-term outcomes over a longer time period than can be obtained from a client survey.

Although this procedure is attractive, it has two important limitations. It can obtain quite accurate employment figures, but these will not tell whether the business assistance program contributed directly to increases in employment. Nor does the system provide information on service quality, as does the client survey procedure. Thus, the UI database should preferably be considered as a complement to client survey procedures, especially for providing data on the amount of job growth for use in PI-8.

■

EXPLANATORY DATA

The program may want to provide explanatory data along with the performance indicator information, to help explain major improvements, or declines, in program performance. For example, various national, state, or local economic indicators are likely to be relevant, since the intermediate and long-term indicators can be affected by economic conditions. The rate of economic growth for the jurisdiction is one indicator of the general economic climate. If the jurisdiction's growth rate slows or increases rapidly, the outcomes of firms receiving assistance would, in general, be expected to also reflect these conditions. Significant external events such as changes in competition from other countries can also affect outcomes for firms in specific industries.

■

REPORTING THE RESULTS

A major need in performance monitoring is for results to be presented to program and other agency managers in clear, informative formats. Exhibits 3.3 and 3.4 present two examples. Exhibit 3.3 illustrates a format designed to show the detailed findings on each specific performance indicator, with breakouts by major client characteristics. The user can quickly identify those categories of clients for whom performance on the indicator was particularly high or low during the period covered by the report. Exhibit 3.4 shows a *summary* report format, presenting data for each performance indicator that compare current performance to prior performance and to targets set by the program. See Section 11, "Analysis and Presentation of Performance Information," for more suggestions on these topics.

EXHIBIT 3.1

PERFORMANCE INDICATORS FOR BUSINESS ASSISTANCE PROGRAMS[1]

Service Quality Indicators:

PI-1 Percentage of clients rating the *accuracy of information* for each service received as excellent or good (Question 2b, Exhibit 3.2).

PI-2 Percentage of clients rating the *timeliness* of the services received as excellent or good (Question 2c, Exhibit 3.2).

PI-3 Percentage of clients reporting that they received the services they requested (Question 3, Exhibit 3.2).

PI-4 Percentage of clients rating the *overall quality* of assistance of each service as excellent or good (Question 2d, Exhibit 3.2).

PI-5 Percentage of clients who would recommend program assistance to other businesses (Question 7, Exhibit 3.2).

Intermediate Outcome Indicators:

PI-6 Number and percentage of clients that (a) decided to start a business; (b) made a significant change in the nature of their business or markets; (c) solved an operational problem; or (d) improved regular business operations or methods; *and,* if any of these occurred, also reported that the business assistance program office's assistance contributed at least somewhat to the outcome (Questions 4a, 4f, 4g, 4h, and 5, Exhibit 3.2).

End (Long-term) Outcome Indicators:

PI-7 Number and percentage of clients that (a) actually started a business; (b) expanded current operations; (c) increased sales; or (d) increased the number of employees; *and,* if any of these occurred, also reported that the business assistance program contributed at least somewhat to the outcomes (Questions 4c, 4d, 4i, 4j, and 5, Exhibit 3.2).

PI-8 Number of additional jobs, as reported by clients (Question 4a, Exhibit 3.2) *and* for which clients reported that the business assistance program contributed at least somewhat to the outcome--or the number of additional jobs indicated by state unemployment insurance data (Questions 4a and 5 of Exhibit 3.2--or unemployment insurance data).

---

1. The information in parentheses refers to the source of data for each indicator.

EXHIBIT 3.2

SAMPLE CLIENT QUESTIONNAIRE FOR BUSINESS ASSISTANCE PROGRAMS

1. For what purpose did you seek assistance in the past 12 months from the Business Assistance Office? **(PLEASE CIRCLE.)**

	Yes	No
a. Business start-up help	1	2
b. Expansion of existing business	1	2
c. Technical assistance on a specific problem	1	2
d. Questions or problems with licensing or government relations	1	2
e. Other (please specify)	1	2

____

2. Please rate the following characteristics for the services you received from the Business Assistance Program. **(PLEASE CIRCLE.)**

RATING SCALE	
1 = Excellent	3 = Fair
2 = Good	4 = Poor

Exhibit 3.2 *(continued)*

Service Received	A. Did not Request the Service	B. Accuracy of Information	C. Timeliness	D. Overall Quality of Assistance
a. Publications	N	1 2 3 4	1 2 3 4	1 2 3 4
b. Seminars/workshops	N	1 2 3 4	1 2 3 4	1 2 3 4
c. Counseling	N	1 2 3 4	1 2 3 4	1 2 3 4
d. Referrals	N	1 2 3 4	1 2 3 4	1 2 3 4
e. Other (specify):	N	1 2 3 4	1 2 3 4	1 2 3 4

f. If you rated any of the characteristics in Question 2 as Fair or Poor, please explain why.

3. Did you get the services you requested? **(PLEASE CIRCLE ONE.)**

Yes... 1

No... 2

a. If no, would you please explain what you wanted but did not get?

Exhibit 3.2 *(continued)*

4. Since the time you began receiving assistance from the Business Assistance Program have you: **(PLEASE CIRCLE ALL THAT APPLY.)**

		Yes	No
a.	Decided to go into business..........	1	2
b.	Decided not to go into business..........	1	2
c.	Actually started a business..........	1	2
d.	Expanded current operations..........	1	2
e.	Decided not to expand..........	1	2
f.	Made a significant change in the nature of your business or in your markets..........	1	2
g.	Solved a specific operational problem..........	1	2
h.	Improved regular business operations or methods..........	1	2
i.	Increased your sales..........	1	2
j.	Increased the number of employees..........	1	2
k.	Gone out of business..........	1	2

l. If you indicated that you had actually started a business (4c) or increased your employment (4j), please indicate the approximate number of additional full-time equivalent employees: **(PLEASE CIRCLE ONE.)**

1 - 4..........	1
5 - 9..........	2
10 - 19..........	3
20 or more..........	4

Exhibit 3.2 *(continued)*

5. To what extent do you feel that the services you received from the Business Assistance Program contributed to the outcomes identified in Question 4? **(PLEASE CIRCLE ONE.)**

Contributed significantly... 1

Contributed somewhat.. 2

Did not contribute to the outcome............................. 3

Service detracted.. 4

Don't know.. 5

a. If in Question 5 you answered that the service did not contribute to the outcome or detracted from it, please explain why.

6. How did you hear about the assistance you received from the Business Assistance Program? **(PLEASE CIRCLE THE SINGLE MOST IMPORTANT SOURCE.)**

Media advertising.. 1

Referral by a Small Business Development Center (SBDC).. 2

Referral by another government agency.. 3

Referral by a private business adviser (such as attorneys or accountants).................... 4

Referral by a bank or lending institution.. 5

A Business Assistance Office publication... 6

Other publications.. 7

Word of mouth (e.g., business acquaintance).. 8

Exhibit 3.2 *(continued)*

7. Would you recommend that other small businesses contact the Business Assistance Program for help? **(PLEASE CIRCLE.)**

Yes... 1

No.. 2

a. If No, would you please explain why not?

8. How available is information on the services of the state's Business Assistance Program in your community? **(PLEASE CIRCLE.)**

Very available.. 1

Somewhat available 2

Only a little.. 3

Not at all.. 4

9. Do you have any other comments or suggestions that would help the Business Assistance Program improve its services to businesses?

Thank you for your help!

EXHIBIT 3.3

EXAMPLE OF A DETAILED REPORT FORMAT FOR BUSINESS ASSISTANCE PROGRAMS

Performance Indicator PI-4: Percentage of clients who rated the overall quality of referrals as excellent, good, fair, or poor.

	Number in Sample	Percentage			
		Excellent	Good	Fair	Poor
Total					
Size (Number of Employees)					
1-9					
10-19					
20-99					
100-499					
500 and up					
Industry Sector					
20					
30					
40					
50					
60					
Region					
Region 1					
Region 2					
Region 3					
Region 4					
Minority Status					
Black					
Female					
Hispanic					
Asian					
Other					

EXHIBIT 3.4

EXAMPLE OF SUMMARY REPORT FORMAT FOR BUSINESS ASSISTANCE PROGRAMS

Performance Indicators	Most Recent Period	Last Period	Year to Date	Year to Date Last Year	Target % for Current Year
Service Quality Indicators					
PI-1 Percentage of clients who rated the accuracy of information for all services as excellent or good.					
PI-2 Percentage of clients who rated the timeliness of all services as excellent or good.					
PI-3 Percentage of clients reporting that they received the service requested.					
PI-4 Percentage of clients who rated the overall quality of all services as excellent or good.					
PI-5 Percentage of clients who recommended program services to other businesses.					

Exhibit 3.4 *(continued)*

Performance Indicators	Most Recent Period	Last Period	Year to Date	Year to Date Last Year	Target % for Current Year
Intermediate Outcome Indicators					
PI-6 Percentage of clients who (a) decided to start a business; (b) made a significant change in the nature of their business or markets; (c) solved an operational problem; or (d) improved regular business operations or methods; *and* reported that the business assistance office's programs contributed at lest somewhat to the outcome.					
Long-term Outcome Indicators					
PI-7 Number and percentage of clients that (a) actually started a business: (b) expanded current operations; (c) increased sales; or (d) increased the number of employees--*and* reported that the business assistance program contributed at least somewhat to the outcomes.					
PI-8 Number of additional jobs for which clients reported that the business assistance program contributed at lest somewhat to the outcome.					

4

FINANCIAL ASSISTANCE PROGRAMS

■

SCOPE

Financial assistance programs have a variety of objectives, funding mechanisms, and organizational forms. This section focuses on financial assistance programs administered by economic development departments that provide direct loans or loan guarantees to private, for-profit businesses for working capital or business expansion. Financing programs to assist exporters are also covered later in Section 6, "Export Promotion Programs."

Objectives for state financial assistance programs commonly include such general purposes as:

1. Creating new jobs or retaining existing jobs
2. Promoting expansion of existing business
3. Promoting creation of new business
4. Facilitating economic adjustment
5. Supporting distressed communities
6. Fostering economic diversification and stability
7. Helping disadvantaged, minority businesses

Groups commonly targeted for financial assistance include businesses of different sizes (separate programs for small versus large businesses), specific industrial sectors, businesses in targeted locations of the jurisdiction, and businesses owned by targeted segments of the population (women and minorities).

A financial assistance program may have more multiple subprograms, with these subprograms providing different types of assistance (e.g., short-term versus long-term funds, etc.) and/or serving different client groups (e.g., small versus large businesses, minority-owned firms, etc.)

The procedures discussed here cover businesses that received a significant amount of assistance whether or not they applied for or received financial assistance. Thus, the procedures cover all firms that had sufficient number and length of contacts with the financial assistance program to be considered clients. (One prerequisite for coverage by these procedures is that the business provides sufficient information to the program so that it can later be contacted for follow-up information.)

Measurement of the results of financial assistance programs involves two special problems of particular concern to government financial assistance to businesses.

The first concern is whether the firm could have obtained financing elsewhere, especially from private sources. Financial assistance programs generally attempt to determine this during the application process to ensure that each firm has made a reasonable attempt to obtain funds. The procedures described here attempt to provide additional information on this question through the client survey procedures. To investigate this fully, however, requires a more in-depth, audit-type examination. Performance monitoring procedures should not be expected to make this determination.

The second concern is whether the firm helped by the program is *displacing* employees at other firms within the state or local community. The financial assistance program's eligibility determination process should attempt to screen out such applicants. To investigate this issue adequately, a more in-depth displacement analysis is needed. Performance monitoring procedures cannot be expected to make this determination.

■

PERFORMANCE INDICATORS FOR FINANCIAL ASSISTANCE

Candidate performance indicators for financial assistance programs are displayed in Exhibit 4.1. The indicators are grouped into three categories: (1) service quality; (2) intermediate outcomes; and (3) long-term (end) outcomes.

Indicators of service quality include characteristics of the way program services are delivered that are important to clients. Quality characteristics to be assessed include:

- The clarity of the applications process, the time and effort needed to complete applications, and the time taken for applications to be processed, reviewed, and funded (PI-1);
- The timeliness of program services, the accuracy and completeness of the information provided, the courteousness of program personnel, knowledge of other agency programs, and the overall helpfulness of the assistance provided (PI-2);
- The number of clients *not* submitting applications because they perceived excess red tape, could not understand what was required to apply, or did not like the reception they received from program personnel (PI-3); and
- The adequacy of coordination among financial assistance programs (PI-4).

The first three of these indicators are each composed of a number of elements. The agency and program can choose to report information on each of these elements separately, or they can combine them into one indicator, as shown for PI-1, PI-2, and PI-3 in Exhibit 4.1, or both. To be most helpful to program personnel in guiding program improvements, the information should be reported on each element as well as in combined form. The combined indicators in Exhibit 4.1 are summary indicators, which are especially useful to upper-level management.

The information for PI-1, PI-2, and PI-4 can be obtained by surveying clients several months after service is provided. The information for PI-1c and d, the time required for applications to be processed, reviewed, and funded, can be obtained by tabulating these times based on program records. A survey of clients, however, is needed to obtain their perspective on the reasonableness of these times (PI-1a and b). A sample questionnaire illustrating how this information can be obtained from clients is presented in Exhibit 4.2.

When respondents give one of the poorer ratings to a service characteristic, the respondent should be asked to explain why. Those reasons should be compiled and examined by program staff to help determine what appears to be the specific problem and what might be done to correct it. Questions 3a, 5c, and 6h in the sample applicant questionnaire in Exhibit 4.2 and Questions 3a, 4a, 5a, 6d, and 8a of the questionnaire in Exhibit 4.3, for clients that did not apply, illustrate such questions.

Intermediate outcome indicators are outcomes that represent positive steps *toward* long-term outcomes, such as increased jobs. Intermediate outcomes include lowered interest costs, increased financial stability, becoming able to obtain subsequent financing from private sources without department assistance, increased competitiveness, increased sales, and increased profitability. The program can measure client progress on these outcomes and determine the extent to which client businesses credit the program's financial assistance for their improvement. These individual outcomes can be reported as individual outcome indicators and/or reported as one summary indicator, as illustrated in PI-5 of Exhibit 4.1. The information on these outcomes can be obtained from the same survey of clients that is used to generate indicators of service quality.

End (long-term) outcome indicators are outcomes that fulfill the long-term mission of the program. These include: increased employment, prevention of layoffs (retained jobs), and more new businesses. The program should measure client progress on these outcomes and determine the extent to which client businesses credit the program's financial assistance for these outcomes. These outcomes are illustrated by indicators PI-6, PI-7, and PI-8 of Exhibit 4.1 (percentage of assisted firms that reported increased employment and percentage of assisted firms reporting avoidance of layoffs that otherwise would have occurred).

The data for these indicators can be obtained from three sources. The survey of clients can generate data for all three indicators. The state unemployment insurance database can be used to determine changes in reported employment from the date before the financial assistance was provided until an appropriate date, such as one year or more, after (for PI-7). And if the program obtains periodic reports on employment as part of its assistance requirements, the data can be obtained from program records. Because applicants for financial assistance usually have to project employment as part of their applications, the program can compare projections to actual employment.

The *contribution* of financial assistance to the outcomes reported by client businesses, both intermediate and end outcomes, can be estimated using the client survey. Businesses receiving financial assistance can be asked to identify the probable impact on their business if they had not received the financial assistance from the state. Second, businesses can be asked to assess the value of the loan or guarantee to their business or project. Clients can be asked at the time of follow-up what they believe their firm would have done if the firm had not received the financial assistance. Question 12 of the sample questionnaire (Exhibit 4.2) illustrates how this might be asked. The tabulations for PI-6 and PI-7 on added employment should include only those responses in which the respondents indicated that they would not have been able to proceed with the project without state assistance.

For loan and loan guarantee programs, an additional indicator of program sources is the occurrence of loan delinquencies or defaults, PI-9. This is an important indicator of the financial condition of assisted firms and provides feedback on the successfulness of awards. However, delinquencies and defaults need to be interpreted carefully. Programs targeting businesses unable to obtain private assistance because they are considered too risky by private lenders can be expected to have relatively high delinquency and default rates. In fact, if the default rate is low, this might indicate overly cautious behavior by the program.

Finally, businesses can be asked to assess the value of the financial assistance to their business or project--PI-10, as illustrated by Question 13 of Exhibit 4.2. Because most, if not all, assistance recipients are likely to perceive the financial help as at least somewhat valuable, the performance indicator PI-4 includes only those who rate the assistance as "extremely valuable."

When client surveys are used, the program also should ask clients to provide comments or suggestions that would help the agency improve its financial assistance program. Question 14 of Exhibit 4.2 and Question 9 of Exhibit 4.3 illustrate how this can be done.

When should clients be surveyed? Clients should be surveyed approximately one year after they begin receiving help. As discussed in previous sections of this manual, this time interval balances client memory problems, on one hand, with, on the other hand, the need to allow sufficient time for significant outcomes to occur. A variation is to survey applicants 9-12 months, for example, after they submitted their applications; the time of application is a convenient point for determining when to administer the client questionnaire. Nonapplicants would be labeled as such if no application was received after a specified time, say 6 months, from the time they began to receive substantial assistance (and provided an address). The nonapplicant questionnaire could be administered soon after the firm becomes a "nonapplicant" since these firms are not asked about service outcomes.

■

DISAGGREGATIONS OF INDICATOR DATA

Breakouts of the indicator data by characteristics of the clients and the services provided can greatly increase the utility of performance indicator information to program personnel. Indicators for the program should be disaggregated by such characteristics as: (1) those firms that: (a) received financial assistance, (b) applied, but did not get financial assistance, and (c) spent time with program personnel but did not apply; (2) the particular subprogram of the financial assistance program; (3) whether the firm was a first-time applicant or not; (4) region, or location, in the jurisdiction (e.g., county or multicounty region); (5) size of business (measured in number of employees and, possibly, in sales); (6) industrial sector of business (SIC code or multi-SIC category); and (7) minority ownership status.

These breakouts will enable program personnel to identify in more detail where the program has been relatively successful or unsuccessful, and permit concentration on those categories that appear most in need.

■

SOURCES FOR PERFORMANCE DATA

There are three sources of performance information for financial assistance programs: program records, surveys of clients, and state unemployment insurance (UI) data. Each source and the procedures necessary to obtain the data are discussed next. More specific details on surveys and UI data are presented in other sections of this manual.

Program Records

Program records are needed to identify and provide contact information for the clients that should be included in the client surveys or UI data search. The records should include such contact data as: the correct names of the clients, addresses, the primary contact person at each business, their titles and telephone numbers, the federal and/or state identification numbers (for tracking the firms' employment using state UI data), and date when the firms become clients.

Program records are also the best source of information on each client for disaggregating the data by such characteristics as the seven identified earlier: the type of assistance provided, which particular financial assistance program provided the service, whether the firm was a first-time applicant or not, the region, size, industry, and minority status.

Records furthermore provide actual performance data for some indicators, such as PI-1c and d (time required for applications to be processed, reviewed, and funded) and PI-9 (number and percentage of recipients delinquent or in default). To the extent that the program, as part of its regular procedures, obtains actual employment figures from firms receiving financial assistance, these data can be used for PI-6 and PI-7.

Client Surveys

Periodic surveys of applicant and nonapplicant businesses are a major source of information on program performance. These surveys are the only efficient way to obtain information on clients' perceptions of service quality. Surveys also seem to be the best way to obtain data on intermediate outcomes. In addition, they can be used to obtain data on employment resulting from the program's financial assistance, and on the firms' perceptions of the extent to which the assistance provided contributed to intermediate and long-term outcomes.

These surveys should cover all businesses applying for financial assistance and at least a sample of businesses contacting the program but not submitting an application. The sample might be a random selection of all clients, or a stratified sample to achieve representation of clients of different services received, size groups, industries, and location within the jurisdiction, in order to later break out the performance data.

The survey should be administered approximately one year after the business applies, or, for businesses that contact the program but do not apply, about 6 months after their first contact with the program. The lag time from the receipt of services by a business to the occurrence of related outcomes averages from one to two years. Memory problems are reduced as shorter time lags are involved. A 6- to 12-month lag time seems to be a reasonable compromise for obtaining outcome information while not taxing the memory of client firms. The agency may choose to mail out the survey questionnaires on each firm's anniversary date of application. Some firms may send in more than one application during a 12-month period. However, the same business facility probably should not be surveyed more frequently than once a year.

Surveys of firms that the program identifies as clients who chose not to apply also can provide data on service quality. As noted earlier, the program needs to define the minimum amount of contact with a business necessary to warrant inclusion in the survey sample (such as a minimum number of hours of contact with program personnel or a minimum amount of program information mailed that defines a business as a client).

Questionnaires illustrative of those that can be administered to program applicants and to nonapplicants are presented in Exhibits 4.2 and 4.3. Program records can be used to identify the primary contact persons at the client businesses and to provide their titles, addresses, telephone numbers, and information on the characteristics of each firm for used in disaggregating the data.

For mailed questionnaires, clients should receive a cover letter from a high-level executive such as the agency director or state governor, encouraging responses and making it clear that responses will remain confidential (responses will be reported only in aggregate form and not be attributed by name to individual firms or persons).

Response rates can be expected to be high from firms receiving financial assistance (e.g., 75 percent or better) but are likely to be lower for firms not receiving assistance. An incentive to respond, such as a valuable departmental publication, can be offered to increase response rates.

Section 9, "Client Surveys," presents more details on surveys, on how they should be administered, and on ways to increase response rates. A sample cover letter for mailed questionnaires is also provided in that section.

State Unemployment Insurance Data

Data available from the state UI system can provide information on the change in employment of facilities receiving financial assistance (i.e., for PI-7). Those records enable the program staff to identify a firm's employment for the month before the firm applied for financial assistance and for the most recently available month. (The UI data, however, do not provide information on the extent to which the financial assistance contributed to any increases in employment that are identified.)

The state UI database also can provide information on some characteristics needed to disaggregate the performance indicator when such data are not available in program records--such as data on the firm's size during the month in which it requested information from the program and its industry (SIC, standard industrial classification).

Section 10, on UI data, provides more detail on the problems with, and use of, this database.

■

EXPLANATORY DATA

Along with the performance indicator data, the program may want to provide explanatory data to help users of the performance reports interpret changes in the data from one reporting period to another. For example, explanatory data for the financial assistance program could include data about general economic conditions that influence business default rates and employment levels. A key explanatory factor is usually interest rates. For example, data on changes in interest rates, such as beginning and ending Treasury bill or prime rates during the period covered by the report, might be used. The program should report explanatory data on a regular basis, not just when performance worsens.

■

REPORTING THE RESULTS

Performance indicator reports should be presented in a clear and informative way. The procedures described in this manual can generate a great deal of data. These data can be presented through the use of both tables that provide *detailed* data and disaggregations and *summary* tables grouping data on services or outcomes for comparison.

Illustrative report formats are presented in Exhibits 4.4 and 4.5 for detailed and summary tables, respectively. Exhibit 4.4 displays a table format containing breakout data for each individual performance indicator. Users of such a report can quickly identify those categories of clients for whom performance on the indicator was particularly high or low during the time period covered. Exhibit 4.5 compares current performance to past performance and to program targets.

The illustrative questionnaires ask businesses to rate each of seven program activities on each of three characteristics: timeliness, courteousness of program personnel, and overall helpfulness. The resulting tabulations provide the program with a total of 21 ratings. This detailed information should be useful to program personnel. However, these can be summarized into: (a) seven indicators (e.g., the percentage of clients who rated all three service quality characteristics as excellent or good for each service activity); (b) three indicators (e.g., the percentage of clients who rated all applicable service activities as excellent or good--one indicator each for timeliness, courteousness, and overall helpfulness); or (c) one overall summary indicator (e.g., the percentage of clients who rated all applicable service characteristics and service activities as excellent or good--as shown in PI-2 of Exhibit 4.5).

Section 11, "Analysis and Presentation of Performance Information," discusses in more detail how the data might be analyzed and reported, including preparation of a written "Highlight Report" that summarizes the major findings for top-level management.

EXHIBIT 4.1

PERFORMANCE INDICATORS FOR FINANCIAL ASSISTANCE PROGRAMS[1]

Service Quality Indicators:

PI-1 Percentage of client firms that rated as satisfactory: (a) the *instructions* for completing applications; (b) the reasonableness of the *time and effort required* to prepare applications; (c) the *time required for applications to be processed* and reviewed; *and* (d) the *time required from approval to receiving the funds.* (Questions 3, 4, and 5 of Exhibit 4.2 and Question 5 of Exhibit 4.3).[2]

PI-2 Percentage of respondents who rated as excellent or good, rather than fair or poor: (a) the *timeliness* of the program's assistance; (b) the *accuracy* of the information they received; (c) the *completeness* of the information received; (d) the *courteousness* of program personnel; (e) the *knowledgeability* of program personnel about other available financial programs; *and* (f) the *overall helpfulness* of the program. (Questions 6 and 7 of Exhibit 4.2 and Questions 3, 4, 6, and 7 of Exhibit 4.3).

PI-3 Number and percentage of respondents that reported that they did *not* submit applications because either: (a) too much *red tape* seemed to be involved; (b) they *could not understand* what was required to apply; *or* (c) they didn't like the *attitude* of the program personnel with whom they spoke (Question 1 of Exhibit 4.3).

PI-4 Number and percentage of respondents who rated the coordination among Economic Development Department programs as excellent or good (Question 8 in both Exhibits 4.2 and 4.3).

Intermediate Outcome Indicators:

PI-5 Number and percentage of respondents that reported that program services either: (a) helped start up business; (b) lowered interest cost; (c) increased financial stability; (d) subsequently helped in obtaining financing from private sources without program assistance; (e) increased competitiveness; or (f) increased profitability (Questions 9b-f and 11 of Exhibit 4.2).

Exhibit 4.1 *(continued)*

End (Long-Term) Outcome Indicators:

PI-6 Number and percentage of financial assistance recipients that reported increased employment *and* indicated that the financial assistance had been an important reason for the increase (Questions 9h and 12 of Exhibit 4.2).

PI-7 Estimated number of additional employees reported because of the financial assistance (UI database or Question 10 of Exhibit 4.2).

PI-8 Number and percentage of financial assistance recipients that reported that the financial assistance prevented layoffs (Question 9g of Exhibit 4.2).

PI-9 Number and percentage of firms receiving financial assistance that are: (a) delinquent (in arrears) on their obligations; or (b) in default (program records).

PI-10 Percentage of firms receiving financial assistance that rated the value of the program to their business as (a) extremely or (b) somewhat valuable (Question 13 of Exhibit 4.2).

---

1. Timeliness can also be determined from program records if the agency keeps records of the time it took to a) process and review applications and b) provide funding after approval.

2. The information in parentheses refers to the source of data for each indicator.

EXHIBIT 4.2

SAMPLE CLIENT QUESTIONNAIRE FOR FINANCIAL ASSISTANCE PROGRAMS: APPLICANT QUESTIONNAIRE

Our records indicate that sometime last year you applied for a loan, loan guarantee, or other financial assistance from the Financial Assistance Program.

We would very much appreciate your opinion on the quality and appropriateness of assistance you received from the program.

1. What is the current status of your application? **(PLEASE CIRCLE ONE.)**

   No determination has yet been made.. 1

   It has been approved but not yet funded.................................... 2

   It was withdrawn... 3

   It was turned down.. 4

   It was funded... 5

2. How did you first learn about these financial programs? **(PLEASE CIRCLE ONE.)**

   Word of mouth... 1

   Banker.. 2

   Attorney... 3

   CPA.. 4

   Realtor.. 5

   Local economic development official.. 6

Exhibit 4.2 *(continued)*

State economic development official.. 7

Business consultants.. 8

Information from TV or newspaper.. 9

State brochures/literature.. 10

Other (please specify)... 11

____

3. Do you feel the *instructions* for completing the application were adequate and clear?

Yes... 1

No.. 2

a. If No, in what way do you feel the instructions could be improved?

4. Overall, what is your feeling about the amount of time and effort involved in your *preparation of the application?* **(PLEASE CIRCLE ONE.)**

Very excessive... 1

Somewhat excessive.................................... 2

Reasonable... 3

Exhibit 4.2 *(continued)*

5. Overall, what is your feeling about the length of time for each of the following activities: **(PLEASE CIRCLE.)**

	Very Excessive	Somewhat Excessive	Reasonable	Too Soon to Tell
a. For your application to be *processed and reviewed?*	1	2	3	4
b. *From approval for funding to being funded?*	1	2	3	4

c. If you rated any of the above in Question 5 as Very Excessive or Somewhat Excessive, would you please explain why?

6. How would you rate each of the following characteristics of each service you received from the Financial Assistance Program? **(PLEASE CIRCLE.)**

RATING SCALE

1 = Excellent	3 = Fair
2 = Good	4 = Poor

Exhibit 4.2 *(continued)*

Service	A. Timeliness	B. Courteousness of Program Personnel	C. Overall Helpfulness
a. Assistance in determining eligibility	1 2 3 4	1 2 3 4	1 2 3 4
b. Assistance in completing the application	1 2 3 4	1 2 3 4	1 2 3 4
c. Assistance with specific questions or problems about the program	1 2 3 4	1 2 3 4	1 2 3 4
d. Assistance in coordinating the financing with participating financial institutions	1 2 3 4	1 2 3 4	1 2 3 4
e. Negotiating the terms and conditions of the financing	1 2 3 4	1 2 3 4	1 2 3 4
f. Information on the status of your application during the review process	1 2 3 4	1 2 3 4	1 2 3 4
g. Processing after approval was given (if applicable)	1 2 3 4	1 2 3 4	1 2 3 4

h. If you rated any of the above as Fair or Poor, please explain why.

Exhibit 4.2 *(continued)*

7. To what extent did the financial assistance personnel with whom you dealt seem to have adequate knowledge of other relevant government financial programs?

   Fully adequate.. 1

   Partially adequate.................................... 2

   Inadequate.. 3

   Don't know.. 4

8. If you worked with more than one part of the Economic Development Agency, how would you rate the adequacy of the coordination among government personnel?

   Excellent... 1

   Good.. 2

   Fair.. 3

   Poor.. 3

   Only worked with one office........................... 4

9. What have been the major benefits for your company from the financial assistance? **(PLEASE CIRCLE ALL THAT APPLY.)**

   Too early to tell..................................... 1

   Helped start up business.............................. 2

   Lowered interest costs................................ 3

   Increased financial stability......................... 4

   Better able to compete in our market.................. 5

Exhibit 4.2 *(continued)*

Increased profitability.......... 6

Prevented layoffs.......... 7

Increased employment.......... 8

Other (Please specify).......... 9

____

Have not received financial assistance **(Skip to Question 14)**.......... 10

10. About how many additional employees (full-time equivalent), if any, do you have as of now because of the financial assistance? **(PLEASE CIRCLE ONE.)**

None.......... 1

1-9.......... 2

10-24.......... 3

25-49.......... 4

50-99.......... 5

100 or more.......... 6

11. Since receiving assistance from the Financial Assistance Program, have you obtained financing from financial private institutions without state assistance?

Yes.......... 1

No.......... 2

Haven't needed any.......... 3

Exhibit 4.2 *(continued)*

12. If your company had not received the financial assistance, what do you believe your company would most likely have done?

Proceeded with the project about as is.. 1

Proceeded on a smaller scale.. 2

Canceled the project.. 3

Taken the project to another state.. 4

Not applicable: approval not yet received.. 5

13. Overall, how would you rate the value of the program to your business?

Too soon to tell.. 1

Extremely valuable.. 2

Somewhat valuable.. 3

Not valuable.. 4

Detrimental.. 5

14. Do you have any other comments or suggestions that would help to improve these financial assistance programs?

Thank you for your help!

EXHIBIT 4.3

SAMPLE CLIENT QUESTIONNAIRE FOR FINANCIAL ASSISTANCE PROGRAMS: NONAPPLICANTS

Our records indicate that you have contacted the Financial Assistance Program over the past year regarding possible financial assistance but did not submit a formal application.

We need your feedback on the quality of the assistance these programs provided to you, so we can improve our services to businesses in the future.

1. Why didn't you submit an application? **(PLEASE CIRCLE ALL THAT APPLY.)**

Was informed that my company was not eligible...................... 1

Too much red tape seemed to be involved................................ 2

Found we didn't need financial assistance; were able to obtain funding from another source.. 3

Couldn't put together the private funding, or other needed elements, and so dropped the project entirely............................ 4

Postponed or canceled project for other reasons........................ 5

Didn't like the attitude of state persons with whom we spoke .. 6

Other (please specify): 7

____

2. How did you first learn about these financial programs? **(PLEASE CIRCLE ONE.)**

Word of mouth from other business firms................................ 1

Banker... 2

Attorney.. 3

(continued on next page)

Exhibit 4.3 *(continued)*

CPA.. 4

Realtor.. 5

Local economic development official.. 6

State economic development official... 7

Business consultant.. 8

Information from TV or newspaper.. 9

State brochures/literature.. 10

Other (please specify)... 7

____

3. When you contacted the agency, did you request information? If Yes, did you receive the information you requested?

Did not request information... 1

Yes, received most or all of the information needed.................. 2

Yes, received some of the information needed.......................... 3

No, received little or none of the information needed................ 4

a. If some, little or none, please explain.

Exhibit 4.3 *(continued)*

4. How *accurate* do you believe the information was that you received? Would you say it was:

Completely accurate.. 1

Mostly accurate.. 2

Mostly inaccurate.. 3

Completely inaccurate.. 4

Did not receive any information.. 5

a. If mostly or completely inaccurate, please explain.

5. If you received written materials from the Financial Assistance Program, such as an application or program description, how helpful were they?

Very helpful.. 1

Somewhat helpful.. 2

Not very helpful.. 3

Not helpful at all 4

a. If not very helpful or not helpful at all, please explain.

Exhibit 4.3 *(continued)*

6. How would you rate each of the following characteristics of the contacts you had with the Financial Assistance Program staff with whom you communicated: **(PLEASE CIRCLE.)**

	Excellent	Good	Fair	Poor
a. The *timeliness* of the information you requested..........	1	2	3	4
b. The *courteousness* of the personnel..............................	1	2	3	4
c. The *overall helpfulness* of the information you received..	1	2	3	4

d. If you rated any of these as Fair or Poor, please explain.

7. To what extent did the Financial Assistance Program personnel with whom you dealt seem to have adequate knowledge of other government financial programs?

Fully adequate..	1
Partially adequate..	2
Inadequate..	3
Don't know..	4

Exhibit 4.3 *(continued)*

8. If you worked with more than one part of the Economic Development Agency, how would you rate the adequacy of the coordination among agency personnel?

   Excellent.. 1

   Good... 2

   Fair... 3

   Poor.. 4

   Only worked with one office.. 5

   a. If you rated Question "8" as Fair or Poor, please explain why.

9. Do you have any other comments or suggestions that would help the department to improve these financial assistance programs?

Thank you for your help!

EXHIBIT 4.4

EXAMPLE OF DETAILED REPORT FORMAT FOR FINANCIAL ASSISTANCE PROGRAMS

Performance Indicator PI-1c: Percentage of clients that rated the time required for applications to be processed and reviewed as very excessive, somewhat excessive, reasonable, or too soon to tell.

		Percentage			
	Number in Sample	Very Excessive	Somewhat Excessive	Reasonable	Too Soon to Tell
Total					
Applicant Status					
Received assistance					
Applied					
Did not apply					
Subprogram					
Industrial development					
Small business					
Other					
First Time Applicant					
Repeat Applicant					
Location Region					
Region 1					
Region 2					
Region 3					
Region 4					
Industrial Sector					
Industrial machinery and equipment (SIC 35)					
Instruments and related products (SIC 38)					
Minority Ownership Status					
Minority owner					
Nonminority owner					

EXHIBIT 4.5

EXAMPLE OF SUMMARY REPORT FORMAT FOR FINANCIAL ASSISTANCE PROGRAMS

Performance Indicators	Most Recent Period	Last Period	Year to Date	Year to Date Last Year	Target % for Current Year
Service Quality Indicators					
PI-1 Percentage of clients firms that rated as satisfactory or reasonable the instructions, time, and effort for obtaining financial assistance.					
PI-2 Percentage of respondents who rated all aspects of service quality as excellent or good.					
PI-3 Percentage of respondents who reported not submitting an application for a reason controllable by the program.					
PI-4 Percentage or respondents who rated the coordination among Economic Development Department programs as excellent or good.					
Intermediate Outcome Indicators					
PI-5 Percentage of respondents who reported that program services either helped or star up a business, improved their financial condition, or increased their competitiveness.					

Exhibit 4.5 *(continued)*

Performance Indicators	Most Recent Period	Last Period	Year to Date	Year to Date Last Year	Target % for Current Year
Long-term Outcome Indicators					
PI-6 Percentage of financial assistance recipients that reported increased employment.					
PI-7 Estimated number of additional employees because of financial assistance.					
PI-8 Percentage of financial assistance recipients that reported that the financial assistance prevented layoffs.					
PI-9 Percentage of firms receiving financial assistance that were either delinquent or in default.					
PI-10 Percentage of firms receiving financial assistance that rated the program as extremely valuable.					

5

TOURISM PROMOTION PROGRAMS

■

SCOPE

Tourism promotion programs are designed primarily to promote the state or locality as a place to visit, so that tourism dollars will be spent there. These programs may also seek to encourage business travel or to encourage the jurisdiction's own residents to vacation near home rather than spending their travel dollars elsewhere. These programs provide information on the jurisdiction and its attractions through a variety of media and, thus, can help tourists plan their visits. Some programs advertise in national magazines or on television and may spend a significant part of their budget on the services of an advertising agency that designs promotional strategies and targets specific audiences. Often these advertisements will refer interested parties to an "800" telephone number or provide a coupon with an address to which prospects may write for additional information on the jurisdiction and its vacation attractions and facilities.

Promotional materials usually provide information about sights of interest, available lodging or other accommodations, and restaurants. The costs for the publications may be shared by businesses that advertise in the literature.

Tourism assistance to individuals is usually provided in one of two ways:

1. The client telephones or writes (perhaps in response to agency advertising) the office and asks for information/literature. The client provides contact information, usually a name and address.

2. The client walks in for over-the-counter assistance or telephones for information. The client does *not* leave a name, address, or telephone number. The client obtains information orally and/or obtains literature. (These tourism offices might be in cities, at highway information offices, or any office that provides tourist information by phone.)

The focus of the performance monitoring described in this section is on assistance to individuals who provide contact information. The major source for performance information is from client surveys. Most tourism programs have some familiarity with this type of survey because of its use for marketing research. The questionnaires used for performance monitoring may also include questions that collect marketing research data of interest to the program (such as detailed information on client characteristics).

In the past, some tourism programs have focused almost exclusively on "conversion" studies as the source of their performance information. Conversion studies are designed to count the number of people who visit an area after receiving tourism information or assistance. Different methodologies have been used to conduct these studies, but they have come under fire because they have been misused and oversimplified to represent the exclusive measure of program performance. Simply counting the number of visitors to a location does not measure the contribution of the services to their decision to visit, unless the survey questionnaire is properly designed to determine that people were influenced by the information or assistance they received.

Clients that come into an office for information, but do not leave contact information, can be given a brief feedback questionnaire and asked to complete it before leaving. This procedure can provide information on the quality of the office's services and on the staff with whom the client came into contact. It does not obtain *outcome* information--on the ultimate helpfulness of the assistance provided and whether the assistance contributed to clients' later decisions as to length of stay, amount spent, or where they visit. Such information cannot generally be obtained until days or weeks later.

This section also provides suggestions regarding procedures for assessing the assistance provided by a *state's* program to local government tourism officials. It does not, however, address procedures relating to public assistance to private tourism agencies, tourism associations, or sponsors of special events. The procedures described here, however, probably can be readily adapted to obtain performance information from these clients.

Some tourism promotion activities are designed to increase the general awareness of outsiders of the state (or local) tourism attractions, rather than seeking only immediate visits. Determining success toward achieving this objective is probably more appropriate for ad hoc studies than for regular performance monitoring, and is not covered by the procedures described here. (Although the information is of interest to the program, conducting regular surveys for this purpose would be costly and would yield only limited performance information. This is the sort of analysis the government's advertising agency might conduct as a part of its effort to assess the effectiveness of a particular promotional campaign.)

■

PERFORMANCE INDICATORS FOR TOURISM PROMOTION PROGRAMS

Exhibit 5.1 presents a list of candidate performance indicators for tourism promotion programs. The indicators are grouped into three categories: indicators of service quality, intermediate outcomes, and longer-term (end) outcomes. A sample questionnaire for obtaining this information is presented in Exhibit 5.2.

Indicators of Service Quality

Indicators of service quality for tourism programs are ratings of such characteristics of program services as completeness, speed (timeliness), and attractiveness of the information received by prospective visitors. These ratings can be presented as separate indicators or combined into one summary indicator, as shown in PI-1. Each characteristic can be rated as excellent, good, fair, or poor by respondents. Other characteristics could be queried in the questionnaire, if desired.

A second way to assess timeliness is to track the time from when the material is requested until it is mailed, and then tabulate these data. A third procedure is to have non-involved staff, or friends of staff, send in requests and record the time from sending in the request until the time the material requested actually arrived. This last procedure, however, is likely to result in a very small sample. However, both these latter procedures provide actual times, rather than client perceptions of timeliness.

Another indicator of service quality that can be included is the percentage of respondents that report they did not receive the information requested before they went on the trip, performance indicator PI-2. This is also an indicator of service timeliness. It is, of course, possible that the reason this occurred was that the client sent in his or her request at the last minute or that the postal service had held up the request. Nevertheless, if a substantial percentage of clients report late arrivals, this is a problem warranting program attention.

A third performance indicator, PI-3, is the percentage of respondents reporting that they went to another location because of some service deficiency, such as not receiving enough information, or the information arrived too late, or the material was not as attractive as that received from other locations. Question 16 of the sample questionnaire (Exhibit 5.2) illustrates the specific wording that can be used. Note that this indicator can also be considered as an end-outcome indicator, since it provides a count of those who did not visit the jurisdiction.

In addition, respondents that give negative ratings on these quality characteristics can be asked their reasons for the poor ratings, as illustrated by question 2d of Exhibit 5.2. Such responses should be compiled and reviewed by program staff to help identify specific problems and obtain clues as to actions to correct these problems. Question 18 of Exhibit 5.2 attempts to distinguish situations over which the tourism program has little or no control--such as respondents deciding to visit other locations to see family--from reasons over which the agency has responsibility.

Intermediate Outcomes

These indicators represent positive action by potential visitors, but they do not indicate that the clients actually visited the state or community. The number of requests for information received by the program, PI-4, is an intermediate outcome for the program. Although this indicator does not actually represent increased travel to the jurisdiction, requesting information is a first step in that direction. Increases in the number of requests for information indicate that the program's marketing techniques are yielding results. Tracking requests from particular regions can indicate the extent to which marketing efforts in those regions are successful. This information does not, in itself, provide a sufficient basis to conclude that the agency's program has affected tourism volume. This indicator is commonly used by tourism offices and is the one indicator where data come from program records (tabulations of requests) and not from surveys of those who requested information.

The second intermediate performance indicator is the percentage of respondents who reported that the information they received from the tourism office had been useful in planning their trip, PI-5. It indicates that the material was helpful, and the extent of its helpfulness, but it does not guarantee that the respondent actually visited the jurisdiction or that the tourism program contributed to the decision to visit.

PI-6 shows the percentage of respondents that indicated that the tourism information influenced their selection of places to visit. Having an influence over places visited does not necessarily mean that the tourist spent added dollars and, thus, is not an end outcome. The client may merely have substituted one location in the jurisdiction for another. Nevertheless, this illustrates an impact on the clients.

Tourism programs may attempt to attract visitors to specific locations within the jurisdiction, such as economically depressed areas. To determine whether the information on a specific campaign increased visits to a particular location, the agency can add a special set of questions to the questionnaire asking respondents whether they had visited the specific area, and if so, the extent to which the information provided had influenced their decision to visit that area.

End (Long-Term) Outcome Indicators

These indicators estimate the extent to which the clients actually visited the state or local jurisdiction and spent dollars there, at least in part as a result of the tourism office's assistance.

The percentage of respondents who visited the jurisdiction partly as a result of the assistance is a primary end-outcome measure for the program. The basic question for the tourism program is whether or not its efforts had a role in motivating the visitor to choose the jurisdiction as a destination, or at least to extend their stay. PI-7 attempts to get at this answer from client responses to questions 5 (influence on decision to visit) and 7 (influence on length of visit) of the sample questionnaire. An affirmative response to one of these questions would indicate that the assistance had a positive impact.

The last indicator in Exhibit 5.1, PI-8, is an estimate of the average number of dollars spent by those clients who both visited the state or local community *and* reported that the information influenced their decision to visit or to lengthen their stay. This indicator is subject to certain accuracy problems. The values would be derived from client responses, such as questions 5, 7, and 14 of Exhibit 5.2. The accuracy of the calculation depends on the ability and willingness of visiting respondents to estimate their daily costs and number of days (nights). This procedure gives "credit" to the tourism program for the dollars expended, so long as the client reports that the information he or she received influenced, at least somewhat, the client's decision to visit or to lengthen his or her visit (even if by only one day).

Other Relevant Information Obtainable from the Client Survey

Regular client surveys also offer tourism programs the opportunity to obtain related market research information such as: how the request was made (question 1 of Exhibit 5.2), number of nights (9), number in party (10), purpose of trip (11), principal activities (12), type of accommodations (13), and locations visited (15). For example, identifying the different sources respondents used to request tourism information can help the program determine the success of its various outreach activities.

■

DISAGGREGATIONS OF INDICATOR DATA

The performance indicator information will be much more useful to program staff if the data on each indicator are broken out by factors such as the state or region of origin of the request for tourism information or, if the agency is assessing requests by residents, the part of the jurisdiction from which the request came. The program should select the geographical units to use in breaking out the data. Greater detail may be desired on locations that are nearby or in which particular marketing efforts have been tried. This information can be obtained from the addresses of those who request information. Indicator PI-8, indicating dollars spent, probably should be disaggregated by the region of the state visited by respondents. The information on destination can be obtained from a question such as question 15 of Exhibit 5.2.

If the program has a number of major services for which it would like to have client feedback on quality (such as certain major publications), it can include such a list on the client questionnaire and ask recipients to rate each item.

The program may also choose to disaggregate performance information by certain marketing research characteristics, such as those contained in questions 10, 11, 12, and 13.

■

SOURCES FOR PERFORMANCE DATA

Program Records

Program records provide the data for tabulating the intermediate outcome indicator, the number of persons requesting information (PI-4 in Exhibit 5.1). In addition, program records are vital for providing the list of clients for the client surveys and the associated contact information (the client's name and address). The client's address is also important for use in disaggregating the findings as to the location from which the clients came.

If the program provides different kinds of information to different clients and records this information in its records, it can subsequently tabulate the data on each indicator for each different kind of information, to estimate the effectiveness of each kind.

Client Surveys

Surveys of those requesting tourism information are the major source of outcome and quality information for tourism programs. The clients to be surveyed each period should have requested information during a specified previous time period, and their mailing addresses should be recorded by the program. It is best to base this period on tourist seasons and, thus, it is likely to cover three- or four-month segments. Clients should be surveyed approximately six to eight months after they receive the tourism information. This allows most respondents enough time to have completed their travel, but does not preclude their remembering the content, quality, and effects of the information they received.

Depending on the number of requests a program receives during a quarter, and the cost of surveying, the program might survey everyone who has requested information or select a sample of all individuals who request information. A total of 200-300 clients each quarter should, in general, be adequate to obtain sufficiently accurate information. This sample might be a random selection of all clients, or a stratified sample of clients to achieve representation from each location where the client originated. A state that has a major objective to encourage residents to spend their tourism dollars in-state might divide its sample into two parts, drawing one random sample from in-state and the other from out-of-state requests.

Once the sample has been selected, the program should provide the necessary information on the clients who are selected (name, address, code for region of origin of request, and services received). The questionnaire should be designed to obtain information both from (a) those who traveled to the state or local jurisdiction and (b) those who did not (to identify reasons). Those who traveled to the state or local jurisdiction can provide information on the outcomes of the services provided and the extent to which these services influenced their decision to visit, the length of their visit, and/or the places they visited. Those who did not visit can be asked to explain why, so that the program can alter its services if it finds that people are traveling to other places for reasons over which the program has some control. The questionnaires for both groups should include questions that allow the recipient to rate the quality of the services they received from the tourism program. Respondents may also be asked to provide additional marketing information, such as the number of people in their party, the length of their stay, the specific region to which they traveled within the state, the purpose of the trip, activities they were involved in while visiting, accommodations used, and demographics of the travelers. As indicated earlier, the sample questionnaire (Exhibit 5.2) contains a variety of such questions (e.g., questions 9 through 13).

A major concern in these client surveys is to obtain an acceptable response rate, of at least 50 percent. This is difficult when dealing with individual clients who have limited contact with the program's services. To achieve reasonable response rates, some form of incentive is likely to be necessary. One effective procedure is to offer those who respond a chance at a $100 savings bond. The program would draw a name at random from those who had responded to the survey each quarter. Financial incentives appear to work well in increasing response rates, at least based on experiences in Minnesota and Maryland. (Minnesota regularly uses client surveys and financial incentives.)

The cover letter used with these surveys is also important in encouraging a response. Having the government's chief executive, or at least another high-level official, sign the letter and using an envelope that identifies the official's office is likely to increase response. People seem less likely to throw away surveys without reading the cover letter if it appears to be official or important business, even if from another state.

Client survey procedures and ways to increase response rates are discussed in more detail in Section 9, "Client Surveys."

■

EXPLANATORY DATA

The tourism program should include explanatory information along with the performance information in its performance reports. For tourism programs, economic and other factors may alter peoples' choices of where to vacation. Major unusual events or circumstances might be identified by the program to help explain performance variations. For example, changes in the value of the dollar relative to other currencies affect the number of Americans who vacation in the United States rather than other countries. The value of the dollar relative to other currencies is quantifiable, and can be routinely reported. Increases or decreases in the cost of travel (i.e., airfares, gasoline prices) may also affect the number of visitors who would consider traveling further distances. This sort of information may help to explain changes in the number of people traveling from different parts of the country. Other factors, such as special occurrences, either positive or negative, such as a world's fair or a major sporting event, or bad publicity at a key time from some type of environmental or other major event within a state, can affect tourism significantly.

■

REPORTING THE RESULTS

The way in which information on performance indicators is reported--its clarity and substance--is crucial in making performance information useful to economic development agencies. Two recommended report formats for tourism are presented in Exhibits 5.3 and 5.4. Exhibit 5.3 shows a detailed format, one that illustrates disaggregations by location of clients, mode of request, and by number in the party. Exhibit 5.4 is an example of a summary format of particular applicability to upper-level managers. It presents the latest data on each performance indicator with comparisons to previous time periods and targets set by the program manager.

Sections 11 and 13, "Analysis and Presentation of Performance Information" and "Uses for Regular Performance Information," respectively, present suggestions on how to analyze and use the information from these reports.

EXHIBIT 5.1

PERFORMANCE INDICATORS FOR TOURISM PROGRAMS[1]

Service Quality Indicators:

PI-1 Percentage of respondents who rated the information they received as to its (a) completeness, (b) speed, and (c) attractiveness as excellent or good (Question 2, Exhibit 5.2).

PI-2 Percentage of respondents who reported that they did not receive the information they requested before they went on their trip (Question 4, Exhibit 5.2).

PI-3 Percentage of respondents who reported as factors leading them to visit *other* locations one or more of the following: did not receive enough information, the information received arrived too late, or the material from other locations was more attractive (Questions 18f, g, and h, Exhibit 5.2).

Intermediate Outcome Indicators:

PI-4 Number of persons requesting information from the tourism program (program records).

PI-5 Percentage of respondents who reported that the information received from the tourism office had been useful in *planning their trip* (Question 8, Exhibit 5.2).

PI-6 Percentage of respondents who indicated that the information they received influenced their selection of places to visit in the state (Question 6, Exhibit 5.2).

Longer-term Outcome Indicators:

PI-7 Percentage of respondents who visited the jurisdiction *and* indicated that the information provided had: (a) influenced their *decision* to visit or (b) increased the *length of their visit* (Questions 5 and 7, Exhibit 5.2).

PI-8 Average dollar amount spent by respondents who visited the jurisdiction and also reported that the information received had influenced their decision to visit or the length of their visit (Questions 5, 7, and 14, Exhibit 5.2).

---

1. The information in parentheses refers to the source of data for each indicator.

EXHIBIT 5.2

SAMPLE CLIENT QUESTIONNAIRE FOR TOURISM PROMOTION PROGRAMS

1. We understand that you requested information from the Office of Tourism sometime during the past six months. How did you make your request? **(PLEASE CIRCLE ONE.)**

   Through the mail (e.g., letter or coupon).. 1

   By calling the Office of Tourism's "800" phone number........................ 2

   By calling the Office of Tourism's regular phone number...................... 3

   Other (please explain).. 4

   ____

2. Please rate the information you received according to the following characteristics: **(PLEASE CIRCLE ONE.)**

	Excellent	Good	Fair	Poor
a. Its *completeness*--the extent to which it contained the information you wanted..	1	2	3	4
b. The *speed* with which you received it after requesting it..	1	2	3	4
c. The *attractiveness/appearance* of the materials you received..	1	2	3	4

   d. If you rated any of the above Fair or Poor, would you please tell us why?

(continued on next page)

Exhibit 5.2 *(continued)*

3. Did you visit [name of jurisdiction] during the past six months? **(PLEASE CIRCLE ONE.)**

   Yes **(Go to Question 4)**.. 1

   No **(Skip to Question 16)**.. 2

FOR THOSE WHO VISITED IN THE PAST SIX MONTHS

4. Did the information you requested from the Office of Tourism arrive before you went on the trip? **(PLEASE CIRCLE ONE.)**

   Yes.. 1

   No **(Skip to Question 9)**.. 2

5. To what extent did the information you received from the Office of Tourism influence your *decision to visit* [name of jurisdiction]? **(PLEASE CIRCLE ONE.)**

   Very much (e.g., attracted your interest in visiting).. 1

   Somewhat (e.g., reinforced tentative plans to visit).. 2

   Not at all (e.g., already had firm plans to visit).. 3

6. To what extent did the information influence your *selection of places to visit* in [name of jurisdiction]? **(PLEASE CIRCLE ONE.)**

   Very much.. 1

   Somewhat.. 2

   Not at all.. 3

Exhibit 5.2 *(continued)*

7. Did the information influence the *length of your visit* to [name of jurisdiction]? **(PLEASE CIRCLE ONE.)**

Lengthened planned visit.......... 1

Shortened planned visit.......... 2

No effect on length of visit.......... 3

8. How useful was the information in *planning* your trip? **(PLEASE CIRCLE ONE.)**

Very useful.......... 1

Somewhat useful.......... 2

Not useful.......... 3

a. If you felt the information was not useful, would you please explain why?

9. How many nights did you stay in [name of jurisdiction]? ____________

10. How many persons were in your party?

Adults (age 16 or over).......... ______

Children (age 15 or less).......... ______

Exhibit 5.2 *(continued)*

11. What was the main purpose of your trip? **(PLEASE CIRCLE ONE.)**

Business trip.. 1

Convention... 2

Pleasure trip, primarily to [name of jurisdiction].................................... 3

Pleasure trip, primarily to some other non-[name of jurisdiction] location 4

12. What were your principal activities while in [name of jurisdiction]? **(PLEASE CIRCLE ALL THAT APPLY.)**

a. Convention or other business.. 1

b. Biking/hiking.. 2

c. Ocean beaches... 3

d. Boating/sailing (except fishing)... 4

e. Fishing (by boat or shore)... 5

f. Skiing/golfing.. 6

g. Enjoying regional events 7

h. Sight-seeing... 8

j. Hunting.. 9

k. Shopping... 10

l. Sporting events.. 11

m. Festivals.. 12

n. Visiting friends or relatives.. 13

o. Other (please specify):... 14

____

Exhibit 5.2 *(continued)*

13. What were the primary overnight accommodations you used? **(PLEASE CIRCLE ALL THAT APPLY.)**

    Hotel/motel/inn.. 1

    Camper/campground.. 2

    Own vacation home.. 3

    Home of friends/relatives.. 4

    Boat.. 5

14. Approximately how much did you spend, on the average, per day on these visits? **(PLEASE CIRCLE ONE.)**

    Less than $25.. 1

    $25 to $50.. 2

    $50 to $100.. 3

    $100 to $200.. 4

    Over $200.. 5

15. Which regions of [name of jurisdiction] did you visit? **(PLEASE CIRCLE ALL THAT APPLY.)**

    [Note to preparer: Each region should be described using common identifiers such as major cities or attractions that will allow persons unfamiliar with the jurisdiction to describe where they visited.]

    Region 1.. 1

    Region 2.. 2

    Region 3.. 3

    Region 4.. 4

    Region 5.. 5

    Region 6.. 6

PLEASE GO TO QUESTION 19

Exhibit 5.2 *(continued)*

FOR THOSE WHO DID NOT VISIT IN THE PAST SIX MONTHS

16. Have you taken a trip for pleasure (e.g., a vacation trip) during the past six months? **(PLEASE CIRCLE ONE.)**

    Yes **(Go to Question 17)**.. 1

    No **(Skip to Question 19)**.. 2

17. What state or city was the primary destination of that trip? ____________________

18. What factors led you to visit that state or city rather than [name of jurisdiction]? **(PLEASE CIRCLE ALL THAT APPLY.)**

    a. Recreational opportunities.. 1

       What type? ____________________________________

    b. Relatives or friends there 2

    c. Distance to [name of jurisdiction] too great.. 3

    d. Convention or business meeting 4

    e. Special or historical attractions.. 5

    f. Information reviewed from [name of jurisdiction] arrived too late......... 6

    g. Did not receive enough information about [name of jurisdiction] 7

    h. Material from other locations was more attractive 8

    i. Cost of trip to other locations was lower.. 9

    j. Other (please specify): 10

       ____

Exhibit 5.2 *(continued)*

FOR ALL RESPONDENTS

19. Do you have any suggestions for improving our service to persons requesting tourism information?

Thank you for your help!

EXHIBIT 5.3

EXAMPLE OF DETAILED REPORT FORMAT FOR TOURISM PROMOTION PROGRAMS

Performance Indicator PI-7a: Percentage of respondents who visited the jurisdiction *and* indicated that the information provided had influenced their decision to visit.

		Percentage		
	Number in Sample	Influenced Decision Very Much	Influenced Decision Somewhat	Influenced Decision Not at All
Total				
Origin of Request				
Out-of-state				
Northeast				
Mid-Atlantic				
Southeast				
Midwest				
West				
In-state				
Region 1				
Region 2				
Region 3				
Region 4				
Request Media				
Mail				
"800" number				
"Regular" telephone number				
Other				
Average Number in Party				
Adult				
0				
1-2				
3-4				
5 or more				
Children				
0				
1-2				
3-4				
5 or more				

EXHIBIT 5.4

EXAMPLE OF SUMMARY REPORT FORMAT FOR TOURISM PROMOTION PROGRAMS

Performance Indicators	Most Recent Period	Last Period	Year to Date	Year to Date Last Year	Target % for Current Year
Service Quality Indicators					
PI-1 Percentage of respondents who rated the information they received as excellent or good.					
PI-2 Percentage of respondents who reported not receiving the information they requested before they went on their trip.					
PI-3 Percentage of respondents who reported one or more factors leading them to visit other locations.					
Intermediate Outcome Indicators					
PI-4 Number of persons requesting information from the program.					
Long-Term Outcome Indicators					
PI-5 Percentage of respondents who reported that the information received had been useful in planning their trip.					

Exhibit 5.4 *(continued)*

Performance Indicators	Most Recent Period	Last Period	Year to Date	Year to Date Last Year	Target % for Current Year
PI-6 Percentage of respondents who indicated that the information received influenced their selection of places to visit.					
PI-7 Percentage of respondents who visited the jurisdiction and indicated that the information provided had either influenced their decision to visit or increased the length of their visit.					
PI-8 Average dollar amount spent by respondents who visited the jurisdiction and reported that the information received had influenced their decision to visit or the length of their visit.					

6

EXPORT PROMOTION PROGRAMS

SCOPE

Export promotion programs are maintained by virtually every state, and most large cities and communities have some form of export promotion effort. Generally, programs are designed to raise business awareness about export opportunities, to encourage export-related activity, and, ultimately, to increase export sales and export-related employment. These programs provide information, contacts, and logistical support to businesses that have, or should have, an interest in exporting. Many programs have overseas staff to help with market development and to provide logistical support for overseas events. The combined export promotion efforts of both the domestic and overseas staff should be included in the performance monitoring process.

Program activities can vary widely. Exhibit 6.1 contains a listing of commonly offered export promotion activities. Most states include some or all these activities in their export program. The basic array of services includes newsletters, other publications, and export-related seminars and workshops, usually held in cooperation with other organizations. Export counseling provides one-on-one contact, either intermittently or on a continuing basis, between program personnel and client businesses. Lists of overseas agents and distributors as well as trade leads are provided to client businesses, and programs may provide introductions to foreign buyers visiting the jurisdiction.

Many export programs assist client businesses to participate in overseas catalog or trade shows, and organize official trade missions to overseas markets. In the latter activity, business representatives are often led by the government's chief executive or other key political figures, who help establish important contacts in target markets. Finally, some programs provide only advice and counseling on export financing, while others provide export financing directly as well. Objectives for export promotion programs usually include: (1) increasing business awareness of exporting, (2) increasing business capability to enter export markets, (3) increasing business contacts with overseas buyers, (4) helping businesses obtain export financing, and, ultimately, (5) increasing sales in overseas markets and export-related employment.

Specific categories of businesses may be targeted for export promotion services. Businesses that are frequently targeted are small- and medium-sized manufacturers, and firms in specific industries with export potential.

Programs to encourage foreign direct investment and services to facilitate joint ventures are frequently part of a government's international effort. These latter programs were discussed in Section 2, "Business Attraction Programs."

■

PERFORMANCE INDICATORS FOR EXPORT PROMOTION PROGRAMS

Performance indicators for export promotion programs are listed in Exhibit 6.2. These indicators include ratings by client businesses of the *quality* of the services they received and of the contribution of services to the export-related *outcomes* they experienced. These indicators are designed to help program managers *determine* the extent to which clients feel that services are of high quality and contribute to their progress in exporting. The information for each of these indicators will need to come from a combination of surveys of program clients and program records. A sample questionnaire for obtaining information from clients is presented in Exhibit 6.3.

Indicators of Service Quality

Ratings of the quality of services received by businesses measure services in terms of whether they have been: (a) timely, (b) relevant and accurate, (c) professionally delivered, and (d) helpful overall. These ratings provide program managers with an indication of recipient attitudes toward these dimensions of service quality, and also help managers identify areas for improvement. These ratings can be requested from clients for each of the agency's major services, as shown in question 11 of Exhibit 6.3.

If the agency wants ratings of the four service characteristics in question 11 (Exhibit 6.3) for each of, say, eight program services, this will result in 32 ratings. This information should be quite useful to program managers; however, for upper-level managers these ratings should be summarized. For example, upper-level officials probably would be satisfied with one summary rating for each service, indicating the percentage of clients giving positive ratings on all four quality characteristics--see PI-1 in Exhibit 6.2. These data also could be summarized into one overall indicator, such as "the percentage of respondents that gave positive ratings to all services they received and to all service characteristics."

Intermediate Outcome Indicators

Intermediate outcome indicators for the program indicate the extent to which export services help clients move toward exporting. Potentially important intermediate outcomes include company decisions to pursue development of an export marketing strategy or plan, establishment of overseas market contacts, or signing of an overseas agent or distributor. These are all examples of pre-export activities that might be undertaken by businesses as a result of program participation. More general intermediate outcome indicators could also be used, such as increased knowledge about exporting and increased commitment to exporting. The program should seek to measure progress in these areas and to determine if client businesses feel that services have had a facilitating effect. These indicators, however, should be labeled "intermediate" outcomes rather than "end" outcomes. Although clients may be encouraged to take actions toward exporting, these actions do not guarantee that increased export sales or increased export-related employment will actually occur.

To obtain the information on these outcomes, it seems necessary to administer systematic surveys of clients. Client firms can be asked if each of these intermediate outcomes occurred, as shown in question 13 of Exhibit 6.3.

However, these outcomes can occur without the program's assistance contributing significantly. Thus, the firm also should be asked about the extent of the program's *contribution* to the intermediate outcomes. The program can choose to ask about all these intermediate outcomes jointly or can ask separately about each outcome. The latter procedure will provide program managers with more information but requires a somewhat more complicated questionnaire. This latter approach is illustrated in question 17 of Exhibit 6.3. Information on intermediate outcomes can be reported as individual outcome indicators for each service, as shown in PI-2 in Exhibit 6.2, or as one summary indicator, such as "the percentage of respondents that reported at least some contribution, of at least one service, to at least one of the intermediate outcomes."

End (Long-term) Outcome Indicators

Long-term outcome indicators include the percentage of responding clients that reported: (1) that increased export sales and export-related jobs resulted (PI-3); or (2) various specific amounts of added sales (PI-4), or (3) added employment (PI-5) resulted at least somewhat due to the program's assistance. It may be more accurate to estimate the amount of added export-related employment from increases reported in export sales than from responses to a direct question (e.g., question 16 in Exhibit 6.3) about the amount of additional employment.

Since information on long-term indicators, as well as on intermediate ones, comes from client responses, the accuracy and validity of the responses are somewhat uncertain. This applies particularly to the data on the amount of export sales (PI-4) and, even more so to the amount of export-related employment that occurred (PI-5)--amounts that were at least partly based on the assistance received from the program. Respondents may be unwilling or unable to provide accurate information on sales and export-related employment or on the extent of the public program's contribution. Section 9, "Client Surveys," discusses ways to increase response rates. Accuracy of responses should also be higher if respondents are asked to provide information about their export sales and employment increases *as ranges* rather than as "exact" numbers, as done in Exhibit 6.3. This means that the agency will not be able to obtain precise numbers, which, in any case, probably cannot be obtained from these (or most other) procedures.

Therefore, the estimates provided for PI-4 and PI-5 should be considered as rough numbers. This information, nevertheless, should still be quite useful in indicating relative performance when comparing performance values from one reporting period to another, or when comparing outcomes among various categories of clients.

Important related outcomes not listed in Exhibit 6.2 but ones that a program may want to tabulate are percentage of firms reporting that they: (1) made their first export sale (beginning exporting); (2) increased exports of current products in current markets; (3) exported new products; and (4) exported to new countries. These distinctions may be important to program managers. For some programs, the signing of licenses and joint ventures also may be important long-term outcomes. As with all these intermediate and end outcomes, the program should link responses to client firms with clients' responses about the extent of the contribution of the agency's service to these outcomes.

Client businesses also should be given an opportunity to provide narrative explanations for their quality and contribution ratings, especially if they give low ratings, as illustrated by questions 12 and 18 on the sample questionnaire. These responses should be compiled and analyzed. Program managers should review these narrative responses to help them identify specific reasons for poor ratings as a guide to program improvement.

■

NONUSE OF PROGRAM SERVICES

Do firms *not* currently using agency services do so because the agency has not provided sufficient information on its services or because the firms believe the agency is not helpful or not accessible? The frequency of such perceptions among firms can be an important indicator of program performance.

To obtain this information, the agency can survey a sample of businesses that have not used the program's services, to find out the reasons why. The reasons should be separated into reasons over which the agency has little or no control and reasons over which the agency has some significant control. For example, if respondents indicate that they have received poor service in the past or did not know about the service, these are problems that the program can work to correct. Question 10 of Exhibit 6.4 illustrates how this information can be obtained. The performance indicator that can be obtained is the percentage of respondents that had not obtained program services for one or more reasons at least partly controllable by the program (PI-6). A survey of nonassisted businesses does not need to be done as frequently as a survey of program clients.

Once-a-year surveys should be sufficient. However, splitting the annual sample into two and surveying twice a year might give program managers more timely information on programs. This survey of nonassisted businesses also can provide data for comparing the outcomes of client businesses to those of nonassisted businesses of similar size and industry (although this is somewhat questionable and probably is more appropriate for a special study than for ongoing monitoring).

A sample of nonassisted firms can be selected at random from a state directory of manufacturers, state unemployment insurance (UI) data files, or other jurisdiction-wide lists of business. A sample size of perhaps 100 to 200 firms should be adequate to provide useful information about reasons for nonuse. More systematic sampling procedures would be required to provide data for comparing assisted to nonassisted businesses, such as closer matching of nonassisted firms to assisted firms as to size and industry.

■

DISAGGREGATIONS OF INDICATOR DATA

Performance indicators for the program should be disaggregated by such client characteristics as: (1) region or location in the state (county or multicounty region); (2) size of business (measured in number of employees and, possibly, sales); and (3) business or industrial sector (SIC, standard industrial classification code or multi-SIC category). These breakouts will provide program managers with information about service performance among businesses in different regions of the state, of different sizes, and in different industrial sectors. This should make the performance information considerably more useful than merely providing the data on an aggregate basis (e.g., for all clients grouped together).

Breakouts also may be used to provide performance information on: (1) whether the businesses are subsidiaries or independent (question 1 of Exhibit 6.3); (2) whether the businesses have overseas plants or not (question 2); and (3) the extent of experience of the businesses in exporting when they began receiving services (e.g., didn't export, were preparing to export, had some experience, or had considerable experience). The extent of experience (export stage of the business) is of interest, since nonexporters, new exporters, and experienced exporters can be expected to differ in the outcomes they achieve. For example, business clients that started out as nonexporters are less likely to show substantial increases in export sales than clients who were experienced exporters. The export stage of a business can be determined through the client survey, illustrated by questions 5 and 6 of Exhibit 6.3, or from the program's own client files.

Exhibit 6.5 illustrates how performance indicator breakout data can be presented.

■

SOURCES FOR PERFORMANCE DATA

Program Records

Program records provide the contact and descriptive information on clients needed to survey clients and to provide data disaggregations. Records should be maintained, preferably in a systematic client information system. The information needed includes: (1) the primary contact persons at client businesses, their titles, addresses, and telephone numbers; (2) the services provided to each client for each reporting period; (3) business location (region or country); (4) size (number of employees); and (5) industrial sector (e.g., SIC code).

Client Surveys

Periodic surveys of clients are the primary source of information on program performance. These surveys should be of all clients, if possible, or if that number is too large, of a sample of clients that began receiving service within a particular time period (such as one calendar quarter). The sample might be a random selection of all clients, or a stratified sample to achieve representation of clients of different services received, size groups, industries, and location in the jurisdiction, in order to later breakout the performance data.

The businesses should be surveyed after a specified time period has elapsed from when the business first received service, such as one year. A one-year lag period provides a balance between (a) opinions of many export promotion professionals that it often takes 12 months or more from the receipt of services by a business to the occurrence of related outcomes, and (b) potential major memory problems if more than one year elapses between receipt of service and the survey. Most intermediate outcomes and at least some of the end outcomes can be expected to have occurred in one year. As the time period increases, the respondent's memory of service quality and the program's contribution to outcomes become weaker.

If a second service to an individual business is subsequently initiated, program managers will need to decide if or when the business should be surveyed again. As a rule, no single business facility should be surveyed more frequently than once a year.

Program managers also need to define the *minimum amount of service* provided to a business before that business can be considered a "client" and warrant being surveyed. Firms that received only a very small amount of assistance from the program should not be included. A simple rule is to select a minimum number of hours of service, such as four or more, that defines a business as a client for performance monitoring purposes.

Clients should receive a personalized cover letter introducing the questionnaire from a high-level official, such as the government's chief executive office or agency head. The letter should make it clear that responses will remain confidential (that responses will be reported only in aggregate form and that program personnel will not have access to individual questionnaires) and that they are important to the agency for improving its service. If possible, an incentive to respond, such as a valuable departmental publication, should be offered. At least two mailings of the questionnaire and telephone reminders should be used to ensure adequate response rates.

Section 9, "Client Surveys," provides more detail on survey procedures and ways to increase response rates. A suggested cover letter for the questionnaire is also presented in that section.

State Unemployment Insurance Data

The state UI database can be used to determine the change in employment of assisted firms. Program personnel should be asked to request the identification number from clients as part of one of the initial contacts. (The UI database contains federal and state identification numbers for each firm that pays taxes on employees in the state.) If the program does not obtain an ID number, it may still be possible to find the firm in the UI database using the firm's name and county code. Because of certain characteristics in the system (described more fully in Section 10), it may not be possible to find all firms using the company name and county code.

The UI database can be used to track the monthly employment of assisted firms. The UI system collects monthly employment figures from firms on a quarterly basis. The program could identify employment change in assisted firms for several quarters. The UI data are useful because they allow the program to track long-term outcomes over a longer period of time than can be obtained from a client survey.

Although this procedure is attractive, it has two important limitations. It can obtain quite accurate employment figures, but this will not tell whether the export promotion program contributed directly to increases in employment. Nor does it provide information on service quality, as does the client survey procedure. Thus, the UI database should preferably be considered as a complement to client survey procedures, especially for providing data on the amount of job growth for use in PI-3b and PI-5.

■

EXPLANATORY DATA

Explanatory data also can be included in the report. Such data would provide users with information about major factors that influence performance, especially factors outside the program's control. The most obvious factor is the *exchange value of the dollar*. The change in the value of the dollar during the reporting period for major export markets can be reported along with the performance indicator data. Top export destination countries can be identified, if needed, through the client surveys.

■

REPORTING THE RESULTS

The resulting performance indicator data should be presented in informative and easy-to-read formats. Exhibits 6.5, 6.6, and 6.7 display illustrative formats for reporting performance results. Exhibit 6.5 presents a detailed report format for reporting performance for one service, using one performance indicator, broken out by industry, size, and location. The user of the report can quickly identify those categories of clients for whom performance was particularly high or low for the period covered by the report. Exhibit 6.6 presents a report format that shows the results for each service on one performance indicator. Exhibit 6.7 presents a summary report format for the program as a whole (all services combined), comparing current performance on each performance indicator to previous performance and against targets established by the program.

Note that in some instances useful information can be more efficiently conveyed by creating performance indicators from the responses to more than one survey question. For example, in Exhibit 6.2, PI-4 and PI-5 are based on combining the responses to Questions 14 and 17, and 16 and 17 (from Exhibit 6.3), respectively.

See Section 11, "Analysis and Presentation of Performance Information," for more suggestions on these topics.

EXHIBIT 6.1

TYPICAL EXPORT PROMOTION ACTIVITIES

1. Seminars/workshops/conferences
2. Staff counseling/technical assistance
3. Introduction to visiting buyers
4. Trade leads
5. Catalog shows
6. Trade shows/fairs
7. Trade missions
8. Trade financing/insurance
9. Referrals for export services
10. Directories of exporters, products, distributors
11. Newsletters/how-to handbooks/other publications
12. Market studies/trade statistics

EXHIBIT 6.2

PERFORMANCE INDICATORS FOR EXPORT PROMOTION PROGRAMS[1]

For Business Assisted Agency Program

Service Quality Indicators:

PI-1 Percentage of respondents that rated each service as either "excellent" or "good" as to: (a) timeliness, (b) relevance and accuracy, (c) professional rendering, *and* (d) overall helpfulness (Question 11, Exhibit 6.3).

Intermediate Outcome Indicators:

PI-2 Percentage of recipients of each service that reported at least some contribution of the service to: (a) a decision to begin exporting, (b) development of an export marketing plan, (c) establishment of overseas market contacts, *or* (d) signing an overseas agent or distributor (Questions 13a, 13b, 13c, 13d, and 17, Exhibit 6.3).

End (Long-term) Outcome Indicators:

PI-3 Percentage of recipients of each service that reported at least some contribution of the service to (a) increased export sales *or* (b) increased export related employment (Questions 13 and 17, Exhibit 6.3).

PI-4 Percentage of respondents that reported various increases in export sales *and* reported that one or more services made at least some contribution to increased sales (Questions 14 and 17, Exhibit 6.3).

PI-5 Percentage of respondents that reported various numbers of new permanent jobs added at facilities in the jurisdiction as a result of increased exporting *and* reported that one or more services made at least some contribution to the added jobs (Questions 16 and 17, Exhibit 6.3).

For Businesses Not Assisted by Agency Programs

PI-6 Percentage of respondents reporting that they did not obtain any services for a reason relatively controllable by the program; that is, because respondents: (a) were not aware of its services, (b) felt that the program did not offer the services they needed, (c) had heard that the program offered poor services, *or* (d) got poor service from the program in the past (Question 10, Exhibit 6.4).

1. Question numbers refer to questions in the sample questionnaire for assisted businesses in Exhibit 6.3.

EXHIBIT 6.3

SAMPLE CLIENT QUESTIONNAIRE FOR EXPORT PROMOTION PROGRAMS (ASSISTED BUSINESSES)

Our records indicate that your firm received assistance from the Economic Development Department to help you consider [name of jurisdiction] as a place to locate a facility.

NOTE: RESPONSES WILL BE HELD ENTIRELY IN CONFIDENCE. RESULTS WILL BE REPORTED ONLY IN AGGREGATE FORM.

1. At the beginning of [year], was your company: **(PLEASE CIRCLE ONE.)**

   Independent? 1

   Headquarters? 2

   A subsidiary or branch? 3

2. At the beginning of [year], did your company (including parent or subsidiaries) have any overseas manufacturing or assembly operations?

   Yes.................................... 1

   No.................................... 2

3. At the beginning of [year], how many people were employed full-time by your company (not including parent or subsidiaries) in: **(PLEASE CIRCLE ONE FROM EACH COLUMN.)**

	The U.S.?	[Jurisdiction] Only?
1 to 9....................	1	1
10 to 19....................	2	2
20 to 49....................	3	3

(continued on next page)

Exhibit 6.3 *(continued)*

	The U.S.?	[Jurisdiction] Only?
50 to 99	4	4
100 to 250	5	5
Over 250	6	6

4. What are your company's total [year] sales in: **(PLEASE CIRCLE ONE FROM EACH COLUMN.)**

	The U.S.?	[Jurisdiction] Only?
Under $500K	1	1
$500K to $4.9M	2	2
$5M to $9.9M	3	3
$10M to $24.9M	4	4
$25M to $50M	5	5
Over $50M	6	6

5. Which of the following best describes your company's export activity as of the beginning of [year]?

   a. We didn't export and weren't interested........ 1

   b. We only exported in response to unsolicited orders........ 2

   c. We were preparing to export........ 3

   d. We had no more than five export transactions per year........ 4

   e. We had six or more export transactions per year........ 5

Exhibit 6.3 *(continued)*

6. Roughly what percentage of total sales from your [name of jurisdiction] facility(ies) *only* were due to exports in [year]?

   None.. 1

   Under 5%.. 2

   5% to 9%.. 3

   10% to 19%.. 4

   20% to 40%.. 5

   Over 40%.. 6

7. Which of the following industries *best* describes your [name of jurisdiction] facility(ies)?

   Food and Kindred Products (SIC 20).. 1

   Industrial Machinery and Equipment (SIC 35).. 2

   Instrument and Related Products (SIC 38).. 3

   Business Services (SIC 73).. 4

8. If your [name of jurisdiction] facility(ies) exported in [year], in which country did you make the largest dollar amount of export sales? ______________________

Exhibit 6.3 *(continued)*

9. Below is a list of [program name] services. Please identify whether or not each service was obtained by your [name of jurisdiction] facility(ies) during approximately [quarter, year].

		Service was obtained	Service was not obtained
a.	Newsletter	1	2
b.	Other publications	1	2
c.	Export-related seminar or workshop	1	2
d.	Individual export counseling/staff assistance	1	2
e.	List of agents or distributors	1	2
f.	Trade leads	1	2
g.	Introduction to foreign buyer visiting [name of jurisdiction]	1	2
h.	Catalog show abroad	1	2
i.	Trade show abroad	1	2
j.	Trade mission abroad	1	2
k.	Export financing	1	2
l.	Other ______________________	1	2

Exhibit 6.3 *(continued)*

10. In approximately what quarter did your [name of jurisdiction] facility(ies) first begin receiving these services from the [program name]?

Did not receive services	1
Before [quarter, year]	2
[Quarter, year]	3
After [quarter, year]	4
Don't know	5

11. Please rate each of the services obtained at your [name of jurisdiction] facility(ies) in terms of the following characteristics? **(PLEASE RATE.)**

RATING SCALE

1 = Excellent		3 = Fair	
2 = Good		4 = Poor	

	Timely	Relevant and Accurate	Profes-sionally Rendered	Overall Helpfulness
a. Newsletter	1	2	3	4
b. Other publications	1	2	3	4
c. Seminar or workshop	1	2	3	4
d. Export counseling	1	2	3	4
e. List of agents or distributors	1	2	3	4

(continued on next page)

Exhibit 6.3 *(continued)*

		Timely	Relevant and Accurate	Profes-sionally Rendered	Overall Helpfulness
f.	Trade lead..	1	2	3	4
g.	Introduction to visiting buyer............	1	2	3	4
h.	Catalog show abroad..........................	1	2	3	4
i.	Trade show abroad.............................	1	2	3	4
j.	Trade mission abroad..........................	1	2	3	4
k.	Export financing................................	1	2	3	4
l.	Other..	1	2	3	4

12. If you rated any of the services Poor or Fair on any characteristic in Question 11, would you please explain why?

Exhibit 6.3 *(continued)*

13. Please indicate whether or not each of the following export-related results occurred at your [name of jurisdiction] facility(ies) *after* you began receiving services from the [program name].

	Did Not Occur	Occurred
a. Decided to export	1	2
b. Developed export marketing strategy or plan	1	2
c. Established overseas market contacts	1	2
d. Signed overseas agent or distributor	1	2
e. Began exporting	1	2
f. Increased sales of current products in current markets	1	2
g. Exported new products	1	2
h. Exported to new countries	1	2
i. Added new export-related jobs	1	2
j. Signed a license or joint-venture agreement	1	2
k. Other	1	2

____

14. By approximately how much did export sales from your [name of jurisdiction] facility(ies) increase *after* you began receiving services from the [program name]?

a. No increase	1
b. $1 to $49,999	2
c. $50,000 to $99,999	3

(continued on next page)

Exhibit 6.3 *(continued)*

d. $100,000 to $499,999 4

e. $500,000 to $999,999 5

f. $1,000,000 to $4,999,999 6

g. More than $5,000,000 7

15. By approximately what percentage do you expect export sales to increase in the next three years? ______________

16. How many permanent new jobs have been added at your [name of jurisdiction] facility(ies) as a result of increased exporting *since* you began receiving services from the [program name]?

a. None 1

b. 1 to 5 2

c. 6 to 10 3

d. 11 to 50 4

e. 51 to 100 5

f. Over 100 6

17. Please circle the numbers below that best describe what you believe to be the contribution that *each* of the following services you obtained from [Program name] made to *each* of the results that occurred at your [name of jurisdiction] facility(ies).

KEY (STRENGTH OF CONTRIBUTION)

1 = did not obtain service
2 = no contribution
3 = modest contribution
4 = substantial contribution

Exhibit 6.3 *(continued)*

a.	Newsletter	1	2	3	4
b.	Other publications	1	2	3	4
c.	Seminar or workshop	1	2	3	4
d.	Staff counseling	1	2	3	4
e.	List of agents or distributors	1	2	3	4
f.	Trade lead	1	2	3	4
g.	Introduction to visiting buyers	1	2	3	4
h.	Catalog show abroad	1	2	3	4
i.	Trade show abroad	1	2	3	4
j.	Trade mission abroad	1	2	3	4
k.	Export financing assistance	1	2	3	4
l.	Other	1	2	3	4

____

18. If you rated any service as making no contribution in Question 17 above, would you please explain why?

(continued on next page)

Exhibit 6.3 *(continued)*

19. Do you have any other comments or suggestions as to how the [program name] can improve its service to [name of jurisdiction] businesses?

Thank you for your help!

EXHIBIT 6.4

SAMPLE CLIENT QUESTIONNAIRE FOR EXPORT PROMOTION PROGRAMS (NONASSISTED BUSINESSES)

NOTE: RESPONSES WILL BE HELD ENTIRELY IN CONFIDENCE. RESULTS WILL BE REPORTED ONLY IN AGGREGATE FORM.

1. At the beginning of [year], was your company: **(PLEASE CIRCLE ONE.)**

   Independent? 1

   Headquarters? 2

   A subsidiary or branch? 3

2. At the beginning of [year], did your company (including parent or subsidiaries) have any overseas manufacturing or assembly operations?

   Yes.......... 1

   No.......... 2

3. At the beginning of [year], how many people were employed full-time by your company (not including parent or subsidiaries) in: **(PLEASE CIRCLE ONE.)**

	The U.S.?	[Jurisdiction] Only?
1 to 9..........	1	1
10 to 19..........	2	2
20 to 49..........	3	3
50 to 99..........	4	4
100 to 250..........	5	5
Over 250..........	6	6

Exhibit 6.4 *(continued)*

4. What are your company's total [year] sales in: **(PLEASE CIRCLE ONE.)**

	The U.S.?	[Jurisdiction] Only?
Under $500K..................................	1	1
$500K to $4.9M..............................	2	2
$5M to $9.9M................................	3	3
$10M to $24.9M.............................	4	4
$25M to $50M................................	5	5
Over $50M.....................................	6	6

5. Which of the following best describes your company's export activity as of the beginning of [year]?
   a. We didn't export and weren't interested.. 1
   b. We only exported in response to unsolicited orders.. 2
   c. We were preparing to export.. 3
   d. We had no more than five export transactions per year....................................... 4
   e. We had six or more export transactions per year.. 5

6. Roughly what percentage of total sales from your [name of jurisdiction] facility(ies) *only* were due to exports in [year]?

   None.. 1

   Under 5%.. 2

   5% to 9%.. 3

   10% to 19%.. 4

   20% to 40%.. 5

   Over 40%.. 6

Exhibit 6.4 *(continued)*

7. Which of the following industries *best* describes your [name of jurisdiction] facility(ies)?

Food and Kindred Products (SIC 20)	1
Industrial Machinery and Equipment (SIC 35)	2
Instrument and Related Products (SIC 38)	3
Business Services (SIC 73)	4

8. If your [name of jurisdiction] facility(ies) exported in [year], in which country did you make the largest dollar amount of export sales? ____________________

9. Below is a list of [program name] services. Please identify whether or not each service was obtained by your [name of jurisdiction] facility(ies) during approximately [quarter, year].

	Service was obtained	Service was not obtained
a. Newsletter	1	2
b. Other publications	1	2
c. Export-related seminar or workshop	1	2
d. Individual export counseling/staff assistance	1	2
e. List of agents or distributors	1	2
f. Trade leads	1	2
g. Introduction to foreign buyer visiting [name of jurisdiction]	1	2
h. Catalog show abroad	1	2

Exhibit 6.4 *(continued)*

		Service was obtained	Service was not obtained
i.	Trade show abroad	1	2
j.	Trade mission abroad	1	2
k.	Export financing	1	2
l.	Other	1	2

____

10. In approximately what quarter did your [name of jurisdiction] facility(ies) first begin receiving these services from the [program name]? **(PLEASE CIRCLE ALL THE FOLLOWING REASONS THAT BEST EXPLAIN WHY.)**

		True	False
a.	Not interested in exporting	1	2
b.	Not aware of [program name] or its services	1	2
c.	[program name] doesn't offer service we need	1	2
d.	Have heard [program name] offers poor service	1	2
e.	Got poor service from [program name] prior to [quarter, year]	1	2
f.	Got poor service from government agencies in past	1	2
g.	Don't need outside assistance in exporting	1	2
h.	Use private sources for export assistance	1	2
i.	Use other public sources for export assistance	1	2
j.	Other	1	2

____

Exhibit 6.4 *(continued)*

11. Please indicate whether or not each of the following export-related results occurred at your [name of jurisdiction] facility(ies) since approximately [quarter, year].

		Occurred	Did Not Occur
a.	Decided to export	1	2
b.	Developed export marketing strategy or plan	1	2
c.	Established overseas market contact	1	2
d.	Signed overseas agent or distributor	1	2
e.	Began exporting	1	2
f.	Increased sales of current products in current markets	1	2
g.	Exported new products	1	2
h.	Exported to new countries	1	2
i.	Added new export-related jobs	1	2
j.	Signed a license or joint-venture agreement	1	2
k.	Other	1	2

____

12. By approximately how much did export sales from your [name of jurisdiction] facility(ies) increase since approximate [quarter, year]?

a.	No increase	1
b.	$1 to $49,999	2
c.	$50,000 to $99,999	3
d.	$100,000 to $499,999	4
e.	$500,000 to $999,999	5
f.	$1,000,000 to $4,999,999	6
g.	More than $5,000,000	7

Exhibit 6.4 *(continued)*

13. By approximately what percentage do you expect export sales to increase in the next three years? ______________________

14. How many permanent new jobs have been added at your [name of jurisdiction] facility(ies) as a result of increased exporting *since* you began receiving services from the [program name]?

    a. None..1

    b. 1 to 5...2

    c. 6 to 10...3

    d. 11 to 50...4

    e. 51 to 100...5

    f. Over 100..6

15. Do you have any other comments or suggestions as to how the [program name] can improve its service to [name of jurisdiction] businesses?

Thank you for your help!

EXHIBIT 6.5

EXAMPLE OF DETAILED REPORT FORMAT FOR EXPORT PROMOTION PROGRAMS

Performance Indicator PI-3: Percentage of clients that rated trade shows as making a substantial, modest, or no contribution to increased export sales *and* increased export-related employment.

		Percentage		
	Number in Sample	Substantial Contribution	Modest Contribution	No Contribution
Total				
Industry Sector				
Food and Kindred Products (SIC 20)				
Industrial Machinery and Equipment (SIC 35)				
Instruments and Related Products (SIC 38)				
Business Services (SIC 73)				
Size (Number of employees)				
1-9				
10-19				
20-49				
50-99				
100-249				
250 and up				
Location (Region)				
Metro				
Nonmetro				
Export Stage				
Uninterested				
Planning to export				
Some experience				
Much experience				

EXHIBIT 6.6

EXAMPLE OF SUMMARY REPORT FORMAT FOR EXPORT PROMOTION PROGRAMS

Performance Indicator PI-3: Percentage of clients that rated each service as making a substantial, modest, or no contribution to increased export sales or employment.

		Percentage		
Service	Number in Sample	Substantial Contribution	Modest Contribution	No Contribution
a. Newsletter				
b. Other publications				
c. Seminar or workshop				
d. Export counseling				
e. List of agents and distributors				
f. Trade lead				
g. Introduction to visiting buyers				
h. Catalog shows abroad				
i. Trade shows abroad				
j. Trade missions abroad				
k. Export financing				
i. Other				

EXHIBIT 6.7

EXAMPLE OF SUMMARY REPORT FORMAT FOR EXPORT PROMOTION PROGRAMS

Performance Indicators	Most Recent Period	Last Period	Year to Date	Year to Date Last Year	Target % for Current Year
Service Quality Indicators PI-1 Percentage of respondents that rated each service as either excellent or good on all four characteristics.					
Intermediate Outcome Indicators PI-2 Percentage of respondents that reported at least some contribution of services to increased pre-export activities.					
Long-Term Outcome Indicators PI-3 Percentage that reported at least some service contribution to increased export sales or jobs.					
PI-4 Percentage of respondents that provided a dollar amount for increased export sales and that services made at least some contribution.					
PI-5 Percentage of respondents that reported a number of new permanent jobs as a result of increased exporting and that services made at least some contribution.					
PI-6 Percentage of respondents that reported that they did not seek program services for a reason relatively controllable by the program.					

7

COMMUNITY ECONOMIC DEVELOPMENT ASSISTANCE

■

SCOPE

Most states have programs designed to improve the capacity of local government economic development efforts. These programs may include a variety of economic development functions aimed at helping local governments in their business attraction, financial assistance, business assistance, and tourism activities. Even if the state economic development agency does not have a formal program to help local governments, it may still want to regularly assess the quality of its informal work with community economic development officials.

The procedures described here can be adapted to most state programs of assistance to local government, such as tourism, technical assistance, or business/financial assistance programs. These procedures have been generalized from those used by Maryland in its procedures for community tourism assistance and by Minnesota in its community technical assistance and grant programs.

The state can undertake a variety of activities to help these local agencies. Services might include conferences and workshops, assistance in analyzing local business needs, identification of assets that may be attractive to prospective businesses (this may include surveys of local businesses or analyses of state unemployment insurance (UI) data to assess the local government's strengths and weaknesses in certain industrial sectors). Additional services include assistance in establishing a revolving loan fund, identification of potential sites for new businesses, provision of data or other information, technical assistance with a particular problem, and brokering incentive packages, as well as assistance to improve general administrative operations, such as help in the development of economic development plans and the setting of priorities and targets.

State efforts are likely to serve communities of different levels of sophistication and experience. The programs may target communities that have no economic development programs, or attempt to assist cities improve their services and/or expand into new areas.

The immediate objectives of these programs generally are: (1) to increase the capacity of local governments to perform certain economic development functions and (2) to improve the assistance received by business clients of local government economic development programs. The ultimate objectives are the same as other state economic development programs: to enhance employment and the economic condition of the state. However, the primary focus of the procedures presented in this section is on assessing the quality of the assistance provided to the local communities rather than the ultimate outcomes, such as the subsequent success of the local communities in adding new jobs.

This section presents procedures for monitoring the state's performance in assisting localities, not procedures for the state to use to determine how well local agencies are performing. Thus, local agencies are the *clients* of the state for programs that are the subject of this section.

■

PERFORMANCE INDICATORS FOR COMMUNITY ECONOMIC DEVELOPMENT ASSISTANCE PROGRAMS

Performance indicators for community economic development assistance programs are listed in Exhibit 7.1. Because community development assistance programs can take on quite different forms in different states, the set of indicators needs to be tailored to the specific activities undertaken by the state to assist local communities. (For example, the Minnesota Star Cities program provides a series of specific services for participating communities. The performance indicators it selected should provide feedback on each of those specific services.)

The information for each of these indicators comes from a periodic survey of each local economic development agency. This appears to be the primary, if not the only, source for this information. A sample questionnaire that might be used to solicit this information is provided in Exhibit 7.2.

Indicators of Service Quality

PI-1 assesses the quality of each individual service provided by the state to the local agency as perceived by local economic development officials. A state may ask respondents for an overall rating of quality and/or a rating of specific service *attributes*, such as the timeliness of the state's assistance, the helpfulness of the state staff, and the accuracy of the information provided (as illustrated in questionnaires included in other sections). For simplicity, the questionnaire in Exhibit 7.2 asks only for an overall rating of quality.

The specific list of *services* to be rated should be geared to each state program. The sample questionnaire in Question 1, Exhibit 7.2, lists eight services (i.e., types of assistance). The activities listed in Question 1 pertain to a technical assistance program, not to a tourism or financial assistance program.

PI-2 and PI-3 provide local officials' perspectives on two particular characteristics of the quality of the state's service: cooperativeness of state personnel and timeliness. Adequate coordination/cooperation/timeliness are often matters of contention between levels of government. If the state agency wants to ask local officials to rate other specific characteristics, it should add relevant questions.

PI-4 provides the local officials' perspective on the adequacy of the state's communication with the community with respect to state plans and policies regarding economic development. Local communities are often concerned about lack of interaction with the state on overall policy issues. This question gives the state the opportunity to identify the extent of this concern.

Respondents also should be asked to indicate their reasons for negative ratings. Questions 1j, 2a, 3a, and 4a of Exhibit 7.2 illustrate how this can be done. These reasons should subsequently be compiled and reviewed by the program to help determine whether, and what, improvements are needed.

Intermediate Outcome Indicators

PI-5 provides local officials' assessments of the state agency's overall contribution to their communities' economic development during the reporting period. Question 5 of Exhibit 7.2 illustrates how this information can be obtained. As demonstrated in Question 5a, respondents also can be asked to provide explanations for their ratings. These responses should be compiled by the central analysis office (CAO) and reviewed by program and other agency officials. These explanations, especially concerning negative ratings, can help state managers identify reasons for problems and suggest needed improvements.

End (Long-term) Outcome Indicators

PI-6 seeks information on the number of additional jobs in the community that resulted from the assistance provided by the state's community assistance program. The accuracy of such responses, however, is probably far from precise. The responses should not be considered as "facts," but rather as local official impressions of the helpfulness of the program. Therefore, as Question 6 of Exhibit 7.2 illustrates, respondents are only asked to give their estimates in ranges, rather than giving one number. Also, as the wording of PI-6 in Exhibit 7.1 indicates, the summary performance indicator might best be expressed only as the percentage of respondents reporting *one or more* added jobs that resulted.

At the end of the questionnaire, respondents should be asked for any further comments or suggestions for improving the state's assistance. This final question also may provide useful suggestions for program improvements.

■

DISAGGREGATIONS OF INDICATOR DATA

Performance indicators for this program should be disaggregated by such community characteristics as: (1) population size of the communities that the state is assisting; (2) type of community (typically urban versus suburban versus rural, or metro versus nonmetro); (3) length of time the community has been involved in economic development activities, or some other estimate of the sophistication of the community's program; (4) region or location in the state (county or multicounty region); and (5) economic condition, perhaps based on economic indicators such as unemployment rates, job, income, or population growth, or number of new housing starts. Exhibit 7.3 presents one set of such categories.

These breakouts will provide state managers with more detailed information regarding how helpful their services are perceived to be by communities of different types and locations.

■

SOURCES FOR PERFORMANCE DATA

Performance data for these indicators would come from regular surveys of communities. The simplest approach is to mail a questionnaire to the lead economic development official in each county or city that is considered a client of the economic development agency. (In smaller communities without a formal economic development agency, the senior official might be a town manager or the town clerk.) In many states, all or most all local governments may be considered clients. For a state with a special program aimed at a subset of cities or counties, the client list will be smaller.

A questionnaire probably should not be sent to any one community more than once a year. However, to provide more timely feedback to agency managers, the total client list might be randomly split into two, three, or four groups, with one group surveyed each six-month period (if the clients are split into two groups), each three-month period (if split into three groups), or quarterly (if split into four groups). More frequent feedback, if only from a portion of all client communities, can provide earlier warnings to staff regarding needed corrections than if feedback is received only once or twice a year.

Second mailings should be sent to communities that do not respond to the first mailing. A telephone reminder might be necessary. In general, the agency should expect a substantial percentage of responses. Agencies should set the target for returns at about 75 percent of questionnaires sent out.

It is preferable to treat the responses as confidential and not make available the name of the person or community giving particular responses. Confidentiality, however, may be difficult with this client group. It is likely, in any case, that most respondents will assume that their responses are not completely confidential and will word their responses accordingly. Although this may inhibit some persons and some answers, most respondents are likely to be reasonably frank. The responses should be returned to a central analysis unit for a tally of the results and compilation of responses to the open-ended questions. (The compilers should screen out wording that might identify individual respondents, unless they have been notified that their responses will not be treated as confidential.) If a local official wants to use the questionnaire to communicate a particular problem to the agency and indicates that he or she is willing to be identified, the appropriate state officials can then be provided a copy of that material so that they may take the necessary steps to resolve the problem or respond to the issue.

To maximize both the likelihood of frank responses and the response rate, the agency head should provide a personalized cover letter for each local government official, encouraging officials to air problems. As with other types of mail surveys, a stamped, self-addressed envelop should be enclosed with the questionnaire.

■

REPORTING THE RESULTS

Exhibits 7.3 and 7.4 display suggested detailed and summary report formats, respectively, for community economic development assistance programs. Exhibit 7.3 is used to provide performance findings on individual performance indicators, within the findings broken out for each category of client. Users of these reports can quickly identify those categories of clients for whom performance on the indicator was particularly high or low during the period covered by the report. Exhibit 7.4 presents summary findings on all the performance indicators. It also provides comparisons of the current period to the previous year and program targets (if any have been set).

See Section 11, "Analysis and Reporting of Performance Information," for more suggestions on these topics.

EXHIBIT 7.1

PERFORMANCE INDICATORS FOR COMMUNITY ECONOMIC DEVELOPMENT ASSISTED PROGRAMS

Indicators of Service Quality:

PI-1 Number and percentage of respondents who rated each service they received as excellent or good (Question 1, Exhibit 7.2).

PI-2 Number and percentage of respondents who rated the cooperativeness of state personnel as excellent or good (Question 2, Exhibit 7.2).

PI-3 Number and percentage of respondents who rated the timeliness of the state's services as excellent or good (Question 3, Exhibit 7.2).

PI-4 Number and percentage of respondents that rated the adequacy of communication with the state about state plans and policies as excellent or good (Question 4, Exhibit 7.2).

Intermediate Outcome Indicators:

PI-5 Number and percentage of respondents who reported that the state economic development agency had contributed at least somewhat to their communities' own economic development in the past 12 months (Question 5, Exhibit 7.2).

End (Long-term) Outcome Indicators:

PI-6 Number and percentage of respondents who reported that additional jobs had resulted over the past 12 months because of the program (Question 6, Exhibit 7.2).

---

1. The information in parentheses refers to the source of data for each indicator.

EXHIBIT 7.2

SAMPLE CLIENT QUESTIONNAIRE FOR STATE COMMUNITY ECONOMIC DEVELOPMENT ASSISTANCE PROGRAMS

1. Which of the following types of assistance have you received from the state Department of Economic Development in *the past 12 months*? How would you rate each of these services? **(PLEASE CIRCLE ONE RESPONSE FOR EACH SERVICE.)**

N = Did not receive this type of assistance
1 = Excellent
2 = Good
3 = Fair
4 = Poor

a.	Attended an annual conference	N	1	2	3	4
b.	Attended at least one workshop or seminar	N	1	2	3	4
c.	Technical assistance from program staff regarding a particular problem or need	N	1	2	3	4
d.	Assistance with targeted marketing	N	1	2	3	4
e.	Assistance in developing economic development plans	N	1	2	3	4
f.	Assistance in identifying potential sites for locating businesses	N	1	2	3	4
g.	Assistance in conducting a survey of businesses	N	1	2	3	4
h.	Received economic/business data (other than that needed for any of the above services)	N	1	2	3	4
i.	Other	N	1	2	3	4

____

(continued on next page)

Exhibit 7.2 *(continued)*

j. If you rated any of the above types of assistance as either Fair or Poor, please explain.

2. How would you rate the cooperativeness of state personnel?

Excellent.. 1

Good.. 2

Fair.. 3

Poor... 4

Don't know.. 5

a. If Fair or Poor, please explain.

3. How would you rate the timeliness of the state's services?

Excellent.. 1

Good.. 2

Fair.. 3

Poor... 4

Don't know.. 5

Exhibit 7.2 *(continued)*

a. If Fair or Poor, please explain.

4. How would you rate the adequacy of the information you received from the state agency regarding *state plans and policies on economic development*?

Excellent	1
Good	2
Fair	3
Poor	4
Don't know	5

a. If Fair or Poor, please explain.

5. Overall, to what extent do you believe the state Economic Development Department has contributed to your community's economic development in the past 12 months?

Has helped considerably	1
Has helped somewhat	2
Has not helped	3
Has hurt	4

Exhibit 7.2 *(continued)*

a. If you indicated that the state's contribution either has not helped or has hurt, please explain.

6. Overall, approximately how many additional jobs do you estimate your community now has that it would not have had without the state's Community Assistance Program's help over the past 12 months?

0	1
1-4	2
5-10	3
11-25	4
Over 25	5
Don't know	6

7. Do you have any other comments or suggestions that might help us improve our economic development assistance to local communities?

Thank you for your help!

EXHIBIT 7.3

EXAMPLE OF DETAILED REPORT FORMAT FOR STATE COMMUNITY ECONOMIC DEVELOPMENT ASSISTANCE

Performance Indicator PI-5: Percentage of respondents who reported that the state economic development agency had contributed at least somewhat to their communities' own economic development in the past 12 months.

		Percentage			
	Number in Sample	Considerably	Somewhat	Not Helped	Hurt
Total					
Population					
0-4,999					
5,000-9,999					
10,000-49,999					
50,000 or larger					
Metro, Nonmetro					
Metro					
Nonmetro					
Region of Origin					
Region 1					
Region 2					
Region 3					
Region 4					
Region 5					
Unemployment Rate					
0-1.9%					
2.0-2.9%					
3.0-3.9%					
4.0-4.9%					
5% or higher					

EXHIBIT 7.4

EXAMPLE OF SUMMARY REPORT FORMAT FOR STATE COMMUNITY ECONOMIC DEVELOPMENT ASSISTANCE

Performance Indicators	Most Recent Period	Last Period	Year to Date	Year to Date Last Year	Target % for Current Year
Service Quality Indicators PI-1 Percentage of respondents who rated each service they received as excellent or good.					
PI-2 Percentage of respondents who rated the cooperativeness of state personnel as excellent or good.					
PI-3 Percentage of respondents who rated the timeliness of the state's services as excellent or good.					
PI-4 Percentage of respondents who rafed the adequacy of communication with the state about state plans and policies as excellent or good.					
Intermediate Outcome Indicators PI-5 Percentage of respondents who reported that the state economic development agency had contributed at least somewhat to their communities' own economic development in the past 12 months.					
End (Long-term) Outcome Indicators PI-6 Percentage of respondents who reported that additional jobs had resulted over the past 12 months because of the program.					

8

GLOBAL INDICATORS

■

INTRODUCTION

Most of this manual focuses on assessing service quality and outcomes for individual economic development programs. This section addresses indicators that relate to all businesses in the jurisdiction, not only those that have been served by the economic development agency.

Traditionally, state or local governments are concerned with jurisdiction-wide indicators of economic development such as employment and earnings. The problem for performance monitoring is that the values of these indicators are largely determined by forces outside the control of the economic development agency and, except for the input into overall economic policy provided by top agency managers, the agency probably has little control over these values. Thus, although state and local jurisdictions will be very interested in these indicators, they often will have little influence over them. These indicators, therefore, are likely to be of limited usefulness in assessing the performance of the agency's programs.

■

DISCUSSION OF CANDIDATE INDICATORS

Exhibit 8.1 presents a set of the candidate "global" indicators. Each is discussed in the paragraphs following.

Indicator 1, state (local) employment, is of key interest to most state and local officials, both economic development officials and others. The source for these data typically will be state unemployment insurance data. As part of state unemployment insurance requirements, each business establishment in the state is required to provide quarterly reports showing employment for each of the three months in that quarter. The data from these unemployment insurance records are by no means perfect. (See Section 10, on unemployment insurance information, for details of problems.) However, on the whole, these data are likely to be relatively accurate and seem sufficiently reliable for most state and local purposes.

Typically these data are collected and reported by industry, by region of the state, and by county. Exhibits 8.2 and 8.3 present formats that might be used for global indicator reports. These formats compare employment for the most recent month for which data are available with that for the last month of the previous quarter, and for the same month of the previous year. The formats also include the percentage change from both the last quarter and the last year.

An important characteristic of these data is that they reflect the *net* change in employment, considering both new jobs that have been added and number of jobs lost. Thus, the difference from one period to another represents the net change in jobs.

Indicators 2 and 3 provide information on the number of new business starts and business failures. The number of new business starts provides one measure of the ability of the jurisdiction's economy to stimulate growth. This information, however, does not indicate *how many jobs* resulted from these new business starts. Data on new facilities' initial employment levels can be obtained from the unemployment insurance database by developing a computer program that will extract the employment for all facilities that appeared for the first time during the quarter or the year.

The number (and percentage) of business failures is another indicator of the strength of the state or local economy. Again, this information does not indicate how many jobs are involved in these business failures, but such information also can be obtained from the unemployment insurance information. For both new business starts and business failures, a problem in estimating the number of jobs involved is how many months after the new business start, or how many months before the business failure, should employment data be sought as a reference point for counting the number of jobs gained or lost. These and other technical details would have to be worked out with unemployment data personnel.

Indicator 4, the unemployment rate, is also of considerable interest. It indicates the percentage of persons who have actively sought work but are not employed. One goal of public economic development programs is to bring these people into the work force. These data can be compared to the same information for other states or localities, to indicate the relative extent of the problem. Unemployment rates usually differ substantially among different demographic groupings of workers and among industries. Thus, the unemployment rate should, if possible, be broken out by such characteristics as age, race, sex, and industry. These figures are collected by the U.S. Department of Labor, with statewide unemployment figures released annually. More limited data are available from the state's unemployment compensation system, such as the number of applicants for, and recipients of, unemployment insurance. Since not all the unemployed apply or are eligible, these figures provide only a partial picture of unemployment.

Indicator 5, the average wage rate, provides some indication of the quality of jobs available in the jurisdiction. The change in wage rate from one period to the next, particularly when adjusted for inflation, indicates progress in this regard. The wage rate, however, is a very gross indicator, and its use has many problems. It is an average that does not reflect the distribution of wage rates. And, in fact, the jurisdiction may need a number of low-wage jobs if it has a pool of persons unemployed whose skills will not permit them to seek higher-level jobs, at least not without extensive training.

Indicator 6, the amount of tax revenue, is another crude indicator of economic activity. Numerous questions exist as to which particular revenues should be included to reflect economic development. Each agency will need to decide which particular tax or taxes to include in this global indicator, such as various corporate taxes, the personal income tax, and sales taxes. Because of variable rates of taxation and various accounting practices, the reliability of such numbers is unclear. However, relative values from one year to the next in the absence of major changes in the tax system should at least provide a rough indicator of trends in the economy and also indicate the size of one direct benefit, revenue, to the government.

Indicator 7, the percentage of businesses that rate the jurisdiction as a good place to do business, provides an indication of business executives' satisfaction with the jurisdiction as a place to do business. These data need to be obtained from surveys of businesses. An easy way to obtain such information is to ask this question of all businesses surveyed by individual agency programs as part of their monitoring efforts. However, it will not be known how representative these firms are of all businesses in the jurisdiction. It can be argued that since these firms have been clients of the economic development agency, their comments will be favorably biased. If the agency also surveys a random sample of firms *not* assisted by programs (to determine reasons why these firms are not using the programs, as discussed in Section 6, "Export Trade Promotion") and asks this question, responses from this sample could provide adequate balance.

Another option, although more expensive, is to conduct a special survey of businesses across the jurisdiction on this issue. A less expensive variation is to attach such a question to another ongoing survey, such as those undertaken regularly in some states by a state university survey research center.

Indicator 8, the "business climate" ranking, produced by one or more private firms, is obviously of concern to state economic development agencies. Most of these business climate rankings (such as the Grant Thornton manufacturing climate rankings and the Corporation for Enterprise Development report card) are somewhat controversial. They collect data on a wide variety of indicators and combine them, using assumptions about the weights (importance) of each particular indicator. Many, probably most, of the components of these rankings are not controllable, or even influenced, by state economic development agencies. Thus, their validity as performance indicators of agency programs is highly questionable. Nevertheless, these rankings are widely publicized across the country and receive considerable public attention, putting pressure on economic development managers to respond.

Indicator 9, total exports, is of interest primarily to the jurisdiction's export promotion program. It is one broad measure of the jurisdiction's competitiveness in the world economy. State export data are available from the U.S. Bureau of the Census. Estimates of the dollar value of exports of manufactured goods produced in the state are available from its Industry Division of the Census, with roughly a three-year lag. Data on the dollar value of exports of merchandised goods shipped from the state are available from its Foreign Trade Division, with roughly a one-year lag. Both of these indicators have important limitations as indicators of the export-related employment and earnings within the jurisdiction. The value of exports of manufactured goods can be significantly understated, because the manufacturers often do not know the ultimate destination of their goods. Conversely, the values may be overstated because the value added by the manufacturer, in some cases, may be small. Also, the figures on goods shipped from the jurisdiction may have little to do with what the shipping jurisdiction actually produced, since the jurisdiction may act only as a shipping point. Finally, neither of these sources includes the value of services exported, which are growing in importance.

■

DISAGGREGATIONS OF GLOBAL INDICATOR DATA

As already described, employment figures should be broken out by industry, region, and county. This breakout information is typically provided in unemployment compensation quarterly and annual reports. Comparisons to previous time periods should also be provided as illustrated in Exhibits 8.2 and 8.3. Users will then be able to compare time trends as well as make comparisons among industries, regions, and counties.

Breakouts by industry, region, and county, and comparisons over time, are also appropriate for most of the other global indicators, to the extent that breakout information is available. For example, corporate tax revenue broken out by industry would indicate trends in sectoral tax revenue returns to the jurisdiction. The last indicator, business climate rankings, generally is available only for the state as a whole.

These global indicators also permit comparisons to other states. For all the indicators other than Indicator 7 (ratings by businesses), data are currently available, at least annually, for all states. And because the data collection procedures are fairly standardized (usually by the federal government), the comparisons are fairly reliable even if their validity is in question.

EXHIBIT 8.1

GLOBAL INDICATORS

1. State (local) employment--(both in total and broken out by region/county and industry)

2. Number of new business starts

3. Number of business failures

4. Unemployment rate (both in total and broken out by region/county)

5. Average jurisdiction wage rate

6. Amount of tax revenue receipts

7. Percentage of businesses that rate the jurisdiction as a good place in which to do business

8. Ranking on various national "business climate" indices

EXHIBIT 8.2

SAMPLE FORMAT FOR GLOBAL INDICATOR REPORT: EMPLOYMENT BY INDUSTRY--FIRST QUARTER, 1988

Industry	Last Month of Quarter	Total Employment		Percentage Change	
		Last Month of Previous Quarter	Same Month of Previous Year	From Last Quarter	From Last Year
Total--All Industries					
Agriculture, Forestry, and Fishing					
01 Agriculture production--crops					
02 Agriculture production--livestock					
07 Agriculture service					
08 Forestry					
09 Fishing, hunting, trapping					
Mining					
10 Metal mining					
13, 14 Oil and gas; nonmetallic minerals					
Construction					
15 Building contractors					
16 Heavy construction contracts					
17 Special trade contractors					

EXHIBIT 8.3

SAMPLE FORMAT FOR GLOBAL INDICATOR REPORT: EMPLOYMENT BY REGION AND COUNTY--FIRST QUARTER, 1988

	Total Employment			Percentage Change	
Region/County	Last Month of Quarter	Last Month of Previous Quarter	Same Month of Previous Year	From Last Quarter	From Last Year
Total State					
Region 1					
Kittson					
Marshall					
Norman					
Pennington					
Polk					
Red Lake					
Roseau					
Region 2					
Beltrami					
Clearwater					
Hubbard					
Lake of the Woods					
Mahnomen					
Region 3					
Aitkin					
Carlton					
Cook					
Itasca					
Lake					
St. Louis					

9

CLIENT SURVEYS

■

USING CLIENT SURVEYS

The previous sections have used periodic feedback from clients as a major source of information on service quality and outcomes. Client surveys are by no means a perfect source, but they are one of the few ways to obtain reasonably accurate information on service quality and the results of services.

Depending on the specific economic development program, these surveys can be either of (a) businesses, (b) community economic development officials who have been clients of a state's department, or (c) citizens who have sought travel or tourism information.

Client surveys may be the only way to evaluate whether services actually contributed to outcomes, as well as to find out businesses' perceptions of the quality of service, such as its timeliness and helpfulness. Surveys of nonclients can be used to identify reasons for nonuse.

Will surveys of clients provide valid information? This depends on a number of elements, such as: whether the survey questionnaire gets to a knowledgeable person (i.e., one who can answer the questions or who was directly involved in the receipt of state services), the person's memory of events (events that may have occurred several months earlier), whether the person answers honestly, whether the survey is of a representative group of clients, and the percentage of respondents who are willing to return a completed questionnaire. Through proper procedures, most of these *concerns can be addressed, so that survey responses can provide reasonably* valid information--certainly better information on service quality and outcomes than was previously available to economic development managers. The procedures described in this section are aimed at increasing the validity of the information obtained.

The use of client surveys by economic development agencies is currently rare (except among tourism offices, which primarily have been using formal surveys for marketing research purposes). Also, some economic development departments in recent years have undertaken special ad hoc surveys, such as of export clients, to identify more about their activities and interests in exporting. However, for the most part, economic development agencies do not undertake surveys on a regular basis. When they do, they generally contract out the work to a university or market research organization. However, since economic development has a very large marketing and market research component, the notion of surveying clients is probably familiar to most economic development professional staffs.

■

DISCUSSION OF KEY CONCERNS FOR SURVEY ACTIVITIES

Some of the principal issues for economic development agencies that plan to undertake client (and nonclient) surveys are listed as follows:

1. A key issue is how to achieve *adequate response rates.* The higher the response rate, the more likely that the information obtained will be valid. Agencies should seek returns from at least 50 percent of the clients surveyed. Later, we provide suggestions for increasing response rates.

2. *The initial start-up effort in implementing a regular survey process* is considerable. Time and effort is needed to develop the questionnaire and survey procedures, to develop computer files, to prepare programs to store and process the data from survey responses, and to handle a myriad of details involved in a survey effort. Many of these tasks can be contracted to a survey firm, but some cannot. The agency should expect to involve many individuals over several months in developing the procedures (and questionnaires) so they are practical, technically sound, and useful to agency managers.

3. The agency will need to maintain the *confidentiality of individual responses.* For the most part, the questionnaires will not involve highly sensitive or proprietary information. Even in those instances where the questionnaires ask for employment or sales figures, the agency usually needs only ranges rather than precise numbers. (Note that more precise employment figures can be obtained, if needed, through other means, such as the unemployment insurance (UI) database discussed in Section 10.) Nevertheless, it is important to maintain the confidentiality of responses so that individual respondents cannot be identified except by authorized personnel. This problem can be alleviated through proper procedures, such as using identification numbers rather than firm names.

4. The *frequency of surveys and reports* needs to be determined. For client feedback to be useful to operating managers, the information should be obtained in a timely fashion. Therefore, performance reports should be provided frequently, approximately quarterly for most economic development programs. For programs where the number of different clients is very small and/or does not change much from period to period, such as programs in which the primary clients are local government agencies (see Section 7), it is probably sufficient for

the surveys to be done semiannually, although grouping a year's clients into quarterly samples might be preferable. The quarterly tabulations can, and should, be accumulated over the year to provide yearly summaries. There are two alternative approaches to conducting client surveys. One involves "flagging" each client in program records so that clients are routinely surveyed at specified intervals (such as 6 to 12 months) after receiving service (continuous processing). The other is to survey clients at the same time during the reporting period (batch processing), so that each client is contacted within plus or minus one-half of the length of the reporting period. We recommend the first approach. It means that each client receives the questionnaire at about the same time, with the same lag time since the clients began receiving services. Reports on the findings can be generated at any time by tabulating the completed questionnaires received to date.

5. *How long after the service has been provided* should the department wait before asking for feedback information? If the feedback is obtained too quickly--such as three months after the service is provided--not enough time will have transpired to obtain information on longer-term results of the assistance. On the other hand, if the department waits too long, such as two years or more, the returning data, although picking up longer-term results, may be unrelated to the priorities of the current managers. Suggestions are included in each section of this manual regarding the specific timing of surveys for individual programs. In general, however, a reasonable compromise would be to seek feedback after about 6 months for tourism programs and usually 12 months for most other programs. Within that time period, for most programs' "end" outcomes can be expected to have occurred, and major "intermediate" outcomes should have occurred if they will occur at all. Even increased jobs and sales can be expected in many instances to occur within 9 to 12 months for many programs.

6. The survey process should *avoid sending more than one questionnaire to clients* (e.g., clients of several programs), and should not survey the same client too frequently. The survey procedures should identify whether (a) a particular client is on more than one list of clients to be sampled or (b) has recently been included in a previous survey. Clients are likely to be willing to be surveyed "once in a while," but do not want to be bothered frequently. The problem will occur most often in agencies with a large number of clients and in those that do not have computerized client lists.

7. A major concern is: *Who does what?* The department can undertake the survey activity itself (as in Minnesota's pilot effort) or it can contract it out (as in Maryland's pilot effort). Most states

will find it advantageous to contract out the work. This saves the agency many headaches and avoids staffing problems. Nevertheless, as discussed in Section 12, the program and central department overseeing the effort will still have several tasks, including making sure that adequate and up-to-date transmittal letters and questionnaires are used, and that the contractor is properly monitored. The effort required by individual program staffs should be kept to a minimum, to avoid overburdening line employees. However, the program will be responsible for ensuring that accurate lists of clients and data on various client characteristics are provided, and for providing occasional questions on topics of special interest for inclusion in the questionnaire.

8. *The letters transmitting the questionnaires* to respondents need to be carefully prepared. Not only is the transmittal letter important for obtaining high response rates, but it also signals the agency's desire to communicate with its clients and to obtain feedback about their past services as input into future services. Thus, the letter is both a public relations element and an integral part of the survey process. The decision as to who signs the letter is an important consideration. In general, a high-level official, such as the department head, or the government's chief executive, should sign the letter. Survey respondents have indicated that a high-level signature reinforces the agency's credibility, and emphasizes a serious interest in obtaining the client's response. (It may also be helpful to have the letter cosigned by an industry association or a chamber of commerce.) Letters furthermore should be individualized, that is, addressed to specific business executives or local government officials. The primary exception is for tourism programs, where a mass-produced transmittal letter to persons requesting tourism information, signed by the top tourism official, will be adequate. This letter does not need to be, and probably should not be, personalized. The wording and content of the transmittal letters for all programs should be designed to encourage the recipient to complete and return the questionnaire. A sample transmittal letter is presented in Exhibit 9.1.

9. *How large should the samples be?* How many businesses, communities, or citizens receiving assistance should be surveyed? The larger the sample size, the more the effort and expense. On the other hand, the larger the sample relative to the full population of clients eligible to be surveyed, the more precise will be the findings. In the pilot tests in Maryland and Minnesota, the number of clients for the time period covered (three or six months) was sufficiently small for each program (usually, under 200) that 100 percent of those clients were surveyed. This situation is likely to be quite common, especially if the reports and surveys are to be prepared relatively frequently, such as quarterly. In

such cases, no sampling effort is needed. Sampling is necessary, however, for those programs where the number of clients served is large, such as for tourism programs. Sampling will also be needed if firms that have *not* been assisted by the agency programs are surveyed (to assess reasons for their nonuse of services). Fortunately, in most cases only relatively small samples are likely to be needed to obtain sufficiently precise results for most agency purposes. For example, samples of 100-200 clients will usually provide sufficient precision even if the number of clients is very large, such as 1,000 and higher. For programs with a small number of clients (around 200 or less), 100 percent coverage is suggested. This will avoid the extra tasks involved with sampling. When sampling is necessary, however, proper *professional random sampling* will avoid bias, or at least the appearance of bias, when outside reviews are made of the process.

10. *Obtaining accurate contact information on clients* is a basic task and involves more problems than might be expected. Many, if not most, economic development agencies do not have in place systematic client information systems. To survey clients who obtained service, say 9 to 12 months ago, the agency should have available a listing of those clients, with accurate information on the service(s) received, the names of the firms, addresses, contact persons to whom the questionnaire can be sent, and, preferably, telephone numbers. In addition, information on such key characteristics as industry and size (at the time the service was provided) and services provided also should be available on each client to enable the program to obtain cross-tabulations of the findings by these characteristics.

    If a client subsequently receives a new, quite different service from a program, the program will need to decide if such new service justifies additional client feedback. If so, the program should record the business or community as a new client for such service in their client records.

    A systematic client information system, particularly one that is computerized, makes the survey process much easier. If such a system is not in place, program personnel will have to expend effort to manually assemble this information, a time-consuming chore that is prone to errors.

11. The *reports presenting the survey findings should be clear, concise, and informative*. The format of survey reports should be carefully developed. Data intended for managerial personnel can be almost incomprehensible--with poor and inadequate labeling, too many numbers compressed together, and so forth. Other sections in this manual provide sample formats that may be useful for summarizing the data from client surveys.

Agencies should require those tabulating the survey results to provide them in a "multiple cross-tab" format, whereby the responses to each survey question are broken out by several key client characteristics (such as region, size category, and industry) and displayed on the same page of the report. This makes reviewing the findings much easier than if the reader has to look at four or five separate pages.

■

CLIENT SURVEY PROCEDURES

How Should Questionnaires Be Administered?

Surveys can be administered by in-person interviews, telephone interviews, by mail, or by some combination of these. In-person interviews are not likely to be practical. Telephone interviews are a good approach if staff time or funds are available, because high response rates are usually achieved. For regular surveys, such as quarterly surveys, telephone interviewing will require more staff time or contract costs than agencies are likely to be able to provide.

On the whole, the most practical and least expensive approach for performance monitoring purposes is the mailed questionnaire. However, *single* mailings will seldom produce adequate response rates. Two mailings should be used, possibly supplemented by telephone reminders to firms that did not respond to these mailings. The latter step can be made contingent on whether or not the response rate from the two mailings reaches the targeted response level, such as 50 percent. In the pilot tests in Maryland and Minnesota, all eight programs achieved greater than 50 percent response rates using two mailings, in some cases supplemented by telephone reminders.

Designing the Questionnaires

Considerable care needs to be applied to designing the questionnaires. The information obtained will be no better than the information requested. The agency needs to ensure that the questions are clear, unbiased, and stated in a manner that encourages honest responses. Effective wording and formatting of questions demands professional skill. Therefore, questionnaire design should be undertaken with the help of experts.

Program personnel should participate in determining the content of the questionnaire so that they get the information they need. Such information includes client characteristics, ratings of service quality, program outcomes, and special information items of interest to agency personnel.

Most questions should have specific response categories, to make responses easier. For these questions, the respondents need only check or circle one of the specified categories. The questionnaire can, and probably should, contain a small number of items to which recipients respond in their own words, such asking for reasons for negative service quality ratings, or asking for suggestions on how the agency can improve its services. These reasons and suggestions subsequently should be examined by program personnel to obtain clues as to program aspects needing modification or correction. Questionnaires should be pretested with several respondents before finalization.

Once a questionnaire has been developed and administered, substantial modification in subsequent reporting periods should be avoided, to enable the agency to compare results over time. The initial investment in developing the questionnaire, thus, should *not* have to be repeated in subsequent surveys.

Of course, changes can be made to correct problems found in earlier versions. Also, programs may want to add a small number (perhaps 1-3) of special, one-time-only questions to the survey. For example, an agency might want to obtain client ratings of a new activity. One or two questions could be added to the regular performance monitoring questionnaire to gain client reactions to that activity.

Although considerable effort will be needed to develop a good client survey questionnaire the first time, subsequent administrations should require little or no added questionnaire development effort. The sample questionnaires contained in this manual can be used as starting points.

Steps to Increase Response Rates

Achieving adequate response rates is a key requirement for a valid survey. Most of the economic development surveys suggested in this manual are of persons whose organizations (or households, for tourist surveys) have been clients of the agency. Thus, higher response rates can be expected than for questionnaires sent "out of the blue" to businesses, government officials, or citizens. Response rates from government (e.g., local) officials can be expected to be quite high, probably 75 percent or better (based on recent experience in Maryland and Minnesota). With a reasonable amount of effort, response rates of at least 50 percent can be achieved from businesses. (The Maryland and Minnesota response rates for businesses varied from a low of 49 percent to a high of 71 percent.) The response rate from citizens receiving tourism or travel assistance also have been satisfactory, particularly where an incentive for responding has been provided (as was done by both Maryland and Minnesota).

The concern with low response rates focuses on the potential for "nonresponse bias." That is, if nonrespondents differ in some significant way in their perceptions of the quality of the service they received or in the results they achieved after receiving assistance, then performance based on information from those responding could be substantially under- or overstated. (It is not clear, however, in which direction this bias would occur. For example, are persons who are dissatisfied with the service *more* likely to return the questionnaires because they want to complain? Or, are they *less* likely to return the questionnaire because they are unhappy with the agency?)

Response rates are also of concern since budgets for surveys may be quite low, constraining the amount of follow-up of nonrespondents, especially telephone follow-up.

Surveys of random samples of firms, communities, or individuals, that have *not* been assisted by the agency (in order to assess reasons for their nonuse of services) are likely to have lower response rates. Section 6, "Export Promotion Programs," presents an example of such a survey. To achieve response rates of up to 50 percent, additional effort, such as telephone reminders or third mailings, may be needed. Fortunately, these samples need not be large. Surveying a random sample of, perhaps, 100 businesses once or twice a year should be sufficient. Thus, the extra cost and effort necessary to achieve adequate response rates is not likely to be large. Further, the shorter length of questionnaires for unassisted firms will help the response rate by making it easier for surveyed businesses to respond.

We recommend the following steps to increase response rates to reasonable levels.

1. The transmittal letter should be signed by a high government official, such as the department head or the governor. For businesses and community officials, the transmittal letter should be personalized and addressed to a specific individual.

2. The transmittal letter should be carefully worded to encourage response. It should emphasize the department's need for the information from clients in order to improve services for themselves and others in the future. (A sample transmittal letter is presented in Exhibit 9.1).

3. Wherever possible, an incentive should be offered to those returning questionnaires. In the case of tourists, an effective incentive has been to offer those returning the questionnaire a chance at a $100 savings bond. (This procedure has been utilized for several years by the Minnesota Office of Tourism and was tested successfully by the Maryland Office of Tourism Development in the pilot tests.) For businesses, an attractive publication or small "gift," such as a copy of a new directory or magazine subscription, might be offered.

4. The questionnaire should be as short and simple as possible. Questionnaires that are complex, cluttered, or much more than four or five pages long should be avoided. A number of sample questionnaires are presented in this manual.

5. A stamped, self-addressed return envelope should be enclosed with the questionnaire at each mailing.

6. The transmittal letter should guarantee that responses will *not* be attributed to individuals or their business or community in any reports.

7. The questionnaire should be as attractive as possible. Preferably, it should be typeset and printed on good-quality paper. Cutting corners such as using office-copiers should be avoided.

8. The agency and each participating program should establish a regular procedure for new clients receiving assistance to be notified by agency staff members about the survey process and encouraged to respond. This procedure, to our knowledge, has not been used in the past, but should help increase response rates.

We do *not* recommend asking program staff to call their clients about the questionnaires when they are sent out. Although this would increase response rates, it could also bias the results, or at least leave the agency open to perceptions of bias by outsiders who learn of this procedure. For the same reasons, it is not appropriate to use program personnel who provided assistance to the client to interview the client for performance monitoring purposes.

A Note on Maintaining Confidentiality of Client Response

Client responses should be kept strictly confidential. For performance monitoring, only grouped data need be reported. Compilations listing individual responses to open-ended questions can be provided to program personnel; however, such listings should not contain names or other information that might permit identification of the specific respondent.

Complete anonymity cannot be guaranteed to potential respondents, since the agency needs to keep track of who does and does not return questionnaires (so that second mailings or telephone follow-ups can be made to those not returning questionnaires). Thus, the mailed questionnaire should contain an identification number for the specific business, community, or individual to whom the particular questionnaire has been sent. The master list that links each identification number to specific clients should be kept confidential.

A Note on Contracting for Client Surveys

Many, if not most, economic development agencies will find it much easier to contract with an outside organization, such as a university or a private survey research firm, for the actual survey work. Exhibit 9.2 identifies a number of elements that the agency should specify clearly in the agreement or contract with these organizations. This will help avoid later disagreements and help ensure that the agency gets what it needs.

■

COSTS OF CLIENT SURVEYS

Client surveys involve effort and cost. Once the questionnaire has been developed and computer programs written for needed tabulations and reports, the subsequent costs for each survey repetition should be small. A rough estimate of subsequent costs, including mailings, tracking of responses, and tabulations, is about $5 per questionnaire mailed. Thus, an agency surveying 500 clients each quarter would require about $2,500 each quarter, or $10,000 each year, if the effort is contracted out. To the extent that current staff are available to undertake some of these tasks, the costs could be reduced.

The effort required for the *initial* development of the questionnaires and computer programming can be considerable. The survey procedures should be developed, as already noted, with considerable staff input (from both program personnel and central agency analysis staff). The computer programming and clerical help needed may require $10,000 or $20,000 for the first-time effort. To the extent that internal staff can do these tasks, out-of-pocket costs would be reduced or eliminated.

EXHIBIT 9.1

MODEL TRANSMITTAL LETTER

Dear :

The [program name] is attempting to improve its services to [name of jurisdiction] businesses. Your responses to the enclosed questionnaire will provide important information to help us judge the quality and usefulness of our services.

Completing the questionnaire should take about 15 minutes.

Your response will be held entirely in confidence. Results will be reported only in aggregate form.

Please return the questionnaire by [date] in the stamped self-addressed envelope we have provided.

In appreciation for your assistance, we are making available at no cost a Department publication entitled ["____________________."] If you would like a copy, please complete and return the enclosed order form describing this publication.

Many thanks in advance for your cooperation.

Sincerely,

Governor/Mayor

or

Department Head

or

Program Head

EXHIBIT 9.2

ELEMENTS THAT SHOULD BE INCLUDED IN A CONTRACT FOR A CLIENT SURVEY

The following elements should be specified in contracts for mail surveys:

1. The size of the samples;

2. Survey administration details, such as whether the mails, telephone, or both are to be used; the number of mailings or number of follow-up telephone calls; and the time between mailings and telephone follow-ups;

3. The role of the contractor in development of the questionnaire;

4. The role of the contractor in pretesting the questionnaire (the agency may want to do some of its own pretesting, but the contractor should also do some);

5. Maintenance of confidentiality of responses;

6. Special coding to be done by the contractor (e.g., transforming county data provided to the contractor into a smaller number of regions);

7. Specification as to how tabulations are to be handled, such as whether "no answers" and "don't knows" should be included in the denominators for the percentages that are calculated;

8. Products to be provided to the government and in what formats (products should include at a minimum: multiple cross-tabulation tables for each question, frequency counts for each question, and a fully legible printout of the input data for each returned questionnaire);

9. The time schedule for the work; and

10. Cost.

10

USE OF STATE UNEMPLOYMENT INSURANCE DATA FOR MEASURING THE PERFORMANCE OF ECONOMIC DEVELOPMENT PROGRAMS

■

INTRODUCTION

State unemployment insurance (UI) programs are a valuable source of data for economic development agencies, providing timely and detailed information on employment and wages that should be accessible to most state economic development agencies. The UI program is a federal-state tax program into which employers pay unemployment insurance taxes directly to the state on their covered employees on a quarterly basis. Authorized and funded in part by the U.S. Department of Labor, the UI program is state-administered. The cooperative agreement between the federal and state governments allows flexibility in how the states collect, measure accuracy, tabulate, and report data on workers covered by the UI programs. This makes it difficult to generalize about the exact data that will be available to a state economic development department from its state UI agency, but there are important commonalities.

■

BUSINESSES COVERED BY THE PROGRAM

State UI programs provide detailed employment information on 90 to 98 percent of all employed workers in the state. Workers who are self-employed, work in some nonprofit organizations (churches, parochial schools), or are employed by interstate railroads are not covered by the program.

■

COUNTY AND INDUSTRY CODES

Employers are assigned county and four-digit standard industrial classification (SIC) codes by the state UI agency, based on their location in the state and the primary product produced. These codes are verified by the state on a three-year cycle (one-third of all firms are updated annually). Employers are routinely asked to identify any changes in their SIC code or location. Businesses with more than one reporting unit (facility) in a state are classified separately as multiunit establishments, in an effort to track the exact location of employment in the state.

■

PROGRAM ADMINISTRATION

The UI program is administered as follows. States collect taxes on a quarterly basis from employers by receiving a tax form from each employer on which the firm reports, at a minimum: (1) the total wages paid to employees during the quarter, (2) the amount of these wages that is subject to taxes, (3) the taxes due, and (4) the number of employees on the payroll for the pay period that includes the 12th day of *each* month. The forms are due at the state department within 30 days after the end of the quarter. Employers with more than one facility in the state (referred to as reporting units) are also sent a form requesting a breakdown of the monthly employment and wage figures *for each unit.*

■

REPORTS TO BUREAU OF LABOR STATISTICS (BLS)

Within five months after the end of the reporting quarter, states are required to submit a machine-readable version of these data to the BLS. At a minimum, states must report, by four-digit SIC code and county, the number of reporting units, monthly and average quarterly employment, and total wages paid. The computer reports submitted are referred to as the ES-202 data report (further discussion of the ES-202 data appears below under "Bureau of Labor Statistics Substate Reports"). For the first quarter of the fiscal year only, these data are also reported by the states to the BLS by size of unit (number of employees).

■

STATE UI DATABASE

In essence, the states are taking a quarterly census of firms, with firm-specific identifiers, four-digit SIC codes, and county codes. States maintain a database of firm-specific information on the number of employees and the amount of wages for each employee. States can potentially identify the exact employment and wages of any firm in the state on a quarterly basis five months after the reporting quarter. For economic development programs aimed at increasing employment of specific firms, specific industries, or specific locations, this information would be very useful in tracking the performance of the agency's programs.

At a minimum, state departments of economic development should be able to access county-level employment and wage data at the four-digit SIC code level, on a quarterly basis, within five months after the reporting quarter.

■

USES OF STATE UI DATABASE

The uses of the UI database for performance monitoring of economic development programs depend on the specific characteristics of each program. Generally, the UI data would appear to be most useful for identifying employment and wage changes for specific firms that have received some type of agency assistance. For agency programs designed to directly increase jobs, such as business attraction and financing programs, the UI data can serve this purpose. For example, most states that have business attraction programs generally report the number of jobs announced by new firms locating in the state. However, states seldom attempt to verify these announcements as to the actual employment of these firms at later dates. The UI database can be used for this purpose by tracking the actual employment of firms locating in the state or adding a new facility. Some state financing programs track the employment of some firms receiving assistance, but the UI data could serve as an important and authoritative verification of these figures.

The UI data can also be used to produce certain global indicators, such as those described in an earlier section. These indicators provide useful information on macroeconomic changes in a state, such as the percentage change in employment in specific industries or counties.

The UI data can be used to select nonassisted firms, based on size, SIC code, or location, in order to survey them about their reasons for nonuse of state services. These firms may be selected randomly or stratified by certain categories. An alternative is to attempt to devise a comparison sample that matches assisted firms on specific characteristics. Each assisted firm would be matched with a nonassisted firm with similar characteristics. As results of the surveyed pairs of assisted and nonassisted firms are analyzed, comparisons between the two groups can be made to determine if there are significant differences.

The UI can also be used to provide information for disaggregating the performance information obtained through client surveys. If program records lack information on size, SIC code, or location, for example, the UI data can be used to provide this information.

The use of *wage data* from the UI system is likely to be of limited value for performance monitoring purposes. The system does not provide information on the hours worked by each employee. Because of the difficulty in identifying full- and part-time workers, and the reporting of multiunit establishments, it is difficult to measure the quality of jobs by the average wage of full-time workers. Unless the state feels it is necessary to track the change in wages for individual employees, these data appear to be of little use for performance monitoring.

Another possible use of the database is as an "early warning device" to track dramatic changes in employment in firms, especially to identify those in need of assistance. The data can also be used to identify rapidly expanding or declining industries or geographic regions targeted by the state.

■

DATA PROBLEMS

As alluded to earlier, because the UI program is state-administered, there are differences in the data that are collected and made available across states. There are also problems and issues regarding the way data are reported and their accessibility to state and local departments of economic development. Although normally resolvable, these problems and issues include: (1) the method of collection used by the state; (2) the information elements collected by the state; (3) the level of automation available for tabulation of data; (4) the time lag in tabulating and reporting data; (5) the classification of firms by the SIC; (6) the classification of multiestablishment firms; (7) the length of the employers' pay period; (8) full-time and part-time employment; (9) the count of workers; (10) the verification of data collected by the state; and (11) the accessibility of data to state departments of economic development and the confidentiality laws and department regulations governing the release of information to other state departments. Each issue is discussed next.

1. Methods of Data Collection and Tabulation. Each state designs its own form for collection of the taxes and required data. Although the basic information collected is the same, the format and structure of questions on the form may be different. Even though states adhere to the same general procedures, the information they collect may be somewhat different.

2. Information Collected. Some states include variables other than those required for BLS reporting. In 38 states, firms are requested to report the total wages paid to each employee during the quarter, to determine an individual's eligibility and benefit without filing a claim. These are called wage reporting states. The other states do not collect this information and, instead, have individuals file claims and then verify this information with the employers. These are known as "wage verification states." In wage verification states it would be impossible to determine the changes in income earned by employees.

3. Level of Automation. Although the BLS requires states to report data in a machine-readable form, the level of sophistication of the systems in each state varies. Some states have levels of automation that allow them to make special calculations of data with relative ease, while other states do not have the capacity to generate analytical cross-tabulations. This difference is important, in that some departments of economic development will be able to obtain special computer runs from their state department of labor, while other states will not.

4. Time Lag in Tabulating and Reporting of Data. Because of their data processing capabilities, some states may be able to tabulate the information collected in advance of the five-month deadline for the BLS. The time lag for data is also affected by the priority placed by the state on the tabulation of UI data. Usually, states give first priority to tabulation of the tax information, then they tabulate the unemployment statistics for the state (compiled from a monthly household survey conducted for the U.S. Department of Labor), and finally, they tabulate the UI data.

5. *Assignment of SIC and County Codes.* In some states, employers assign the SIC and county codes to their firms. All new firms are required to fill out forms designed by individual states to classify firms by SIC, but there are no set standards for classification. In cases where firms manufacture several different products or are involved in different types of businesses, the state must determine which product or activity comprises the majority of the unit's production and must assign the appropriate SIC. This assignment is verified every three years, with one-third of the units in the state being verified annually. This may be problematic, in that units may change their major product or business within this three-year period, which the state is usually not able to detect.

6. *Multiestablishment Reporting.* A related problem is the reporting of multi-establishment firms. States make an effort to classify multiestablishment firms so that the exact location of workers employed by the firm may be identified. States treat each location of a multiestablishment firm with 50 workers employed in secondary locations and with at least 6 in any single location or industry as separate reporting units, making it easier to tell where individuals are employed but more difficult to identify the number of separate "firms" in the state. If the state asks the multiestablishment firm to identify the number and location of all of its workers in the state but the firm fails to report this, all workers will be identified as employed at the location of the reporting unit, which may have few of the individuals actually employed by the firm in the state.

7. *Length of the Pay Period.* The employment figures reported by establishments represent the number of employees paid wages "during the pay period that includes the 12th of the month." Therefore, it is not possible to identify total employment at a specific time. Most pay periods, according to state UI program administrators, tend to be two weeks in length; however, they may be of any length. The longer the pay period, the greater the likelihood that the employment figures will be inflated by the number of workers who are no longer employed but who earned some wages during the reporting period. It is difficult to say how much the employment figures are affected by worker turnover, but it is important to recognize that length of the pay period can cause some discrepancies.

8. *Full-time and Part-time Employment.* The information collected does not specify the amount of time during the pay period that any person is employed; therefore, businesses that employ several part-time workers may appear to have as many employees as businesses that employ only full-time workers, even though the actual amount of time employed may be much less. Using the firm's wages to calculate the average wage per worker may help identify establishments that employ many part-time workers.

9. *Count of Workers.* In total, the dataset counts the number of different workers on the payroll during the payroll period. It does not count the number of people actually working at any one time, because turnover may

have resulted in more than one person working a particular job. The count will include all part-time and temporary workers. It is possible for the count of total employment to rise, as reported in the database, without any new full-time, or even part-time workers entering the labor force. On the other hand, the count will not include positions available that have not been filled by either full- or part-time workers during the payroll period.

10. Verification of Data. There are no set mechanisms for quality control to assure that all employers are reporting. Neither are states required to verify the quality of reported data and its accuracy. Because the information is collected for tax purposes and not for statistical use, states give priority to verification of the taxes paid, and not to the other information reported. Employers may also file for an extension on reporting if they are unable to pay their quarterly taxes. States *estimate* the employment and wages for known nonreporting firms. These elements introduce questions about the accuracy and reliability of the data.

11. Data Access. States differ in the laws and departmental regulations governing the release of UI data to other state departments and the general public. Because of the concern about release of proprietary information, some states may not allow the release of state data on a firm's employment level under any circumstances, and may require that county reports be aggregated to obscure employment levels and make identification of any individual firm's employment or wages impossible. Some states may not even allow the release of the data reported to the BLS under any circumstances, and state departments of economic development have to make requests to the BLS for substate reports. (In Maryland and Minnesota, economic development agencies have access to their state's UI data and are developing the policies and procedures necessary to protect the confidentiality of the data.) We do not know whether *local* government agencies would be able to obtain access to the state's UI information at all or under what conditions (needed to protect the confidentiality of data provided by individual businesses).

■

BUREAU OF LABOR STATISTICS SUBSTATE REPORTS

For state departments of economic development that are not able to gain ready access to their own state's data, or if their state does not have the capacity to perform the data manipulations they require, ES-202 data are available on a substate level directly from the BLS. Although the BLS only reports these data at the state level (in *Employment and Earnings,* a BLS monthly publication), they will tabulate them at the four-digit SIC and county level, at additional cost, for those states that request these reports. Usually, these reports will be aggregated at employment levels that will protect against disclosure of proprietary information (the rule for reaggregation is that if two firms comprise 80 percent of a four-digit SIC, the data will be aggregated at a higher level), but a state department of economic development may request a waiver that will allow them access to the original dataset.

The ES-202 reports, although offering very useful information, are obviously less useful than the state UI database. In using the BLS substate reports, state departments of economic development will have to include the additional time necessary for the BLS to tabulate substate reports, which may be more than 90 days after the state submits its ES-202 data. And the BLS substate reports will not enable the state to verify employment levels.

■

CONCLUSION

The state UI database offers state departments of economic development useful data for measuring the performance of many economic development programs. Although some problems exist in accessing and using these data, most departments of economic development should be able to gain access to the data in the future. Once access is gained, economic development agencies need to take steps to ensure that the data remain confidential.

11

ANALYSIS AND PRESENTATION OF PERFORMANCE INFORMATION

■

ANALYSIS OF INFORMATION

This section discusses key tasks in analysis of the data. Suggested ways to help transform the information into usable, helpful, and informative reports are presented. Five analytical steps are suggested:

1. Examination of cross-tabulations;
2. Examination of information from open-ended questions;
3. Preparation of composite summary tables;
4. Preparation of summary highlight reports; and
5. Special in-depth analyses.

The first four steps are integral parts of the performance monitoring process. The fifth step is outside the process, but can be an important adjunct to it. These steps are discussed below.

1. Examination of Cross-Tabulations

The basic tabulations resulting from the performance monitoring process present the findings on each performance indicator, tabulated against the various characteristics ("breakout variables") that are important to the program, division, and/or department, such as the outcomes achieved by firms from each service in each region or industry. Exhibit 11.1 illustrates the report format that can be used to display each performance indicator by the breakout information obtained from surveys of businesses or local government clients. The example in Exhibit 11.1 is adapted from the format used for export promotion programs in the Maryland and Minnesota pilot tests. This format, or at least a close variation, should be generated by computer, using appropriate software. The first row of the exhibit presents overall totals for all surveyed clients. Subsequent rows break out responses by selected client characteristics (region of the state in which the clients are located, type of location, business size, industry category, and stage of exporting of the firm when it began receiving the program's assistance). These breakout data are likely to be particularly important to program managers for guiding program improvements.

The breakout information enables the department to consider whether performance has been particularly successful or unsuccessful in several areas, such as among clients located in various regions of the state, clients of certain sizes, or clients in particular industries. The program manager or other department personnel should examine the percentages to determine where the values for the performance indicator are particularly good and particularly poor. (When displaying this level of detail, the central analysis office (CAO) should be careful to avoid very small cell sizes that might permit readers to identify individual respondents and thus violate confidentiality requirements. Such cases should be combined with other appropriate categories, such as "other" or "don't know" categories, to maintain the confidentiality of the information.)

Exhibit 11.1 also illustrates a useful presentation technique: highlighting figures that "stand out" as having unusually high or unusually low levels of performance for each performance indicator. In this exhibit, unusual performance is indicated by circled figures. Program personnel who review the performance tables might thus circle unusual figures to call readers' attention to them. (Color coding is even more effective.)

Generally, the performance indicators for data obtained from client surveys are expressed in percentages rather than absolute numbers. Percentages usually provide more meaningful information. However, the total number of clients responding should be indicated in these tables to alert managers to situations where the number of responses is low--as illustrated by the first column in Exhibit 11.1. (In calculating these percentages, the numbers used in the denominators should include those respondents giving a "don't know" answer, but should exclude respondents giving a "not applicable" answer. For respondents who skip a question or whose answers cannot be deciphered, the coder will need instructions to determine whether the implied response is "don't know" and included in the denominator, or "not applicable" and not included in the denominator.)

Outcome indicators obtained from the unemployment insurance (UI) database (such as employment in various regions and industries) are tabulated and displayed somewhat differently. Exhibit 11.2 illustrates such a tabulation, showing both employment and changes in employment for various regions and counties within the state. For data on gross statewide changes (covering unassisted as well as assisted business), the absolute size of employment should be presented, as shown. Percentages or numbers of the amount of added or reduced employment can be used to indicate changes from previous time periods (along with the appropriate "plus" or "minus" sign). Similarly, for indicators showing changes in employment of *assisted* firms (from before and after state assistance), both absolute size and percentage changes should be presented.

2. Examination of Information From Open-ended Questions

Each of the client survey questionnaires illustrated in this manual, whether administered to businesses or local communities, contains a number of open-ended questions. These questions ask respondents to augment their ratings by giving reasons for their ratings and suggestions for program improvement. The organization tabulating the survey data should provide each program with a list of the verbatim responses for each open-ended question (in a manner that preserves confidentiality).

Program personnel should examine these responses carefully, since they may identify specific problems in the program's service delivery and provide important clues about how to improve the service.

An option for the department is to ask the organization doing the tabulations to code responses into various categories (e.g., categories of reasons why respondents gave poor ratings to a particular service characteristic) and tabulate the findings for these new categories. Although this coding will facilitate examining the data, it takes extra effort and adds to time and cost requirements. Also, the process of coding is likely to lose some information (and miss subtleties) that could be helpful to program personnel. If resources can be made available, we recommend that the organization responsible for the data tabulations present both the verbatim responses and tallies of those responses grouped into useful categories.

3. Preparation of Composite Summary Tables

In addition to the detailed tabulations, the department also should prepare summary tables of the performance indicators. Each program should identify summary performance indicators likely to be of particular interest to division and department managers. Examples of the summary performance indicators are presented in the exhibits in the program sections of this manual. An example of a summary indicator table is shown in Exhibit 11.3, taken from Section 6, "Export Promotion Programs" (Exhibit 6.7).

The data for these summary indicators should come from the computer-generated tabulations. The program may choose to include additional summary performance indicators manually calculated from the basic detailed data reports. (If so, these values should probably be programmed for machine tabulation in later reports.)

The performance indicators included in the program sections of this manual are characterized as to whether each indicator is:

a. An indicator of service quality, that is, a characteristic of the state's service delivery that is of importance to clients;

b. An intermediate outcome indicator, indicating that clients of the department have taken significant steps that are likely to lead eventually to increased job or sales; or

c. A long-term outcome indicator, indicating changes in jobs or sales resulting, at least in part, from the department's services.

As illustrated in Exhibit 11.3, these indicator labels should be used in reports distributed outside the program, to help users of the reports keep the findings in proper perspective. These labels also should convey to outside readers that the program and department are attempting to put the findings into perspective.

After performance reports have been prepared for more than one time period, the summary reports can be used to present trend data on the indicators. When a program sets targets for the coming year on performance, the summary reports can subsequently be used to present comparisons of actual performance to the targets. Exhibit 11.3 illustrates a format for presenting both types of comparisons. In the exhibit, results for the most recent quarter, and year to date, are compared to the results of the previous quarter and year to date. The last column of the exhibit also illustrates comparisons of actual performance to the target for the time period.

This format, over the long run, is likely to be a major management performance review format. It permits program, division, and department management to assess recent time trends as well as performance relative to established targets. Preparation of this table requires that program managers identify targets for the performance indicators at the beginning of the period in question and, for time trend data, that the program collect and maintain data for previous time periods. Use of trend data also requires reasonable stability in the indicators and data collection procedures so that the comparisons over time are fair and valid. A major change in the questionnaire or in the procedure used to draw samples, for example, could reduce the comparability from one time period to another.

Exhibits 11.4 and 11.5 illustrate special-purpose summary tables, demonstrating how a program can compare each of its primary services on a number of characteristics. Such information should help identify which services appear to be performing well and which appear to be having problems in serving clients. These particular tables can be generated by the computer. Each combines in one table the data on a number of specific program services (export promotion services in these examples). The format in Exhibit 11.4 is intended to display client ratings for each of the survey questions on service quality. The format in Exhibit 11.5 provides client responses for each service as to the extent of contribution of each service to changes in clients' exports.

As noted earlier, when clients give poor ratings, they should be asked, in an open-ended question, to explain the poor rating. These explanations should enable the program and department to better interpret respondents' concerns and to obtain clues for improving particular services that have received poor ratings.

Exhibit 11.6 illustrates a presentation of findings on a summary performance indicator where the data are not only shown for all clients in total but also are broken out by key client characteristics, such as location, size, and industry. As indicated earlier, such breakouts are likely to be of major interest and use at all levels within the department as well as of considerable interest outside the department. Thus, selected breakouts of the major summary performance indicators, such as those in Exhibit 11.6, probably should be provided to department management.

There are many possible variations for these reporting formats. The ones selected will depend on the particular information that the agency wishes to emphasize. Once selected, however, the report format should remain reasonably stable so that the agency cannot be accused of manipulating presentation formats to display only favorable information.

4. Preparation of Summary Highlight Reports

The purpose of the summary highlight report is to provide top managers with a brief review of key findings from the latest time period. Each program should prepare a highlight report, less than three pages long if possible, and providing both numerical and interpretive information. "Bullets" should be used to present major findings, supported by backup tables. The report should extract the principal findings on:

- The type of clients receiving services, gleaned from the descriptive data collected;
- Service quality indicators, identifying improvements that have occurred from previous periods, and service characteristics for which the results have been particularly good during the current reporting period and those where the service has not done well or has worsened substantially;
- Outcome indicators, both intermediate and long-term, including improvements in results from previous periods, and service areas where outcomes have been particularly good or poor during the current reporting period; and
- An indication of actions that the program believes are warranted in response to the performance data, such as reductions in obstacles or service adjustments.

The highlight report should address key client breakout characteristics, identifying performance indicators for which special categories of clients appear to have been served particularly well or poorly--such as clients located in specific regions of the state, in certain industries, or in certain sizes of business.

The individual programs should be responsible for these highlight reports. Program managers may feel that they have insufficient time to prepare the report and may wish to delegate it to a member of their staff or, perhaps, ask for assistance from an analysis office elsewhere in the department (such as a CAO). No one, however, has more insight into the program activities and operations than the program personnel themselves, and the highlight report should include this perspective.

Elsewhere, this manual has emphasized the importance of having the program manager review the performance reports coming from the data collection procedures before widespread dissemination. The highlight report gives the program manager the opportunity to indicate the program's rationale for negative findings and for presenting positive findings it believes are appropriate. This opportunity to review the data and provide interpretations to upper-level management is vital for assuring constructive use of the data. Program managers should consider preparation of these highlight reports as a major management task for their office. They should draw on resources within their program and perhaps outside (particularly on analytical details), to help them with the preparation of the highlight reports.

Program managers, prior to preparing this highlight report, will find it valuable to hold a "How Are We Doing?" session with their staffs. At this meeting, the staff can review the various performance report materials, identify causes of poor performance, identify problems and obstacles that may be contributing to poorer than desired performance, and suggest changes. In addition, the meeting can be used to pinpoint areas of good performance and suggest how this good performance might be transferred to other areas with poorer outcomes (e.g., to other industries, other size businesses, or other regions of the state).

When a program reviews the detailed performance reports and prepares the summary highlight report, it should take the following steps:

- *Look for large differences* in responses among categories and highlight those differences. (Exhibit 11.1 illustrates one method of highlighting: shading or circling those figures that appear particularly large or particularly small.) Also *look for substantial changes*, either positive or negative, from previous performance reports. Differences of 10 percentage points or more are likely to be important.[1] Differences of less than 5 percentage points between the various categories of clients, or from previous time periods, are not likely to be of importance to the agency. Program and other department officials should recognize that a small percentage of negative responses relating to the quality of service delivery is inevitable. It is virtually impossible to be successful with all clients.

- *Examine responses to open-ended questions* obtained from the client surveys. The surveys should ask respondents to explain their ratings of various service characteristics, especially negative ratings, and should also ask for suggestions on how services could be improved. The responses can reveal particular aspects of current services that trouble clients and can provide suggestions for improving services. The verbatim responses to each open-ended question should be provided to each program by the CAO, along with the response tabulations for the other survey questions. If there is a large number of responses to a particular open-ended survey question, the program should assign someone to analyze the responses, group them by type of responses, and summarize them.

- *Consider possible "explanatory factors."* The department and program should include in their reports the data or other information on key external factors outside the program's control. For example, foreign exchange rates (the value of the dollar) influence business exports; interest rates influence financial assistance programs; and national economic condition indicators certainly are related to business growth within the state. Explanatory datasets can routinely be included along with the performance tables.

5. Special In-depth Analyses

In addition to these formal performance monitoring activities, the program or other department offices can undertake special in-depth analyses of the performance data to learn more about the results observed. Two types of studies can be used.

In the first approach, analysts examine the basic data, such as the various data printouts, in more detail, to look for relationships that have not been explicitly examined in the formal, regular reports. For example, a program manager might suspect that a problem in a region is due to special circumstances in a few counties within the region. Using the basic database for the tabulations, analysts can examine that possibility, either manually or by using the computer, by breaking out the performance data relating to those particular counties. Similarly, the program manager might suspect that an industry located in a particular region of the state is associated with a problem. Again, the program manager, or others, can obtain special tabulations and analyze the data to confirm those suspicions.

A second, more complex form of analysis is to undertake more in-depth study of a program area where the results appear to have been deficient. This involves conducting a supplemental study, including *special data collection*, to examine the particular problem and explore why the problem is occurring. This latter type of analysis requires more resources than the first type.

If the economic development agency has an ongoing performance monitoring process, such has been described in this manual, it may also be able to use, on occasion, a "random-assignment, controlled experiment" to evaluate program performance. In this case, the program could test one or more different ways to assist clients, randomly assigning different methods to different clients. The performance monitoring process could provide evaluation information on each method if the clients are coded by the method used and the findings tabulated by method.

■

OTHER VARIATIONS FOR PRESENTING PERFORMANCE INDICATORS

This section has presented examples of specific tables showing various performance indicators broken out by various categories of businesses (or communities). Clearly, there are many possible variations. In addition, as the program managers, division managers, and other department personnel gain experience with this kind of information, they are likely to seek other reports, either in addition to, or replacing, their initial performance report formats. This is reasonable, so long as the department maintains sufficient stability in its reports for trends to be examined over time. Too much change from year to year in reporting formats can raise suspicions that the department is manipulating the reports to present information in as favorable a way as possible.

The performance data can be tabulated against data elements included in survey instruments or data obtained from program records or UI (as discussed in the individual program sections). New data elements can be added as circumstances warrant. For example, a program may be interested in distinguishing performance with business (or local community) clients by the type and amount of assistance provided to them. So long as the program provides the data for each business or community to be added to the database for each respondent, such tabulations can be made, and the information can be readily analyzed and reported by these additional service characteristics.

Note, section 11

1. Statistical tests (such as the chi-square test) can be used to assess the level of *statistical* significance, especially of client survey data. Note, however, that in many cases the economic development agency is likely to be surveying all, or a large proportion, of its clients. In such cases, *sampling* errors will not be an issue.

EXHIBIT 11.1

SAMPLE PERFORMANCE REPORT--SECOND QUARTER, JANUARY 1989

Percentage of recipients who reported *the contribution to increased employment from export counseling as:*

	Number in Sample	Percentage		
		Considerably	Some	None
Total	116	38	26	36
Region of Origin				
Region 1	38	18	29	53
Region 2	25	48	28	24
Region 3	53	47	23	30
Metro versus Nonmetro				
Metro	80	43	20	15
Nonmetro	36	28	38	33
Employment Size				
1-19	58	45	25	30
20-49	18	22	22	56
50-99	12	33	17	50
100-250	10	55	22	22
250 or more	10	20	40	40
Industry Type				
Agriculture and food products	22	27	27	45
Machinery and equipment	32	50	25	25
Instruments	14	14	29	57
Other	50	40	28	32
Export Stage				
Uninterested	14	29	0	71
Partially interested	12	83	0	17
Exploring	12	50	33	17
Experienced small	44	27	23	50
Experienced large	34	47	41	12

EXHIBIT 11.2

EMPLOYMENT BY REGION AND COUNTY--FIRST QUARTER, 1988

Region/County	Last Month of Quarter	Total Employment		Percentage Change	
		Last Month of Previous Quarter	Same Month of Previous Year	From Last Quarter	From Last Year
Total State					
Region 1					
Kittson					
Marshall					
Norman					
Pennington					
Polk					
Red Lake					
Roseau					
Region 2					
Beltrami					
Clearwater					
Hubbard					
Lake of the Woods					
Mahnomen					
Region 3					
Aitkin					
Carlton					
Cook					
Itasca					
Lake					
St. Louis					

EXHIBIT 11.3

EXAMPLE OF SUMMARY REPORT FORMAT FOR EXPORT PROMOTION PROGRAMS

Performance Indicators	Most Recent Period	Last Period	Year to Date	Year to Date Last Year	Target % for Current Year
Service Quality Indicators					
PI-1 Percentage of respondents that rated each service as either excellent or good on all four characteristics.					
Intermediate Outcome Indicators					
PI-2 Percentage of respondents that reported at least some contribution of services to increased pre-export activities.					
Long-Term Outcome Indicators					
PI-3 Percentage of respondents that reported at least some service contribution to increased export sales or jobs.					
PI-4 Percentage of respondents that reported a dollar amount of increased export sales and that services made at least some contribution.					
PI-5 Percentage of respondents that reported a number of new permanent jobs as a result of increased exporting and that services made at least some contribution.					
PI-6 Percentage of respondents that reported that they did not seek program services for a reason relatively controllable by the program.					

EXHIBIT 11.4

EXAMPLE OF SPECIAL PURPOSE SUMMARY TABLE (EXPORT PROMOTION SERVICE QUALITY RATINGS)

E/G = Percent rating the service quality as either excellent or good
F/P = Percent rating the service quality as either fair or poor

	Number in Sample	Percentage							
		Timeliness		Relevance and Accuracy		Professionally Rendered		Overall Helpfulness	
		E/G	F/P	E/G	F/P	E/G	F/P	E/G	F/P
Newsletter									
Other publications									
Seminar or workshop									
Export counseling									
List of agents and distributors									
Trade lead									
Introduction to visiting buyers									
Catalog shows abroad									
Trade missions abroad									
Exporting financing									

EXHIBIT 11.5

EXAMPLE OF SPECIAL PURPOSE SUMMARY TABLE (EXPORT PROMOTION SERVICE CONTRIBUTION RATINGS)

Performance Indicator: Percentage of clients that rated each service as making a substantial, modest, or no contribution to increased export sales.

		Percentage		
	Number in Sample	Substantial Contribution	Modest Contribution	No Contribution
a. Export counseling				
b. List of agents and distributors				
c. Trade lead				
d. Introduction to visiting buyers				
e. Catalog shows abroad				
f. Trade shows abroad				
g. Trade missions abroad				
h. Export financing				
i. Other ____________				

EXHIBIT 11.6

EXAMPLE OF DETAILED REPORT FORMAT FOR SUMMARY PERFORMANCE INDICATOR (FOR EXPORT PROMOTION PROGRAMS)

		Percentage				
	Number in Sample	Most Recent Period	Last Period	Year to Date	Year to Date Last Year	Target for Current Year
Total						
Region of Origin						
Region 1						
Region 2						
Region 3						
Metro versus Nonmetro						
Metro						
Nonmetro						
Employment Size						
1-19						
20-49						
50-99						
100-250						
250 or more						
Industry Type						
Agriculture and food products						
Machinery and equipment						
Instruments						
Other						
Export Stage						
Partially interested						
Exploring						
Experienced small						
Experienced large						

12

RECOMMENDATIONS ON ORGANIZATION, ROLES, AND RESPONSIBILITIES

■

INTRODUCTION

This section discusses roles and responsibilities in an ongoing performance monitoring process. It covers the functions of operating divisions, the central analysis office (CAO), and the department head. Some future steps that can be undertaken to improve performance monitoring after full implementation are also described, such as forming an overall department advisory committee to annually review the procedures.

A CAO should probably be assigned responsibility for the various administration and data processing tasks. Making one central office responsible for these duties relieves operating program personnel of added work, improves the efficiency of these procedures, and should increase quality control. Exceptions to this approach may be appropriate for divisions that have worked independently in the past to implement satisfactory performance monitoring systems. Such divisions may prefer to conduct client follow-up surveys themselves. Similarly, if only one or two of the agency's programs decide to introduce these performance monitoring procedures, these programs may have to do these tasks themselves. However, to the extent that the performance data are to be used by the department head or other offices in the department, their procedures should be subject to periodic quality control review by the CAO.

■

ROLES AND RESPONSIBILITIES OF THE OPERATING DIVISION

1. Each participating division is responsible for providing to the CAO the appropriate sample of businesses or communities that need to be followed up through procedures such as client surveys or unemployment insurance (UI) data analysis. For each client, the program is responsible for providing designated descriptive information, such as that described in other

sections of this manual. A major problem for many economic development programs throughout the United States is the lack of systematic recordkeeping on clients, leading to gaps in client records. Program personnel generally recognize this problem, and some agencies are attempting to improve their record-keeping, if only for their own internal operating purposes. A program's data base on clients probably should be mechanized and needs to be kept up-to-date. Preferably, a common client intake form should be used by all programs that have business clients. This would form the basis for a department-wide data base. This would help the department in many ways, such as avoiding multiple questionnaire mailings to a client. Over the long run, data base linkages across programs and divisions will provide more comprehensive information to department personnel on the needs, characteristics, and services provided to individual business clients. A routinely updated and mechanized client information system will also make it much easier to implement the performance monitoring process and will increase the procedures' accuracy.

2. Each division and its programs has a primary responsibility to determine the characteristics against which it wishes the performance indicators to be cross-tabulated--and to provide the data on those characteristics. If and when the program or division wishes to add to or modify these characteristics, it should notify the CAO.

3. The program is the *primary user* of the performance findings, and thus has responsibility for their careful review and examination (other than the quality checks done by the CAO). Because program management and staff are most familiar with the program, they are in the best position to identify areas needing improvement and to suggest ways to correct problems. After performance reports begin to arrive regularly, the program should be able to identify trends, emerging problems, successes, and the outcomes of prior actions.

4. The program should prepare a summary of highlights shortly after receiving the basic performance reports. A discussion of the summary's contents was presented in Section 11. This highlight report should focus on the major successes and problems indicated by the detailed reports, and should point out any trends for the various performance indicators. It should emphasize the outcomes for key program services and identify particular regions of the state, industries, and size of firms for which services appear to have been particularly successful or unsuccessful. Programs may choose to seek assistance in preparing their highlight reports, perhaps from the CAO. This highlight report gives program managers an opportunity to present their perspective on the outcomes reported, to indicate reasons for problems that have appeared, and to describe any actions that the program is undertaking or plans to undertake to correct problems indicated in the detailed reports.

5. The program is responsible for expeditious dissemination of the performance report, including its summary of highlights, to division and department managers, and others as appropriate. The program should distribute the performance report approximately two weeks after receipt. This should allow sufficient time for the program team to review the findings and prepare its highlights summary. These performance reports are basically similar to other reports that traditionally have been generated by individual programs on program operations, even though in this case the data collection effort may have been undertaken outside the program. The division chief is responsible (within department-wide guidelines) for defining the policy regarding distribution of the reports.

6. Once each year the division and program should review the performance monitoring process (including performance indicators, questionnaires, cross-tabulations, and report formats) and recommend modifications.

7. The use of client surveys, such as those included in this manual, also provides programs with the opportunity to add a small number of special questions each time the survey is mailed out. This permits programs to obtain timely, ad hoc information from its clients. For example, a program might have issued a new publication and wants feedback from clients as to its usefulness. The survey questionnaire could be modified to ask a few questions about the new publication.

■

ROLES AND RESPONSIBILITIES OF CENTRAL ANALYSIS OFFICE

The CAO has the following roles and responsibilities in the performance monitoring process:

1. The CAO establishes the annual schedule for the process. The schedule should cover such elements as the following: periodic due dates for submission of client information to the CAO by the programs, the time frame for mailing the client survey questionnaires, the dates performance reports are due to be provided to program managers, and the dates performance reports are to be submitted to the department head's office by the program.

2. The CAO ascertains that the needed information is obtained from each participating program on each client in the client sample. It maintains special department-wide data element codes and notifies the individual programs about special department-wide data elements that are needed (such as identification of county and business size categories and codes). This, however, does not preclude individual programs from adding other special data elements or data categorizations believed helpful to the program. The CAO should also ensure that there are not duplicate entries on the client list.

3. The CAO is responsible for collecting the data on the clients identified by each program through client surveys and from the UI database (as described elsewhere in this manual). The CAO may complete this task on its own or it may contract for them. Contracting has the advantage of saving staff time and avoiding the need to monitor the many details involved in surveys. The desirability of contracting will depend on the availability of reasonably priced contractors.

4. The CAO is responsible for providing tabulations of the findings (from both the client survey and the UI database) to the programs in legible and usable form. The materials the CAO should provide to the programs include the agreed-upon data tabulations and compilations of responses to the questionnaires' open-ended questions. Some tables may need to be prepared manually. (In some instances, the *program* staff may want to prepare additional summary tables.)

5. The CAO is responsible for taking the necessary steps to ensure that survey response rates are sufficiently high (e.g., at least 50 percent) to achieve adequate validity of the findings and external credibility. Achieving adequate response rates, however, will not always be easy, particularly from businesses. The CAO can use the following steps to encourage response (see the section on client surveys for more details): telephone reminders (or telephone interviews when necessary), more effective wording of transmittal letters, and strengthening incentives to encourage client responses. Alterations in transmittal letters or in the type of incentives offered, however, should be agreed upon by the divisions and the respective programs. The CAO may need to take additional steps, such as reducing the length of the questionnaire if this is suspected as a major deterrent to responding. Again, this modification should be worked out with the division and respective programs.

6. The CAO is responsible for quality control of the department's overall performance monitoring process. This responsibility encompasses obtaining adequate response rates, periodically reviewing the samples provided by the programs to ensure that they represent the department's clients, checking the accuracy of clerical data entry and computer programming, and reviewing and approving changes (whether additions, deletions, or modifications) to client survey questions that are requested by the divisions.

7. The CAO reviews the detailed reports generated from the computer or other sources, to ensure that they are readable and free of major errors.

8. The CAO assures that the data received from clients is kept confidential, according to legal and internal departmental ground rules.

9. The CAO helps guarantee that individual program managers are the first to review reports on performance data. The individual program, not the CAO, is responsible for disseminating the information to

appropriate personnel elsewhere in the department. This includes the CAO analysts themselves (other than for quality control purposes), the division heads, legislators, and media. It bears reemphasizing here, however, that no one should see the reports before the program has had the opportunity to review and comment on them. An exception would occur if the program unduly delays dissemination of the report. "Undue delays" should be defined in departmental guidelines.

10. The CAO helps the individual divisions and programs to understand the data's technical nature and reliability. The office should instruct program personnel in using the data and, if requested, help them prepare summary highlight reports.

11. The CAO should review the quality and accuracy of external statements to be used outside the department regarding technical aspects of the data. It should provide needed footnotes to external reports (and probably internal reports as well), indicating the scope and limitations of the data. (This is done by major newspapers and other pollsters throughout the country when describing the results of surveys.)

12. The CAO should participate in the department's performance monitoring advisory committee. The representative of the CAO might chair the committee. This committee, as described later, should annually review the procedures and recommend improvements in both the procedures and the department's use of performance information.

■

ROLES OF DEPARTMENT HEAD'S OFFICE

Ultimately, the department head is responsible for the performance monitoring process. The day-to-day overview of the process will need to be delegated to the CAO; however, the department head's office assumes the following special roles:

1. It provides written policy regarding the performance monitoring process. This policy should emphasize the importance of the process and the department head's support for it as a vital management tool. The policy should also specify confidentiality requirements, document the distribution of the various reports, and emphasize that the program and program manager should be the first to review the outcome reports. At the same time, the policy should specify time limits for holding reports within the program. (The programs should be responsible for transmitting the reports each reporting period within a reasonable amount of time.)

2. It approves the wording of transmittal letters sent by the department to clients, including any incentives promised to clients for their response. This ensures that the wording will conform to department policy.

3. It reviews, and appropriately comments on, the performance reports provided to its office from the divisions, using the information to help guide policy decisions. This function has the important secondary benefit of providing encouragement and incentives (by congratulating successes and improvements and encouraging corrective effort when performance is inadequate).

■

NEEDED FUTURE ACTIVITIES AFTER FULL-SCALE IMPLEMENTATION

A decision to implement performance monitoring on an ongoing basis does not signal the end of the need for review and improvement of the process. Performance monitoring, especially of outcomes, is the focus of this manual. It is a new process and can still be considered somewhat experimental. Program managers, division heads, and other department personnel will most likely want to modify on occasion the data sought, perhaps the data collection procedures, and the specific uses of the information. Thus, the following future steps are recommended:

1. At least annually, the department should *review the performance monitoring process for possible modification.* This review can be undertaken by an advisory committee, perhaps chaired by the CAO and consisting of representatives from each division. The committee should examine the technical procedures and the report formats for their usefulness and validity. Major issues to address are survey response rates and the clarity and utility of the reports. The frequency of reporting should also be periodically reviewed. (For programs whose primary clients are businesses, reports probably should be provided quarterly to furnish timely information to program managers. However, surveys of communities, where the samples during any one quarter are small, might be tabulated less frequently such as only semiannually.) The committee should also review how, and to what extent, department managers are using the information from the performance reports and make appropriate recommendations for improving usage.

2. The department needs to *provide training* to department managers in the nature and use of performance reporting. A major obstacle to using information on program outcomes is managerial inexperience. Some degree of management training will be needed to encourage managers to understand the reasons for, and uses of, this information. A small training module on the performance monitoring process could be included in department management training programs. Managers should be encouraged to use the data for a number of purposes, such as motivating their staff (perhaps by establishing performance targets for each performance indicator) and identifying needed program improvements. Both uses could be promoted by holding "How Are We Doing?" sessions after each quarterly or semiannual report is received. These sessions can be utilized

by program managers to identify problems and obtain staff suggestions regarding further actions to correct these problems. For example, by examining performance data broken out by characteristics such as location in the state, industry, size of business, and key services provided by the program, the program manager's staff should be able to obtain insights on specific problems and their solutions. (See Section 13 for a more detailed discussion of uses for performance information.)

3. This outcome-focused performance monitoring process should *become part of a more comprehensive performance monitoring process*. Although information on outcomes and service quality has been the major missing link in performance reporting for economic development programs, other key performance data are also important to department managers. These include:

   - Information comparing actual expenditures to budgeted expenditures.

   - Information on the amount of work activity undertaken during the period. This includes data on the number of various activities (e.g., number of reports or other materials sent out, number of trade missions held, number of prospects identified). Work activity data do not reveal much about the quality or results of the work, but they do provide information about the quantity of program activity. This information is useful and already widely collected managerial information.

   - Information on efficiency (productivity). There has been little efficiency measurement in most economic development departments throughout the country. An exception has been the occasional use of estimates of the amount of tax revenue or added jobs achieved per dollar of expenditure. These estimates have often been highly questionable because of questionable data sources. The information from an outcome-focused performance process, however, should provide more reliable (but still by no means perfect) data on outcomes that can be used to better estimate the magnitude of the numerator (revenues or jobs) for the efficiency indicator.

In the long run, the desired product should be a comprehensive management information system providing information on inputs, work activity, outcomes, service quality, and efficiency.

13

USES FOR REGULAR PERFORMANCE INFORMATION

■

INTRODUCTION

The preceding sections have identified specific performance indicators and data collection procedures, and have discussed performance reports. This section discusses how such information can be used by the department.

There are multiple users of performance information: program managers (and their staffs), division heads, central analysis office (CAO) staff, and the department head's office. Inevitably, concerns and conflicts will surface at each level as to how the data should be used. Program personnel should focus on using the information to improve their programs. Higher-level managers will tend to use the information to help explain their programs and justify their budget requests to the governor and legislature, who in turn will use them as assessment tools.

The procedures described here are aimed foremost at helping the department, particularly program managers, to improve program performance. Other uses of performance information, no matter how desirable they are, should be considered secondary and should not be allowed to impede the primary purpose of improving programs.

The sections following describe ways that department managers can use performance information. Each management level has similar uses; the major difference is one of emphasis. The CAO is potentially an additional user, such as when undertaking department program and policy analysis. Inevitably, too, performance information will be of interest to persons *outside* the department, including the governor, members of the legislature, and the media.

■

USE OF PERFORMANCE INFORMATION BY PROGRAM MANAGERS

The performance monitoring process attempts to provide reliable, valid information on service quality characteristics and various outcome indicators, broken out by key characteristics of clients, such as location of the clients within the state, industry, and size of the firm or community. In addition, for most programs the performance data are also broken out by particular types of services (for example, for small business assistance services, whether the service was counseling, seminar/training activities, or primarily literature).

With such information, program managers should be able to make the following uses of the performance information:

1. The information will help identify aspects of the program that have, and have not, resulted in satisfactory results and for which client services have been particularly helpful or not helpful. This information, along with that obtained from the various open-ended questions in client survey questionnaires (such as why respondents rated a particular program characteristic as being poor), should provide the program with specific clues as to where changes are likely to be needed and what clients feel is wrong with the program's services and, therefore, needs improvement. This, in turn, should help the program manager determine how to allocate the program's resources.

   The various report formats, illustrated in previous sections of this manual, are intended to help program personnel identify aspects of their service that are not performing as well as desired. The program manager can identify and focus on certain specific characteristics for which outcomes have not been adequate, such as service timeliness to clients located in particular regions of the state or in specific industries, or problems with particular services that the program provides. Thus, performance information should help program managers improve the quality of their program.

2. After the data have been obtained for more than one time period, the program manager will be able to examine trends. This will enable managers to detect whether service quality and outcomes are worsening, thus indicating the need for corrective action.

3. Performance information can help motivate program employees and increase their interest in better serving their clients by obtaining their input into the process of improving services. Individual program managers can use the receipt of the quarterly/periodic performance reports to hold staff "How Are We Doing?" sessions. The manager might schedule a session with his or her staff after they have had a chance to look at the latest report. The staff should: (a) discuss where the program has been successful and whether that success might be transferred elsewhere and (b) examine aspects of their services where performance has not been as successful as desired, identifying the "whys" and what might be done to improve performance. The program manager can use this occasion to have staff begin development of an action plan for making improvements. In later periods, the manager and staff will be able to review whether the actions taken have led to the hoped-for results. Program staff should, ultimately, be major users of the performance information, such as by using the data to help guide their own allocation of time and effort.

   For example, if the program personnel find in a particular region of the state that results (based on information from the client surveys and/or unemployment insurance (UI) data) are less than desired, the staff could explore why the program has not been as successful in those regions and identify (and take) steps needed to provide revised or additional services for that region.

4. Performance information can help program managers develop program plans and budget requests, and subsequently help justify these plans and requests. As already stated, the performance reports should help to indicate needed actions. Thus, the evidence provided by the performance reports can assist program managers to justify their plans and budget requests.

5. Program managers can use previous performance information to set program targets for individual performance indicators for future periods. (Normally, such target setting is done at the beginning of a calendar or fiscal year.) Later, performance reports showing the targets along with the actual results can be used to indicate the extent to which the program achieved its targets. Target setting can, in some situations, be done on an individual staff basis, especially if staff, such as marketing representatives, each have their own clients, or they can be set on a group basis. In general, group targets are likely to be the better approach because they encourage cooperation among staff. Group targets, however, do not provide as intense incentives for each individual. Constructive competition could be introduced through group incentives if, for example, different teams serve different regions or different industries. Differences in difficulty in serving particular regions or particular industries can be compensated for by giving each group their own targets and measuring the "winners" of the competition by the extent to which they reached their targets. Awards for winners of competitions need not be monetary, but can be a symbolic award, such as a plaque for each member of the winning team or a luncheon for them sponsored, say, by the division manager.

6. Program managers can use the performance data to delve further into the nature of particular problems. The program manager and program staff can tap into the performance database for more detailed information, beyond that provided in the basic performance reports. For example, the program might find that the performance of clients in a particular region was not as high as desired. The program personnel might request special data runs that break out clients in that region by industry, size, and specific services. The information would permit program staff to identify more clearly the particular problems existing in that region, as well as providing an indication of what might be done to improve the services. The information might also indicate the extent to which less than satisfactory results were due to *external* factors, such as plant closings or economic problems in the region or industry.

In many instances, program staff will believe that they know the reasons for certain problems and anticipate poor outcomes even before the performance reports are received. However, even highly knowledgeable program staff receive only partial information on their programs. In any case, the data provided by a process known to be objective and reliable can provide program personnel with strong evidence to help them support their recommendations.

For example, the following actions by Minnesota programs resulted from examination of their performance reports:

- The Trade Office initiated a strategy to increase the number of nonmetropolitan area clients served (after the report showed low numbers of such clients and concerns expressed by these businesses).

- The Trade Office created a Trade Lead task force that developed a set of recommendations to improve the delivery of trade lead services (after the report showed relatively low levels of satisfaction among businesses about this particular activity).

- The department's Star Cities program, which provides technical assistance to local economic development agencies, revised its manual on the program, incorporating findings from the survey, and used the results to help develop its annual work plan.

- As a result of the next year's follow-up survey, a new trade show marketing plan was developed for Star Cities' clients.

■

USE BY DIVISION AND DEPARTMENT MANAGEMENT

Divisional and departmental managers have similar uses for performance information, although the emphasis may vary. Division heads may be especially interested in program management issues, whereas departmental executives may focus more on policy issues and on overall performance of entire program units. Four principal uses for these levels of managers are listed next.

1. The performance information can be used to help develop and improve division and department programs and policies. Division chiefs are more likely to be concerned with attempts to improve their programs than the department head. The department head's office will likely be more heavily concerned with department policy relative to performance elements, such as which types of clients, which regions and which industries are being adequately served.

2. Division heads and the department head's office may emphasize using performance information to hold division and program managers accountable. Higher-level managers, on the other hand, are not likely to have time for detailed, day-to-

day review of individual programs. They are more dependent on objective and independent information for identifying the extent to which their programs are performing at high levels of quality. Thus, they can use the periodic (i.e., quarterly) performance reports to keep abreast of overall divisional performance.

3. Top department officials can use the information to motivate their managers to improve performance. As with program managers, relative to their own staffs, a department head may want to use the data to encourage division heads to continue good performance or to improve performance in the face of disappointing results. One specific approach, as discussed under program manager uses, is to work with lower-level managers to establish performance targets for each major performance indicator for the forthcoming year and, subsequently, to compare actual performance to targeted performance (by using report formats such as that shown in Exhibit 11.6 in Section 11).

   Similarly, the performance information can be included in annual performance appraisals of lower-level managers. Individual performance appraisal tends to be highly subjective, that is, heavily based on the rating manager's judgment. Heavy dependence on qualitative judgments can be quite controversial, particularly in cases in which an upper-level manager provides low ratings of the lower-level manager. Because the performance data provide objective information, not subjective judgments by the manager doing the employee rating, both parties may feel less defensive. Nevertheless, the performance data will still need some subjective interpretation. Often external reasons, such as economic factors or foreign exchange rates, account for less-than-targeted performance.

4. Performance information can be used to help design policies and budgets and to help explain these to the governor and legislature. The performance information can be used as evidence to support department proposals for expansion or modification of programs. The fact that the department is attempting to assess systematically and objectively the results and quality of its programs on a regular basis, and is listening to its clients, should help assure the governor and legislature that the program is responsive, and should add credibility to the department's proposals.

■

USES BY CENTRAL ANALYSIS OFFICE

The CAO (by whatever organizational title) has a major role in the performance monitoring process, acting as the chief clerical and data tabulation arm for the department, and having responsibility for quality control over the data collection and reporting processes.

In addition, the CAO will, on occasion, use the performance data as a starting point for more in-depth evaluations and analyses of various programs and policies. The information obtained in the performance monitoring process can be a rich source of data about programs, outcomes, and quality, as well as about the nature of the clients served by the department. By undertaking special studies, program and policy analysts can also assist individual programs, divisions, and top management by providing insights into what is happening, why, and what changes might be desirable.

Performance monitoring procedures can also enable policy analysts and program managers to conduct a special type of study: *systematic experiments in ways to improve program services*. For example, if a program wishes to test a new practice before a full-scale implementation, the CAO and program officials could design an experiment in which a sample of randomly selected clients is provided the service in the new way while other clients are provided service in the old way. Subsequently, the routinely collected performance data would be analyzed to compare the results for clients who received the new service approach with the results for clients who received the old approach. The staff would have to add only one additional data element for each client, a code indicating whether or not the client received the new service.

■

EXTERNAL USES AND USERS

Inevitably, the governor, legislature, and media will be interested in, and will use, the data from performance reports for their own purposes. These purposes will not always appear beneficial from the department's viewpoint. For instance, performance reports will invariably contain "bad news" on some performance indicators, and external users will on occasion misuse this information, whether intentionally or unintentionally.

To some extent, the department can alleviate this problem of "bad news" by the following steps:

1. Do not overstate the significance of performance data that show favorable results. Good results as well as poor results can occur because of external factors and internal actions. For example, in "good times," performance indicators will tend to improve because of a favorable external economic environment, whereas during economic downturns, results can be expected to worsen. Department managers should recognize the importance of such uncontrollable factors when claiming success in good times, so that, in turn, they can point more credibly to external factors during bad times.

2. The department should be constructive in presenting negative findings. Program officers should attempt to identify the problem, explain why performance was poor, and indicate what corrective actions are planned or being taken to eliminate the problem. Of course, if performance reports continue to show the same problem, listeners will become dubious about excuses and corrective plans.

3. As described in previous parts of this manual, the department should provide a "Program Manager Review" step that per-

mits lower-level management to review performance reports first, so as to provide upper-level management with reasons for less than desirable performance and indicate any planned or recent corrective actions. Upper-level management can add this to the information released outside the department. It is very important that the program manager, division manager, and department managers be given the opportunity to review and comment on the information from the performance reports before the reports are released outside the department.

■

CURRENT LIMITATIONS ON UTILITY

Users should recognize that performance monitoring procedures are inherently limited in terms of what they can show, and therefore, in terms of what they can be used for. They can identify how well programs are doing and where they are doing well, such as in what regions of the state, in what industries, and in what size businesses (or communities). However, the performance information does not explicitly identify *why* the outcomes are the way they are. The procedures merely provide clues (such as by asking clients to explain why they have given a rating of "poor" to some aspects of the program's service). By identifying particular service characteristics and particular client characteristics (such as region, business size, and industry) where outcomes or service quality are highly rated or not highly rated, the data may suggest reasons for a negative rating (e.g., inadequate communication with businesses or communities in a particular region of the state).

Performance monitoring does not replace the need for periodic in-depth examination of individual programs, but it does provide important information to support such efforts. In-depth examinations can utilize extensive statistical analysis and provide much more qualitative and quantitative information about what is happening in the program and about what improvements are needed.

Furthermore, not until the outcome monitoring procedures have been repeated over a period of at least two to three years will it be possible to examine *time trends* in service outcomes and quality. This is a major use of the outcome information: to help department managers determine whether program outcomes and quality are improving, and to what extent.

Some other potential uses, such as having department management set targets on individual performance indicators at the beginning of the year and subsequently comparing actual outcomes against those targets, also cannot be tested until at least one to perhaps three more years.

■

CAUTION: KEEP EXPECTATIONS REASONABLE

All parties (the department head, division, and program managers) should avoid assuming that performance monitoring will automatically improve programs, or that every report, or every number, will lead to new actions. As with most regular reports, only some information will require action. Over time, however, department managers should expect performance reports to lead to actions improving departmental programs. If this does not happen, the process will not be valuable and should be terminated.

■

NEED FOR MANAGERIAL TRAINING IN USE OF PERFORMANCE INFORMATION

Ongoing performance monitoring provides department managers with valuable information to identify where problems are occurring and to help improve services to clients--particularly when performance information is broken out by such key client characteristics as location in the state, type of industry, and size of firm, for each major service. Collecting the information on a regular basis also indicates to others outside the department, such as the governor, the legislature, and communities and businesses in the state, that the department is indeed trying to identify, and be responsive to, their needs.

The design of the performance monitoring process, though far from perfect, can yield considerably more and better information on service outcomes and service quality than has yet been made available to department managers. The major impediment to exploiting the process is probably the inexperience of department managers in using the resulting findings. Such information has not been routinely made available in the past to managers. Many of the uses discussed here have not been generally applied in any state. Managers need to be informed about the nature of the performance information and about how it might best be used to improve services. Such information should be included by the department in its management training programs, for both current and new managers.

Collecting performance data on a regular basis requires staff time and money. Clearly, if the information emerging from the performance monitoring process does not lead to improved services, the process will be ineffectual. For managers who are willing and able to use the information, however, the costs of the effort are modest compared to the considerable potential returns it can bring.

14

IMPLEMENTING A PERFORMANCE MONITORING PROGRAM

INTRODUCTION

This section provides suggestions to economic development agencies about the how to initiate a performance monitoring system. The material draws heavily upon the experiences of the economic development departments of Maryland and Minnesota in pilot testing their own systems.

START-UP STEPS

We suggest the following basic start-up steps:

1. Secure top agency management support and form an agency-wide steering committee.

2. Identify a central department office to oversee and coordinate the implementation effort.

3. Hold a series of "focus groups" with agency clients to obtain their views on desirable performance characteristics.

4. Select programs to be included in the initial effort.

5. Establish working groups for each program for which performance monitoring is to be implemented; assign them the responsibility for establishing performance indicators, data collection procedures, and report formats.

6. Provide central support and technical help for each working group and ensure compatibility with other parts of the performance monitoring system.

7. Pilot test the procedures.

8. Modify the procedures based on pilot test findings and prepare an operating manual to guide the ongoing system.

The sections following discuss each of these steps.

■

STEP ONE: SECURE TOP AGENCY MANAGEMENT SUPPORT AND FORM AN AGENCY-WIDE STEERING COMMITTEE

Without the support of the department head and division heads, the performance monitoring process is not likely to maintain an adequate commitment of time and resources to be properly implemented and operated. Thus, those individuals in charge of establishing the performance monitoring system should ensure that they garner the necessary top-level support.

The commitment from top-level management is needed to obtain:

a. *Sufficient resources.* A number of agency personnel, including representatives from the programs participating in the performance monitoring effort, will need to allocate several hours each month for at least the first six months of the project. This should not require additional out-of-pocket expenses to the agency. However, some technical assistance is likely to be needed, including help with focus groups (Step 3) and with computer programming for a variety of clerical/administrative operations--particularly for the pilot testing phase (Step 7)--such as for processing client surveys and obtaining data from the unemployment insurance (UI) database. For these tasks, additional resources are likely to be needed. Over the long run, maintaining a performance monitoring process is likely to require about the equivalent of two person-years of mostly clerical-level effort.

b. *An adequate length of time for implementation.* A 12- to 15-month period should be planned for deployment, testing, modifications, and initial implementation of the performance monitoring system for a typical state agency, but less for a local government agency.

The agency head should establish a steering committee of representatives from each of the major divisions within the department. This committee would guide the project, especially on issues of concern to the entire department. Each division should be represented on the committee, even if no program from a division is selected initially for performance monitoring. Having representatives from other divisions will provide the project with objective assessments of its progress and will ease the inclusion of programs from those divisions in the future.

■

STEP TWO: IDENTIFY A CENTRAL DEPARTMENT OFFICE TO OVERSEE AND COORDINATE THE IMPLEMENTATION EFFORT

The department head should select an office that can represent the whole department, such as the office of analysis or research, and that can oversee and coordinate the effort--to ensure that the system components are compatible and are carried out efficiently. Preferably, one senior person should be assigned to supervise the effort. This person should have access to resources that can assist in the various steps. A first task for this office is to establish a schedule, including milestones. A sample schedule is presented in Exhibit 14.1.

■

STEP THREE: HOLD FOCUS GROUP MEETINGS WITH AGENCY CLIENTS

Obtaining clients' perspectives on the characteristics of the agency's performance that are important to them is highly desirable for determination of performance indicators. One way to obtain this input is through "focus groups," in which small groups of perhaps 8 to 12 clients are invited to discuss the qualities they believe are important elements of the department's program assistance. These sessions normally last about two hours.

The focus group sessions should be led by an experienced focus group leader, preferably not a department employee. (However, our past experiences indicate that one or two representatives of the department can be present at these meetings to listen and, on occasion, to ask for clarification of comments. If so, the participants should be told that department personnel are present.) An assistant to the focus group leader should take notes and prepare a report summarizing the views of the focus group.

The participants might be randomly selected from the roster of agency clients. Preferably, clients should be invited from each of the the major programs of the department. A small number of participants should also be selected from businesses that have *not* used the department's services. The individual programs can be asked to provide a list of "nonclients" to the central coordinating office. These would be firms that appear to be likely to benefit from state assistance.

If the department considers local government economic development programs to be clients of some programs, the department should hold one or more focus groups comprising representatives from some of these local governments. These focus groups should be separate from those for businesses because of the diverse concerns of these two types of clients. Representatives from the tourism industry might be included.

The focus group meetings should be held in a variety of locations throughout the jurisdiction, not in only one major city in a state. This will permit the agency to obtain a wide variety of relevant viewpoints.

The focus group leader should pose questions such as the following:

- What are the major strengths of the services you have received?
- What are the major weaknesses and problems in the services you have received (or not received)?
- Why have you not made more use of the department's services?

Given an effective focus group leader, such questions should provide adequate stimulation to obtain the information desired. The focus group leader should seek feedback from each participant, allowing each adequate time to express his or her viewpoint. Inevitably, participants will air their gripes about the department, many of which will be relevant to the basic purpose of determining what performance characteristics should be measured on a regular basis. But many of these gripes will not be relevant to this purpose. The agency should consider the focus group sessions as providing an additional benefit: an airing of complaints, some of which may require early action by the agency. A summary of these complaints should be included in the report on the focus groups.

■

STEP FOUR: SELECT PROGRAMS TO BE INCLUDED IN THE INITIAL EFFORT

The department head, with advice from the steering committee, should identify and select the programs to be included in the initial effort. Trying to include every program in the performance monitoring process is likely to be overly ambitious and may greatly dilute the quality of the effort. The agency probably should focus on a small subset of programs, perhaps four or five at most, for the initial effort.

The programs chosen should be representative of the many types of programs the agency offers. One strategy is to select one program from each major unit (e.g., division) in the department. The following criteria might be used to help select these programs:

a. The extent to which the program has sufficiently accurate information on program objectives and clients. The purposes of the program should be reasonably clear. Also, at least a rough database on clients, including addresses, principal contacts, and dates of services, should be available in the program's records.

b. The extent of support for the performance monitoring effort by the program manager and division head. Program support is tremendously important to operational success. Although initial reluctance is a normal reaction, and should not preclude inclusion, hostility toward the effort may doom it to failure.

c. The perceived importance of the program. The more important or more costly programs should be given priority.

d. Substantial improvements appear needed in existing procedures. Some programs may already be involved in regular monitoring of client outcomes. Resources are better expended on programs that have little performance monitoring in place.

Once programs have been selected, the steering committee should establish working groups for each.

■

STEP FIVE: ESTABLISH WORKING GROUPS FOR EACH PROGRAM INCLUDED IN THE PERFORMANCE MONITORING PROCESS

For each program selected, a process for the development work and pilot testing needs to be established. One promising approach is a "working group" approach, in which the department establishes for each program a group chaired by someone representing the program, probably the program manager or a senior official above the program level. The working group should consist of approximately 4 to 10 people (depending on the size and complexity of the program). Membership should include the program manager and one or two other staff from the program. The group also should include at least one representative from outside the program, but in the same division or branch, and it should include one person from the central coordinating office. If feasible, the agency also should include one person outside the department, such as a consultant who can provide independent insights and technical know-how.

The central office representative or outside consultant should be responsible for helping the working group move the sessions along, including preparation of an agenda for each meeting and materials for working group members to review, preferably well before each meeting.

It is extremely important that the working group meet regularly during the first few months (at least monthly, but preferably more frequently). Each working group should address the following issues:

- Which performance indicators are appropriate?
- What specific data sources and data collection procedures should be used?
- What specific client characteristics and service characteristics should be included in the performance monitoring process (e.g., so that the individual performance indicators can be broken out by such characteristics as location, size, and industry categories)?
- What procedures should be used to determine which clients should be included in the monitoring process? What data will need to be provided by the program on each client, such as what contact information will be needed (e.g., addresses and telephone numbers) for such procedures as client surveys and examination of the UI database--as discussed in other sections of this report?
- What should be included in performance reports and in what formats?

An example of the major topics the working groups should discuss and when, approximately, they should be scheduled is given in Exhibit 14.2.

■

STEP SIX: PROVIDE CENTRAL SUPPORT TO WORKING GROUPS

As noted in Step 5, independent technical assistance should be provided to each working group. Working groups without external help will have trouble on some of the technical issues (such as the details of data collection procedures). Outside assistance will help ensure that the group focuses on indicators of service quality and outcomes, rather than process indicators; that the technical quality of the work is high, and that the working group's recommendations are compatible with those of other working groups. (For example, the basic framework of any survey work and related data processing should be compatible across programs.)

■

STEP SEVEN: PILOT TEST THE PROCEDURES

Approximately six months after the beginning of this effort, the agency will probably be able to begin pilot testing the procedures. This testing should be a full-scale test of the procedures. (For example, if it is intended that all eligible clients of a particular program are to be covered in each reporting period, the pilot test should cover all eligible clients; by the same token, if a 30 percent sample is to be drawn, this size sample should be used in the pilot test.) Not only will this ensure a fully realistic test, but if the pilot test is reasonably successful, the data obtained can then be used for initial performance reports and serve as a baseline for identifying trends in subsequent data.

As discussed elsewhere in this report (especially in Section 12, which covered roles and responsibilities), the agency will need to decide whether to undertake data gathering by using its own personnel (perhaps supplemented by temporary staff) or to contract out selected tasks, such as the client surveys. It may be easier over the long run to contract out these tasks (which, for the most part, are not familiar activities for most economic development agencies). However, either approach might be used in the pilot test. If the agency decides to contract out the survey work in the pilot test, it should allow time for such contracting in its schedule. The use of a state or local university or college to undertake the survey work is likely to reduce the time needed for the contracting process.

The agency should expect to find many bugs and problems in the procedures during the pilot test. Even if the agency adopts procedures and survey questionnaires very similar to those provided in this manual, it should expect the pilot testing to uncover numerous problems with specific procedures or with the phrasing of questions in its own jurisdiction. However, once the system has been tested, modified accordingly, and implemented, client surveys can probably be completed relatively quickly.

■

STEP EIGHT: MODIFY THE PROCEDURES BASED ON PILOT TEST FINDINGS AND PREPARE OPERATING MANUAL

After the pilot test has been completed, the various participants should review the procedures and results (including the information obtained and the formats for reporting the information), to identify needed modifications. Once these modifications have been determined, and the agency has decided to continue the monitoring as a regular agency process, the central office should develop an operating procedures manual that spells out who needs to do what and when for each reporting period.

■

FINAL COMMENT

The procedures presented in the other sections of this manual are aimed at describing what an *ongoing* performance monitoring system would look like. These procedures can be used by a state or local economic development agency as a starting point for developing or revising its own system. For example, the performance indicators presented here for a particular type of program might be provided to working group members examining a similar program--to serve as a starting point for the working group. The sections on roles and responsibilities, analyses and reporting, and uses of the performance information probably would also be useful to working group members to provide background for the performance measuring process.

EXHIBIT 14.1

SAMPLE PROJECT SCHEDULE

Project Steps	Months 1	2	3	4	5	6	7	8	9	10	11	12	13	14	15
Step 1: Secure top agency management support	■														
Step 2: Identify a central department office to oversee and coordinate the implementation effort	■														
Step 3: Hold focus group meetings with agency clients		■	■												
Step 4: Select programs to be included in the initial effort			■												
Step 5: Establish working groups for each program included in the performance monitoring process				■	■										
Step 6: Provide central support to working groups				■	■	■	■	■	■	■	■	■	■	■	■
Step 7: Pilot test the procedures									■	■	■	■			
Step 8: Modify the procedures based on pilot test findings and prepare operating manual													■	■	■

EXHIBIT 14.2

TOPICS FOR FORMAL WORKING GROUP MEETINGS

Meetings One and Two:

1. Define program goals and objectives.
2. Select performance indicators for the program.

Meetings Three and Four:

3. Select data collection methods.
4. Choose and define client population.
5. Develop survey instruments and procedures.

Meetings Five and Six:

6. Review results of data collection.
7. Select final performance indicators and report formats.
8. Review procedures for ongoing performance monitoring.

Note: This is an "idealized" agenda. In practice, the working group is likely to discuss the indicators and revise data collection instruments many times before they are finalized.

SOCIOLOGY of Leadership

LARRY F. ROSS

Kendall Hunt
publishing company

Kendall Hunt
publishing company

www.kendallhunt.com
Send all inquiries to:
4050 Westmark Drive
Dubuque, IA 52004-1840

ISBN 978-1-5249-2208-5

Published in the United States of America

Contents

Preface

There are two things that I love talking about; one of them is sociology, and the other is leadership. Intrigued by both subjects as I got deeper into the understanding of their theories, I found myself wondering why there was not a book on the sociology of leadership because they seem so connected to each other. When I taught a strategic leadership class at the graduate level, one of my students made a bold statement as to what would Karl Marx say about this particular situation? Of course, I would say this is a great question and begin to share with him my answer. This is the question that he asked: What would Karl Marx say if leadership, particularly strategic leaders, controls most of the society? In this case, I told that Karl Marx would have suggested that those in strategic leadership positions at various Fortune 500 level organizations are the capitalists, who control the "means of production". Further, Marx would have added that the working class people are labeled the proletariat in this organization. A graduate of the U.S. Army Military Academy at West Point, he stated that the Academy had been teaching several sociology courses so that a student could now major in sociology. I recall telling him that there should be a course on the sociology of leadership and he said sir, based on your background, you should publish a book on the subject. As a retired military U.S. Army officer myself, I found the conversation intriguing because I remember the days when individuals graduating from West Point could only obtain engineering degrees. After talking to this person, I discovered that one could get a degree, not only in sociology but also in leadership development science. I finished teaching that course for the period and started to conduct some research on the matter of sociology of leadership. When we met again, I told him that I had gathered some pretty good data on Max Weber regarding power and authority, which indicated that sociologists have something to say about leadership. However, after several weeks had gone by, I could only see one clear-cut article on the sociology of leadership. However, the report also covered educational administration. The rest is history in that this book is an accumulation of research completed over a two-year period.

Sociology of Leadership

Thinking Critically!

1. No doubt that understanding the role and impact of leadership in society makes for an interesting study.
2. Leadership is instrumental to achieving social change within society and when sociologists ask those famous words "what holds society together," it is its leadership.

Introduction

- Leadership Connection in Society
- Social Forces affect all of us!
- We are social animals!
- It's all about you!

As You Read

- I sincerely hope that this book will add to the body of knowledge on leadership and sociology, but all the social sciences as a whole to bring a clear understanding of the "Sociology of Leadership."

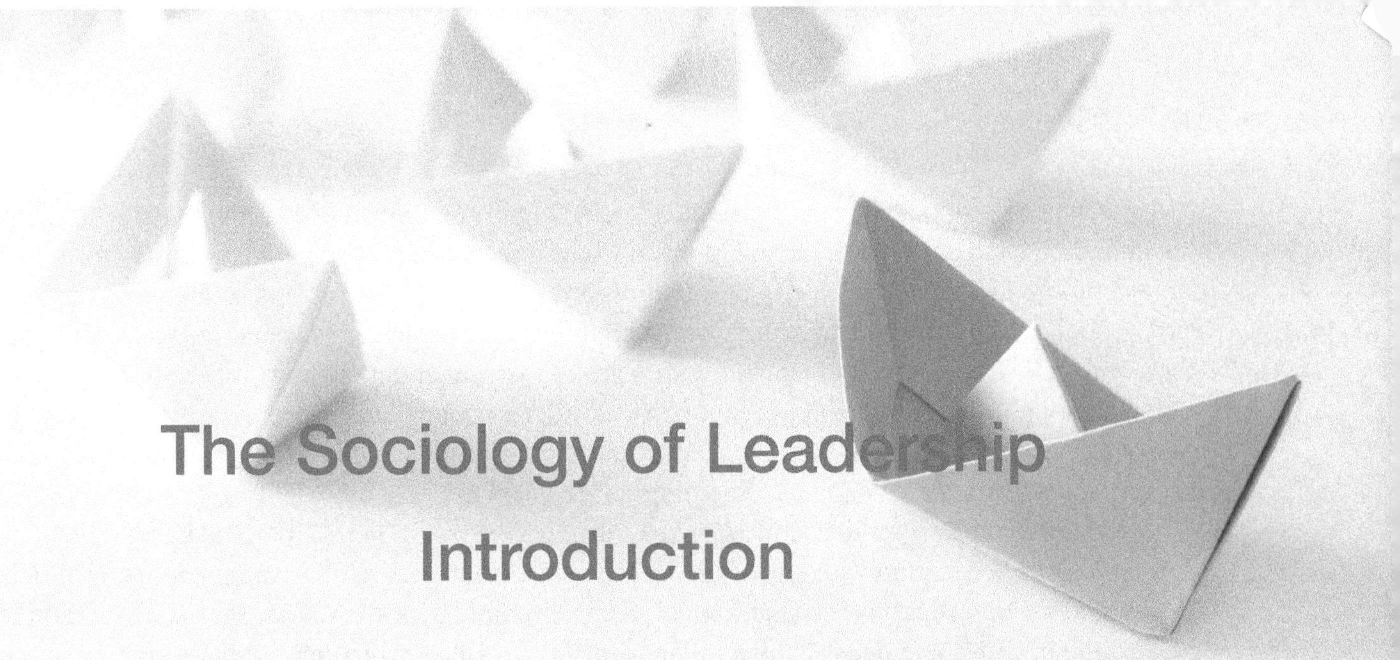

The Sociology of Leadership Introduction

Academic sociologists have been trained to conceive of their discipline—sociology—as the scientific study of society, and to remit to the sister discipline of psychology the study of individuals.

Richard Wall

One thing that sociology and leadership theorists would agree on is that when it comes to societal changes, it will not happen without some leadership. Just like sociologist's argument for "What holds society together?" Leadership theorists will argue that the direction of leadership brings stability to society. Therefore, leadership is vital to success of groups, organizations, institutions, and businesses. Even we can surmise that when it comes to social change, it will not happen without leadership and one's ability to lead is essential to this process. Leaders are important social actors in organizations and this is the main reason to look at leadership through the lens of sociology. The great philosopher Aristotle once said that man is by nature a social animal. Not only is it important to learn leadership from a particular discipline like sociology, but then a synthesizing approach also is needed to help integrate them together. Looking at ***Sociology of Leadership*** from a sociological perspective, there is a need to integrate various aspects of history, business, economics, psychology, leadership, and of course sociology studies. Each plays a significant role in our quest to understand sociology of leadership.

Everywhere you look, one can argue that leadership in some form occurs in everyday life, and this includes self-leadership. Leadership infers commitment to social change. In other words, we can also argue that social change is designed to bring awareness to various social problems that exist in society and without leadership people cannot unite to change. Leadership is a process that starts with self. It's designed to interact with a group to bring about changes for the betterment of society as a whole. There is a link when it comes to sociology and leadership. However, the biggest event that inspires changes in society is led by a social movement. This book is a capitalization of research on what is characterized as Sociology of Leadership.

A remarkable piece published in *Harvard Business Press*, Guillen (2010), addresses the issue of *Sociology of Leadership* with great skill. Guillen states that leadership in organizations, political parties, and nation-states has been the subject of much sociological work since the very inception of the discipline; with sociologists publishing more articles on leadership than scholars in other fields, particularly management and psychologists' scholars. However, sociologists basically disagree on the relationship between leaders and followers, whether leadership is about meaning or domination, or is it about the performance implications of different leadership styles. He goes on to say that there are theoretical assumptions and arguments of the four main schools of sociological thought on leadership: Weberian approach, institutional functionalism, neo-Marxist, and relational.

There are those who support my philosophy in that leadership is a relationship that involves the people who make up all facets of society regardless of what position he or she may hold. I am quite sure that Hughes, Thompson, and Terrell (2009) would have no argument with my position, because they agree that there is one fundamental point, which is that leadership is a relationship. They further state that it is a relationship between those who aspire to lead and those who choose to follow. And, regardless of how many people are involved in the relationship, he or she must be willing to engage each other. "How sweet the sound" but one thing I would like to add from these scholars is no matter how much formal power or authority you may have, you will only leave a lasting legacy if others want to be in that relationship with you.

Some questions that also need to be considered is how leaders succeed in various groups, businesses, organizations, institutions, and society as a whole. Moreover, what is the historical significance of those who played a pivotal role, not only in American society, but also elsewhere in the world? What type of leadership style did those leaders use to conquer success? For example, an understanding of leadership and group dynamic theories indicates that in its earliest stages, the strongest influence on a social movement will be the charismatic leader who personally symbolizes its values. At some point, intellectuals play a **leadership** role by contributing to the developing ideology of the social movement, and if a movement takes off, it is because of its leadership. Sociology provides for the study of social and organizational aspects of leadership. In this view, issues such as why people act as they do in stressful and extreme situations (social movements) or what constitutes the nexus between leadership/followership, organizations, institutions, culture, etc. would also need to be addressed. For many years, scholars have almost exclusively concentrated on purely psychological aspects of leadership. Today, sociological research enriches the traditional strand of leadership studies by bringing in both an organizational and societal perspective. As a result, there is a new phenomenological sociological approach we can add to the body of knowledge. There are also numerous case studies of leadership carried out in this field of social science research. We hope that one can agree that nothing happens without direction, and you can't lead others if you cannot first lead yourself. I also agree with Blanchard's (2014) position on an individual knowing their points of power. Specifically, one can argue that if you are good at communicating and motivating people, you have personal power. If you find that people have a tendency to like being around you or associated with you, you have relationship power. Relationship allows a leader to have significant influence over others in groups and this leads to the overall success in achieving your goal as a leader. If you realize that you have specific expertise or skills in a particular area, you also have knowledge power. Knowledge is golden when one is a leader. And finally, if you're the "go-to" person in the office or at home because people understand and know that you can get things done, you have task power. For the most part, these are leadership terms. However, going deeper into this argument, one can surmise that this person would also need to have a keen grasp of the socialization process that occurred in their life to help them ascertain the overall influence that made them a leader. There is also something unique about the social relationship between leaders and followers and the ability to tie it to the sociology of leadership. Unfortunately, many scholars in sociology and leadership have failed to connect this powerful combination to the point that literature is lacking. Whiteford and Ganem (2015) posit that sociologists favor the study of social forces, organizational dynamics, and the relative lack of agency that individuals have in these contexts. They go on to say that this means leaders matter less than the structures surrounding them. The big question here is how can this be? For example, the Great Man theory argues that leadership is inherent, meaning that great leaders are born and not made. Well, we have seen the effective training of leadership, and we have only institutions like West Point and Harvard to thank for this answer. When taught on how to be a leader, many of them rise to the occasion (President Theodore Roosevelt, General Douglas MacArthur, and Secretary of State/General Colin Powell). We should be intrigued by the position put forth by *Scott C. Whiteford* and *Natasha M. Ganem* when they say that there is an advantage of having "A Sociology of Leadership." In other words, studying this aspect of sociology allows students to learn specifically how leaders with charisma influence individuals, organizations, and movements. Moreover, sociologists would be in a better position to add to the body of knowledge of organizational psychology, as well as leadership and management thought. A sociology of leadership course would increase enrollment not only for sociology departments, but also draw students from other disciplines (psychology, business, economics, and history) eager to learn the connection of leadership from a sociological perspective. The sociology of leadership will assist participants in developing a personal philosophy of leadership, mindfulness of the moral and ethical responsibilities of leadership, and provide awareness of one's own ability and style of leadership from a sociological perceptive.

There is more in that as stated before, society cannot function without leadership. However, when people talk about leadership, they always talk about good or bad leadership. Organizations are always looking for people to lead their members and hope that the person doing the leading is a good leader. The organization even sends their potential leaders to school or put them through a leadership development course in hopes that they will stand out among their peers and lead the organization to great heights. One must understand that leadership is not just limited to the work frontier, but it also extends to all of society. In fact, we can trace leadership back to the beginning of civilization in that Egyptian rulers, Greek heroes, and biblical patriarchs, all having one thing in common and we call it leadership (Stone & Patterson, 2005). In other words, leadership began as a societal phenomenon before it evolved into a professional one. Moreover, many of the leadership qualities that corporate and professional leaders aspire to are based on the social and political leaders of the past.

As I stated before, Aristotle, the Greek philosopher, stated that man is a social animal and he who lives without society is either a beast or God. We should not be biased in this premise, so let's conclude from this statement that all human beings are social animals and as such, are required to live together in large groups. However, in order for social animals to live together, they must adapt to different roles to accomplish different things, but in this process, we find that people not only have a commitment toward each other, they also have this same commitment to those chosen to lead. Selnick (2010) states that there is a difference between leadership and commitment, because if an organization's roles can be specified in advance, and if the rote prevails, then there may not be a need for leadership. However, there is something to be said for an organization that is staffed with workers who know where they stand and are able to do their jobs efficiently based on the roles they play inside the organization. Nevertheless, on the basis of this behavior, leadership is necessary whenever roles change by experience (2010). Therefore, in order to give structure to society and help society grow and develop, we must naturally divide these social animals (people) into leaders and followers. Leaders must pave the way and move people from one place to another, directing the others as they move forward, whereas the followers complete the various tasks assigned to them which helps to bring changes, in this particular case, to society.

Alain (2012) furthers the argument of leadership connection to society in that he too believes that human beings are social animals but "in order to give structure to society and help society grow and develop, people were naturally divided into leaders and follower" (p. 1). He also agrees that leadership is needed to facilitate not only social change (power to influence how people feel and serve as an advocate to meet the goals of that change), but to also assert leadership by acting as the face of society and serve as its symbol.

And what about societal changes? Leadership is instrumental to achieving social change within society and when sociologists ask those famous words "what holds society together," it is its leadership. We know that all throughout history, whether it was for ending social norms, overcoming social evils or modernizing history, social change is difficult without the right kind of leadership. Alain (2012) states that it has to be good leadership because it is that type of leadership that allows leaders to pave the way and move from one frontier to another, directing others, while followers complete tasks assigned to them which brings forth changes desired by members of a group. Put simply, when it comes to rallying the multitudes, igniting passion in people to facilitate a common goal and motivating them to achieve it, we find it isn't possible to unite the people and inspire action without leadership. One person has to step up to the plate or be chosen to spear the movement. The person may not professionally be a leader, and he or she does not have to be a political leader, but one thing is clear in that the person should have the charisma to inspire people and motivate them.

No doubt that understanding the role and impact of leadership in society makes for an interesting study. Hence, this is where the sociology of leadership comes into play. Although it is easy to break down the overall effects of leadership in the work environment into small, simply identifiable structures, analyzing how leadership affects society is somewhat complex. In my view, this is the main reason why sociologists and leadership theorists alike have failed to tackle these phenomena. I wholeheartedly think that Whiteford and Ganem (2015) would support this argument because their research indicates only one chapter in a book that addresses what a sociology of leadership might look like. The bottom line is that society is a multiphenomena structure, with a myriad of social forces, features, and influences at play all the time and leadership plays an important role in this process. Therefore, we have to recognize that society is not limited to a few defined goals. Nevertheless, to address the sociology of leadership presents an intangible, yet great phenomenon to add to the body of knowledge for sociologist and leadership theorists alike.

Social forces or factors have an intended effect on those placed in leadership positions. For example, those who grow up and end up going to the best schools are more likely than not to be put in leadership positions. However, it goes deeper than this in that we find that if groups, organizations, or companies are going to be successful, it is not only because of their normative and strong culture, but more importantly their leadership. Although the sociological perspective of leadership tends to include various aspects of history, business, economics, and psychology, most of these disciplines center primarily on the leader's talent, knowledge, and behavior. According to Whiteford (2016), the crucial part of the study of leadership from a sociological perspective is understanding how leaders thrive in groups, organizations, society, and for the most part, throughout history. The sociology of leadership is for those future leaders who are interested in a variety of the field to include but not limited to business, history, economics, psychology, and of course sociology, as it will provide a well-rounded understanding of sociology of leadership. I sincerely hope that this book will add to the body of knowledge on leadership and sociology, and all the social sciences as a whole to bring a clear understanding of the "*Sociology of Leadership*."

References

Alain, P. (2012). The impact of a good leader and good leadership in society. Retrieved from Https://www.industryleadersmagazine.com/the-impact-of-a-good-leader-and-good-leadership-in-scoiety/

Blanchard, K. (2014). 3 ways to be an effective self-leader. Retrieved from http://www.fastcompany.com/3026046/leadership-now/3-ways-to-be-an-effective-self-leader

Guillen, M. F. (2010). Classical sociological approaches to the study of leadership. In N. Nohria, & R. Khurana (Eds.). *Handbook of leadership theory and practice: A Harvard business school centennial colloquium* (pp. 223–305). Boston, MA: Harvard Business Press.

Hughes, M., Thompson, H. L., & Terrell, J. B. (Eds.) (2009). *Handbook for developing emotional and social intelligence: Best practices, case studies, and strategies.* San Francisco, CA: Pfeiffer.

Selnick, P. (2010). *Leadership in administration: A sociological interpretation.* New Orleans, LA: Quid Pro Books.

Stone, G. A., & Patterson, K. (2005). The history of leadership focus. Retrieved from http://www.regent.edu/acad/sis/publications/conference_proceedings/servant_leadership_roundable/2005/pdf/stone_history.pdf

Whiteford, S. C. (2016). Sociology 398: Sociology of leadership. Retrieved from http://soc.unl.edu/SOCIOLOGY/Soc%20of%20Leadership%20Syllabus.pdf

Whiteford, S. C., & N. M. Ganem (2015). Is there such a thing as "A Sociology of Leadership?" Retrieved from https://workinprogress.oowsection.org/2015/10/27/is-there-such-a-thing-as-a-sociology-of-leadership/

Sociology of Leadership

Think about Self!

As you read throughout this book, I want you to critically think on how you might go about applying what you have learned about the sociology of leadership and its relationship to your life.

Chapter 1

- A General Overview of Sociology
- The Principal Divisions and Theories
- Sociological Studies
- Applying Sociology and its Benefits

As You Read

- What is sociology?
- Name the three sociological paradigms.
- What are the benefits of sociology?

Chapter 1

A General Overview of Sociology

© Panos Karas/Shutterstock.com

Man is by nature a social animal: an individual who is unsocial naturally and not accidentally is either beneath our notice or more than human. Society is something that precedes the individual. Anyone who either cannot lead the common life or is so self-sufficient as not to need to, and therefore does not partake of society, is either a beast or a god.

Aristotle

There are benefits one can receive from studying sociology. You can amass specific knowledge and apply it to your everyday life. Learning various aspects of the sociology of leadership will help in your quest to gain more knowledge about the society and its different relationships. Sociology is the science of society, and it permits us to look at our everyday lives as if we were visitors seeing our new society for the first time. Observing our social lives enables us to understand the patterns surrounding our lives and those of others. Peter Berger (1963) was right when he first said that society is not what it appears to be. I can just imagine that *Auguste Comte* echoed something similar during the period of the French Revolution which he grew up to observe. It was the human drama that appeared to surround him which he later described as sociology, the study of society. Sociology emerged in the late 19th century as a product of its discipline, philosophy, rather than as applied research. *Max Weber*, *Emile Durkheim*, and *Vilfredo Pareto* formed an intellectual triad of sociological theorists of the 19th century. Although it was Max Weber who gave us a theory of bureaucracy as well as the notion of the Protestant ethic, it was Emile Durkheim who divided societies into two primary types: mechanical, those dominated by a collective consciousness, and organic, those characterized by specialization and division of labor and social interdependence (Henslin, 2017). From Durkheim, we can ascertain that mechanical societies are bound together by what he called kinship, friendliness to others, and being a good neighbor. However, it is the lack of such solidarity in organic societies that led to anomie, a sense of what he called "normlessness" or confusion. Durkheim posits that to restore social solidarity in organic societies, they had to come through a new "collective consciousness," which led to the establishment of values and norms levied on members of society. You see in an organic society that people must cooperate, love one another, and be

© maximmmmum/Shutterstock.com

willing to sacrifice the self for the group to promote solidarity (Durkheim, 1947). Moreover, Durkheim substituted the group as the source of values and norms and as the new collective consciousness.

Another major sociological school of thought is that of social behaviorism. This school of thought introduces the idea of the social person as the object of study and establishes what is now called social psychology as an essential branch of sociology. Charles Horton Cooley, in his famous work known as the "looking-glass self" or the idea that the social self, arises reflectively regarding a person's reactions to the opinions of others. It is through a person's group experience that he or she forms the first notions of both self and social unity. Also, the famous George Herbert Mead, a social psychologist, suggested that a person learns himself or herself through a process of taking the role of others in various interactive situations. Society serves as a process of interaction by which self is always in what Charles H. Cooley describes reshaped through these encounters or interactions. A person is shaped by society's one-on-one interactions.

We define sociology as the study of human society. Specifically, sociology is the scientific study of the structure, the functioning, and the changes in human groups as they operate in society. Society is a vast and complex phenomenon, and therefore, it has been long debated as to which sociology should study the part of society. There is a significant degree of difference of opinion regarding the definitions, scope, and subject matter of sociology. However, one thing is for sure in that when we think of sociology, we must grasp what Wright Mills (1959) called the "vivid awareness of the relationship between personal experience and the wider society" (p. 2). We must also add that although most people consider their lives unique, sociologists take, to some extent, an unpopular view that people behave in somewhat predictable ways. Therefore, this particular understanding of the interchange of man and society is the primary goal of sociology. The patterns of behavior are crucial to the study of sociology as you will see in my attempt to wrestle and gain knowledge of the sociology of leadership. As you read throughout this book, I want you to critically think on how you might go about applying what you have learned about the sociology of leadership and its relationship to your life.

Principal Divisions and Theories

The school of thought in sociology centers on functionalism, conflict theory, symbolic interactionism, social exchange theory, and formalism. However, the three most important paradigms are functionalism, conflict theory, and symbolic interactionism.

Functionalism is the top-down examination of society as a complex of interrelated and interdependent parts. Talcott Parsons claimed that society must fulfill the criteria of adaptation to the environment. Goal attainment facilitates this as a result of a collective vision. Parsons also reminds us that mediating conflicts between individuals are just part of the process for human survival. And, it was Emile Durkheim (the first professor of sociology) who argued that sociology has broadly three main divisions which he terms as social morphology, social physiology, and general sociology. Social morphology covers the geographical settings, the density of population, and other preliminary data which are likely to influence the social aspects of society. Social physiology concerns with such dynamics processes such as religion, morals, law, economic, and political issues and these may be the subject matter of a particular discipline. General sociology is an attempt to discover the general social laws which form the specific social processes. Durkheim considers these social processes as the rational part of sociology.

The great Max Weber combines two schools of thought which centers on the historical and systematic parts of society. However, it is his analysis surrounding the relationship between economics and religion which enables him to use both historical as well as the systematic method. The sociologies of law, economics, and religion are the special sociologies which are part of both usual and historical methods of the study.

According to Pitirim A. Sorokin (Russian American sociologist), we can divide sociology into two branches which include general sociology and special sociology. General sociology studies the specifics that are common to all social and cultural phenomena in their structural, dynamic, and the interrelationships between the sociocultural and biological aspects. In the structural part, sociology studies various types of groups and institutions as well as their interrelations toward one another. Moreover, we also investigate the dynamic side sociology studies in which different social processes such as social contact, interaction, socialization, conflict, domination, and subordination are reviewed. Special sociologies study a particular sociocultural phenomenon for more information on the subject matter. Some of the most developed sociologies are the sociology of population or demography, sociology of law, sociology of religion, rural sociology, sociology of knowledge, sociology of fine arts, and many others.

Morris Ginsberg argued that there is a relationship between history and sociology (Ginsberg, 1934; 2016). He has listed the problems of sociology under four aspects: social morphology, social control, social processes, and social pathology. Social morphology includes investigation of the quantity and quality of population, the study of social structure, or the description and classification of the principal types of social groups and institutions. Social control includes the study of law, morals, religion, conventions, fashions, and other sustaining and regulating agencies. Social processes refer to the study of various modes of interactions between individuals or groups including cooperation and conflict, social differentiation and integration, and development and decay. Social pathology relates to the study of social maladjustments and disturbances.

Raymond Aron was better known for his skepticism of ideological orthodoxies. He mentioned six schools in sociology, and they included historical, formal, society and community, phenomenological, universalistic, and general. He was hard on Karl Marx (renowned conflict theorist). Aron suggested that Marxism is mental opium and that many scholars create and believe false myths. One of these myths centered on the belief that history is progressive and liberating, which led to totalitarian controls. Karl Marx states that the proletariat is the collective savior of humanity, whereas in fact most workers, relatively than becoming bearers of Marxism, just want a universal or middle-class standard of living.

Sociological Studies

Theoretical Sociologists tap into the theories from a micro or macro level of analysis. When we think of sociological theories, we start off with the big three and their associations with famous sociologists: conflict theory (Karl Marx), structural-functionalism theory (Emile Durkheim), and symbolic interactionist theory (Max Weber/George Herbert Mead). The first two theories, conflict and functionalism, are associated with research conducted on a macro level, whereas the last theory, symbolic interactionism, is related to research performed at the micro level.

© S-F/Shutterstock.com

Criminology is the branch of sociology that studies the criminal behavior of individuals or groups. The concept "Criminology", derived from the Latin *crimen*, which means accusation, and the translated Greek *logia,* meaning "the study of," is the study of crime. To give you an idea of some of the areas that sociologists might look into include, but is not limited to, the following; the frequency, causes, types, and location of crimes. Some sociologists also look at the social and individual reactions to crime and the ability of government control and oversite of laws to control crime.

Global Sociology seeks to compare other societies with our own (United States). As we study and compare other societies, we might find that there are other ways to live. Global sociology gives us an understanding of the diversity of the world's cultures. As Schneider and Silverman (2013) suggest, when you understand how sociological concepts can be applied to different societies, you will understand the concepts much better. Some of the sociological concepts we are referring to include: values, norms, roles, socialization, deviance, social control, social stratification, social change, inequality, modernization, etc. However, leadership should be added as one of the concepts in that as we dig deeper into this concept and its connection to sociology as a whole, you will find that leadership in other countries differs based on the culture (as discussed in Chapter 4) of that particular country. The bottom line is that global sociology is concerned with human relationships from a

© Iakov Kalinin/Shutterstock.com

cross-cultural approach and the complex social environment in which we live. Understanding that it is within the social environment that our relationships with other people take place and with the advent of globalization, we find that the surroundings are not only smaller, but we are also closely connected than ever before because of technology.

Group Relations concerns with the problems arising out of the coexistence in a community of diverse racial and ethics groups. Frankly, new areas and subareas of sociology are continuously evolving over the period.

Political Sociology studies the social implications of several types of political movements and beliefs and the origin, expansion, and functions of the government and the state. In particular, political sociology studies the power and the relationship among societies, states, and political conflict from a macro or micro component level.

Social Psychology seeks to comprehend human motivation and behavior as society determines them and its values. The field studies the socialization process of the individual on how he or she becomes a member of society. This concept also explores the public, crowd, the mob, and various other social groupings and movements. Analysis of mass persuasion or propaganda and public opinion has been one of its primary interests. It is also about how others influence people's thoughts, feelings, and behaviors and in this case, the leader's influence on the individual. To be clear, Fiske (2010) states that it's all about people influencing other people. However, she states that the classical definition of social psychology for which Gordon Allport wrote back in 1954 says it the best in that it is "the scientific attempt to explain how the thoughts, feelings, and behaviors of individuals are influenced by the actual, imagined, or implied presence of other human beings."

Social Psychiatry deals with the relationships between social and personal disorder, and its general hypothesis that society, through its extreme and conflicting demands upon the individual, is to a large extent responsible for his or her instabilities such as various types of mental disorders and antisocial behaviors. As one highlights the effects of socioeconomic factors on mental illness, there is a need for therapeutic communities to help with this situation. With the many factors associated with mental illness in society, the argument would be for those in community leadership positions to step up to the plate. In its applied aspects, social psychiatry wants to solve this problem.

Social Disorganization deals with the problems of instability. This might lead to problems of crime and delinquency, physical and mental, poverty and dependency, and population movements. Of these subdivisions, it is *crime and delinquency* that have received the most attention. This also led to the development of the bright field of criminology.

Sociology of Demography is the scientific mathematical and statically study of the population. These studies center on the size, situation, composition, density, distribution, and measurement of the population. Simply, this branch of sociology studies the distribution of the human population with the analysis of population change based on sociological perspectives. It also investigates trends and other factors determining population change.

Sociology of Education is a concept symbolizing ideologies that study the objectives of the school as a social institution. Sociology of education also looks deeper into the curriculum and extracurricular activities, its relationship to the community and other institutions that may have an impact on the educational system as a whole. *Sociology of Education* addresses mass schooling systems of modern industrial societies, including the expansion of higher, further, adult, and continuing education. We can trace the systematic sociology of education to Emile Durkheim's pioneering studies of moral education as a basis for organic solidarity and Max Weber's analysis of the Chinese literati as an apparatus of political control.

Sociology of Knowledge is the branch of sociology which studies the relationship between thought and society. We can also state that it is concerned with the social or existential conditions of knowledge. Scholars in this particular field tend to study the philosophies and ideologies, political doctrines, and theological thought. There is an attempt to relate the ideas it explores to the sociohistorical settings in which they are produced and received. Although tied to Marxian-thought patterns, Karl Mannheim and Max Scheler developed the first systematic elaboration of the sociology of knowledge as a new scientific discipline (Sociology of Knowledge, 2016). And it was Mannheim who defined the sociology of knowledge as a theory of the social or existential conditioning of thought (2016). We note that the sociology of knowledge incorporates into the general sociology theory both in America and in Europe, and it is often merged with other areas of research and is frequently no longer explicitly referred to as sociology of knowledge. Some questions to be addressed in explaining the sociology of knowledge might include but is not limited to:

- How might we come to know about who and what we are through knowledge?
- How does the economy and consumer goods shape our knowledge?
- Is there a connection between knowledge and social order; what is your role?
- What are the connections between knowledge and social movements on the advent of social change?
- What role do the media play in knowledge production in society? (2016)

Sociology of Law concerns itself with formalized social control efforts, with processes whereby members of a group attain uniformity in their behavior through the rules and regulations imposed upon them by society. It enquires into the factors that bring about the creation of regulatory systems to facilitate control of society. In other words, sociology of law centers on a multidisciplinary area of research interested in the interrelationship of legal practices, institutions, doctrines, and the related social contexts.

Sociology of Leadership seeks to understand the ***social relationship*** between leaders and their impact on followers, organizations, businesses, institutions, and social movements. Sometimes called social interaction, a social relationship is a relationship between two or more persons. New to the realm of sociology, sociology of leadership recognizes that society cannot function without leaders. The notion of the sociology of leadership seeks to divide people into leaders and followers that give rise to the overall structure and survival of society. For example, we can use the leadership of Jesus as a great example in that he saw the ability of a few, whom he later called his disciples, to help him lead the Christianity movement. The Christian community and the way people were drawn to it were the key to society growing with Jesus as a leader. Pagels (2016) stated that the community took care of people and we know this because they would feed the destitute, take care of individuals who were widowed so that they wouldn't become prostitutes and orphans, and so forth. She goes on to say that this was a primary obligation of Jewish piety. And Jesus' followers certainly understood that because when people joined the Christian communities in Rome, for example, they would be buried. However, this is not something anyone could take for granted in the ancient world. Nevertheless, this is a society where people tend to take care of one another. Hence, the enormous appeal of Jesus and the Christian movement.

So when you think of the spread of Christianity from a sociological point of view, we find that it distinguishes itself from all the other religious options in the Mediterranean, except Judaism. We know that both groups meet at least once a week and have very clear ethical norms, an ethic of community charity, and both groups have revealed ethical patterns of behavior. In other words, there was no promiscuity centering on don't do certain things that will bring shame. Sociologically speaking, this is the reason why Christianity would appeal to members of society and why the movement continues today, and it centers on the leadership of Jesus, whom some argue, was the greatest leader ever.

Sociology of Religion looks at the church as a social institution and seeks to discern its origin, expansion, and changes in its structure and function. In other words, we find that the sociology of religion looks to understand the belief, practices, and organizational forms of religion using the roots and methods of the discipline of sociology. Emile Durkheim contributed significantly on this subject during his studies of suicide, specifically, looking into the suicide rates among Catholic and Protestant populations.

Applying Sociology and its Benefits

Most of you have taken one or more courses in sociology. During that time, you learned a great deal about the field and became familiar with such concepts as socialization, cultural, social stratification, minorities, institutions, sociological research, sociological theories, social movements, and social change. However, studying these concepts helped you to learn a lot regarding society and human relationships. You also learned that society and relationships involve patterns, and it is these patterns that help you make appropriate decisions at some point during your life journey. Making decisions requires self. However, if participating in a group or organization, the pleasure to make decisions is charged to leaders. Although applying sociological concepts to one's life is not new, studying the many facets of sociology can help one succeed in your life journey. For example, if you can understand the nature of sociology of leadership, then this situates you to benefit from it when elevated to a position of leadership. Looking at it another way, if you understand that this college is part of the social institution of education, you will have a better idea of what you must do to be successful. On the flip side, you will also be aware of what is likely to happen if you fail. What we know allows us to be successful, not only in society but also in all of our endeavors.

Sociologists have learned in the study of sociology that we tend to develop relationships with people who attend the same school, work at the same place, attend the same religious services, or are in the same economic bracket. The bottom line is that we become involved with people around us who have similar characteristics. Knowledge of this fact enables one to develop a positive expectation for future relationships.

We also know, for example, that relationships tend to last longer when the people involved have many things in common. Moreover, if two people share interests, commitments, and values, their relationships gather strength from these common elements. Moreover, we must understand that applying sociological knowledge to gain the most from each situation is simply a personal means of using sociology.

Chapter Summary

Sociology is a fast-growing social science divided into subdivisions. It is a very complex and exciting field of study. New sociological topics are being added all the time with the focus on giving us more knowledge about the various roles we play in society and the effect of those roles in our social interactions. Leadership is a role that some of us play in society. Sociology of leadership is one of those new subdivisions that, in my view, has an impact on society and individuals, especially those who may ascend to leadership positions. Sociology is about social life, and we live in a rapidly changing global society, defined by many cultures. However, we recognize that humans are rational beings who desire to control their environment, and depend, on some aspects of leadership (rather it be the leadership of self or those placed in that role) to help manage their environment. My inquisitiveness has led me to explore sociology of leadership in an attempt to explain the leadership and sociology connection by first giving you a general overview of the many facets of sociology. The next chapter will look into the many facets of leadership as we begin to blend these two concepts to add to the body of knowledge of leadership and sociology.

Glossary

Social Relationship Sometimes called social interaction, it is the relationship between two or more persons.

References

Berger, P. (1963). *Invitation to sociology*. New York, NY: Anchor Books.

Durkheim, E. (1947). *The division of labor in society*. (G. Simpson, Trans.). New York, NY: Free Press.

Education, Sociology of. (2016). A Dictionary of Sociology. Retrieved from Encyclopedia.com: http://www.encyclopedia.com/social-sciences/dictionaries-thesauruses-pictures-and-press-releases/education-sociology

Federico, R. C. (1979). *Sociology*. (2nd ed.). Reading, MA: Addison-Wesley Publishing Company. Fiske, S. T. (2010). *Social beings: Core motives in social psychology*. Hoboken, NJ: John Wiley & Sons, Inc.

Fredriksen, P. (2016). The spread of Christianity. Retrieved from http://www.pbs.org/wgbh/pages/frontline/shows/religion/why/appeal.html

Ginsburg, M. (1934). *Sociology*. London: Oxford University Press.

Ginsberg, M. (2016). A Dictionary of Sociology. Retrieved from Encyclopedia.com: http://www.encyclopedia.com/social-sciences/dictionaries-thesauruses-pictures-and-press-releases/ginsberg-morris

Hall, C. S., & Lindzey, G. (1957). *Theories of personality*. New York, NY: John Wiley & Sons, Inc.

Henslin, J. M. (2017). *Essentials of sociology: A down-to-earth approach*. (12th ed.). Boston, MA: Pearson Education.

Knowledge, Sociology of. (2016). International encyclopedia of the social sciences. Retrieved from Encyclopedia.com: http://www.encyclopedia.com/social-sciences/applied-social-sciences-magazines/knowledge-sociology

Kouzes, J. M., & Posner, B. Z. (2007). *The leadership challenge.* (4th ed.). New York, NY: John Wiley & Sons, Inc.

Mills, C. W. (1959). *The sociological imagination.* Oxford: Oxford University Press.

Pagels, E. H. (2016). The great appeal: What did Christianity offer its believers that made it worth social estrangement, hostility from neighbors, and possible persecution? Retrieved from http://www.pbs.org/wgbh/pages/frontline/shows/religion/why/appeal.htmlSchneider, L., & Silverman, A. (2013). *Global sociology: Introducing five contemporary societies.* (6th ed.). New York, NY: The McGraw-Hill Companies, Inc.

Shamir, B., & Eilam, G. (2005). What's your story? A life-stories approach to authentic leadership. *The Leadership Quarterly*, 16, 395–417.

Chapter 1

Leadership Skill-Building Exercise

The Making of a Leader

The making of a leader begins with writing about self. You might recall the social psychological concept called the "Looking-glass Self" developed by Charles Horton Cooley in his argument that a person's self grows out of society's interpersonal interactions and the perceptions of others. He argues that individuals tend to shape their self-concepts based on their understanding of how others perceived them. Leaders are very concerned as to how they are seen in the eyes of others, not only in their business endeavors but also the community as well as society as a whole. This leadership exercise allows you to take a good look at "self" and in an attempt to see how others perceive you in society, school, and workplace to include those who are close to you and the family. Go deeper and ask yourself how you would view self?

I once read a great book by the name of *Authentic Leadership*, written by Bill George. I want to tell you that this book not only moved and propelled me forward as a person, but also helped in my leadership walk to discover who and what I am as a leader. In other words, after reading his book, I used what C. Wright Mills had stated long ago: use your sociological imagination to write the history and biography of yourself. I looked into the looking-glass self and developed an image of myself and the perceptions that went along with it and began to write my story.

This exercise requires you to do the same in that use your sociological imagination and taking into consideration the looking-glass-self-concept, determine how people perceive you, and write down your specific story to be told later in the training event/course. As a suggestion, I would think that you would want people to see you as being real, genuine, and authentic in your leadership walk. Therefore, I want you to also pay particular attention to what George (2005) state in that "how do you become an authentic leader? . . . Although we may be born with leadership potential, all of us have to develop ourselves to become good leaders. The medium for developing into an authentic leader is not the destination but the journey itself a journey to find your true self and the purpose of your life's work" (p. 27). You might find, as I did that it all started with self, the day you were born and begin to become socialized into the role and person that you would become later in life. You might ask why authentic leadership? Shamir and Eilam (2005) argue "that authentic leadership rest heavily on the leader's life story and the construction of a life-story is a major element in the development of authentic leaders" (p. 395). They further assert that it is these life-stories that provide followers with major data on which to base their perceptions about a leader's genuineness or authenticity. I couldn't agree more in that we want individuals to perceive you as being genuine, real, and authentic to the point they will ask you to lead them some day.

As you tell your specific story as a social person or social self, you too will begin to recognize through the looking-glass self that one is a social being. Shamir and Eilam (2005) take this a bit further when they state leaders are social beings, influenced by social norms and values, parental and peer socialization, schooling, role models, and other social inspirations.

To start this off, I want you to write about something significant that changed in your life and as you begin to put pen to paper be real, authentic and remember to write whatever comes to mind. You might also want to prioritize certain events. This leadership skill can serve a variety of purposes, particularly during following exercises as you attempt to learn more about self. This activity starts the beginning of your development of self-knowledge and self-clarity, including simplicity about values and your overall opinions about self.

© G7 Stock/Shutterstock.com

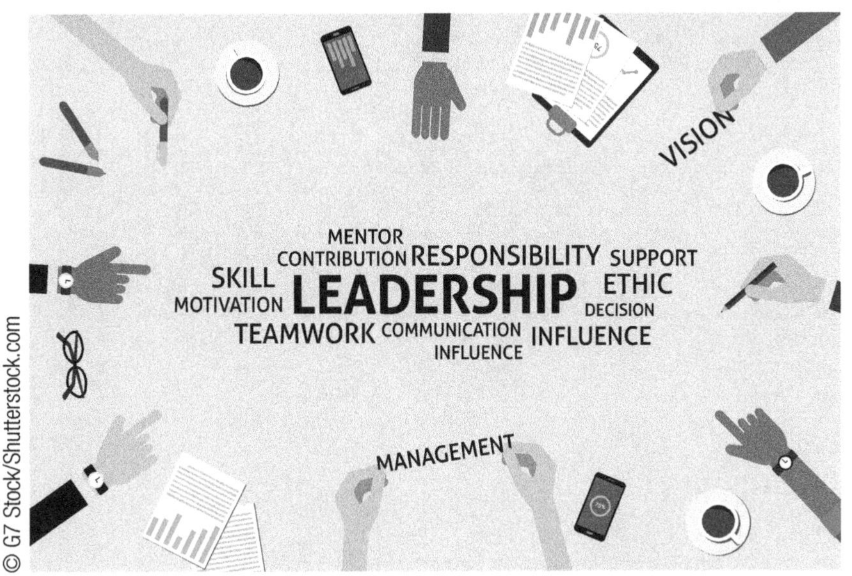

Sociology of Leadership

Thinking Critically!

From the conflict perspective, what is the goal of leadership in society, an organization, or self?

Chapter 2

- A Review of Leadership
- Characteristics of Leadership
- The Paradigms of Leadership

As You Read

- Do you think leaders are born or made?
- What leadership theory do you like best?
- What is your take on the ability to influence others?

Chapter 2

A Review of Leadership

© Panos Karas/Shutterstock.com

Every few hundred years in Western history, there occurs a sharp transformation. Within a few short decades, society—its worldview, its basic values, its social and political structures, its arts, its key institutions—rearranges itself . . . We are currently living through such a time.

Peter Drucker

Everyone can attest to the importance of leadership. At the bookstore, you will find a host of books on display talking about this subject. Nevertheless, each of those books will have its definition of what leadership is and what it is not. One can also discover that there are several schools of thought in regards to the theory of leadership. While sociologists do not view leadership as a collection of qualities existing in a person, they see it as a social role that various people engage in now and then in given societal settings. Nevertheless, the overall focus is on leadership behavior, and not on the individuals as leaders. Leadership is about change and how the leader is uniquely aware of what's important to facilitate that change. From a leadership theorist perspective, Northouse (2014) suggests that a leader who is socially perceptive can create this change more efficiently if he or she understands how the proposed change may affect all the people involved. We also find that the early sociological theorists tended to explain leadership regarding either the person or the environment and went on throughout the 19th century to view leadership as an aspect of role differentiation or as an outgrowth of social interaction (Bass, 1990). So, there is no doubt that if we examined history, we would find that leadership has played a vital role in social history. Even today, we still conclude that leadership is essential. In other words, despite the skepticism about the reality and the importance of leadership, all social and political movements require leaders to begin them, and the bottom line is; a leaderless movement is out of the question (1990).

Slater (1995) wrote a remarkable article about the sociology of leadership and educational administration, and one of the first things he asserts is that among the many questions scholars ask about leadership, there are three asked most often: (1) What is leadership? (2) Why does it matter? (3) What are the conditions for its existence and effectiveness? The problem of trying to define leadership has had its problem for years, never mind the fact we are making a stand to connect it with sociology. However, everyone who studies the concept of leadership tends to come up with their definition. Bass (1981) once wrote that there are almost as many different definitions of leadership as there are persons who have attempted to define the concept. Leadership is necessary regardless of how one defines the concept. For example, having served in the military for many years, I know firsthand that leadership is crucial to the success of military operations. In addition, leadership is also critical to businesses. Bass (1990) asserts that the importance of leadership as demonstrated in social science research is to lead others effectively. If a person who is in charge of others can convince them to follow and accomplish a critical mission-oriented task, I consider that person a leader. Therefore, leaders can influence others (followers) to follow and perform tasks for the organizations for which they serve. There is a host of research on leader–follower activities in their quest to accomplish the goals of the organization.

It is the leader who acts in a way that persuades or influences followers to perform their mission-oriented tasks for the team. What has intrigued the school of theorists is the unique ways in which the leader can act or behave to facilitate this process. We must also understand that there is a difference between the persuasion and power of the leader. Bass (1990) asserts the definition of leadership as a form of persuasion tended to be favored by students of politics and social movements and also by military and industrial theorists who were opposed to authoritarian concepts. However, he goes on to say that power is regarded as a form of influence relationship in that some leaders tend to transform any leadership opportunity into an extensive power relationship. Although many theorists have rejected the notion of authoritarian leadership, one can argue that there is a connection between the two concepts (leadership and power). There are those out there who exercise leadership because they do in fact have the authority to do so, but this does not make it right. However, history has shown that we need the power to exercise leadership because a leader with no power will not get anything to accomplish.

Leadership is about interactions and the relationships with others. A sociologist by the name of Bogardus (1929) stated that as a process, leadership is that social interaction which causes some people to set out toward an old goal with new zest or a new target with hopeful courage, gathering different individuals to accomplish the new goal. Overall, the new leadership grows out of this interaction process. Bass (1990) asserts that we also need to understand that leadership may be regarded as an aspect of role differentiation in that according to role theory, each member of society occupies a position in the community as well as in various groups, organizations, and institutions. He follows this up by saying that leadership appears as a manner of interaction involving the behavior by and toward the individual lifted to a leadership role by other persons. Slater (1995) offers us another twist to the relationship equation in that he states that "leadership is really a social relationship, a social dyad" (p. 450). Although the relational and dyadic nature of leadership seem is addressed in the literature, scholars tend not to pay too much into the followership role as a whole. Slater supports this notion when he suggests that the primary reason could be the history of the study of leadership as well as cultural bias. He backs this up with the assertion that throughout history, the field of psychology and its historical tendencies have always been interested in individuals and their individual-level phenomena. For some particular reason, the U.S., according to Slater, has a bias against followership. You see, being a follower runs against the grain of individualism because it is part of the core of American character (1995).

Characteristics of Leadership

© Dusit/Shutterstock.com

There is no doubt that leadership denotes a mutual expression pattern between the leader and his followers. For the most part, leadership is considered a two-way affair in that members influence the behavior of the leader just as much as the leader changes their behavior. For example, although there are rarely any formally selected leaders, a crowd may follow anyone who begins giving orders in an authoritative and assured manner. Federico (1979) states that a leader is often a crucial factor in determining whether an aroused crowd turns into an aggressive, angry mob or is calmed and diverted. Moreover, if we were to use Martin Luther King as an example, we would find that he had the power to inspire and fill his audiences with zeal through powerful oratory. Even during the election of Barrack Obama, we found him to be a great oratory to rally. By using his oratory skills well, young adults were inspired and rallied around him and were one of the groups that played a key role in his election results. Like Martin Luther King, he too had the ability to calm and reassure participants when the issue of race began to dog his campaign during the 2008 election period. Nevertheless, a leader must be able to maintain order and discipline under the most provoking circumstances (1979). We call that leadership at its best.

Viewing characteristics of leadership from the sociological perspective, one has to recognize that the concept of leadership is understood only in the context of followers and their relationship with the leader. If a leader looks behind him or herself and no one is following, one should conclude that this person is not a leader. In other words, without followers, there can be no leader (Federico, 1979; Ross, 2008, 2012). A leader's job is to seek and establish rapport with their audiences by gaining their trust and directing their behavior toward a particular goal levied by society or in some cases an organization. Leadership is distinct to a given situation, and we know this to be true by the mere fact that under certain conditions, the effectiveness of a leader will be evident when the leader can direct the collective mood to their purpose which is the fulfillment of the overall goal. This is also why the leader must have good judgment.

We must understand that followership is critical to leadership. Van Knippenberg and Hogg (2003) support this premise by stating that studies of subordinate attributions by leaders reveal that decisions are guided by the traditional factors of distinctiveness, consistency, and consensus as are other forms of attribution. They further state that a particular aspect of the leader–follower relationship adds to a powerful additional factor to this judgmental process. This leader–follower connection is a serious business when it comes to the social dimensions of leadership, particularly when one has respect for the leader's judgment. Psychology is a major contributor to the study of leadership, but leadership is not only psychological but also sociological in nature. However, with that said, we should be able to address leadership in sociological terms and categories. So how do we do this?

Historically, sociologists have used the three most critical theories, functionalist theory, conflict theory, and symbolic interaction theory, to address various aspects of society, relationships, and social behavior. No doubt that if you spend lots of time studying these principles, you will begin to form different opinions about the world around us. Mainly, you will start to grasp a solid understanding of society, relationships, and of course social behavior.

The Classical Sociological Aspects of Leadership

Following sociological traditions, we need to address sociology of leadership through four sociological paradigms with the understanding that one might consider other sociological theories to entertain the subject matter:

Functionalist Perspective

Sometimes introduced as the structural functionalist perspective, the great Herbert Spencer, Emile Durkheim, Talcott Parsons, and Robert Merton are considered the architects of this point of view. For them, society is a system of interconnected parts, working together in harmony to continue a state of balance and social stability for the whole. Their argument is that all social institutions exist for the benefit of society, therefore, playing a vital role. For example, the institution of the family plays a critical role in reproducing, nurturing, and socializing children and the institution of education exists to transmit society's knowledge, skills, and the development and understanding of culture to its youth. Likewise, there is the institution of politics which helps to govern members of society and publish laws, the do's and don'ts of society, as a, means of social control. Let's not forget the institution of economics, which serves a vital role in the production, distribution, and consumption of goods and services. And, if you want to seek something higher than yourself, you look to the institution of religion which provides moral guidance through a place of worship. The bottom line is that all of these institutions work for the benefit of helping society to maintain its balance or social equilibrium. You must also understand that as far as the functionalist perspective is a concern, functionalist's theorists use terms such as functional or dysfunctional to describe the effects of social components on society. What is the leadership's take here?

If we look at leadership from a functionalist theory perspective, we have to tap into the tradition of thought as illustrated by Emile Durkheim. In this case, leadership must be seen as an essential function of society, separated by various parts, but promoting social integration. There cannot be social order without direction or leadership of some kind. Leadership provides order and integration for society. In the eyes of Durkheim, if there is no leadership, chaos or anomie will ensure destroying the institution. Functionalist's theorists

Thinking Critically

From the conlfict perspective, what is the goal of leadership in society, an organization, or self?

will also argue that the concept of leadership is shaped by taken-for-granted symbolic, normative, and cognitive institutions (Nohria & Khurana, 2010).

> It is not because he is a leader of industry that a man is a capitalist; on the contrary, he is a leader of industry because he is a capitalist.
>
> *Karl Marx*

Conflict Perspective

Although the functionalist perspective interpretation of society is composed of different parts working together as a whole, the conflict perspective views society as composed of various groups and interests competing for different resources and power. Simply, the conflict perspective looks at not who has the power, but who benefits from it in regards to a particular social arrangement. Derived from the works of Karl Marx, conflict sociologists emphasize the role of coercion and power in constructing social order. The only way social order is maintained is by the domination of those who have the greatest power, and this is done through political, economic, and various other large-scale institutions that make up society. Marx's argument is that industrialization led the development of two classes of people in society: the bourgeoisie (the haves or owners of the means of production) and proletariat (the have-nots or workers who earn wages). In his eyes, it is the haves versus the haves-nots who are always in conflict. The bourgeoisie who are rich use their power to control the various institutions of society. As a result, the workers are denied access to many resources that are afforded to those who are rich, the capitalists as he calls them. Marx being concerned with social change made it clear that he was no fan of the capitalists. Conflict exists because of the relationship between the capitalists (wealthy/owners of the means of production) and laborers (proletariat/poor/workers). Marx states "It is not because he is a leader of industry that a man is a capitalist; on the contrary, he is a leader of industry because he is a capitalist" (Marx, 2013, p. Loc 7974). The argument here is that this is just another means of keeping the less fortunate, poor, or in his words, the proletariat in place. Leadership is about being in charge of others to accomplish a goal. Could this be one of the goals of leadership? It may be cynical to suggest that those in leadership positions are placed there to hold others down. Truly, this could not be the case. However, use your sociological imagination and think about what Karl Marx was trying to say here. This is his leadership take on a capitalist society. Let's flip the script a bit, how is leadership displayed in a communist or socialist society? The point here is that someone has to be in charge, am I right?

Symbolic Interactionist Perspective

In what is called macro-sociology, functionalist and conflict perspectives are concerned about the broader aspects of society, the large institutions, or large groups that influence the social world in which we live, whereas symbolic interactionist perspective is centered on micro-sociology. In other words, this aspect is concerned with what sociologists call the social psychological dynamics of individuals interacting in small groups. This view was widely influenced by the works of George Simmel, Charles Cooley, George Herbert Mead, and Erving Goffman. However, it was sociologist William Isaac Thomas (1966) who emphasized the importance of definitions and meaning of social behavior and its consequences. Also known as symbolic interactionism, this theory centers on the symbolic meaning that people cultivate and depend upon various social interactions. Using symbolic interactionism as a framework to address our understanding of the sociology of leadership, one would need to think of this in terms of leader–follower interactions. The overall meaning that one places on a leader's behaviors by followers is the key to understanding a leader's ability to influence followers. Herbert Blumer coined the term symbolic interactionism in 1937 to address what he called an interpretive sociologic approach to the study of human behavior (Blumer, 1969). Blumer, like other members associated with the Chicago school of symbolic interactionism (Robert E. Park, John Dewey, Charles Horton Cooley, William James and William Isaac Thomas), believed that "... individuals could never be understood apart from the social situations in which they were participating ... knowing the individual's own interpretation of those situation characteristics was indispensable for understanding his behavior" (Meltzer & Petras, 1970, p. 5). Society cannot exist without the individual, and the individual cannot be without society. Nevertheless, symbolic interactionism is based on the fact that human beings act toward things based on the meanings associated with them. These meanings are derived from social interactions one has with others. In other words, the joining of people through what we call interaction is a social reality. As a result, an interpretative process begins, which allows one to deal with the various things he or she encounters during this social reality. These meanings are anything that a person can notice, allude to, or otherwise indicate. As Charon (1979) asserts, these things that we place meaning to are actually *social objects* because they are "pointed out, isolated, cataloged, interpreted, and given meaning through social interaction" (p. 38). Using social interactionist language, leadership, the character of a leader, a specific leader, and a particular leader's behavior are all labeled as social objects. Simply, as people begin to interact, the associated meanings become a social product. What is so unique about this overall process is that the meaning is formed through social interaction and through self-communication processes, and one can interpret and transform the meanings.

Leadership involves a leader's ability to influence followers, and intentional leader behaviors are social actions. As Charon (1979) makes it clear, "action is social action when the individual orients his or her acts to others besides self" (p. 127). Moreover, Paul (1996) supports this conclusion when he states that it is these leader behaviors that are symbolic when the acts are intended to communicate the meaning to followers. He further concludes that because leaders and followers each separately assigns meanings to these acts, the degree of congruence between leaders and followers' assignment of meaning is critical to the effectiveness of leader's influence attempts (1996).

The Vertical Dyad Linkage Model

Although the symbolic interactionism perspective is seldom addressed in relationship to the study of leadership, it has been discreetly recognized by many leadership theorists (Dansereau, Graen, and Haga, 1975; Hollander, 1993; Northouse, 2016). Developed by Scholar's Dansereau, Graen, and Haga (1975), the vertical dyad linkage is consistent with the symbolic interactionist view of leader–follower relations. Also, research does indicate that social interaction between leaders and followers does create shared meanings toward other social objects, and this is based on the overall quality of the relationship between them. Northouse (2016) asserts that in assessing the characteristics of the vertical dyads, research indicates two general types of linkages (or relationships): those that were based on expanded and negotiated role responsibilities (extra roles), which were called the *in-group*, and those that were based on the formal employment agreement (defined roles), which he called the *out-group*. We should also note that during an organizational setting, followers become a part of the in-group or out-group based on how well they work with the leader and how well the leader works with them (2016). Symbolic interactionism provides a great deal of theoretical structure with which to study the social phenomena of leadership. The historical aspects of leadership are designed to get you thinking about leadership as a whole, and this might be the key to identifying your particular style. However, Chapter 9 will center on self-leadership, and it is designed to help you focus in on your leadership style.

Great Man Theory (the 1840s)

We have all heard the expression that great leaders are born and not made, and this is the argument behind the great man theory of leadership. In other words, great leaders will emerge when there is a great need for them. The premise that one must be a natural born leader is associated with those who were male, mainly when it came to military leadership. Famous during the 19th century, this theory took shape with the early research on leadership, and it was based on people who were already leaders and it was easy to verify by pointing to people like Alexander the Great, Abraham Lincoln, Julius Caesar, Eisenhower, Churchill, or going further back to even Jesus.

Gender adds a new twist to the equation in that one could not support this notion at the time because most leaders were male and also those who conducted the research were also male. One should also note that some of these individuals included aristocratic rulers who came to power through birthright, and because people of lesser social status had fewer opportunities to exercise and attain leadership roles, it supported the idea that leadership is an inherent ability. Some still support the argument today that prominent leaders have the right qualities or personality for the position, thereby implying that built-in features are what makes these individuals capable leaders.

From a sociological perspective, there is the argument put forth by sociologist Herbert Spencer, who suggested that these leaders were the products of the society in which they lived. In his book, The Study of Sociology, Spencer (2002) posits that you must admit that the genesis of a great man depends on the long series of complex influences which have produced the race in which he appears, and the social state into which that race has slowly grown, and before he can remake his society, his society must make him. I agree with the argument. In his example of Julius Caesar, Spencer goes on to say that Caesar would never have made his conquests without disciplined troops, because he inherited their prestige and tactics and organization from the Romans who lived before them. In my example, Eisenhower assumes the Presidency of the United States because of four generals in World War II: General George S. Patton, General Omar Bradley, General Henry Arnold, and England's General Bernard Montgomery. Therefore, we can conclude from Spencer's argument that a leader's success also depends on the material and mental accumulations which society inherits from the past. Other than that, the leader is powerless in the absence of the coexisting population, character, intelligence, and social arrangements (2002).

Trait Theory (the 1930s to 1940s)

Still making that assumption that leaders are born with something, trait theory is similar to the great man theory in that it supports the argument that leaders are born with inherited traits. Trait theory also attempts to understand the nature of behavior about situational influences. Called personality traits by social science scholars, they center on ways of perceiving, thinking, feeling, and behaving that are usually stable over time and across situations.

According to Digman (1990), there is a host of different trait theories, and they all come to the same conclusion in that people genetically inherit traits from their biological parents. He also asserts that some of these traits are predominantly suited for leadership, and people who make good leaders have a correct if not sufficient combination of attributes. Simply put, one might argue that some of these traits are uniquely suited to leadership and leaders who possess the right mix of traits are good leaders. Human resources personnel use what is known as the big-five personality dimensions as a placement for employees to include leaders, because they are considered well-thought-out, underlying traits that make up an individual's overall personality. The big-five includes being open, agreeable, emotionally stable, conscientious, and extroverted. All of these are great leadership traits. A leader must be open to any experience that helps him or her to accomplish the mission of the organization efficiently. Therefore, a leader who is highly open to experience tends to be more approachable, very creative, imaginative, and shows a sense of curiosity. On the flip side, a leader who is lowly open to experience will prove that he or she is uncomfortable, practical, traditional (status quo), down-to-earth, and conservative. By the way, lowly open to experience may not help a leader to facilitate change. As an extrovert, the person is considered assertive, outgoing, talkative, and of course open compared to an introvert, who is timid, quiet, and reserved. If we were to conduct a compare and contrast analysis of agreeableness, we would find that high-agreeableness means good nature, cooperative, and trusting compared with low agreeableness, which is cold, antagonistic, and distant. Emotionally stable refers to one's ability to control his or her emotions at the time of crisis. A person who has what we call positive emotions tend to be calm, self-confident, and secure. Negative emotions center on those who are nervous, depressed, and insecure. Consequently, a person with negative emotions will have serious problems leading others in an organization. Conscientiousness refers to an individual who shows consistent and reliable behavior when working in a team. Frankly, a person who shows high conscientiousness is considered to be highly responsible, dependable, organized, and persistent compared with low conscientiousness, which is unreliable, disorganized, inconsistent, and easy-going.

Stogdill (1974) identified the following traits (13) and skills (9) as critical to a leader's success:

Traits	Skills
1. Adaptable to situations	Clever or intelligent
2. Alert to social environment	Conceptually skilled
3. Ambitious and achievement/oriented	Creative
4. Assertive	Diplomatic and tactful
5. Cooperative	Fluent in speaking
6. Decisive	Knowledgeable about group task
7. Dependable	Organized (administrative ability)
8. Dominant (desire to influence others)	Persuasive
9. Energetic (high activity level)	Socially skilled
10. Persistent	
11. Self-confident	
12. Tolerant of stress	
13. Willing to assume responsibility	

He once said that traits considered singly hold little diagnostic or predictive significance. However, collectively, one can generate personality dynamics or patterns that are advantageous to the person acting in a leadership role.

McCall and Lombardo (1983, 1988) conducted a research on the success and failure of leaders and came up with four primary traits by which they could succeed or derail:

1. Emotional stability and composure—Calls for a leader who is calm, confident, and predictable, particularly when he or she is under pressure;
2. Admitting error—A leader must own up to the mistakes, rather than putting energy into covering up;
3. Excellent interpersonal skills—The leader must be able to communicate and persuade others without resorting to harmful or coercive tactics; and
4. Intellectual breath—A leader who can understand a broad range of areas, rather than having a narrow and narrow-minded area of expertise.

Leadership theorists support the idea that under trait theory, good leaders will have the right or sufficient combination of attributes. Northouse (2014) states that leadership is a relationship and as far as traits are concerned, he too associates this theory with leaders who are born. However, as he puts it "all of us are born with a wide array of unique traits and that many of these traits can have a positive impact on our leadership" (p. 114). There is evidence to support the trait theory, but this theory remains one of the most criticized in relationship to other leadership theories. Then, there is the argument that leadership is a behavior. Although not all inclusive, there are those who displayed important leadership traits that made them very successful. These include great names like George Washington, Harriet Tubman, Eleanor Roosevelt, Winston Churchill, Mother Teresa, Nelson Mandela, Bill Gates, and Oprah Winfrey (2014). When we think of the social science link to leadership, we should start by reviewing the concepts of intelligence, confidence, charisma, sociability, and integrity.

Intelligence

To accomplish their endeavors successfully, leaders need to be smart, not only on the job but off as well. There are those who support the idea that social intelligence is critical whereas others have talked about emotional intelligence. Social intelligence is the ability to understand relationships, the various social situations that one might be involved in a given situation. This is another reason why the socialization process is so important as one moves through his or her life cycle. Although psychologists spend a lot of time talking about intelligence, sociologists and leadership theorists have another view. In most cases, we find that sociologists are speaking about intelligence regarding its validity. In other words, they might argue what are valid measures for intelligence tests or just what is intelligence? Nevertheless, there are some who claim that intelligence tests are designed to keep the social class system intact (Henslin, 2017), and more recently, the attempt by some sociology scholars to link intelligence with socioeconomic inequality.

Leadership theorists, for the most part, relate intelligence to what they call a leader's emotional state with the understanding that one can develop this concept through learning. There would not be an argument if one were to say that all the famous people addressed in this book have one thing in common in that all of them have a high degree of emotional intelligence. Daniel Goleman (1998), in a remarkable article tying emotional intelligence to leadership, stated: "IQ and technical skills are important, but emotional intelligence is the sine qua non of leadership" (p. 1). He states explicitly:

> The most effective leaders are all alike in one crucial way: they all have a high degree of what has come to be known as emotional intelligence. It's not that IQ and technical skills are irrelevant. They do matter; but . . . they are the entry-level requirements for executive positions. My research, along with other recent studies, clearly shows that emotional intelligence is the sine qua non of leadership. Without it, a person can have the best training in the world, an incisive, analytical mind, and an endless supply of smart ideas, but he still won't make a great leader.

Like what constitutes leadership, defined by many definitions, there is no standard definition for intelligence or what precisely constitutes intelligence. However, the academic point of view might suggest that intelligence is nothing more than one's ability to learn. If one goes through his or her life cycle and completes their schooling along the way, then, of course, they are intelligent. An intelligent person then can be a leader. Researchers have suggested that intelligence is a single, broad ability whereas others believe that intelligence involves a range of aptitudes, skills, and talents. Now, a little about IQ tests.

Research indicates that IQ scores are broken down similar to those shown here. Although the 68% of IQ scores fall within one standard deviation of the mean, the majority of people have IQ scores in the range of 85–114. The scores are:

- 1 to 24: Profound mental disability
- 25 to 39: Severe mental disability
- 40 to 54: Moderate mental disability
- 55 to 69: Mild mental disability
- 70 to 84: Borderline mental disability
- 85 to 114: Average intelligence
- 115 to 129: Above average; bright
- 130 to 144: Moderately gifted
- 145 to 159: Highly exceptional
- 160 to 179: Remarkably gifted
- 180 and up - Profoundly gifted

(Terman, 1916a, 1916b)

French psychologist Alfred Binet was the first to devise a test to study intelligence. This test was never designed to measure knowledge in areas such as math and reading, the ACT and SAT type of knowledge. Although you can study to take the ACT or SAT, the IQ test is not something you can train on to get a better score. The IQ is designed only to reveal your ability to use logic to solve problems, distinguish patterns, and make quick links regarding various points of information. Of particular interest, there are those who classify brilliant individuals like Albert Einstein who possessed IQ's of 160 or higher or that only Presidents like Thomas Jefferson, or Abraham Lincoln have high IQs, there is nothing to indicate that these famous people ever took an IQ test.

Confidence

A leader has to be confident in his or her ability. Put plainly, being self-confident allows one to grow as a leader. You can find a lot of books that teach a leader to communicate, solve problems in an efficient manner, to coach and mentor others, and also hold others accountable for their actions. However, if the leader is not confident that he or she can accomplish these acts, then real leadership will exist only in title.

Being confident does not mean one can be overly aggressive, taken to this extreme might classify the leader as a bully. There is no doubt people like to work with others who are confident in their abilities because trust comes into play, and the leader will extend a hand to make sure individuals are confident in his or her abilities. Making those tough decisions implies that one is confident. I would suggest that there is something to be said for the confident leader because people will find that he or she has better relationships. They are also happy, more motivated to get the job done, open to risks, accept negative feedback without reservations, and seek out ideas for helping the organization change to maintain the competitive advantage.

Charisma

Leaders must have some charisma if they expect people to be enthusiastic about their leadership. More about this concept is introduced later during the discussion of Max Weber.

Sociability

Sociologists describe this as a personality trait whereby one can seek out the opportunity of social contact with others. This contact is face-to-face or through media communication events. Northouse (2016) identifies sociability as one of the five characteristics of an effective leader. He further states that a leader who processes this trait is friendly, outgoing, courteous, tactful, and diplomatic.

Leadership theorists argue that sociability traits are characteristics which individuals possess that inspire productive relationships. In most situations, we naturally display sociability traits, an approachable and outgoing attitude, self-will, flexibility, integrity, and unity. Although others may adopt sociability skills over a period, leaders must demonstrate those skills to succeed. Those workers who display sociability traits are more likely to be selected to lead others in an organization. These attributes allow employees to communicate ideas well and gain the respect of colleagues and staff. We might also add that traits such as self-determination, self-motivation, self-management, self-leadership, and overall ability to take personal responsibility for actions are sociability qualities of organizational leaders.

Integrity

Integrity is where leadership begins, and it serves as the top trait for a leader. An organization cannot have success unless its leader has integrity. In a research question designed to address what, one looks for most in a leader? Kouzes and Posner (2007) found that it was honesty. Honesty and integrity are linked. In my view leaders must show honesty and integrity when they are in office. Richard Nixon had serious problems with honesty.

Behavioral Theory (the 1940s to 1950s)

Leadership is a behavior that is centered on what they do. There is also the assumption that leaders can be made, rather than being born as some suggest. In other words, behavioral theories of leadership do not pursue innate traits or competencies. It is concerned about what leaders do to accomplish the mission. One can learn leadership behaviors because they are relatively easy to develop. As you might guess, this theory opened the floodgates to what is now understood as leadership development. Using an extensive study to correlate statistically significant behaviors, one can ascertain successes as well as failures to leadership based on one's behavior as a leader.

A key figure in the conduct of leaders is the great *Burrhus Frederic Skinner (1904–1990).* Skinner (1974), a psychologist, once stated that leadership is a learned behavior that is influenced by genetics but not by the existence of spirits within the body. He later indicated that reinforcement of leadership behaviors and punishment or nonreinforcement of leadership behaviors determine who will become a leader. The founder of behaviorism, he developed the theory of operant conditioning, the idea that behavior is determined by its consequences, either by reinforcement or punishments. The argument here is that results make it more or less likely that the behavior will occur again. For Skinner, the only scientific approach to psychology was one that studied behaviors, not internal (subjective) mental processes (1974). It should be noted that Skinner's approach to leadership was not popular among some psychologists because they argued that those behaviors can be explained and controlled purely by manipulating the environment (Hall & Lindzey, 1957). In the objection, Skinner states that if leadership practices could be identified, they could be taught and learned.

Speaking of teaching individuals to be leaders, this supports the same argument presented by *Sharon Daloz Parks* who identifies ways in which leaders can be taught. However, Parks (2005) identifies a growing crisis in leadership with five key thoughts: (1) Within every person there is a hunger to exercise some sense of personal agency, to have an effect, to contribute, to make a positive difference, to influence, help build, and this knowledge to lead. (2) Throughout human history, within every social group, there is a hunger for authority that will provide orientation and reassurance, particularly in times of stress and fear. What is new is that there is now hunger for leadership that (3) can deal with the intensification of systemic complexity emergency from the cybernetic, economic, political, and ecological realities that have created a more connected and interdependent world; and (4) can respond adaptively to the depth, scope, and pace of change that combined with complexity creates unprecedented conditions. Finally, (5) this new landscape creates a new moral moment in history. Critical choices must be made within significantly changed conditions, a greater diversity of perspectives must be taken into account, assumed values are challenged, and there is a deepened hunger for leadership that can exercise a moral imagination and moral courage on behalf of the common good (p. 2). This connected and independent world is perpetrated by the advent of globalization, because it has changed the rules of the game for what is now being called global leadership. Globalization means that companies are allowed to sell goods and services outside the national boundaries, hence, the birth of the global leader who must understand the culture where these goods and services might be delivered. Globalization demands efficient and consistent leadership development, and one must learn leadership behaviors to help in this process. There are many shortfalls with trait leadership theory.

Contingency Theories (the 1960s)

The contingency leadership theory argues that there is no particular way for one to lead and that every leadership style is based on certain situations. Mainly, contingency theories take the approach that a leader's actions should vary to match the situation. Sure, people perform at their maximum level in some locations, but taken out of their comfort zone; the performance is minimal. Leadership theorists support the position that leaders employing a contingency theory tend to express their leadership when feeling that their followers will be receptive to ideas. Fiedler (1964, 1967) gave us the contingency model of leadership effectiveness by studying the styles of many different leaders who worked in various settings, mainly military organizations. He did this by assessing leader's methods, their situations in which they worked, and how effective they were in organizations. Looking at the leader's styles to determine who were good or bad, Fiedler and group were able to lay the groundwork for which styles of leadership were best and in which styles were worst for a given organizational setting (Northouse, 2014). Contingency theory takes styles and situations and matches them together. However, the leadership styles are task-motivated or relationship motivated with the intent of reaching its goal through work or relationship motivation. According to Northouse (2014), to measure leadership leader styles, Fiedler developed the Least Preferred Coworker (LPC) scale. Leaders who score high on this magnitude are motivated, and those who score low on the scale are identified as task-driven. Put another way, a leader who is usually critical in rating the least favored coworker will obtain a low LPC score whereas one who is strongly motivated to have close personal relationships with other people will receive a high LPC score. Although there are those who find *Fred Edward Fiedler's* theory to be somewhat narrow, critics argue that it is an essential formula for success. There is a lot of empirical research that supports this theory.

Situational Approach to Leadership

At this point, we would be remiss if we did not talk about the situational approach to leadership. Situational leadership first appeared in 1969 when the great Paul Hersey and Ken Blanchard published the Life Cycle Theory which was based on their understanding of empirical evidence at that time. They later changed their views and came up with the Situational Leadership Model, published in 1977. Although leadership theorists feel that it is connected to the contingency approach to leadership, Hersey and Blanchard never called it a theory for the simple reason that it did not explain why things happen. Nevertheless, there are some who call it a theory (Graeff, 1983; Northouse, 2016; Yukl, 2006).

The situational approach comprises a directive and supportive dimension, addressing that different situations call for different kinds of leadership. Overall, this calls for the leader to make changes in their leadership style to accommodate the abilities of their followers. This is the same argument put forth by Fiedler's contingency model in which he postulates that there is no single best way for leaders to lead, because the situation tends to create different leadership styles (Fiedler, 1964, 1967; Hersey & Blanchard, 2010).

Nohria and Khurana (2010) openly state, "leadership is a diagnostic activity requiring a person to ask, in each situation, what is the maximum and unique value that a leader could bring to this situation?" (p. 161). Although the Situational Leadership Model is well-thought-out in this situation, such methods stress the importance of precisely understanding various situations and how the leader demands vary with them. The ability of the leader to adapt to a particular situation is paramount to successful leadership. We can ascertain from the research that in certain circumstances, the leader will need to focus more on the task at hand whereas in other cases, there is a need for the leader to be focused on the people.

The SLII Model

Created in 2002, Situational Leadership II (SLII) pays attention to the follower. Arguing that no one size fits all, a leader must adapt his or her leadership style to the situation. Blanchard (2008) uses competence and commitment to determine a followers' ability to accomplish a particular task. Naturally, to perform this work, the leader must evaluate his or her followers and assess their capability to perform a given goal. The suggestion is that the leader should change his or her behavior as the supporters can accomplish their assigned mission. The assessment will come to reveal members' knowledge of or experience with a particular goal. One cannot give guidance to members without this evaluation. In the end, the leader will come to know the optimum amount of direction to provide to accomplish the goal. Overall, SLII has four leadership styles (S1, S2, S3, and S4) which are known as directing, coaching, supporting, and delegating. The other central part of the situational leadership approach includes four development levels (D1, D2, D3, and D4).

Blanchard (1985) asserts that the development level is the degree to which followers not only have the competence to complete the task, but they also show a sense of commitment. Papworth, Milne, and Boak (2009) also support Blanchard statement when they say that the effectiveness is maximized by matching the level of leadership style with follower readiness. Therefore, a D1 indicates that a member is enthusiastic and would respond better to directing as connected to the leadership style of S1. The D2 member has some ability to complete the task but needs some coaching which is connected to S2 leadership style. Moving to D3, we find that the follower has the knowledge to perform the function but often disappoints the organization. This follower better responds to the S3 leadership style. D4 respond better to delegating because they not only have a commitment and competence to work independently, but they also do not need any guidance to get things done, being self-sufficient. Therefore, we can associate this with S4. As you can see, the situational leadership approach is based on task and relationship behavior between the leader and follower. Overall, it is the leader who must determine the nature of the situation, and then adapt his or her style as suggested by SLII model.

Transformational Leadership

Transformational leaders are considered change artists. They can motivate and inspire people by helping them to see something higher than themselves. Focusing on the overall performance of groups members, transformational leader's goal is to ensure that all associates fulfill his or her potential. One unique thing about this type of leadership is that it is designed to take followers and develop them into leaders. Therefore, the transformational leader must align followers with tasks that enhance their performance.

Designed around political leaders, James MacGregor Burns (1978) introduced the concept of transformational leadership to describe a process in which "leaders and followers raise one another to higher levels of motivation and morality" (p. 396). In other words, the relationship becomes "moralistic" in that it raises, as Burns suggests, human conduct and ethical aspiration. Burns alluded to the difficulty in one understanding management and leadership and went on to claim that these differences are in characteristics and behaviors. At this point, Burns described two concepts: transformational leadership and transactional leadership. In his explanation of these concepts, Burns explained that transformational leadership centers on creating a significant change in the life of people and organizations. However, transactional leadership is about a leader's personality, traits,

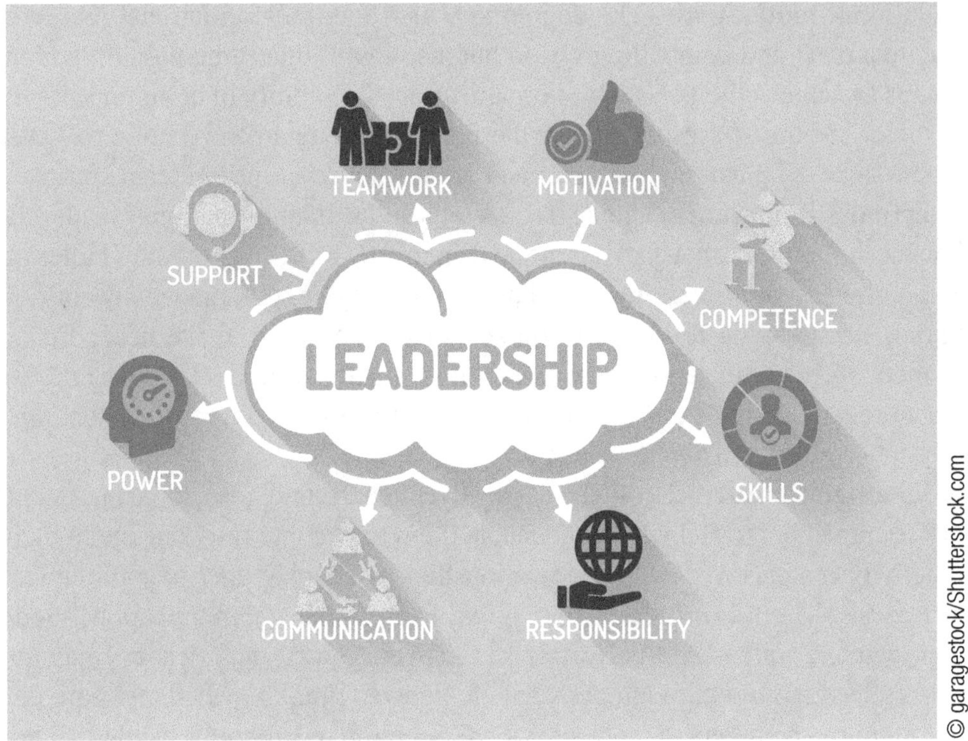

© garagestock/Shutterstock.com

and his or her ability to make change through example by the articulation of a compelling vision, strategy, and challenging goals. Although transformational and transactional leadership are equally select styles, transformational leaders are idealized to the point they set the tone with a sense of morality, arguing that one must work as part of a team, organization, or community to get things accomplished. This idealized process is spearheaded by the fact that transformational leaders have charisma. To facilitate cultural change in an organization, transformational leaders are the best, because transactional leaders do not strive for cultural change but work with existing cultures. To (or "intending to") being successful, transformational leaders understand the mechanics of moving forward, sustaining motivation through the use of ceremonies, cultural symbolism, and other rituals that pump up people to facilitate real progress.

Four transformational leadership behaviors facilitate inspiring positive change in followers:

1. **Individualized influenced—**The degree in which the transformational leader serves as a role model for members. Inspired by the transformational leader's charisma, members learn to trust and respect this person and in time, emulate this leader and internalize his or her principles. Although Antonakis (2012) calls this the emotional component of transformational leadership, the leader is following charisma that gives him or her an edge to create this strong emotional bond with followers. Moreover, when transformational leaders articulate this compelling vision of the future, they can influence followers by arousing these robust emotions in support of the idea. Northouse (2016) posits that this behavior "is measured on two components: an attributional component that refers to the attributions of leaders made by followers based on perceptions they have of their leaders, and a behavioral component that refers to followers observations of leader behavior" (p. 167). On the basis of high standards of moral and ethical conduct, the transformation leader can be counted on to do the right thing, at the right time, for the right reasons.

2. **Inspirational motivation—**The degree to which the transformational leader can not only articulate a clear and compelling vision but also instill that same passion and motivation to followers to achieve the goals of the organization. The ability to communicate high expectations, he or she transforms to support the future of the team and inspire followers to pledge to do the same. Enthusiasm and optimism are displayed, arousing team spirit.
3. **Intellectual stimulation—**The degree to which the transformational leader can stimulate followers to the point that they create and innovate so that he or she challenges the status quo. Instilling creative learning techniques so that they explore new ways of doing things is essential. Encouraging followers to think outside the box to make needed changes for the betterment of the organization and not oneself is vital to all survival. Public criticism or embarrassment regarding one's mistakes is not a virtue for this leader, nor is criticizing a member's idea because it differs from the leader.
4. **Individualized consideration—**The degree to which the transformational leader offers support and encouragement to followers that enable them to become fully engage in their endeavors. This activity centers on growing the relationships by keeping lines of communication open so that ideas are shared. In other words, two-way exchange in communications should always be encouraged and welcomed. As Northouse (2016) suggests, these leaders may use delegation to help followers grow through personal challenges. Frankly, when tasks are delegated, this leader monitors members to see if additional direction or support is needed without followers feeling they are micro-managed.

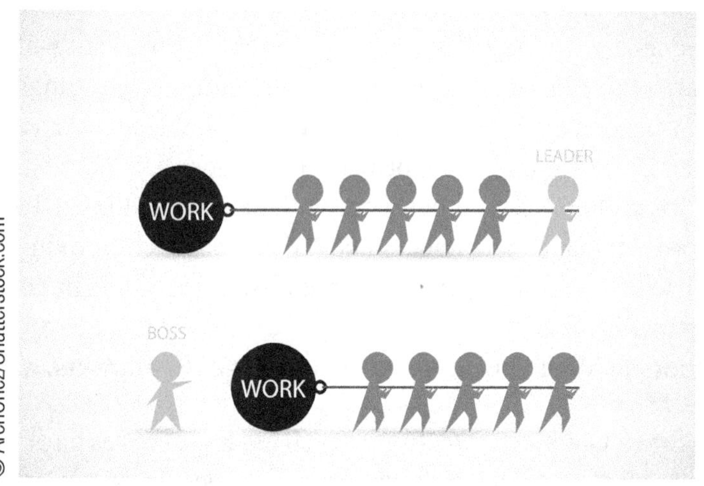

Lussier and Achua (2001) make clear that transactional leadership is transitory in that once a transaction is completed, the relationship between parties may end or be refined, whereas transformational leadership is more enduring, especially when the change process is well articulated, designed, and implemented. In the end, it is the transformational leader who inspires followers to go beyond their self-interest for the good of the group (2001). It is the transformational leaders who move their people into a position to go that extra mile because he or she sees something higher than themselves with the understanding that it not about them but the entire organization's survival. Becoming a transformational leader makes you good, but becoming a servant leader makes you great (Ross, 2008).

Servant Leadership

This author is biased when it comes to servant leadership, because he feels that all leaders must serve. As leaders, one must serve, and this is why servant leadership is unique. Robert Greenleaf (1904–1990) got it right when he wrote: "The servant-leader is a servant first . . . It begins with the natural feeling that one wants to serve, to serve first. Then conscious choice brings one to aspire to lead . . . The difference manifests itself in the care taken by the servant, first to make sure that other people's highest priority needs are being served . . . And, what is the effect on the least privileged in society? Will they benefit, or at least not further be harmed? (Greenleaf, 1977, p. 7, 1996, p. 2)." This is a profound statement in that it does not get any better than this, the charge to a leader that he must first be a servant to all. Greenleaf went on to refine his thinking on servant leadership by suggesting that the concept had implications for institutional structures, trustees, foundations, churches, governments, educational institutions, and the human spirit. The overall premise is that everything must begin with a conscious choice by an individual who wishes to serve first. Greenleaf's ideas resonates with management and organizational thinkers like Max Depree, Peter Senge, Peter Block, and of course the great Stephen Covey, and many others who emphasize the importance of an ethical base for organizations, the power of trust and stewardship, and the personal depths that authentic leaders must honor as they empower and serve others (1996). Like Greenleaf, I too believe that we have a crisis in leadership.

If we were to take the simplest definition of the leader as one who goes ahead to guide the way, a leader, as Greenleaf saw it, might be a mother in her home, any person who wields influence, or the head of a vast organization (Greenleaf, 1996). I would add self-leadership to the equation. As you move forward in the book, one must lead self before leading others. The bottom line is this, as servant leaders empower and develop people, they show a sense of humility, appear authentic in the eyes of followers, have a tendency to accept people for who they are, know how to provide direction, and are good stewards who work for the good of the whole.

Chapter Summary

Clearly, it would be impossible to address the many facets of leadership in this book. This is just a palate of what's out there that in this author's view has an association with major parts of society. There is something to be said for the sociological approaches to leadership: functionalist, conflict, and symbolic interactionalism. We have learned some of the histories of leadership and why some believe that leaders are born and not made. We discussed the impact of race, geographic location, class status, and other things that make us appear different when speaking about leadership. However, when we learn to lead by serving, it is the key to leadership. As we learn to lead through servanthood, we defy the conventional wisdom of leadership and fall into an unusual group of people who possess a particular love for humanity. A servant leader moves beyond the typical attitudes of the traditional leader and now finds himself or herself in a unique position of elevation from others. Anyone who has the heart for his or her fellow human being can be a servant leader. The Bible even makes this clearer in that he whom shall become king must first become the slave to others. Jesus was once asked which commandment was the greatest and he responded by saying "to love the Lord God with all your mind, heart, body, and soul; to love your neighbors as yourselves as all of the commandments hinges on these two. We call this leadership at its best."

We live in a futuristic world that can create its structure. Unfortunately, there are no models to use which may enlighten us as to which direction to follow. The leadership examples here give us the knowhow to lead in a constantly changing, interconnected, and increasingly complex society. There is no doubt that the world is moving through a period of profound transition. I wholeheartedly agree with Peter Drucker's assertion that every few hundred years in Western history, there occurs a sharp transformation. Within a few short decades, society changes its fundamental values, social and political structures, parts of key institutions, thereby, rearranging itself. We are currently living through such a time; however, we must understand that sociology of leadership is more about the relationship between the leader and follower than just looking at the institution to ascertain why leaders act the way they do in various organizations.

References

Antonakis, J. (2012). Transformational and charismatic leadership. In D. V. Day & J. Antonakis (Eds.), *The nature of leadership.* (2nd ed.) (pp. 256–288). Thousand Oaks, CA: Sage.

Bass, B. M. (1981). *Stogdill's handbook of leadership: A survey of theory and research.* New York, NY: The Free Press.

Bass, B. M. (1990). *Bass & Stogdill's handbook of leadership: Theory, research & managerial applications.* (3rd ed.). New York, NY: The Free Press.

Blanchard, K. H. (1985). *SLII: A situational approach to managing people.* Escondido, CA: Blanchard Training and Development.

Blanchard, K. (2008). Situational leadership. *Leadership Excellence*, 25(5), 19.

Blumer, H. (1969). *Symbolic interactionism: Perspective and method.* Berkeley, CA: University of California Press.

Bogardus, E. S. (1929). *A history of social thought.* Los Angeles, CA: University of Southern California Press.

Burns, J. M. (1978). *Leadership.* New York, NY: Harper & Row.

Charon, J. M. (1979). *Symbolic interactionism: An introduction, an interactionism, an integration.* Englewood Cliffs, NJ: Prentice-Hall.

Dansereau, F., Graen, G., & Haga, W. (1975). A vertical dyad linkage approach to leadership within formal organizations: A longitudinal investigation of the role making process. *Organizational Behavior and Human Performance*, 13, 46–78.

Digman, J. M. (1990). Personality structure: Emergence of the five-factor model. *Annual Review of Psychology*, 41, 417–440.

Federico, R. C. (1979). *Sociology.* (2nd ed.). Reading, MA: Addison-Wesley Publishing Company.

Fiedler, F. E. (1964). A contingency model of leadership effectiveness. In L. Berkowitz (Ed.), *Advances in experimental social psychology*, 1, pp. 149–190. New York, NY: Academic Press.

Fiedler, F. E. (1967). *A theory of leadership effectiveness.* New York, NY: McGraw-Hill.

Goleman, D. (1998). What Makes a Leader? *Harvard Business Review*, 76(6), Retrieved April 4, 2016.

Greenleaf, R. (1996). *On becoming a servant leader.* D. M. Frick & Spears. (Eds.). San Francisco, CA: Jossey-Bass.

Graeff, C. L. (1983). The situational leadership theory: A critical view. *Academy of Management Review, 8*, 285–291.

Hall, C. S., Lindzey, G. (1957). *Theories of personality.* New York, NY: John Wiley & Sons, Inc.

Henslin, J. M. (2017). *Essentials of sociology: A down-to-earth approach.* (12th ed). Boston, MA: Pearson Education.

Hersey, P., & Blanchard, K. (2010). Life cycle theory of leadership. In J. T. McMahon (Ed.), *Leadership classics*, pp. 294–305. Long Grove, IL: Waveland Press, Inc.

Kouzes, J. M., & Posner, B. Z. (2007). *The leadership challenge.* (4th ed.). New York, NY: John Wiley & Sons, Inc.

Lussier, R. N., & Achua, C. F. (2001). *Leadership: Theory, application, skill development.* Australia: South-Western College Publishing.

Marx, K. (2013). *Complete works of Karl Marx.* Minerva Classics.

McCall, M. W. Jr., Lombardo, M. M., & Morrison, A. M. (1983). Off track: Why and how successful executives get derailed. Greensboro, NC: Centre for Creative Leadership.

Meltzer, B. N., & Petras, J. W. (1970). The Chicago and Iowa schools of symbolic interactionism. In T. Shibutani (Ed.), *Human nature and collective behavior: Papers in honor of Herbert Blumer*, pp. 3–17. Englewood Cliffs, NJ: Prentice-Hall.

Nohria, N, & Khurana, R. (2010). *Handbook of leadership and practice: A Harvard business school centennial colloquium.* Boston, MA: Harvard Business Press.

Northouse, P. G. (2016). *Leadership: Theory and practice* (7th ed.). Thousand Oaks, CA: Sage Publications, Inc.

Northouse, P. G. (2014). *Introduction to leadership: Concepts and practices.* Thousand Oaks, CA: Sage Publications, Inc.

Pagels, E. H. The Great Appeal: What did Christianity offer its believers that made it worth social estrangement, hostility from neighbors, and possible persecution? Retrieved October 28, 2016, from http://www.pbs.org/wgbh/pages/frontline/shows/religion/why/appeal.html

Papworth, M., Milne, D., & Boak, G. (2009): An exploratory content analysis of situational leadership. *Journal of Management Development, 28*(7), 593–606.

Parks, S. D. (2005). *Leadership can be taught: A bold approach for a complex world.* Boston, MA: Harvard Business School Publishing Corporation.

Paul, J. (1996). A symbolic interactionist perspective on leadership. *The Journal of Leadership Studies*, 3(2), 82–93.

Ross, L. F. (2012). *Leadership: So what makes you think you can lead.* Philadelphia: Xlibris Publishers.

Ross, L. F. (2008). *So you want to be a strategic leader: Here are the essentials to get you started.* Philadelphia, PA: Xlibris Publishers.

Skinner, B. F. (1974). *About Behaviorism.* New York, NY. Alfred A. Knopf.

Slater, R. O. (1995). The sociology of leadership and educational administration. *Educational Administration Quarterly,* 31(3), 449–472.

Spencer, H. (2002). *The study of sociology.* London: University Press of the Pacific.

Stogdill, R.M. (1974). *Handbook of leadership: A survey of theory and research.* New York, NY: Free Press.

Terman, L. M. (1916a). *The measure of intelligence.* Whitefish, MT: Kessinger Publishing.

Terman, L. M. (1916b). *The use of intelligence test.* Boston, MA: Houghton Mifflin.

Thomas, W. I. (1966). On social organization and social personality: Selected papers. Chicago, IL: Phoenix Books, University of Chicago Press.

Van Knippenberg, D., & Hogg, M. A. (2003). *Leadership and power: Identity processes in groups and organizations.* London: Sage.

Yukl, G. (2006). *Leadership in organizations.* (6th ed.). Upper Saddle River, NJ: Pearson.

Chapter 2

Leadership Skill-Building Exercise

How to Tell a Story

Great leadership is the ability to tell a compelling story, and this takes skill and, of course, practice. We tell stories when the need arises, and this can be to get others to support a change in the organization or just support a project. Nevertheless, the whole idea is to persuade others to support your actions. For a leader, this is an essential skill. How can you tell that the story makes all the difference in the world. According to O'Hara (2014), the best storytellers are the ones who can use various memories and life experiences to illustrate their point. I agree, having served in many countries around the world, I can think of a lot of stories that show various positions. Like myself, many of you have been to places and can also provide vivid details or illustrations about something that may have had an impact that is worth telling a remarkable story.

Use these stories to get your point across because, at the end of the day, you will look back and say I persuaded them to walk with me on my leadership journey and we were successful. The bottom line is that telling this compelling story gives us this unique power to persuade and motivate because it does appeal to our capacity for empathy (Guber, 2007; Hsu, 2008; Jensen, 2014). It is okay for the audience to feel your emotion because your story can reveal you authenticity. If you are partaking in a class or training exercise, use this activity for participants to tell their story. Use the steps below to help you in this process by identifying who, what, when, where, why, and how:

Step 1. Start off with the where and when in that give us the location and period when the situation occurred (position the drama).

Step 2. Give us a sense of all involved parties, the people who make up the story.

Step 3. State the problem and describe the involved parties' participation. Hopefully, it will lead to how they addressed or handled the problem. Make sure that you are specific about each person's involvement and what they did exactly.

Step 4. Identify any "props" that may illustrate the problem so that you can bring the story home. By the way, your prop could be a surprise or some amazement that fascinates your audience to the point that they get excited enough to ask you to go deeper into the story.

Step 5. Now give us that ending that tells why it is important for us to know the story in the first place.

> **Note:** If your training exercise lasts for more than several weeks, one or two participants should engage in storytelling each week so that everyone will get a chance, but more importantly, they get a sense of how important this leadership activity can be in persuading change or promoting their project in an organization. Tell us a story as to why it is important to you!

The above steps were adapted from the Storytelling Checklist which can be found at www.amacombooks.org/leadershipact.

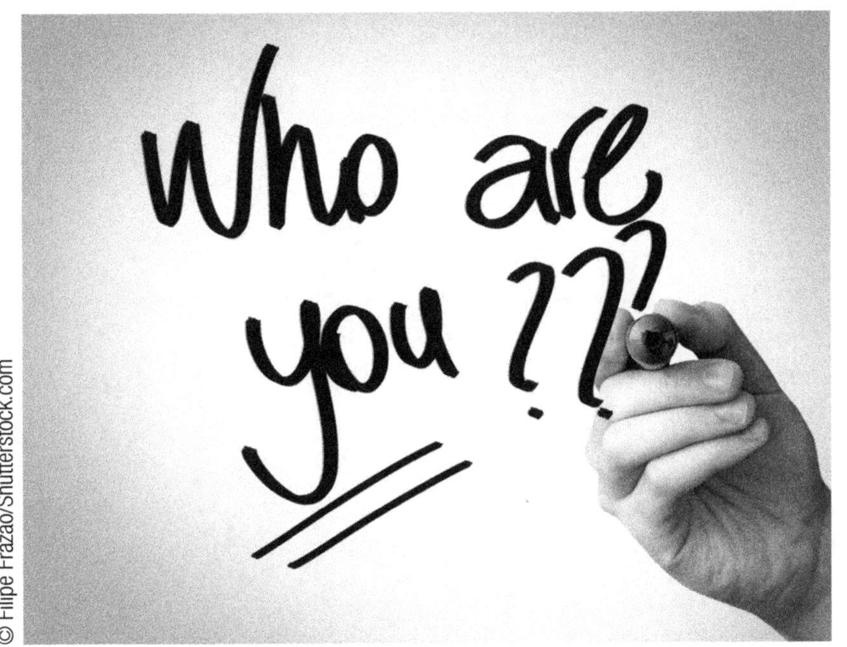

Chapter 3

As You Read

- Why is the socialization process so important to leadership?
- Why Know thyself?
- Is social power important to a leader?

Sociology of Leadership

Thinking Critically!

What happens when we connect power and authority? Think about the Weber debate.

Chapter 3

A Leader's Socialization, Social Identity, and Power

© Heartland Arts/Shutterstock.com

No society can surely be flourishing and happy, of which the far greater part of the members are poor and miserable.

Adam Smith

Sociologists and leadership theorists will not argue over the notion that there is a socialization process to leadership. Society makes us human. However, the social environment, the entire personal experience of having direct contact with others, is what makes us human. We learn from others through our many associations. The process by which we learn the ways of society is directly dependent on the characteristics of our social group. The debate over which leaders are born or made comes into focus here through the discussion of the socialization process of leadership. There is no question that the socialization process has everything to do with an individual's upbringing, their knowledge, skills, attitudes, values, norms, beliefs, and overall actions. Although leadership skills for some are innate and inborn, the overall process of socialization plays an essential role in the growth of these skills. Sociologists and leadership theorist's ability to address whether or not one makes a great leader must start with the premise on how a leader is socialized.

As children, we learned in gender socialization what behaviors society is willing to accept. Initially, this process sets us on a life course contingent upon our gender. The result of this method set the tone for labeling of what is maleness and femaleness in a social setting. Simply put, this also applies to leadership, where the environment, social settings, culture, beliefs, and traditional work parallel in shaping what kind of a leader one will become. Socialization is a complex, lifelong process connected to leadership. We learn how to define ourselves through interactions with others. As socialized leaders, we seek to make our lives and the lives of others fairer and more workable, not only in the workplace but also through activities that may affect a person's environment in general. If a leader neglects this primary area of responsibility, he or she will fail. You found in Chapter 2 that a leader must be a servant first and this alone demonstrates to members of the group that he or she will need to take this responsibility seriously. You also learned in the same chapter that transformational leaders offer some unique skills to inspire and motivate those they lead. For both servant and transformational leaders, one of the unique skills is their socialization process.

A socialized leader succeeds in transforming a group by focusing on the needs of others. To help in this effort, it does not hurt to enlist the support of those outside the group. Socialized leaders have respect for themselves and the people they lead. They will often make choices that are in the best interests of all involved parties. Well-socialized leaders exhibit several traits including courage, determination, experience, humility, vision, and integrity. Working to advance the leadership principles in place, a socialized leader makes a concerted effort to organize his followers and encourages creativity in them rather than suppressing their needs and interests. Put simply, a socialized leader doesn't always have to tell members what to do but to a decent degree, let them guide their expectations of him or her. In this case, dictatorship is not an option, but he or she rather creates a dialogue with their followers to accomplish the goals of the group.

The leader who demonstrates values like honesty, integrity, justice, fairness, as well as accountability sets the tone for high or real leadership. Gupta and Krishnan (2004) state that within the last decade and a half, exceptional leaders who infuse ideological values and moral purpose into organizations and who have remarkable effects on their followers and organizations have captured the attention of leadership scholars. Just to name a view, some of these scholars include Bernard M. Bass, James M. Burns, Jay A. Conger, Rabindra N. Kanungo, and Robert J. House. A leader who exhibits true leadership displays the center of integrity in that its very core helps to influence their followers.

As illustrated by Jesus, real leadership is above all, a servant. The question is, however, what makes us social and how can leaders use this to their advantage to lead others? It is the identity of the leader that helps move society forward, particularly if that leader is part of what C. Wright Mills the power-elite. The perfect example that we can put forward comes from the office of the President of the United States. Inevitably, once elected, the President becomes part of the power-elite. Nevertheless, for many, he is the "Leader of the Free World." We hear this all the time from members of Congress as well as other heads of state in many nations. However, most people fail to recognize how a leader is often the face of their society and a symbol for it. For example, when people elect a leader they are proud or placed under the care of a leader who in particular, does a great job, there is a sense of pride and identification with the individual, and this helps to blend society together. Keep in mind that an effective leader is one that people of society are pleased to be associated with for the simple reason he or she has the ability and does bring the society together. This positive identity leads other people, not just in the society for which the leader is from, but elsewhere around the world in the case of the United States President. Remarkable leaders are extraordinary, and as such, their countries remember them. The leader can be part of a unique social phenomenon, shaping lives, and stringing the bonds of society. By the way, this is a unique identity of being an excellent and efficient leader. Therefore, a leader's social identity and its impact on leadership are necessary (Fielding and Hogg, 1997). It's more than just one's ability to understand social identity; the leader must be acutely aware of his or her culture and power. Simply, it is the power that influences others, and its use and how its components can affect them will define effective versus ineffective leaders. However, let's go deeper into the socialization of a leader.

Socialization and Leadership

If we are to engage in a sociology of leadership debate, we must also come to the conclusion that we must connect the socialization process to leadership. **Socialization** is the process by which people learn, through interaction with others, which they must know to survive and function in society. Through this process, we learn our roles and the roles others play in society, and as a result, we develop a self-image. According to sociology scholars, at its simplest form, socialization is about our ability to learn norms, attitudes, values, and behaviors and this, by the way, is a lifelong process (Anderson & Taylor, 2010; Collins & Makowsky, 1993; Witt, 2016). Leadership scholars think of the socialization process in regards to team, group, or organizational development and a leader having cultural competence (Antonakis, Cianciolo, & Sternberg, 2004; Kellerman, 1984; Marshall & Oliva, 2006; Ross, 2012; Zaccaro & Klimoski, 2001).

The building of one' self-identity sets the tone for the socialization process, and this overall has an impact on leadership as a whole. Ross (2012) states that this starts when we begin learning from our early days of life through our interactions with others, and this will continue all through life unless something happens that interfere with our ability to learn. Although we will discuss in Chapter 4, we find that different cultures contribute to learning social skills. For example, one's peers, the community, and other institutions, as a whole, have an impact on the socialization process. The bottom line is that socialization process will determine who you are, what you will become or stand for, and how one views himself or herself.

Not forgetting the nature versus nurture debate, it would be wrong to leave the mechanics of human behavior out of the equation. We should not overstate the relative importance of nature and nurture in shaping human behavior. It was Pines (1985) who argued that human behavior is a product of one's genetic or hormonal makeup. Freud (2015) and Hogg (2010) both support the natural instincts or drives that act as influences on the behavior of all human beings and Piaget (1952, 1926) compliments this saying it is physiological processes of development that place limits on the range of thought and behavior of which a person is capable at any given age. Although these theories do not all argue that human behavior is entirely a product of nature, they do posit that nature has significant influence over human behavior.

The nurture refers to the impact of social forces in shaping human behavior. Those who emphasize nurture as the primary influence over human behavior asserts that behavior is a product of interactions with other people. There are strong opinions coming from Mead (1934) and Cooley (1964) and the situation in which people find themselves, including their share of scarce resources and the relationship of their circumstances to larger societal needs. It should be noted that in no area of human behavior has this debate been more compelling than in childhood socialization.

Mentioned earlier, it is the parents who play a significant role in this process, and we find that later when the child becomes a teenager or young adult, they are pretty good at imitating their parent's speech or actions and makes a concerted effort to pattern themselves after them. However, we find that these children are also affected by their peers, and they get to come in contact with others who might have been in an entirely different environment. What better place to start this process off with an educational institution. It is when they go to a school that they are overwhelmed with diverse cultures and a variety of new personalities. In most cases, this socialization process seems to overtake those of the parents. The one reason for this is because the individual is spending more time with peers than parents. Naturally, teachers are also involved in this process, but it is the peers or in most cases, friends that have the most impact.

Years ago, Bates (1967) stated the sociological model of human behavior is not inherently harder to grasp than are others, yet in practice, problems are often encountered. He also states that this is so primarily because more familiar perspectives interfere. We hope that the leadership perspective as addressed here does not interfere with the basic understanding of human behavior but adds to the body of knowledge to help understand sociology and leadership as it relates to each other. As far as leadership is a concern, we contend that when it comes to children or young adults who have a high self-esteem as it pertains to leadership skills, they are less likely to be influenced by their peers. The advent of peer pressure does come into play here because many of those are trying hard to blend in with their associates. However, individuals with leadership skills will control their destiny, whereas guiding those who follow in their footsteps. Leaders can have a solid impact on other people's nature and how they are affected by their environment. Nevertheless, this is what leaders do because they guide others and if correctly done, one can lead a team, group, or organization to succeed. Those with a lot of leadership skills and those who need to have a leader follow each other and create a sort of cycle. Leaders guide others, but they also need the support of those they govern to be a leader. Sometimes this happens in smaller businesses, and the leader has to rely on them or those who utilize their business.

Leadership is not only taking control and being able to guide people but also being able to relate to people. Nature could be a significant factor in the leadership traits one possesses. Their genes and natural traits they possess could be part of their dynamic and directing personality, and it can also be part of how an individual relates to others and if they genuinely care for them. Also, nurture can be an influence. Life experiences can strengthen a person, so they learn to be an active individual who stands up for their beliefs and opinions and guide others to do the same. People have to understand their self before they try to understand others. A leader has to take control of his or her emotions. Once they can control themselves, they can more effectively guide others and be a leader. We need to talk about one more thing for just a moment and this is the connection of socialization and its impact on an organization.

Socialization and Organizational Integration

We should not forget about the power of socialization and its overall impact on the organization. We know that socialization is a key ingredient of culture. However, when it comes to leadership in an organization, there is another twist and that is strategy. Gibson, Ivancevich, Donnelly, and Konopaske (2003) suggest that we must view socialization as a form of organizational integration. If we do, we will see an example of enhanced strategy to facilitate goals. Specifically, they allege that it is socialization, as an integrated part of a strategy, which allows for achieving congruence of not only organizational goals but individual objectives as well. The bottom line is that the common thread recommended to organizational leaders is the active role played by the leader and the group members in integrating goals and objectives (2003).

Social Identity and Leadership Dynamics

A leader must have something in common with members of the group, and if one takes the social aspects of leadership seriously, we can provide keen insights into the process of leadership both within and between those groups. ***Social identity*** is one who acknowledges he or she belongs to a particular group and through its connection echoes the same values, and emotional support afforded other members. Therefore, the social identity aspects of leadership are just another key to this overall process. The totality of a leader's social identity and how that serves as a centerpiece to our overall understanding of leadership interaction with various groups helps to define what leadership is and give the interpretation of skills needed for a person to become a better leader.

© Gustavo Frazao/Shutterstock.com

A person's self-identity is part of the social science debate. We find that the psychological identity of a person tends to center on one's self-image (mental model of the individual), and his or her self-esteem, and their individuality. On the other hand, sociologists look at the concept of identity from the learning of social roles and him or her personal experiences. One thing for sure is that we cannot just investigate the social identity aspects of leadership by itself in that we must look at it within the scope of the situation on which it lies. As Altheide (2000) suggests, it is deeper than that because one must review the self, identity, and the definition of the situation as critical concepts for the investigation and analysis of social behavior. He qualifies this statement by saying that all human sciences concerned with the role of meaning in human behavior implicitly and explicitly deal with identity and definitions of the situation. I couldn't agree more in that one must review self-identity in a relationship with the situation to understand the workings, in this case, leadership and the person in charge, which is the leader. Sociologists like to refer to the ***definition of the situation*** as what people use to know or what one expects of them and others in a situation. It is the definition of the situation that people sense their status and the role they play in a particular situation so that they know how to behave in that situation. Waller (2014) supports this in that he states:

> Many persons living together in a common group life for many overlapping generations have mapped out precisely the limitations of behavior inherent in the social situations most common in their culture. From their experience has arisen a consensus concerning what is and what is not thinkable in those situations. From these situations as they have been defined and generalized by particular group products which have in turn become essential conditions of life in that group. We may refer to these group products as definitions of situations (p. Loc 5141).

On the basis of the situation and through symbolic communications, we form new habits and routines (Berger & Luckmann, 1967; Cooley, 1964; Mead, 1962; Schutz, 1967). We need to understand that as the group action begins to form, individual lines of work may appear. As a result, each aligns one's action to the actions of others by understanding not only what he or she is doing, but what he or she intends to do, thereby, getting the meaning of their acts. For George Herbert Mead, this is done by the individual as he or she takes the role of others. In other words, one either takes the role of a particular person or the role of a group (Mead's "generalized other") (Mead, 1934). In doing so, the individual seeks to ascertain the intention or direction of the acts of others. Mead (1962) also asserts that this is the fundamental way in which group action takes place in human society. Nevertheless, we exist as social beings in the midst of a process in that we do not have or own an identity, but rather identity emerges and is acknowledged in the situations (Altheide, 2000). As a group thinks about leadership as a whole, it is at this point that the organization may see an individual who emerges as someone who could lead the group. Hence, the person begins to align his or her actions with that of the group. The group subsequently begins to see that person as its leader or one who is classified as their leader. Moreover, what a person does when acting in a leadership role coupled with their understanding of the group's situation makes him or her ready to lead. Put another way, what a person does when acting in a leader's role is largely dependent upon the situation in which he or she resides. Hemphill (1949) agrees with this position in that he posits that under the situational theory, what an individual does when acting as a leader is in large part reliant upon the various characteristics of the situation in which he functions. So when one's social identity emerges as him or her being the leader, one can ascertain that it is due in part to the situation that made this happen. It is the group that defines the ***self-leader***; the person who can garner enough support to lead the group toward achieving a particular goal. As Messick and Kramer (2005) assert from the social identity perspective, a group exists psychologically when people share a self-conception regarding defining features of a self-inclusive category. They also argue that the effect of social identity processes on leadership is quite straightforward. Just, "as group membership becomes increasingly salient, leadership perceptions, evaluations and effectiveness become increasing based on how groups the leader is perceived to be" (p. 57). The relationship between leaders and the led becomes critical if the group is going to be successful in their actions.

Leadership has changed over the years. No longer are leaders just concerned about the many cultures in their organizations, they are tasked to figure out a host of many things to include bringing people with very diverse backgrounds, values, and cultures together to achieve a common goal. However, for leaders to be successful in their endeavors, they not only need an awareness of their social identity but others as well. You cannot lead others if you can't lead yourself. To do this, one must know thyself. ***Know thyself*** is not new in that Plato, and Socrates promoted this concept. Nevertheless, it was Socrates who argued that to be wise, one must know thyself. Part of a leader's social identity is his or her ability to know thyself to (or "intending to") ascertaining why it is that they belong to a particular group or organization. It is a shared sense of identity that makes leadership possible because people you lead may be different from you and others in the group. However, as the group comes together and determine that the overall future of the group is in its leadership, it is the leader who must contribute to the effectiveness of the group, thereby raising the group's identity and giving the group power to succeed.

Max Weber believed that leadership is a creative and transformational process in that his argument on charismatic leadership continues to inspire many leadership theorists today. Reicher, Haslam, and Hopkins (2005) presents a significant issue; can we explain how leaders can transform people's thinking and behavior without denying the ability of individuals to think for themselves? They go on to state that keeping in line with a social identity approach, leaders and the led must rely on each other to create the conditions under which mutual influence is possible. It is the mutual influence that gives the group its power over other groups. However, to be more specific, they make the following four points that we must consider:

1. They place emphasis on the creative and transformational aspects of leadership, which were inspired by Weber. For us to sidestep these points ignores the very elements that make leadership socially and intellectually significant.
2. The overall impact of leaders on the led must address the context of their joint involvement in an individual social relationship. Moreover, it is this mutual identity-based relationship which both enables and constrains the practice of leadership and which provides the basis for overcoming the traditional opposition between the leader and the led.
3. They argue that existing social identity models of leadership need to be developed to account for the efficient manner in which (a) leaders seek to shape identities and (b) the led response to these attempts.
4. Finally, there is a suggestion that the balance between autonomy and constraint in leadership is a dynamic process that tends to unfold over time (2005).

A leader's social identity reveals, for the most part, because he or she models a set of group social norms. Modeling a group social norms is just one of the elements that elevate a person to the leadership position of the group. Hogg (2001) states that we confer leadership when one strictly adheres to group norms. ***Social norms*** are the rules that govern behavior in groups. The social sciences have conducted a tremendous amount of research on this matter. For example, sociologists tend to focus on norms social functions and how they motivate people (Coleman, 1990; Durkheim, 1950; Hechter and Opp, 2001; Parsons, 1968), whereas anthropologists have centered on how social norms operate in different cultures (Geertz, 1973). When speaking about social norms, there is a difference when it comes to the ingroup and outgroup.

Knippenberg and Hogg (2003) indicate that norms tend to be displaced away from outgroup positions in an attempt to emphasize ingroup similarity while at the same time maximizing how the ingroup differs from salient outgroups. They go on to say that leadership emergence is thought to occur when group identification and group salience is high. When one group draws on their association as a primary source of self-identification, the salience of one's group membership is kept extremely high by such means as physical separation, distinctive panel dress, jargon, and so on (2003). An exquisite example of this would be college fraternities and sororities. Most leaders of social groups think that they have it all figured out and this is the primary reason they have the position of leader. Again, it is members of the group who give us this sense of social identity. It is the leader who emerges in such settings because they are viewed as models and accorded high social status, thereby, enhancing their extraordinary power to be in charge of the group. However, leaders who receive such praise will often have a condition that marks them as different from the rest the group (2003). Once afforded this unique opportunity, the leader has the power to influence not only the actions of the group but also has the ability at his or her discretion to change the group's social norms. It takes a period for a group to clarify its attitudes, beliefs, values, goals, and behaviors that characterize its collective norms. A typical leader will not only be effective but might have some charisma, whereas a leader who deviates from the social norms of the group are perceived to be ineffective and might find themselves out of a job.

We understand that social identity relates to how we identify ourselves with others and what we have in common with them. For example, some of us identify ourselves according to religion or where we are from (Asian American, easterner, Windy City), or political affiliation (Democrat, Republican, Environmentalist), vocation (writer, artist, surgeon), or relationship (mother, father, great-uncle). In some cases, a person can have multiple identities, and this can center on the roles that we play in society. Nevertheless, the different roles a person plays can help them realize their overall identity. Social identity can provide individuals with a sense of self-esteem and a framework for socializing with others, and it can influence their overall behavior. Using the term social identity not only allows us to understand who the person is, it also helps us to ascertain various roles the person plays, in this case, society as a whole.

Social identity approach premise is simple in that leadership is a function of the group instead of the individual, and we find that people who are leaders in their groups tend to be closer to the typical group member rather than followers. If a leader is socially attractive, it becomes easier for group members to accept their authority and comply with his or her decisions. Others view leaders as the leader and as such, group members attribute leadership traits to the person and not the situation. When done, we find that our understanding that the distinction is between the leader and others because the group views him or her as very special. Consistent with this view of leadership, researchers have found that individuals can manipulate their leadership status in groups by portraying themselves ideally to the group (Messick & Kramer, 2005).

There is considerable data on the social identity of leadership. Most of the research centers on a group or organizational aspects of leadership. One of the key elements of being a leader is for the person to galvanize a group or organization around a higher purpose or shared vision to accomplish whatever the mission. However, if we were to flip the script so to speak, we could point out that someone else from within the group or organization could elevate themselves to assume the role of leadership from the current leader. The current leader could lose the position if one begins to set himself or herself apart from the hierarchical structure of the group or organization. If one understood the complexity of the society as a whole, one might change the relationship before another leader could give rise and take over the group. The need for the leader to understand the social identity of the group is critical because leaders who set themselves apart in fortresses or castles may realize that people want more from leadership. Kerfoot (2008) states that a relevant field in leadership research is that of the social identity of the group and what that means for leadership. The key is to analyze the social identity of the group and their relationship with the leader.

Reicher, Haslam, and Platow (2007) suggest that the great leaders examined and identified the social identity of the group and on the basis of this status can guide the team from within the organization. These leaders not only appear to belong to the group, but they also display the perfect characteristics that make the group distinct from others. Leaders who separate themselves and who hold very different social identities than the group are less efficient than those who can exhibit the group's identity and lead from within rather than from the outside (2007). We know that the essence of leadership is the ability to influence followers to meet the overall goals of the organization. Hogg (2001) said it best when he asserts that leadership is a relational term and this is why some people can persuade others to adopt new values, attitudes, and goals, thereby, exerting leadership on behalf of those values, attitudes, and goals. The overall relationship is almost configured by and played out within the parameters of a group because of a small group like a team, a medium-sized group like an organization or a large group like a nation (2001). It is important to understand the social orientation of leadership and its impact on the group or organization. We should not neglect the social systems and the significant amount of influence that leadership may have on its structure. For example, we know that transformational leadership approach causes a change in individuals and social systems. This leadership approach can create valuable and positive change in followers with the overall goal of developing followers into leaders. These include linking the follower's sense of identity and self to the mission and the social identity of the group or organization. For a transformational leader, this helps him or her to convince followers to take greater ownership for their work and also facilitate the leader's ability to align followers with tasks that optimize their performance.

There is also a social or cultural attraction that comes into play here in that the person who holds a leadership position must be socially attractive to the group. According to Messick and Kramer (2005), this empowers the leader and publicly confirms his or her ability to influence those in the group. Leaders who act like they are a member of the group are not only more socially attractive but also endowed with a sense of legitimacy or genuineness. Social attraction works alongside attribution and information processing to help influence leadership (2005). As a result, the leader can understand the behavior patterns of the group. In other words, the command nature of this action and the relative prominence of the group is likely to encourage an internal acknowledgment to essential leadership ability or charisma. There are many attributes of leadership, and these include, put are not limited to one's status, charisma, popular support, and capacity to influence. However, they are vital to a leader ability to actively maintain his or her leadership position. We could say that the longer an individual remains in a leadership position, the more they will be socially liked, the more consensual will social attraction be, and the more entrenched will be the primary attribution effect (2005).

There is empirical support for social identity of leadership. Simply put, the core idea of social identity analysis of leadership is that as groups become salient, leadership processes become more strongly influenced by perceptions of examples that work in conjunction with social attraction and attribution processes (Messick & Kramer, 2005). There is a critical test that has shown as a group becomes more salient emergent leadership procedures and leadership effectiveness perceptions become less dependent on leader schematic congruence, the more dependent the group becomes on leadership. Although there is indirect support from a range of studies of leadership that is in the social identity tradition, there is also support for the idea that prototype-based depersonalized social attraction may facilitate leadership (2005). One more thing is that a leader's social identity can lead to power in society.

Social Identity and Power

There is also a linkage between social identity and power. For groups or organizations to survive, they have to use their power to influence behaviors by providing information on how to behave and exert pressure to encourage compliance. By the way, this is a leader's responsibility. These forces typically come in the form of rules and regulations that members must subscribe to if they want to belong to the group or organization. Overall, members gain power from personal characteristics and their positions and can use a variety of power tactics to influence other members. The dynamics of this power within the members of the groups or organization has a significant impact on leaders' behaviors. How the member's interact, the impact of minorities, and the number of influenced members have on one another, play a role in leadership behavior. Empowerment also plays a role in that it is at the core of work where members have power and authority over operations. Within the group, members need to learn how to use their power to work together efficiently. Learning how to act assertively, rather than passively or aggressively, encourages open communication and effective problem-solving in the group. When it comes to social identity, we must understand that it's connected with issues of power and privilege (Hannum, 2007). At some point and time, you may experience feeling the power and privilege associated with being a member of a dominant or "in" group. On the flip side of this, you may have also felt the powerlessness and disadvantage of being a member of a nondominant or "out" group. Nevertheless, membership in the same social identity group can make you part of the ingroup or outgroup. For example, let's say you are a man in a primarily male-led organization, with a mostly male clientele, in an industry that is considered to be Masculine. In that context, you are part of the ingroup and probably feel comfortable and accepted in the framework of the culture; you are part of the dominant social identity group. This overall power gives the leadership the authority it needs to move the group or organization forward. In other words, there is also a sense of the power of authority.

The power of authority organizes and pushes itself through the concept of identity. Therefore, it defines by the cohesion of people's collective identifications. Simultaneously, we can construct identity according to the interest of power. Thus, the interaction between power and identity is nonlinear. Cartwright (1959) argues one finds in sociology, a variety of distinctions among different types of social power or qualitatively different processes of social influence. Leaders use this social influence to maintain support and order with their subordinates. Although not an easy task, the leader is affecting a subordinate's emotions, opinions, or behaviors for that matter. The ability to influence a subordinate's behavior is needed to achieve the groups' goal and vision. I am saying this about the concept of social power and leadership because of its ability to influence the overall aims of the organization.

Social Power

Power is a central part of social life. The most basic form of power is a sheer force. If we express social power in this manner, society cannot exist. Force may produce compliance but always does so by generating fear or, in extreme cases, terror. On the other hand, an enduring society can engineer a significant agreement among its members on proper goals (in the form of cultural values) and the appropriate means of attaining them (in the shape of cultural norms). The influence that a leader has among their peers and within the group or organization as a whole is essential. However, leaders must have an explanation for their power and superiority, and there are only three types of legitimate (legal and accepted) authority. The social strength of a person or organization often results in others zeroing in on it, and such power is about the level of the skill, knowledge, information, or fame that they possess in a desirable area of expertise. In other words, social power is the ability to achieve goals even if other people oppose those goals. We can associate all societies with some form of power, and power typically resides with the government. Nevertheless, some governments in the world exercise their power through force, which is not legitimate. Nevertheless, considering ways in which power might be perceived regarding justice rather than coercion, prominent sociologists Max Weber defined authority as power widely seen as legitimate rather than coercive. He went on to say that there are only three legal avenues to social power and it's connected to the concept authority. Although Weber identified three major types of authority: charismatic, traditional, and rational-legal, often the legitimacy of leaders depends on primarily upon only one (Witt, 2016). However, all three can be present at one time. The work of Weber helped to influence social theory research and the discipline of sociology significantly.

Power and Leadership

What happens when we connect power and authority? We recognize that Weber was evident of the various types of power. However, I think that we need to have a better understanding of power and authority and the overall sociological impact on those who would be leaders. Coleman (2016) states that we know that the concepts of power and authority are central to sociological analyses of society as a whole. Power is the ability of one person or group to exercise influence and control over others. Most would recognize that leaders use this power and authority. Moreover, the exercise of power is about relationships ranging from the interaction of two people (husband and wife) which one can, as an example, use of power and control, to a nation threatening or dominating other countries. We have seen when it comes to various countries. Sociologists are most interested in the structure of power in society. Although sociologists are very concerned about who has the power, they also want to know how institutions and government use their power. In the United States, society is stratified by race, class, and gender; we also find that power is part of the structured and essential social institutions in ways that reflect these inequalities. Furthermore, a traditional power in society influences the social dynamics within the individual and group relationships.

For the leader, the exercise of authority may be persuasive or coercive. For example, a firm political leader may persuade the nation to support a military invasion or a social policy through popular appeal. We might also conclude that sheer force may exert this power. Looking at Karl Marx argument, those who control the means of production controls the power in society. In other words, it is about those who have all the assets rather it be political, military, and economic. In some aspects, it does not have to be large assets. Although a large group (e.g., one associated with a social movement), might be able to exercise power to facilitate a social protest to promote some aspect of social change. We cannot say that smaller groups cannot use power because they can with the right resources.

Power can be legitimate as Max Weber has noted in his historical writings. If the power is deemed to be legitimate, members of society will accept it as right and just and whatever the leader's actions are will stand. Leave no doubt that authority is power, perceived by others as legitimate. For example, the United States President has the power to enforce the laws of the United States and his or her powers are legal, not because he or her was elected President, but because the constitution gives him or her that power. There is no argument that most people in the United States understand that the President has legitimate power. Going further, we can also conclude that the law is perceived by most as a legal system of authority.

I think that leadership and power questions lie at the center of group life in a diversity of contexts. I also suggest that most informal of groups have some form of leadership and the understanding of leadership and power from a sociological standpoint can enlighten a greater understanding of group dynamics, and this includes both inside and outside of the workplace. Leadership and power is a synthesis of contributions from leadership theorists, sociologists, and organizational scientists as well that address these issues from a fresh perspective. In recent years, these themes have stood the test of time. The reason is that many theorists look through the lens of social categorization approaches, which highlight people's social identity and the social roles they play as group members. At the end of the day, we should understand the processes that influence perceptions of and expectations for individuals and groups from a sociological and leadership point of view. However, I am the first to admit that there is little information as to the impact on organizations, groups, and society as a whole. With the understanding that the context of leadership has changed, traditionally, leaders worked in groups in which people mostly associated with their mutual culture and values. However, today leaders are required to bring groups of people together who may have very different backgrounds, perspectives, values, and cultures. In other words, the people you lead are likely to be different from you and from each other in significant ways. I recognize that this is the primary reason for leaders to have an awareness of social identity, their own, and that of others. We will discuss more on Weber's authority and power in Chapter 7.

Social Identity Theory and Transformational Leadership

Leadership is affected by the social identity of the leader. The emergence of leadership occurs because a member portrays the norms of the group and is, therefore, selected to be its leader. The ability to influence group members can be attractive in some aspects sense of attractiveness pushes some to leadership positions. However, the ***social identity theory of leadership*** as described as a group process, generated by social categorization (social comparison, intergroup relations, and self-enhancement motivation) tends to focus in on leadership. To some extent, social identification may alter the basis of liking others who are in charge. We have seen how media plays a part in this endeavor. Groups, mainly established groups, who elevate a person to a leadership role, give him or her the power to influence because of what we said before, this social attractiveness, thereby, letting the person secure compliance with suggestions and recommendations he or she makes to facilitate success. As Berscheid and Reis (1998) clearly point out, if you like someone you are more likely to agree with them and comply with requests and suggestions. Why not put someone in charge that you like? You are saying that this person can do the job of the leadership of the group.

Hogg (2001) puts forth an argument by Henri Tajfel who introduced the idea of social identity in which he theorized how people conceptualize themselves in intergroup context, how a system of social categorizations creates and defines an individual's place in society. We connect the person to the group because of the emotional and value significance to him. A group will compare itself to other groups. Because of this notion, groups only exist about other groups in that they derive their descriptive and evaluative properties or social meaning in connection with these other groups (2001). This social comparison between groups levies a competition among them, which attempts to enhance each positive distinctiveness and positive social identity. Again using fraternities and sororities as an example, we see this exact thing happening to them with the idea of recruiting individuals to join their group. It is the distinctiveness and positive social identity that stands out among these groups that allow for successful recruitment of new members. When we personalize things, people notice or pay particular attention to what is going on. However, depersonalization affects people's feelings about one another (2001). In this case, people are not interested in the activity or group as a whole and will likely not join. One can surmise that ingroup members are more likable than outgroup members. One of the reasons for this is because of self-liking (self-esteem) in which ingroup members will have more so than outgroup members based on social attraction. It is a universal appeal and in some cases self-liking, which enables one to not only join the group but also to later become its leader.

Hogg (2001) states that social identity processes influence leadership to the point that some leaders have a disproportionate power and influence to set agenda define identity, and mobilize people to achieve collective goals. To illustrate this better, we should use the connection with transformational leadership. Transformational leadership emphasizes the charismatic features of leaders, and this theory is highly relevant to groups. Using Bass (1998) theory of transformational leadership that we learned earlier if a leader has certain charismatic traits, he or she ought to be able to convince followers to work toward common goals while ignoring his or her vested interests. The overall exhibition of transformational leadership skills allows the leader to stimulate and inspire his followers with a sense of imagination, thereby, being confident in his or her decision-making and the ability to depict an optimistic future. Transformational leadership style arouses and heightens the motivation of followers, and this leads them into action to do great things for the organization. More specifically, the transformational leader relies on emotional charms and inspiring discussions to arouse his or her followers.

Chapter Summary

This illustrates the complex dynamics associated with the relationship between the leader and the led. Primarily, as leaders understand these relationships, the better he or she can influence those they lead. As we discussed earlier, it can be difficult to comprehend a person if we don't even know ourselves. Again, know thyself is critical, not only for the leader but also for him or her to know others. There are unique differences when talking about power in society, not only for who has, but the bigger question is by what authority as well.

Glossary

Definition of the Situation What people use to know or what is expected of them and others in a situation.

Know Thyself To be wise; one must know thyself.

Self-leader The person who can garner enough support to lead the group toward achieving a particular goal.

Social Identity One who is acknowledging he or she belongs to a particular group and through its connection echoes the same values and emotional support afforded other members.

Social Identity Theory of Leadership Described as a group process generated by social categorization (social comparison, intergroup relations, and self-enhancement motivation) and it tends to focus in on leadership.

Social Norms Rules that govern behavior in groups.

References

Altheide, D. L. (2000). Identity and the definition of the situation in a mass-mediated contex. *The Sociological Quarterly*, 23(1), 1–27.

Anderson, M. L., & Taylor, H. F. (2010). *Sociology: The essentials.* (6th ed.). Belmont, CA: Wadsworth.

Antonakis, J., Cianciolo, A. T., & Sternberg, R. J. (2004). *The nature of leadership*. Thousand Oaks, CA: Sage Publications.

Bass, B. M. (1998). *Transformational leadership: Industry, military, and educational impact*. Mahwah, NJ: Erlbaum.

Bates, A. P. (1967). *The sociological enterprise*. New York, NY: Houghton Mifflin Company.

Berger, P., & Luckmann, T. (1967). *The social construction of reality*. New York, NY: Anchor Books.

Berscheid, E. & Reis, H. T. (1998). Attraction and close relationships. In D. T. Gilbert, S. T. Fiske & G. Lindzey (Eds.). *The handbook of social psychology* (4th ed.), Vol. 2, pp. 193–281. New York, NY: McGraw-Hill.

Cartwright, D. (Ed.). (1959). *Studies in social power*. Ann Arbor, MI: Institute for Social Research.

Coleman, J. (1990). *Foundations of social theory*, Cambridge, MA: Belknap.

Coleman, J. A. (2016). Authority, power, leadership: Sociological understandings. Retrieved from http://newtheologyreview.com/index.php/ntr/article/viewFile/563/746

Collins, R., & Makowsky, M. (1993). *The discovery of society.* (5th ed.). New York, NY: McGraw-Hill, Inc.

Cooley, C. H. (1964). *Human nature and the social order*. New York, NY: Schocken.

Durkheim, E. (1950). *The rules of sociological method.* Glencoe, IL: The Free Press.

Fielding, K. S., & Hogg, M. A. (1997). Social identity, self-categorization, and leadership: A field study of small interactive groups. *Group, Dynamics: Theory, Research, and Practice*, 1, 30–51.

Freud, S. (2015). *Beyond the pleasure principle*. New York, NY: Dover Publications, Inc.

Geertz, C. (1973). *The interpretation of cultures: Selected Essays*. New York, NY: Basic Books.

Gibson, J. L., Ivancevich, J. M., Donnelly, J. H., & Konopaske, R. (2003). *Organizations: Behavior, structure, processes.* (11th ed.). New York, NY: McGraw-Hill.

Gupta, V. & Krishnan, V. R. (2004). Impact of socialization on transformational leadership: Role of leader member exchange. *Journal of Management*, 11(3), 7-20.

Hannum, K. (2007). *Social identity: Knowing yourself, leading others*. Greensboro, NC: Center for Creative Leadership.

Hechter, M., & Opp, K. D. (2001). *Social norms.* New York, NY: Russel Sage Foundation.

Hemphill, J. K. (1949). *Situational factors in leadership*. Columbus, OH: Ohio State University, Bureau of Educational Research.

Hogg, M. A. (2001). A social identity theory of leadership. *Personality and Social Psychology Review*, 5(3), 184–200.

Hogg, M. A. (2010). Influence and leadership. In S. T. Fiske, D. T. Gilbert & L. Gardner (Eds.), *Handbook of social psychology* (5th ed.), pp. 1167–1207. Hob

Kerfoot, K. (2008). Leadership: Social identity and guiding from within. *Nursing Economics*, 38(1), 24–26.

Kellerman, B. (1984). *Leadership: Multidisciplinary perspectives*. Englewood Cliff, NJ: Prentice-Hall, Inc.

Knippenberg, D. V., & Hogg, M. A. (2003). *Leadership and power: Identity processes in groups and organizations*. Thousand Oaks, CA: Sage Publications.

Marshall, C., & Oliva, M. (2006). *Leadership for social justice: Making revolutions in education*. Boston, MA: Pearson Education.

Mean, G. H. (1934). *Mind, self, and society*. Chicago, IL: University of Chicago Press.

Mead, G. H. (1934). *Mind, self, and society*. C. Morris (Ed.). Chicago, IL: University of Chicago Press.

Messick, D. M., & Kramer, R. M. (2005). *The psychology of leadership: New perspectives and research*. Mahwah, NJ: Lawrence Erlbaum Associates.

Parsons, T. (1968). *The structure of social action: A study in social theory with special reference to a group of recent European writers*. New York, NY: Free Press.

Piaget, J. (1926). *The language and thought of the child*. New York, NY: Harcourt, Brace.

Piaget, J. (1952). *The child's conception of number*. London: Routledge and Kegan Paul Ltd.

Pines, A. (1985). *The burnout measure*. Park Ride, IL: London House Management Press.

Reicher, S., Haslam, S. A., & Hopkins, N. (2005). Social identity and the dynamics of leadership: Leaders and followers as collaborative agents in the transformation of social reality. *Leadership Quarterly*, 16, 547-568. The new psychology of leadership. *Scientific American Mind*, 18(4), 22–29.

Reicher, S., Haslam, S. A., & Platow, M. (2007). The new psychology of leadership. *Scientific American Mind*, 18(4), 22–29.

Ross, L. F. (2012). *Leadership: So what makes you think you can lead*. Philadelphia, PA: Xlibris Publishers.

Schutz, A. (1967). *The phenomenology of the social world* (G. Walsh and T. Len-Bert, Trans.). Evanston, IL: Northwestern University Press.

Waller, W. (2014). *The sociology of teaching*. Eastford, CT: Martino Fine Books.

Witt, J. (2016). *SOC*. (4th ed.). New York, NY: McGraw-Hill Education.

Zaccaro, S. J., & Klimoski, R. J. (Eds.). (). *The nature of organizational leadership: Understanding the performance imperatives confronting today's leaders*. San Francisco, CA: Jossey-Bass.

Chapter 3

Leadership Skill-Building Exercise

The Qualities of a Great Leader

List of Qualities	1	2	3	4	5
Tolerance					
Calmness					
Empathy					
Sense of humor					
Problem solving					
Charisma					
Listening					
Self-discipline					
Humility					
Fairness					
Knowledgeable					
Positive attitude					
Creativity					
Relationships					
Assertiveness					
Responsibility					
Servanthood					
Character					
Wise					
Dependability					
Curious					
Commitment					
Communication					

Sensitive
Strong values
Genuine
Role-model
Social consciousness
Dedication
Results-driven
Loyalty
Adaptable
Passion
Teachability
Diplomatic
Focus
Courage
Goal-oriented
Self-reliant
Motivation

From the list of qualities, rate each according the scale below. Be prepared to address your rating. Positive qualities are just another piece of the puzzle when it comes to the making of a great leader.

Scale

1. I need some serious help in this area.
2. I could use some minor improvement in this area.
3. There is some hope for me yet in that I can do this without help.
4. I normally display this quality when interacting with people.
5. I absolutely have this quality under my belt and always hit a homerun.

Chapter 4

- Culture and Leadership
- Sociological and Leadership Perspectives on Culture
- Racial Identity, Cultural, and Leadership
- The GLOBE Study

Sociology of Leadership

Thinking Critically!

As a student, consider the obstacles to cross-cultural interaction here on campus. Why might people be unwilling to interact with others who have alternative cultural practices? How might it perpetuate inequality? What is your response to others who engage in this type of behavior?

As You Read

- Why is understanding culture so important to leadership?
- Is one country better at leadership than another?
- Explain your take on the Leader's role in creating culture that supports diversity.

Chapter 4

Culture and Leadership

© Everett Historical/Shutterstock.com

The best leader is the one who has sense enough to pick good men to do what he wants done, and the self-restraint to keep from meddling with them while they do it.

Theodore Roosevelt

Understanding culture and its relationship to leadership are critical. Just as we discussed with the other concepts introduced in the Sociology of Leadership, we must also break down the relationship that exists between culture and leadership from a sociological and leadership perspective. Sociologists and leadership theorists look at this from a different viewpoint. We will specifically address each and then bring them together referencing their importance. Culture is an abstract term, which makes it very hard to define. However, for the purpose of this book, we will define ***culture*** as a set of rules, values, norms, symbols, beliefs, language, and traditions which are learned and carried over from generation to generation. There is no substitute for building relationships across cultures. We must recognize that culture permeates conflict, no matter what we do as a leader. A leader understands that a culturally diverse staff can strengthen any group and push them to new heights regardless of its environment. Everyone, irrespective of their background or culture, can bring ideas to the table; use them.

The Components of Culture

Every society has its distinctive customs and practices. All of the social sciences use the term culture to refer to a population's characteristics of beliefs, language, symbols, technology, norms, and values, which are preserved and transmitted from generation to generation. Simply put:

- A ***belief*** is a declaration about reality that one accepts as true. Beliefs are someone's observation, opinions, custom, or faith. However, people who share a given tradition may not take or share those ideas. Beliefs can produce lethal effects or supply the framework for one's perceptions.

- A ***language*** is a system for communicating facts, ideas, and feelings. The language uses standardized symbols in a linguistic framework recognized by society. We use language to not only transmit culture by recording its knowledge, beliefs, and values, but members of society also use it to share skills and experiences up close and far from generation to generation.
- ***Symbols*** are anything used to exemplify something else. For example, words, signs, and gestures are part of the fabric of society.
- ***Technology*** is the vehicle used to transmit culture at a faster pace. Technology is any recurring operation that we use to influence the environment to achieve some specific goal. For example, some of the engines of technology include Facebook, Twitter, or Snapchat. These social media sites serve to transmit culture through relationship networks, discussion forums, media sharing networks, personal networks, and interests-based networks. As society changes, so do the technology, which is an upgrade.
- ***Norms*** are standards of behavior. They are rules that we are expected to follow in our relationship with others. Sometimes called laws or legal regulations, norms not only provide guidelines for appropriate behavior in a given situation but also supply people with expectations of how others will respond to their actions. When we violate norms, then sanctions may be applied to enforce them as a means of social control.
- ***Values*** purport what is good or bad, right or wrong, appropriate or inappropriate in society. Values are broad behavioral preferences used to guide behavior in particular situations. Values are important because they affect the content of norms. Values are critical to understanding the culture.

Sociological Perspective

For sociologists, culture is a way of life, passed on from generation to generation. It is a system of values, beliefs, behaviors, and artifacts that one preserves for generations. It's a way of life for a particular group of people that acts as a lens through which to view the world. Culture is the key to the sociological perspective, because it is used to influence our behavior and beliefs in society. We are all influenced by the language and gestures we use to interact with one another. Society cannot exist without culture, and there is a noticeable difference as one moves from one community to another. Therefore, culture and society are interrelated. It is the values we hold dear for our children that are passed down to them through the learning of culture. In other words, the concept of culture includes all those aspects of human life that we learn and share across generations. For example, there are certain ways in which we meet and greet in America, how we engage in romantic love or the belief that hard work will lead to success. Sociologists call these more intangible aspects of culture as a ***nonmaterial culture (or symbolic culture)***. However, they associate ***material culture*** with things like a person's hair, jewelry, tools, or physical objects (food to clothing) which people make to satisfy their needs. When we use our culture as a means or standard by which to evaluate another group or individual, it leads to the view that other cultures are inferior or abnormal. By the way, this type of judgment is called ***ethnocentrism,*** and it leads to problems. Therefore, we must always remember that culture is something that is learned and never uses it as a measuring stick for judging others, because there is nothing inherently better about ours.

The founder of Anthropology, Tylor (2016a, b), once stated that culture or civilization, taken in its ethnographic sense, is that complex whole which includes knowledge, belief, art, morals, law, custom, and any other capabilities and habits acquired by man as a member of society. We find this to be important because every sense the arrival of modern civilization cultural development has been rapid from the industrial revolution, information age, and now globalization, which is out of control. We are more sophisticated than ever before through the changes of technology, and this has allowed culture to change our lives dramatically. It had not only an impact on individuals but also organizations, some of which have not kept up and later caused their demise.

Leadership Perspective

Leadership theorists see culture as a part of the overall structure of organizations. Culture affects how leaders respond in various situations. There is a clear relationship between organization culture and leadership behavior as well as job satisfaction. For example, Nohria and Khurana (2010) support this position, but they also state that the globalized business world of today not only provides firms with unprecedented opportunities but also formidable challenges because it represents a higher level of complexity resulting from conditions of multiplicity, interdependence, and ambiguity. You just can't transform a global organization without a complete understanding of a worldwide network of interconnected and integrated operations from a cultural perspective. "From a leadership perspective, it requires the ability to work with and influence individuals inside and outside the corporation, representing a diversity of cultural backgrounds, to help achieve the corporation's goal" (p. 336).

As we put leadership and culture into context, the literature suggests that are different levels of analysis with one being the relationship between organizational culture and leadership, and the other being the relationship between national culture and leadership. Although there is a little or empirical linkage, the two streams of research appear to be mutually exclusive (Nohria & Khurana, 2010). There is the support that leaders have an impact on organizational culture with their actions and behaviors. For example, with the advent of social tools elevated by technology, it is much easier to facilitate this process. We illustrated Culture by the actions and behavior of leaders, what they pay attention to in the organization, who get rewarded and punished, and the allocation of resources to accomplish the mission. For leadership, this is the making of culture. As Schein (2017) posits, the organizational life cycle is a key determinant of the connection between leadership and organizational culture. Leaders are an essential element in the success of the organization, because if the culture is sick, the group or organization will fail. In other words, if the culture is bad, it will not maintain its competitive advantage long (Ross, 2012).

When it comes to the national culture and leadership, one can also say something equally prevailing. In this era of globalization, most companies or organization, especially Fortune 500 companies, are connected in some way globally. However, for them to be effective, they have to enter those markets understanding what they will bring to the table from a cultural point of view. They are unable to be operative in goods and services if they have no clue about the global culture they will enter. Research indicates that there are differences across cultures, differences regarding effective leadership behaviors, actual patterns of leadership behavior, and the relationship of leadership behavior to outcomes (Yukl, 2012). There is also a general agreement among researchers that national culture refers to cognitive systems and behavioral repertoires and are shaped as a result of individuals' everyday experiences (Hofstede, 1980). There are consequences for not understanding the cultures of various countries in which organizations have a global stake in goods and services.

Racial Identity, Culture, and Leadership

Misunderstanding race and culture impact your leadership. We recognize this as one of the reasons why it is crucial to understand various cultures. The complexities of a modern society require today's leaders who encompass many characteristics that past leaders did not need to possess. Today's leaders need to be not only politically and socially savvy, but also culturally sensitive. However, it does help to know just a little about various cultures to put you above the rest of your peers. We might also add that sociologists understand race as a social rather than a biological category and we recognize that some, particularly students, will find this confusing. Nevertheless, think of it this way in that we acknowledge that there are those who understand race and its association with a person's skin color, which is an inherited physical trait that one has at birth. However, sociologists point out that no physical attribute will always accurately identify what race someone is associated with in society. This position is supported by Omi and Winant (1994) as they point out in *Racial Formation in the United States* when they wrote "Although the concept of race invokes biologically based human characteristics, it is always and necessarily a social and historical process" to identify who and what is the race of a person. (p. 55). Yes, it is because the definition of race is not firm and can change regularly as racial categories are challenged and established. There is one thing that allows us to point to a person race and it would be to look at the culture a person emulates, and this can help guide us in our process of identification.

The African-American Culture

We find for the most part that African-American culture comes, not just from the traditions of Africa, but also from the fact that most were from descendants of slaves. Taylor Quintard, an African-American history teacher at Washington University, teaches a course designed to trace African-American history from the period 1619 to 1890. The statements that he makes is intriguing to this author in that Quintard (2000) states the history of African American has been a paradox of incredible triumph in the face of tremendous human tragedy. How true it is to make that statement in that it has to resonate with many who claim that they are African American. Many would argue that a ***slave*** is a person held in bondage of another. Although the European slave trade began in 1441, it was not until the mid-1500s when Europeans started to bring black Africans to America as slaves. Apparently, one must consider this as a forced migration. Slaves were regarded as a commercial business for their owners because most were plantation workers. Despite the hardships inflicted on slaves, they managed to develop a strong cultural identity. Slaves looked after each other, particularly the children, and they managed to maintained strong family ties. They learned spiritual music and developed their form of Christianity. Over a period, African culture enriched America with music, theater, and dance. Meltzer (1993) states that "in any society, slavery cannot escape the influence of the given culture" (p. 5). In other words, as the institution of slavery develops, a distinct African-American experience accumulated, and traditions of resistance and accommodation developed as slaves worked to create the world for themselves. The African-American culture was forged in response to the realities of slavery and manifested in music, religion, family and kinship structures, and other aspects of everyday life that we still find today, passed on from generation to generation (Baptist, 2016; Blassingame, 1972; Genoverse, 1972). Culture is the mold in which slavery formed.

Gender Relations

The southern agricultural areas of society developed into a complex social system that became stratified by race, gender, and class. The result of this activity led to the plantation elite, small in numbers, but wealthy and politically powerful, sitting on top of the structure (Healey & Stepnick, 2017). During the slave period of society, racial groups were stratified by gender. For example, white women were subordinate to men, and the slave community echoed the same. However, at the bottom of the system were African-American women slaves, which led to a double jeopardy of being oppressed through their gender and race (2017). Some view it as a triple play: "Black in a white society, a slave in a free society, and women in a society ruled by men, female slaves had the least formal power and perhaps the most vulnerable group of antebellum America" (White, 1985, p. 15).

The Native Americans Culture

Indians were here first, and their culture was highly visible, particularly the language. Although big in size, they had limited technology. As contact begins to surface, conflicts followed, and in the late 1800s, they were defeated as a people. The diminishment of approximately 10 million Native Americans by 1890 was devastating. Native Americans were not enslaved during the colonial period, because their competition with whites centered on land, not labor (Healey & Stepnick, 2017). As a result, Native Americans ended up being forcibly removed from their territory that they had occupied for generations. Specifically, those who had not died in the many battles with U.S. Soldiers were forced into Indian reservations west of the Mississippi. In 1838 and 1839, the state of Georgia and the federal government forcibly marched approximately 17,000 Cherokees westward over 800 miles, which later became known as the Trail of Tears, because of the conditions during the journey. An estimate indicated that over 4,000 of them died of hunger, exposure, or disease.

Gender Relations

Native Americans practiced various forms of slavery and had a strict gender-based division of labor, but this did mean that women were subordinate to the men. In many tribes, women held positions of great responsibility and controlled the wealth (Healey & Stepnick, 2017). There were cases in which women were adversely affected by their environment. They were responsible for gardening and other chores while the men went off to hunt. The introduction of houses by the Europeans led to a great increase in hunting ventures for the people. However, women in the Cherokee nation lost much status and power under pressure to assimilate. Like African Americans, Native Americans also sharply differentiated from the dominant group by race, and in many cases, were internally stratified by gender. They were simply powerless and subordinate to white society and the federal government.

The Mexican American Culture

During the early 1800s, Mexican Americans began to settle in areas, which came to be known as Texas, California, New Mexico, and Arizona. According to Healey and Stepnick (2017) social and political life was organized around family and the Catholic Church, and based on farming and herding, tended to be dominated by an elite class of wealthy landowners. They also state that Mexicans were racially a mixture of Spaniards and Native Americans, and differences in skin color and other physical attributes provided a convenient marker of group membership. However, once observed, it was evident to which group they belong too. As far as religious preferences are a concern, the majority of the Mexican Americans were Roman Catholic, whereas Anglo Americans were Protestant. Even today, this still stands. Although Anglo Americans used their superior numbers and military power to acquire control of the political and economic structures and take the resources of the Mexican American community, only in New Mexico were they able to retain a measure of power for decades, because they were evenly split (population wise) in that area (2017). As with African American and Native Americans, they too were labeled a minority group and their culture and language suppressed, and property rights revoked, and their status lowered.

Gender Relations

In southwest America, an apparent gender-based division of labor existed among Mexican Americans. The women cared for the family, child-rearing, and household tasks. However, Mexican Americans as a whole became part of a landless labor force, and women and men suffered the economic devastation that accompanied military conquest by a foreign power (Healey & Stepnick, 2017). There was strain among the families because of poverty and economic instability. For the household to survive economically, women had to work outside the house. In comparison to black women slaves, Mexican American women also became the most vulnerable part of the social system (2017).

Culture Affects Leadership

According to Schein (2017), 90% of a person's behavior is motivated by social rules and not personality. When it comes to leadership impact on culture and vice versa and through the association of both of these complex concepts, we still do not know what a leader is or what one is supposed to do at this stage in the research. We can state, however, that culture and leadership are two sides of the same coin. When groups or organizations start, there is always a leader in charge who prefers to do things his or her way. As a result, those preferences are going to be passed on and executed by the group members. Moreover, the leader's values and preferences are the first behaviors that a group or organization learns how to do, and if that works those actions ultimately become the culture of that team. Actually, it is the leaders of the group who creates its culture. As you learned in the previous chapters, there is a host of research on what a leader should do on various occasions or the competencies or traits one should have demonstration when sitting at the wheel of leadership. As Schein (2017) puts so elegantly "part of the confusion derives from the fact that there is no clear consensus on defining who a leader is . . . or anyone who takes the initiative to change things. Leadership as a distribution function is gaining ground, which leads to the possibility that anyone who facilities progress toward some desired outcome is displaying leadership" (p. 12).

It is very easy to link leadership and culture because together, there is no doubt that leaders create culture, but if the culture becomes dysfunctional, blame it on the leader. The leader is responsible for changing it. As Northouse (2016) suggests, the concept of leadership and culture both have an impact on how leaders influence others. However, he flips the script a bit and replaces culture and leadership with ***ethnocentrism*** and ***prejudice***. He defines ethnocentrism as a tendency for individuals to place their group (ethnic, racial, or cultural) at the center of their comments of others and the world, whereas prejudice is a mostly fixed attitude, belief, or emotion held by an individual about another person or group can be based on faulty or unsubstantiated data. Sociologists like to describe ethnocentrism as a propensity to assume that one's culture and way of life represent what is customary or are superior to all others. Witt (2016) states that when we hear people talking about our culture versus their culture, we are sometimes confronted with statements that reflect the attitude that our culture is best. Ethnocentrism is like a lens through which a person looks at one culture to examine another. People using this type of evaluation have a tendency to give priority and value their beliefs, attitudes, and values over others. Nevertheless, this can lead to problems if one is closed-minded and will not entertain the value of what other cultures might bring to the group. As far as leadership is a concern, ethnocentrism can be a major obstacle to effective leadership, because it not only prevents people from fully understanding or respecting the viewpoint of others, but it can also hinder an experienced leader's successful accomplishment of his or goals for the group.

Thinking Critically!

As a student, consider the obstacles to cross-cultural interaction here on campus. Why might people be unwilling to interact with others who have alternative cultural practices? How might it perpetuate inequality? What is your response to others who engage in this type of behavior?

We can link culture and leadership, but we can also do this for ethnocentrism and prejudice. Prejudice involves inflexible generations that are resistant to change or evidence to the contrary. It can also refer to someone's judgments about others based on previous decisions or experiences (Northouse, 2016). Let's remind us from time to time that we all hold prejudices to some degree, but one must be aware that prejudice is self-oriented rather than other-oriented. As suggested above, ethnocentrism and prejudice can interfere with our ability to lead. Effective leadership is the capacity to understand and appreciate the human experience of others, ability to fight our prejudice, and that of those we lead. However, leadership at its best is the capacity to find ways to negotiate with those you lead who are from various other cultures, other than your own. However, this is even more important in this era of globalization.

Globalization and Leadership

We went from the industrial age, the information age, to what is now called the globalization age. Leaders must be competent in various cultures. The Fortune 500 hundred companies that we hear so much about are multinational corporations that sell goods and services beyond their borders. Northouse (2016) states that globalization has created the need for leaders to become competent in cross-cultural awareness and practices. ***Globalization*** is the process by which the integration of government policies, cultures, social movements, and financial markets, facilitates the transfer of capital, goods, and services across national borders. According to Held and McGrew (2002), globalization denotes the expanding scale, growing magnitude, speeding up, and deepening the impact of transcontinental flows and patterns of social interaction. This overall process links remote communities like never before. Moreover, we find that its origins lie in the work of many 19th century scholars and early 20th century intellectuals. The association comes from Karl Marx and sociologists such as Saint-Simon and students of geopolitics such as MacKinder, who recognize how modernity was integrating the world (2002). As Witt (2016) reports, conflicts with roommates, classmates, and professors are often chalked up to personality clashes and other individual attributes, but they cannot be fully understood or dealt with apart from coming to terms with the ways our social background have shaped how we think, act, and feel. Times are changing to the point that globalization has resulted in the world becoming one place and one system used to distribute commerce, driven by mutual interactions for various good and services. Robertson (1992) supports this notion when he states that cultures and societies, along with their members and participants, are being squeezed together and driven toward increased mutual interactions. He further "describes this as the compression of the world" (p. 27). Being socialized throughout life up until this point, we know the social position that one occupies and realize that it does shape the opportunities and obstacles we face as a person and leader. Sociology provides us with the tools to better understand, interpret and respond to the world around us. It is one's leadership behaviors that we must address if leadership is to expand globally to facilitate the success of the organization.

The GLOBE Study

The GLOBE study is the most significant cultural study of leadership covering 62 societies. According to House, Hanges, Javidan, Dorfman, and Gupta (2004), the 21st century may very well become known as the era of the global world. We couldn't agree more, and with the advent of globalization, we have the means to be globally connected like never before. Therefore, it is important that we address leadership behaviors and their impact on other cultures. The researchers divided the 62 counties they studied into regional clusters. The clusters provided a way to evaluate the similarities and differences between cultural groups (clusters) and to make eloquent generalizations about culture and leadership. Researchers used the following factors of common language, geography, religion, and historical accounts to divide the world into 10 distinct clusters: Eastern Europe, Middle East, Confucian Asia, Southern Asia, Latin America, Nordic Europe, Anglo, Germanic Europe, Latin Europe, and Sub-Saharan Africa. Shown in Figure 4.1 is the country clusters/groupings used in all GLOBE studies.

Figure 4.1 Country Clusters According to GLOBE

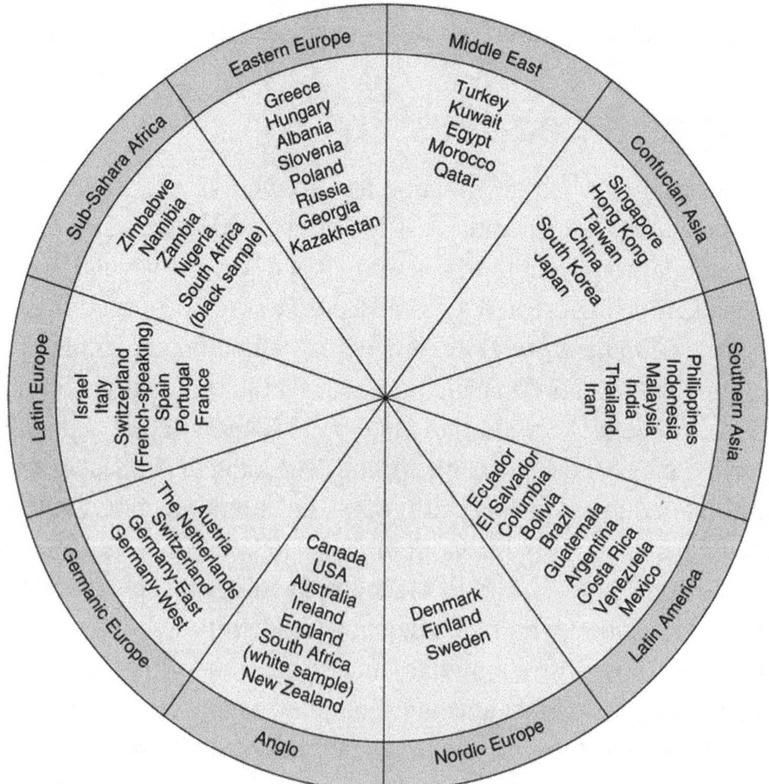

Source: "Republished with permission of SAGE Publications, from *Culture, Leadership, and Organizations: The Globe Study of 62 Societies*, by R. J. House, et al, 2004; permission conveyed through Copyright Clearance Center, Inc."

As a result, the study identified six leadership behaviors that various cultures determined were useful in an individual's leadership walk. The leadership profiles and associated behaviors are addressed below:

1. Charismatic/value-based leadership reflects the ability to inspire, to motivate, and to expect high performance from others based on firmly held core values. This kind of leadership includes being visionary, inspirational, self-sacrificing, trustworthy, decisive, and performance-oriented.
2. Team-oriented leadership emphasizes team building and a common purpose among team members. This kind of leadership includes being collaborative, integrative, diplomatic, non-malevolent, and administratively competent.
3. Participative leadership reflects the degree to which leaders involved others in making and implementing decisions. It includes being participative and nonautocratic.
4. Humane-oriented leadership emphasizes being supportive, considerate, compassionate, and generous. This type of leadership includes modesty and sensitivity to other people.
5. Autonomous leadership refers to independent and individualistic leadership, which includes being autonomous and unique.
6. Self-protective leadership reflects behaviors that ensure the safety and security of the leader and the group. It includes leadership that is self-centered, status conscious, conflict inducing, face-saving, and procedural (House, Hanges, Javidan, Dorfman, and Gupta, 2004, p. 675).

If one want to be successful across various cultures, it is important for a leader to exhibit the specific leadership behaviors of that culture.

Eastern Europe Leadership Profile

The Eastern Europe Leadership Profile describes a leader who is very independent and takes an individualistic approach to leadership. However, the research also indicates that the leader is very strict when it comes to protecting ones' position as a leader (Figure 4.2). Although the leader is

Figure 4.2 Eastern Europe Leadership Profile

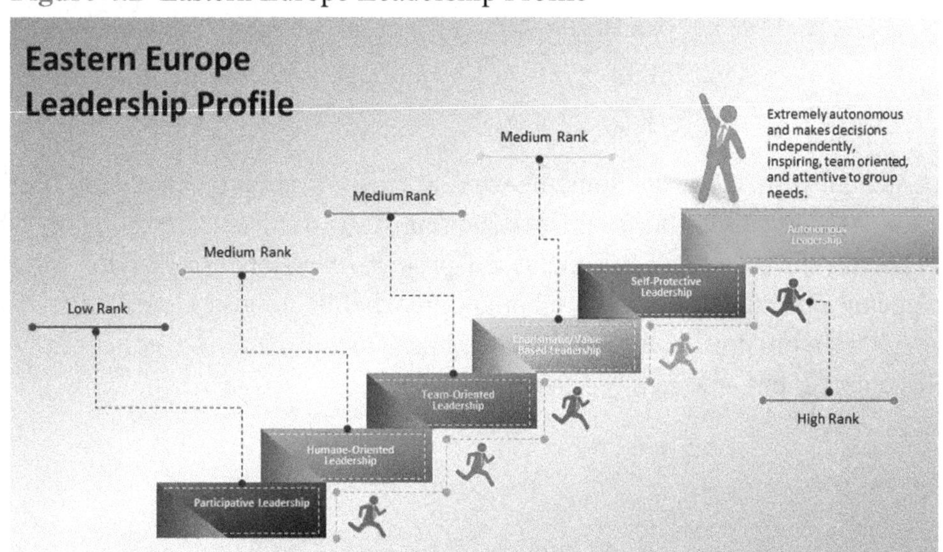

Source: Adapted from House, Hanges, Javidan, Dorfman, and Gupta (2004).

considered to be moderately charismatic/value-based, team-oriented, and humane-oriented, he or she seems disinterested in involving others in the decision-making process. Only, the culture describes a leader who is extremely autonomous, makes decisions independently, and is to some extent inspiring, team-oriented, and attentive to group needs.

Latin American Leadership Profile

Latin American Leadership Profile appears to be somewhat different compared to its Eastern European Leaders. Although charismatic/value-based, team-oriented, and self-protective leadership is vital, autonomous leadership seems lacking (Figure 4.3). There is reasonable support for leadership that is participative and humane-oriented. Nevertheless, the profile indicates a leader who is charismatic/value-based, can inspire and motivate others, while also collaborating to get things done, yet self-seeking in some aspects. The leaders in Latin American like to participate in decision-making. However, they take a middle-of-the-road approach to dealing with people.

Figure 4.3 Latin American Leadership Profile

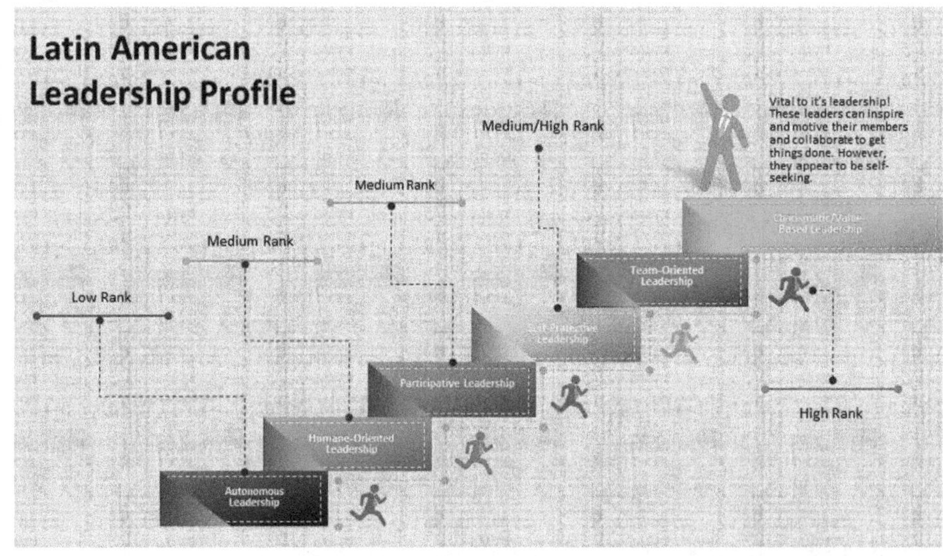

Source: Adapted from House, Hanges, Javidan, Dorfman, and Gupta (2004).

Latin Europe Leadership Profile

Latin Europe Leadership Profile has some likeness to Latin American Leadership Profile in that it does flip the script so to speak with participative and self-protective leadership behaviors (Figure 4.4). Latin American may have a slight edge on the self-protective leadership behavior. Notably, there is a lack of independence and sensitivity to other people when it comes to leadership. However, like the other Latin leadership profile, there is a leadership, which is inspiring, collaborative, participative, and self-centered, but moderately compassionate.

Figure 4.4 Latin Europe Leadership Profile

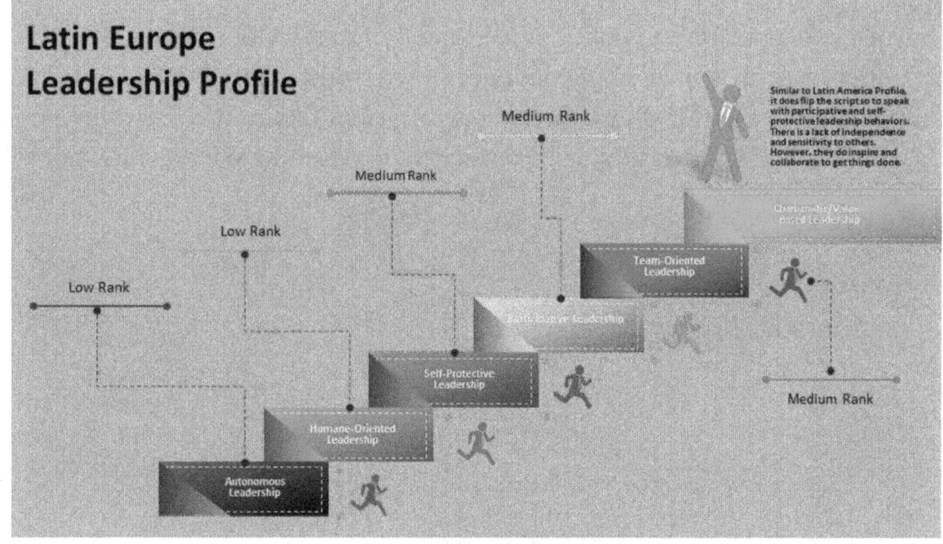

Source: Adapted from House, Hanges, Javidan, Dorfman, and Gupta (2004).

Confucian Asia Leadership Profile

Like the other profiles above, the Confucian Asia Leadership Profile is also unique. For this profile, self-protective, team-oriented, and humane-oriented score the highest rank for leadership (Figure 4.5). Although moderately able to inspire and motivate people, this leader will not involve others in making and implementing decisions. Simply put, he or she is a loner when it comes to getting others involved in setting goals and acting on them. This leader protects oneself and the group, but again, uses his or her position to make decisions alone.

Figure 4.5 Confucian Asia Leadership Profile

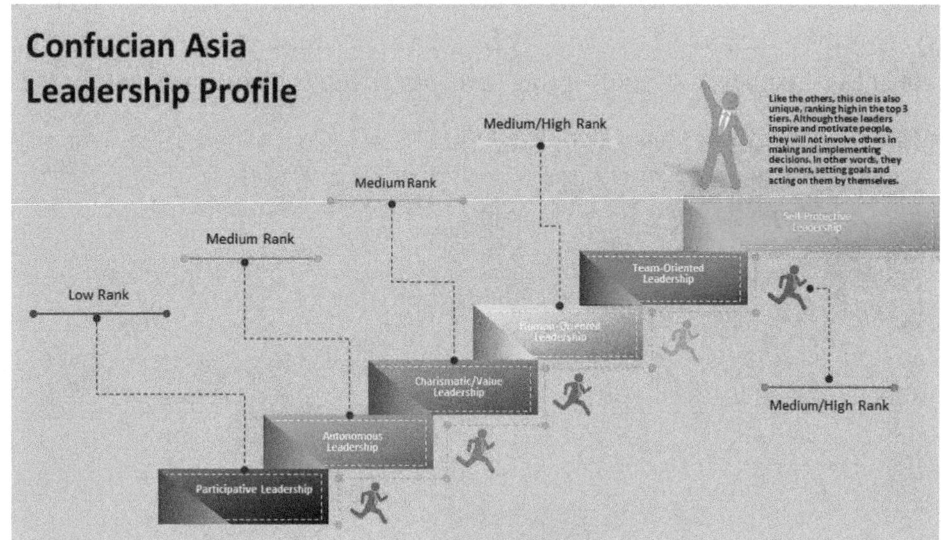

Source: Adapted from House, Hanges, Javidan, Dorfman, and Gupta (2004).

Nordic Europe Asia Leadership Profile

For Nordic Europe countries, one can argue that leadership starts with a vision. They believe in high performance from others as well as being decisive in their outcomes (Figure 4.6). The leaders are moderately diplomatic in their dealings. Leaders in this area like to involve others in making and implementing decisions. However, they lack sensitivity to other people and are very self-centered.

Figure 4.6 Nordic Europe Leadership Profile

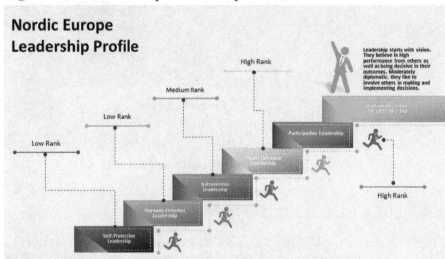

Source: Adapted from House, Hanges, Javidan, Dorfman, and Gupta (2004).

Anglo Leadership Profile

The Anglo Leadership Profile places emphasis, which is the charismatic quality of an individual as perceived by others, to be his or her connection with some very central feature and in this case, we call it charisma. Leadership in these areas of the world reflects a high ability in charismatic/value-based, participative, and a keen sense of sensitivity to other people (Figure 4.7). The leaders are motivated and visionary. However, they appear to be very ineffective because of being prone to face-saving or status consciousness. In other words, self-protective leadership is less significant for these countries.

Figure 4.7 Anglo Leadership Profile

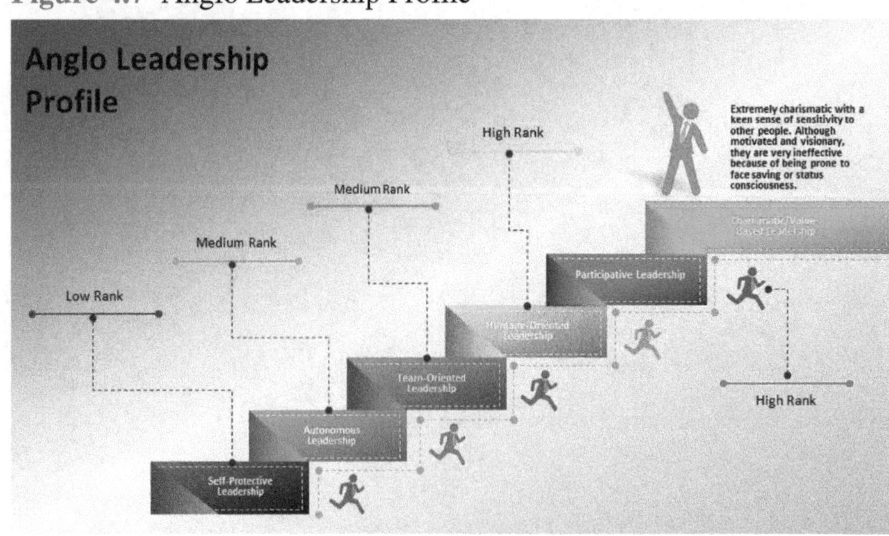

Source: Adapted from House, Hanges, Javidan, Dorfman, and Gupta (2004).

Sub-Saharan Africa Leadership Profile

Leadership in these countries center on people in that the leader is supportive, considerate, and compassionate to people needs (Figure 4.8). Moreover, the leader should have charisma, be team-oriented, and let others get involved in the decision-making process. Of particular note, leaders who act alone or autonomously tend to be not useful in these countries. They cannot be excessively self-centered but should be visionary, inspirational, and trustworthy.

Figure 4.8 Sub-Saharan Leadership Profile

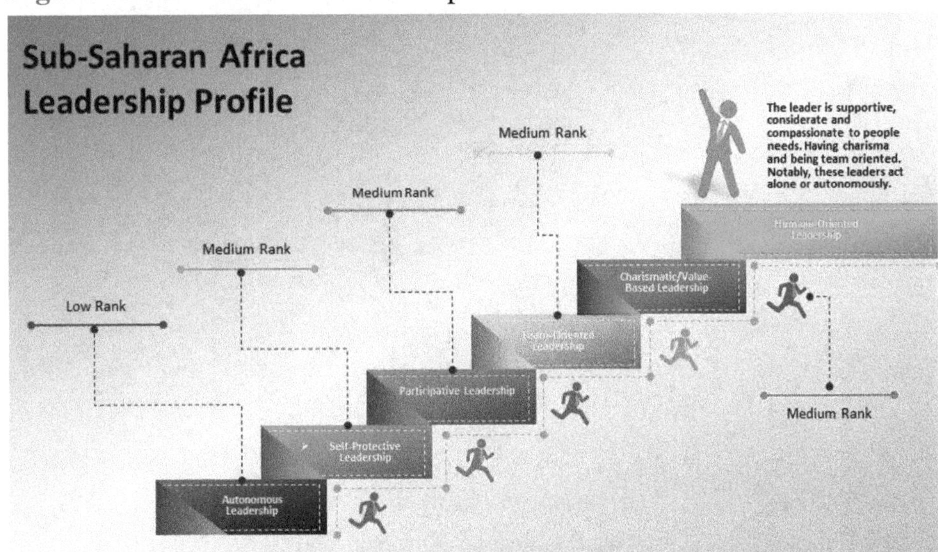

Source: Adapted from House, Hanges, Javidan, Dorfman, and Gupta (2004).

Southern Asia Leadership Profile

Like Confucian Asia, to Southern Asia, self-protective is crucial (Figure 4.9). Charismatic/value-based, humane-oriented, and team-oriented leadership are also vital. Also, like Confucian Asia, they both find participative leadership to be ineffective. In other words, they don't believe in involving others in the

Figure 4.9 Southern Asia Leadership Profile

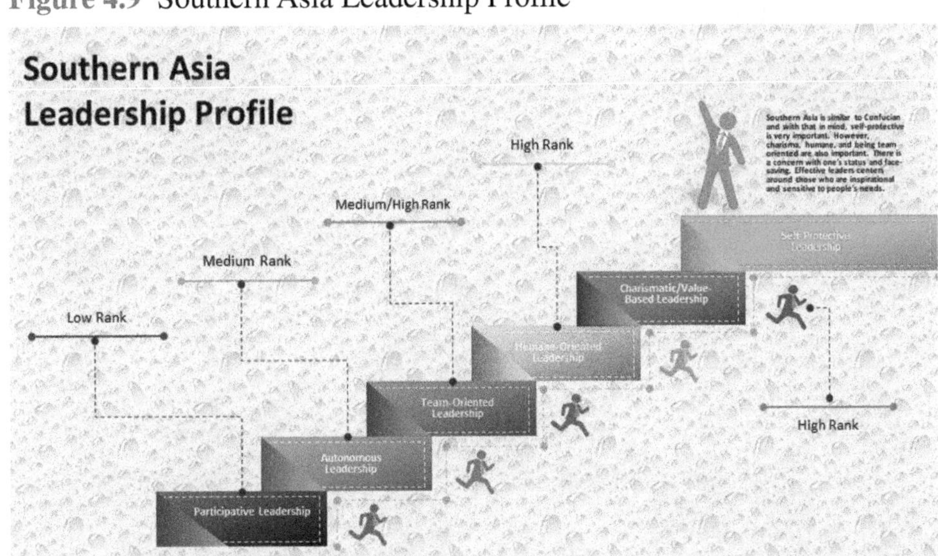

Source: Adapted from House, Hanges, Javidan, Dorfman, and Gupta (2004).

decision-making process. Although they appear to be concerned with status and face-saving, they feel that effective leadership tends to come from leaders who are inspirational and sensitive to people's needs.

Germanic Europe Leadership Profile

We can tailor leaders in this area to a style that is very participative in that they want everyone involved in the decisions, from making them to implementation (Figure 4.10). The leader is visionary,

Figure 4.10 Germanic Europe Leadership Profile

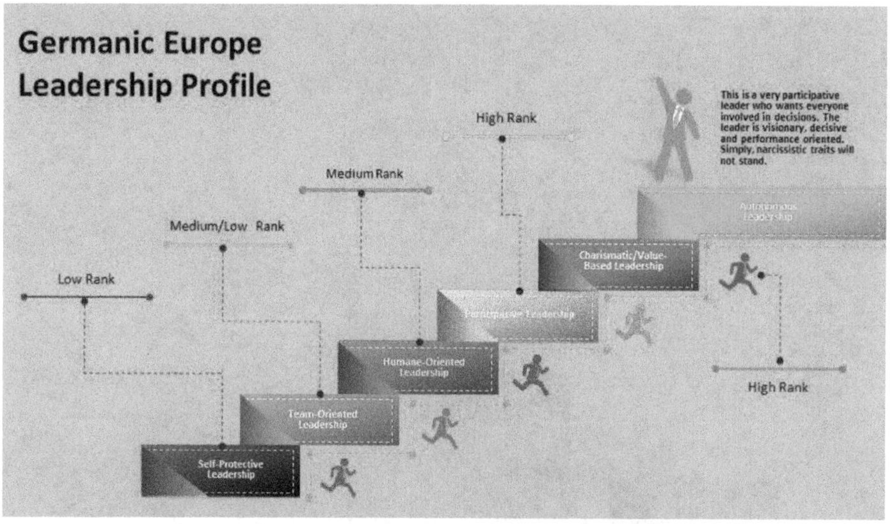

Source: Adapted from House, Hanges, Javidan, Dorfman, and Gupta (2004).

decisive, and performance-oriented. However, leadership is not concerned with their status or entertaining face-saving matters. Put simply; narcissistic traits will not stand.

Middle East Leadership Profile

Middle Eastern leadership is different. These countries believe that a person status, as well as face-saving, is crucial (Figure 4.11). They are less interested in charismatic/value-based, team-oriented,

Figure 4.11 Middle East Leadership Profile

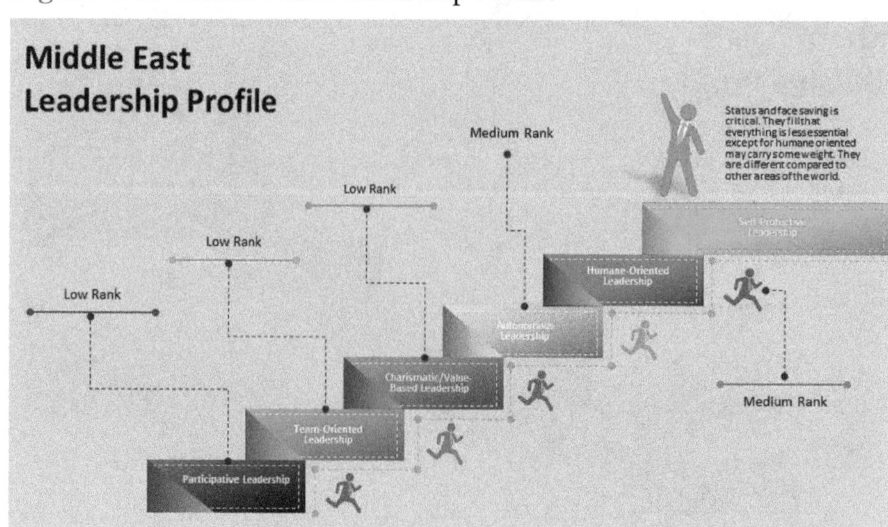

Source: Adapted from House, Hanges, Javidan, Dorfman, and Gupta (2004).

and participative processes, because they find them as nonessential in regards to effective leadership. The bottom line is that these countries are very different from others previously addressed.

The significance of the GLOBE gives us an idea of how to view leadership across the globe. If an organization is a multinational organization, then the importance of leadership in these countries are evident in that a leader who decided to venture into these countries must understand the culture of the area to be successful. Notably, this study covered 62 countries, and the list of leadership attributes was universally endorsed by 17,000 people in those countries.

Chapter Summary

This chapter introduces culture and its relationship to leadership. Culture is complicated even for a society of the United States. The many people who live here, some of which have come from many lands and nations, make our culture complex. The contrast of values between what people call the traditional way compared to those new to the historical aspects of U.S. human relationships takes its toll on many inhabitants in this complex society. However, we must understand that simply having relevant information does not mean we clearly understand this complexity. It does give us an advantage that is designed to help us in our leadership walk.

The GLOBE study is of particular importance because there is evidence to support interconnections national, organizational culture, and leadership attributes. Overall, we must understand that there are implications for global leaders in their attempt to influence people and groups from around the world, particularly if associated with an organization. Globalization is the trigger point that drives this cultural trait for leaders.

Glossary

Culture A set of rules, values, norms, symbols, beliefs, and traditions, which are learned and carried over from generation to generation.

Ethnocentrism A tendency for individuals to place their group (ethnic, racial, or cultural) at the center of their comments of others and the world.

Globalization A process by which the integration of government policies, cultures, social movements, and financial markets, facilitates the transfer of capital, goods, and services across national borders.

Prejudice A mostly fixed attitude, belief, or emotion held by an individual about another person or group based on faulty or unsubstantiated data.

Slave A person held in bondage of another.

References

Baptist, E. E. (2016). *The half has never been told: Slavery and the making of American capitalism*. New York, NY: Basic Books.

Blassingame, J. W. (1972). *The slave community: Plantation life in the Antebellum South*. New York, NY: Oxford University Press.

Genoverse, E. D. (1972). *Roll, Jordan, roll: The world of slaves made*. New York, NY: Pantheon.

Healey, J. F., & Stepnick, A. (2017). *Diversity & society: Race, ethnicity, and gender*. (5th ed.). Los Angeles, CA: Sage.

Held, D., & McGrew, A. (2002). *Globalization/Anti-Globalization: Beyond the great divide*. Malden, MA: Polity Press.

Hofstede, G. (1980). *Culture's consequences: International differences in work-related values.* Beverly Hills, CA: Sage publications.

House, R. J., Hanges, P. J., Javidan, M., Dorfman, P. W., & Gupta, V. (Eds.). (2004). *Culture, leadership and organizations: The GLOBE study of 62 societies.* Thousand Oaks, CA: Sage Publications, Inc.

Meltzer, M. (1993). *Slavery: A world history.* Chicago, IL: Da Cape Press, Inc.

Nohria, N., & Khurana, R. (2010). *Handbook of leadership theory and practice: A Harvard business school centennial colloquium.* Boston, MA: Harvard Business Review Press.

Northouse, P. G. (2016). *Leadership: Theory and practice.* (7th ed.). Los Angeles, CA: Sage.

Omi, M., & Winant, H. (1994). *Racial formation in the United States from the 1960s to the 1980s.* New York, NY: Routledge & Kegan Paul.

Quintard, T. (2000). *The African-American experience: A history of black Americans.* Unpublished.

Robertson, R. (1992). *Globalization: Social theory and global culture.* London: Sage.

Ross, L. F. (2012). *Leadership: So what makes you think you can lead.* Philadelphia, PA: Xlibris Publishers.

Schein, E. H. (2017). *Organizational culture and leadership.* (5th ed.). San Francisco, CA: Jossey-Bass.

Tylor, E. B. (2016a). *Primitive culture volume I.* New York, NY: Dover Publishers.

Tylor, E. B. (2016b). *Primitive culture volume II.* New York, NY: Dover Publishers.

White, D. G. (1985). *Aren't I a woman? Female slaves in the plantation south.* New York, NY: Norton.

Witt, J. (2016). *SOC.* (4th ed.). New York, NY: McGraw-Hill Education.

Yukl, G. (2012). *Leadership in organizations* (8th ed.). Upper Saddle River, NJ: Prentice Hall.

Chapter 4

Leadership Skill-Building Exercise

Social Leadership Skill-set

Social Leadership Skill-set

There is no doubt that culture has an impact on social skill development. This Leadership Sill-Building Exercise is designed to make you aware of your social skills. I suggest that you be honest answering the question, because there are no right or wrong answer.

Step 1. This questionnaire contains statements about Social Leadership potential. Using the scoring system below, you are asked to place a checkmark in the box that represents how you feel about each statement:

- Totally Agree (TA)
- Mostly Agree (MA)
- Neutral (N)
- Mostly Disagree (MD)
- Totally Disagree (TD)

Again, you will want to be honest in that this tool is only as good as the quality of your answers. Some skills you will be good at while others not. The hope is that the ones you are not good at, you can get help working on the skills to make you a better leader. In other words, this will help you to reflect on your strengths and areas that need improvement. You do not have to be in a leadership position to participate in this exercise. However, if not acting in leadership, manager, or supervisor position, you should still complete the activity. You may also be able to relate the questions to something similar in your environment.

	Social Leadership Skill-set	TA	MA	N	MD	TD
1.	I can feel what others feel and will walk in their shoes if I need to provide an example of my concern.					
2.	People see me as a change agent, able to predict what needs to change and motivate others to participate in the process.					

	Social Leadership Skill-set	TA	MA	N	MD	TD
3.	I am not rigid in my ability to adapt to changes. Being flexible is a hallmark of my leadership ability in that adjusting my leadership skills to support organizational goals is key to my performance.					
4.	I connect with each member of the group, and they see me as a coach who can communicate and resolved conflicts with ease. I serve as the go-between to mediate conflicts.					
5.	I welcome other's opinions even those whom I may not want to identify with in various situations.					
6.	I have the ability to lessen the impact of the change in my organization through my communications skills with my group.					
7.	Adapting to change does not alter my personal values and desires. My ethical behavior stands firm regardless of the situations placed in front of me.					
8.	When challenged to facilitate organizational change, I make a concerted effort to communicate every precise detail so that group members can also meet the challenged.					
9.	Learning from others to enhance their lives is one of my trademarks.					
10.	To react to various challenges or difficulties in the organization, I must understand my group's principles and desires as generated by their ideas.					
11.	I can change or adapt my behavior if need be to keep my group from failing and also help them develop themselves.					
12.	Communicating direction in words and deeds is the underpinning of vision. However, teaching and guiding the group to comprehend the purpose to accomplish the vision fully is essential.					
13.	One must relate to people to understand their approach to achieving an objective.					
14.	I can articulate how group members will respond to change because I understand not only what's essential to, or persuades them.					

	Social Leadership Skill-set	TA	MA	N	MD	TD
15.	I have good instincts which tell me how to respond to new situations. To find a concrete solution, I often realize that it is healthier to think the problem out thoroughly.					
16.	I recognize the importance of listening to group members carefully to facilitate using their ideas into the plan so that the vision becomes ours.					
17.	I make a concerted effort to ensure group members understand the culture of the organization through various techniques.					
18.	I recognize that core values are important and it is essential that I aligned my values with the core values of the organization.					
19.	I participate in events designed to share knowledge and learning.					
20.	I wholeheartedly agree with fostering an open culture.					
21.	I completely understand the motivation of myself to the point of being able to instill healthy habits in others.					
22.	I am considered being forward looking to the point of knowing the dreams and aspirations of others.					
23.	I can challenge myself and others to push the limits to change the social condition for which we are placed.					
24.	I realized that leadership is everyone's business and I always moves forward to facilitate that argument or process.					
25.	I like making others feel powerful and have no problems with relinquishing my power in the process.					
	Add the total number of checkmarks in each column:					

Source: Adapted from http://www.nwlink.com/~donclark/leader/social_leader_survey.html

Step 2. Using the tallied checkmarks above, multiple each column total by the assigned number below (12, 9, 6, 3, or 0):

1. Sum the responses for "Totally Agree (TA)" multiple by 12 = Score _____
2. Sum the responses for "Mostly Agree (MA)" multiple by 9 = Score _____
3. Sum the responses for "Neutral (N)" multiple by 6 = Score _____
4. Sum the responses for "Mostly Disagree (MD)" multiple by 3 = Score _____
5. Sum the responses for +Totally Disagree (TD)" multiple by 0 = Score zero

Step 3. Add all five columns totals to establish your final score _________. Looking at the chart below, you will find your social leadership skill-set. Be prepared to discuss with your instructor your next course of action.

270–300	Excellent social leadership skill-set
225–269	Good social leadership skill-set
150–224	Average social leadership skill-set
Below 150	Low social leadership skill-set

© Syda Productions/Shutterstock.com

Sociology of Leadership

Thinking Critically!

1. What are prejudice and discrimination and how do they operate today in society?
2. Is there an illusion that the glass has already been shattered because women have climbed to top-level positions?
3. What is the impact on minorities when it comes to the glass-ceiling debate?
4. To what extent do race and ethnicity influence the opportunities you have or the obstacles you face to become a leader, manager, or supervisor.
5. Who makes a better leader male or female?
6. Lastly, can you imagine a world in which racial classification had no importance? Why or why not?

Chapter 5

- Race, Ethnicity, and Gender Leadership
- Exploring the Leadership Styles of Racial Groups
- The Development of Racial Justice
- Gender Leadership

As You Read

- What will it take to elect a woman President of the United States?
- What is Race?
- What are the consequences of race and ethnicity for leadership opportunities?
- What is racism?

Chapter 5

Race, Ethnicity, and Gender Leadership

© Hogan Imaging/Shutterstock.com

The first responsibility of a leader is to define reality. The last is to say thank you. In between, the leader is a servant.

Max Depree

There is no argument that humans come in a range of colors and shapes. When we break down the concept of ***race***, we need to understand that it is a unique group of people with inherited physical characteristics that distinguish it from another group, whereas in contrast to race, we discern that ***ethnicity or ethnic group*** refers to cultural characteristics or shared cultural heritage. In other words, their sense of belonging may center on their country or ancestry and cultural tradition, which include, but may not be limited to language, music, religion, clothing, distinctive foods, family names, and relationships. The concept race continues to create problems in society. As Omi and Winant (1994) suggest, social actors become inserted into a structure permeated with social meanings that affect how we comprehend, explain, and act in the world. However, people have a tendency to confuse the terms race and ethnic group. Nevertheless, race continues to play an essential role in shaping and representing the social world in our society. People tend to classify each other racially based on physical characteristics such as facial features, hair texture, skin color, and body shape. When sociologists address race and ethnicity concepts, they go a bit further and talk about minority and dominant groups.

Sociologist Wirth (1945) defined a ***minority group*** as people singled out for unequal treatment and who regard themselves as objects of collective discrimination. Sociologists point to those who do the discriminating as the ***dominant group***, for this is the group that has the significant power and privilege in society. For example, according to the U.S. Census, in the year 2050, Hispanics will have the majority, but they will not be the dominant group because of lack of power in society. Notably, some laws protect minorities from discrimination. These laws appear under various Federal statutes. For example, Ross (2012) posits that Equal Employment Opportunity (EEO) laws are designed to protect minority groups from discrimination. Leadership in organizations plays a significant role when it comes to EEO laws because they are charged with the enforcement of these statutes specifically in and outside the Federal government. Overall, The Equal Employment Opportunity Commission enforces EEO laws. Nevertheless, can we say that there is a difference when it comes to male or female leadership? What happens when you through race into gender equation?

African American Leadership

During a review of history, you will find documented studies on leadership and the development of leadership theories that has its primary focus on Caucasian males, particularly if you go back to mid-1800 to early 1900. However, as one moves forward through history, you will see the emergence of African American leadership (Walters and Smith, 1999). For example, there is biographic literature on African Americans leaders like Frederick Douglass and Martin Luther King, Jr. (civil rights reformers), Nat Turner (famous slave insurrectionist—rebellion in 1831), Harriet Tubman (led slaves to freedom), Booker T. Washington, W. E. B. Du Bois (educational reformers), Frederick Douglass (a national leader of the abolitionist movement in Massachusetts and New York), to Barack H. Obama, Jesse Jackson, and Malcolm X (political leaders with charisma).

African Americans began their tenure in the United States as slaves. Nevertheless, as time moved on, African American leaders began to emerge, and with the help of liberal white American citizens, they began to realize their worth and intellect. As stated by Watson and Rosser (2010), "This realization brought about a change in the mindset of blacks in America" (p. 1). They go on to say that having a new frame of mind, African Americans began to take a stand against prejudices and injustices that beleaguered them. As a result, this allowed leadership in the African American community to emerge, in spite of the adversities the minority group faced. A review of African American leadership did not seem too materialized until after the civil rights during the 1960s.

In another twist to African American leadership, Collins and Makowsky (1993) state that Weber and Marx had a greater influence on the development of Du Bois thought and politics than the fin-de-siècle Social Darwinist climate of opinion. Famous Sociologists like Weber did characterize parts of Du Bois' work. However, the Marxist undercurrent of his writing comes out increasingly in his considerations of the African slave trade (1993). According to Du Bois, Frederick Douglass (1817–1895) is considered the first national black leader. However, others classified him as the leading abolitionist who escaped from slavery in 1838, and later became a writer and lecturer (1993). After the passing of Douglass in 1895, Booker T. Washington emerged as a charismatic leader who also became known as a great orator. Du Bois had both praise and criticism for Washington, but he did establish Alabama's Tuskegee Institute, which now serves as a major African American university.

Founded by Booker T. Washington in 1881, Tuskegee now acts as a historically black university. I had the pleasure of meeting several Tuskegee Airmen during a civil rights event for the U.S. Department of Agriculture, National Resources Conservation Service at our headquarters in Beltsville Maryland. During that time, I served as Chief of Investigations for the Civil Rights Division. Every year during the same period, we would hold a civil rights event to coincide with the Black History Month celebration. The month and year were February 2005, and the guests were members of the Tuskegee Airman. Several of these distinguished gentlemen lived in Hampton Virginia area. Astonished by the conversations that I had with them, I was just amazed by the stories they told of heroic leadership events. The two Tuskegee Airman movies that I have seen over the years correspond to the facts said to me by those wonderful patriots. Euphoric to meet them, I recognized the sacrifices that these and many others in uniform have made for our country. The point is this, African American leadership has played a significant role in the history and building of this great nation, and I could not be more proud.

Early leadership theories and styles excluded African Americans. For example, The Great Man Theory goes back to the year 1869 when racial tensions were widespread. Watson and Rosser (2010) posit that during that period, "the thought that a Negro could be a great man, a leader, was almost inconceivable" (p. 2). The argument put forth by commentators is that leadership of great man shapes history. Unfortunately, those Great Men named in history, articles, and studies are Caucasian (Bass, 1990). For example, Jews left Egypt because of the leadership of Moses, and the leadership of Winton Churchill inspired him to rally his nation not to give up during World War II. However, Bass (1990) goes a bit further in that:

> For the romantic philosophers, such as Friedrich Nietzsche, a sudden decision by a great man could alter the course of history (Thomas Jefferson's decision to purchase Louisiana, for example). To William James (1880), the mutations of society were due to a great man, who initiated movement and prevented others from leading society in another direction. The history of the world, according to James, is the history of Great Men; they created what the masses could accomplish. Carlyle's essay on heroes tended to reinforce the concept of the leader as a person who is endowed with unique qualities that capture the imagination of the masses. The hero would contribute somehow, no matter where he was found. Dowd maintained that "there is no such thing as leadership by the masses. The individuals in every society possess different degrees of intelligence, energy, and moral force, and in whatever direction the masses may be influenced to go, they are always led by the superior of few" (p. 37).

You learned in Chapter 2 that the overall argument for Great Man Theory is that leaders are born and not made. True, but not for a reason articulated by Great Man Theory in that I do have a news flash which is that everyone is born when they come to society, not just leaders. There is also research out there that considers the Great Man Theory's argument to be a myth and some previous Great Men (Lee Iacocca, John F. Kennedy, Douglas MacArthur) were found to be great people because of the situations that took placed during their leadership tenure (Cawthon, 1996; Northouse, 2016; Watson & Rosser, 2010). Put simply; situational leadership supports this notion because this theory is all about situational demands which will determine who will rise to the leadership position. Many also assert that educational scores and socioeconomic status may contribute to African Americans lack of leadership.

Bass (1990) argues that lower rates of achievements and leadership can be attributed to possible personal inborn deficits or educational or cultural deprivation. The many years of cultural conflict, coupled with discrimination also add to the problem. However, the advent of African American fraternities and sororities and the National Association for the Advancement of Colored People (NAACP) in the 1900s, helped give rise to the development of leadership for blacks. Those recognized Black Greek Letter Organizations and date of establishment include: Alpha Phi Alpha Fraternity, Inc. (1906), Alpha Kappa Alpha Sorority, Inc. (1908), Kappa Alpha Psi Fraternity, Inc. (1911), Delta Sigma Theta Sorority, Inc. (1913), Omega Psi Phi Fraternity, Inc. (1911), Phi Beta Sigma Fraternity, Inc. (1914), Zeta Phi Beta Sorority, Inc. (1920), Sigma Gamma Rho Sorority,

Inc. (1922), and Iota Phi Theta Fraternity (1963) (Cuyjet, 2006; Kimbrough, 2003; Kimbrough and Hutcheson, 1998).

Bass (1990) also states that early research tended to propose that stress created by marginality is likely to be a constraining effect on African American leaders. He also indicated that these leaders might lack contact to major networks and appreciation and encouragement from their superiors. In another twist in the conversation, Bernard Bass speculates that racial prejudice, a cultural background that stresses modesty, and the stereotype of Asians as passive and retiring, may all contribute to the reasons they are not found in leadership positions in higher numbers, despite their larger representation in the technical and professional fields (1990).

There is still that covert and overt racism that many African American leaders still feel even today in the 21st Century. Knight, Hebl, Foster, and Mannix (2003) suggest that society may be engaged in an aversive racism, a modern form of racism that avoids complete white supremacy while more insidiously rationalizing white dominance. They further state that it is perhaps the most difficult barrier for African American to conquer. However, Rosette, Leonardelli, and Phillips (2008) present another answer to the problem in that they identify the existence of negative racial bias and stereotypes. Overall, they believe that another mechanism may also be at play here in what they call "being white." In other words, race itself rather than stereotypes about race is part of the business leader sample, and this triggers organizations to see whites as the more likely choice for leadership positions. There is also other leadership research that suggests African Americans feel they are held to a higher standard. In an extensive study of white and black women leaders, some African American contributors described incidents of outright racism, indirect challenges to their authority, and being held to a higher standard (Bell & Nkomo, 2001; Hill-Davidson, 1987).

Exploring the Leadership Styles of Racial Groups

There is a host of research that compares the leadership styles of blacks and whites. For example, research conducted in the 1970s indicate that blacks are less likely to deploy harsh punishment than their white colleagues (Bass & Bass, 2008; Shull & Anthony, 1978). However, whites exhibited better human relation and administrative skills than blacks (Bass, 1990; Richards & Jaffee, 1972). Blacks lead differently than whites, and one of the reasons is the way they are perceived while being in charge. Ospina and Foldy (2009) supports this notion in that studies of predominantly white work environments document the constraints that leaders of the color face based on how others perceive them. They also assert that affirmative action policies alone are not enough to advance leaders of color to positions of power. There must be more programs that generate inclusive environments where diversity is valued, and people are prepared to learn from a different perspective. We must also note that when blacks are in charge of whites, they seem to be more considerate and less directive. However, when whites are in charge of whites or blacks, research indicates they are directive, although, one study reported that whites exhibit intimidation or coercion when dealing with blacks (Kipin, Silverman, & Copeland, 1973). When subordinates were mixed, there were no clear patterns associated with the leader. Overall, minority leaders intentionally and consciously draw on their racial identity to execute their leadership. As you learned in Chapter 3, leadership and identity are closely linked, and because leadership is a social process, one's identity and particularly his or her race/ethnicity are important for us to understand. However, other relevant articles investigated the leadership styles of Native Americans, Latinos, Asians, and African Americans.

According to Alston (2005), these leaders can turn mechanism of oppression into "effective vehicles for constructive change" (p. 677). In a system where race seems to matter when it comes to leadership, the above racial groups find the skill to turn their ethnic identity into a strength due in part that they are aware of how others perceive them. Bell (1990) also asserts that these minority leaders must be biculturally fluent in that they must be able to lead in ways that not only resonate with followers of their racial-ethnic group but also connect with the dominant means of working in their white-majority environments.

Native Americans lead with the notion that leadership is about creating and expanding a sphere of influence, rather than merely exercising authority. Native Americans are less likely to be placed in a position to lead in that there is no way of leading given enormous variation in tribal norms and traditions (Warner & Grint, 2006). In other words, the chances of being a leader are very slim in tribal communities. Moreover, Muller (1998), in his description of Native American women managers (Navajo), asserts that they "are not brought up to be assertive and competitive" which places them at a disadvantage (p. 12).

The Development and Support of Racial Justice

Prejudice and discrimination are facts of life in the United States. If I may also say, prejudice is an attitude whereas discrimination is an action because one singles out a person or persons for unfair treatment and this type of treatment is, to some degree, based on almost anything. For example, we have seen discrimination based on appearance, age, race-ethnicity, sex, height, weight, or disability. We also know that income, religion, or political beliefs are other common reasons for discrimination. However, in most organizations, leadership positions are typically chosen by the dominant group. The dominant group has more power and privileges and the higher social status as the minority group. Nevertheless, what might we stay about race at this point? We know and understand that Adolph Hitler tried to convince people that race, the inherited physical characteristics that identify a group of individuals, was a reality. In other words, he believed that a race called the Aryans was responsible for the cultural achievements of Europe, these tall, fair-skinned, mostly blond haired people, biologically superior, a super race destined to establish what he called a new world order. Although race remains a social reality, the ideas of racial superiority that justifies one group's rule over another may be less popular today than ever before. Furthermore, in modern biology, the pure race is a myth because people show so great a mixture of physical characteristics; skin color, hair texture, nose and head shapes, eye color, and just about everything else as far as the biological makeup, hence, the main reason why we live in a multicultural world. However, because the idea of race is so rooted in our culture, race is a social reality that social scientists must challenge.

Many of us build on and take pride in our racial and ethnic identities. There is evidence to support that our life chances, for the most part, is determined by our race and ethnicity. Keeleher et al. (2010) suggest that differences in racial or ethnic identity remain, and in some cases are growing, particularly in areas of well-being that include wealth, income, education, health, and even life expectancy. They also assert that these differences result in historical and current practices which produce and reproduce the racialized outcomes in a way that does not, to some extent, allow us to look into the old lens of race. Leadership can play a precarious role in either contributing to racial justice or supporting healthy patterns of racial inequality and execution in our society. There should be a change to facilitate the development of leadership programs that contribute to racial justice which in the end will support solutions to racial inequalities.

As Keeleher et al. (2010) make very clear, failure to pay attention to structural racism in leadership development programs and nonprofit leadership leaves several unchallenged issues that undermine the effectiveness and sustainability of community-based organizations and racial justice work. They identify some of these issues that may have an impact on racial justice:

- A disproportionate percentage of executive directors and board members who do not reflect the general population;
- The professionalization of nonprofit management in a way that overlooks the lack of connection between leaders and the communities they serve; and
- The unchallenged assumption that people of color can improve their leadership only as beneficiaries of highly prescriptive intervention from outside their communities, rather than from resources that support collective work and responsibility for self-determination in their cultural context (2010).

Leadership development programs must forge the way and continue to adapt approaches that rethink and retool practices to facilitate this process. Prior leadership thinking on race, to a large extent, centered on the following:

- Personal responsibility and individualism—The belief that people control their fates regardless of social position, and that individual behaviors and choices determine material outcomes.
- Mediocracy—The idea that resources and opportunities are distributed according to talent and effort, and that social components of "merit," such as access to inside information or powerful social networks, are of lesser importance or do not matter much.
- Equal opportunity—The belief that employment, education, and wealth accumulation areas are "level playing fields" and that race is no longer a barrier in these areas (2010).

We must also note that the dominant culture of the United States influences the values and beliefs associated with the current leadership philosophy and training.

Gender Leadership

Research on gender and leadership indicates good news for some and bad news for others. For example, Eagly (2007) notes that despite barriers, women are increasingly achieving positions of leadership and are effective the ones elevated to these posts.

For some particular reason, people not only prefer male bosses, but it is also still harder for women to be promoted into leadership roles than it is for men. Furthermore, research also indicates that women are not as effective leaders than men, and leadership hurdles are higher for women of color than white women and men, despite the advancement of women to Fortune 500 companies (Eagly & Carli, 2007; Holvino & Blake-Beard, 2004). Although corporate America has some female CEOs, the number is minuscule. For example, only 14% of the top five leadership positions at companies in the S&P 500 are held by women and progress is likely to continue to be slow (Egan, 2015).

The U.S. Bureau of Labor Statistics (2015) reported the following percentage of women in managerial positions by ethnicity: Whites 43%; African Americans 35%; Asians 49%; and Latinas, 26% (Table 5.1).

These percentages are up compared with previous years. The report also indicates that women occupy more managerial positions than men (42% compared to 35%). According to Chemers (1997), white male researchers tended to ignore democratic differences between the concepts of gender and race and its overall inequality in leadership. However, the study of these concepts is critical mainly because gender differences play a significant role in the workplace. One should note that this is evident because of the different number of women and men occupying key leadership positions, particularly CEO jobs in organizations. We have already discussed the fact that sex role socialization starts early in life. However, social learning theory argues that during that process, girls and boys learn the overall limits of their particular gender. It is the behaviors associated with women and men leadership styles that are important here.

Responses between women and men are different because of the way they influence and shape decisions as well as the outcomes employed by their particular leadership style. According to Groysberg (2013), the differences become more distinct in the leadership styles of women and men, which reflect the consequences of their actions and decisions as leaders. There is other evidence when women and men deal with specific tasks in various situations. In an examination of 201 Norwegian companies, researchers found that women and men do not differ in their ability to perform operational tasks, but when it came to strategic level decision-making tasks, women decisions are made based on sensitivity to others compared with men (2013). In a related development, women excelled in all but one category of leadership competencies including taking the initiative, practicing self-development, developing others, inspiring and motivating others, building relationships, teamwork, integrity/honesty, and driving results, during a leadership evaluation survey of 7,280 leaders (Folkman, 2012). The men edge out the women in only one category, developing a strategic viewpoint. However, why is it still so hard for women to shatter the glass ceiling? When African

Table 5.1 Employed women by management occupation, race, and Hispanic or Latino ethnicity, 2014 annual averages (Numbers in thousands)

		Percent of Total Employed			
Occupation	**Total Employed**	**White**	**Black or African American**	**Asian**	**Hispanic or Latino Ethnicity**
Management occupations	28, 931	43.2	34.7	46.7	26.1

Source: Adapted from U.S. Bureau of Labor Statistics (2015).

Americans saw their first black President of the United States, many women chanted that the next President would be Hillary Rodham Clinton with the expectation that the glass ceiling would be shattered forever. However, as you already know this did not happen in that Donald Trump was elected President of the United States in 2016. Now the question remains in that what will it take to elect a woman President of the United States?

Ely and Rhode (2010) assert that when women perform consistently and substantially above expectations in male-dominated context, their effectiveness may carry particular weight. Notwithstanding, this effect applies in particular to women of color, who routinely encounter lower expectations of competence. Another issue of concern is that women receive special scrutiny. In other words, research indicates even when a small group of women occupies prominent roles, they are subject to special scrutiny and polarized assessments (2010). There are those who believe that Hillary Clinton is a polarizing figure. Even winning the popular vote by over 3 million, she still failed to get the 270 votes in the Electoral College necessary to secure the presidency, not once, but twice. Can it be that the problems of women ascending to various leadership positions center on their overall style of leadership coupled with their effectiveness? Northouse (2016) suggests not, because he asserts that any substantial leadership style differences between women and men should not disadvantage women and can even offer a female advantage.

Chapter Summary

For years researchers have had problems with race or ethnicity because they rarely defined or operationalized the concepts adequately. We might also add that race became a part of our sociological and philosophical understanding as we struggled to analyze the impact of multicultural ideology on battles for equality in the domains of gender, race/ethnicity, and sexuality as a whole. Moreover, research indicates that race became a part of our culture and consciousness as people sought to distinguish themselves or attempted to separate one another. As people became more cynical about their attitudes about race, arguments begin to ensue, thereby causing disconnections among the individuals in society. We have seen an accumulation of this disconnection during the 2016 general election, as we have seen more race problems since the period associated with the civil rights movement. There are those who would like to elevate the differences between blacks and whites when it comes to values, socioeconomic background, and intelligence. However, should we because as President Barack Obama once said "there is not a liberal America, and a conservative, there is the United States of America. There is no a black America and white America and Latino America, and Asian America—there's the United States of America." Think about how unique this would be if we all believe this to be true in our hearts. Although sociologists take into consideration the social reality of race, the connection to leadership is very clear. Race shapes individuals' psychological makeup, but it is also an intrinsic part of their collective identities, connected to the larger social structures within which leadership emerges. However, leaders must be able to recognize their limits in these environments, and if they can, leading becomes more successful. We can learn a great deal regarding race/ethnicity and leadership and the overall differences in leadership styles and effectiveness. One must be cognizant of their leadership style when leading others regardless of their race because it is an important human source function.

Although women continue to make progress by ascending to top-level positions in many corporations, when can society see its first woman President of the United States? Is there an illusion that the glass ceiling is not broken because women have climbed to some top-level positions? Do women still see this as a problem when it comes to leadership positions? Overall, there is a gender gap when it comes to leadership. And, because most of the findings regarding female leaders stem from culturally distinct roles of women in society, there is a generalization well across cultures in which the roles of women and men differ (Northouse, 2016). In this case, women can clearly differentiate themselves from people who will, in the end, lead men to accept them as leaders; hence, breaking the glass ceiling forever.

Glossary

Race A group of people with inherited physical characteristics that distinguish it from another group.

Ethnicity or Ethnic Group Refers to cultural characteristics or shared cultural heritage.

Minority Group People who are singled out for unequal treatment and who regard themselves as objects of collective discrimination.

Dominate Group This is the group that has the greater power and privilege.

References

Alston, J. A. (2005). Tempered radicals and servant leaders: Black females persevering in the superintendency. *Educational Administration Quarterly*, 41(4), 675–688.

Bass, B. M. (1990). *Bass & stogdill's handbook leadership: Theory, research, & managerial applications.* (3rd ed.). New York, NY: The Free Press.

Bass, B. M., & Bass, R. (2008). The *Bass handbook leadership: Theory, research, & managerial applications.* (4th ed.). New York, NY: Free Press.

Bell, E. I. (1990). The bicultural life experiences of career-oriented black women. *Journal of Organizational Behavior*, 11, 459–477.

Bell, E. I., & Nkomo, S. M. (2001). *Our separate ways: Black and white women and the struggle for professional identity.* Cambridge, MA: Harvard Business School Press.

Cawthon, D. L. (1996). Leadership: The great man theory revisited. *Business Horizons*, 10, 44–48.

Chemers, M. (1997). *An integrative theory of leadership.* Mahwah, NJ: Erlbaum.

Collins, R., & Makowsky, M. (1993). *The discovery of society.* (5th ed.). New York, NY: McGraw-Hill, Inc.

Cuyjet, M. J. (2006). *African American men in college.* San Francisco, CA: Jossey-Bass.

Eagly, A. H. (2007). Female leadership advantage and disadvantage: Resolving the contradictions. *Psychology of Women Quarterly*, 31, 1-12. DO1:10.1111/j.1471-6402.2007.00326.x

Eagly, A. H., & Carli, L. L. (2007). *Through the labyrinth: The truth about how women become leaders.* Boston, MA: Harvard Business School Press.

Egan, M. (2015). *Still missing: Female business leaders.* Retrieved from http://money.cnn.com/2015/03/24/investing/female-ceo-pipeline-leadership/

Ely, R. J., & Rhode, D. L. (2010). Women and leadership: Defining the challenges. In N. Nohria, & R. Khurana. (Eds.), *Handbook of leadership theory and practice: A Harvard business school centennial colloquium*. Boston, MA: Harvard Business Press.

Folkman, Z. (2012). A study in leadership: Women do it better than men. Retrieved from http://www.zengerfolkman.com/media/articles/ZFCo.WP.WomenBetterThanMen.033012.pdf

Groysberg, B. (2013). Gender differences in leadership styles and the impact with corporate boards. Retrieved from http://www.cpahq.org/cpahq/cpadocs/Genderdiffe.pdf

Hill-Davidson, L. (1987). Black women's leadership. *Signs: Journal of Women in Culture and Society*, 12(2), 381–385.

Holvino, E. & Black-Beard, S. (2004). Women discussing their differences: A promise trend. *The Diversity Factor*, 12(3), 1-7.

James, W. (1880). Great men, great thoughts, and their environment. *Atlantic Monthly*, 46, 441-459.

Keeleher, T., Leiderman, S. Meehan, D., Perry, E., Potapchuk, M, Powell, J. A., & Yu, H. C. (2010). Leadership & Race: How to develop and support leadership that contributes to racial justice. Retrieved from http://leadershiplearning.org/system/files/Leadership%20and%20Race%20FINAL_Electronic_072010.pdf

Kimbrough, W. M. (2003). *Black Greek 101: The culture, customs, and challenges of black fraternities and sororities*. New Jersey, NJ: Fairleigh Dickinson University Press.

Kimbrough, W. M., & Hutcheson, P. (1998). The impact of membership in Black Greek-letter organizations on Black students' involvement in collegiate activities and their development of leadership skills. *The Journal of Negro Education*, 67, 96–115.

Kipin, D., Silverman, A., & Copeland, C. (1973). The effects of emotional arousal on the use of supervised coercion with black and union members. *Journal of Applied Psychology*, 57, 38–43.

Knight, J. L., Hebl, M. R., Foster, J. H., & Mannix, L. M. (2003). Out of role? Out of luck: The influence of race and leadership status on performance appraisals. *Journal of Leadership and Organizational Studies*, 9(3), 85–93.

Muller, H. J. (1998). American Indian women managers: Living in two worlds. Journal of Management Inquiry, 17, 4-28. DO1:10.1177/105649269871002

Northouse, P. G. (2016). *Leadership: Theory and practice*. (7th ed.). Los Angeles, CA: Sage.

Omi, M., & Winant, H. (1994). *Racial formation in the United States: From the 1960s to the 1990s*. New York, NY: Routledge.

Ospina, S., & Foldy, E. (2009). A critical review of race and ethnicity in the leadership literature: Surfacing context, power and the collective dimensions of leadership. *The Leadership Quarterly*, 20, 875–896.

Richards, S. A., & Jaffee, C. L. (1972). Blacks supervising whites: A study of interracial difficulties in working together in a simulated organization. *Journal of Applied Psychology*, 56, 234–240.

Rosette, A. S., Leonardelli, G. J., & Phillips, K. K. (2008). The white standard: Racial bias in leader categorization. *Journal of Applied Psychology*, 93(4), 758–777.

Ross, L. F. (2012). *Leadership: So what makes you think you can lead*. Philadelphia: Xlibris Publishers.

Shull, F., & Anthony, W. P. (1978). Do black and white supervisory problem-solving styles differ? *Personnel Psychology*, 31, 761–782.

U.S. Bureau of Labor Statistics. (2015). Women in the labor force: A databook. Retrieved from https://www.bls.gov/opub/reports/womens-databook/archive/women-in-the-labor-force-a-databook-2015.pdf

Walters, R., & Smith, R. (1999). *African American leadership*. South Carolina: SUNY.

Warner, I. S., & Grint, K. (2006). American Indian ways of leading and knowing. *Leadership*, 21(2), 225–244.

Watson, A. C., & Rosser, M. (2010). The emergence of Africa-American leaders in American society. Retrieved from http://www.leadershipeducators.org/Resources/Documents/Conferences/FortWorth/Watson.pdf

Wirth, L. (1945). The problem of minority groups. In. R. Linton (Ed.), *The science of man in the world crisis*. New York, NY: Columbia University Press.

Chapter 5

Leadership Skill-Building Exercise

Leadership Behavior Skill-set

Leadership Behavior Skill-Set

The leadership behavior skill-set will give you data about your task and people orientation. You are asked to complete the exercise and have three people you know to fill out the exercise thinking about you in the process.

Step 1. The Leadership Skill-Building Exercise is designed to assess your leadership behavior. You will need to carefully evaluate the statements below and circle one of the five numbers to the right of each statement based on these criteria:

- Never = 1
- Rarely = 2
- Sometimes = 3
- Frequently = 4
- Always = 5

	Authentic Leadership Skill-Set					
1.	I communicate to team members the requirements for the job.	1	2	3	4	5
2.	I am friendly with members of the team.	1	2	3	4	5
3.	I set the criteria for job performance of team members.	1	2	3	4	5
4.	I help members of the team to feel comfortable.	1	2	3	4	5
5.	I offer recommendations to solve problems.	1	2	3	4	5
6.	I reply positively to recommendations made by others.	1	2	3	4	5
7.	I make my views very clear to others.	1	2	3	4	5
8.	I treat people fair.	1	2	3	4	5
9.	I develop a course of action for the team.	1	2	3	4	5
10.	I perform in a likely manner toward team members.	1	2	3	4	5
11.	I define the duties for each members.	1	2	3	4	5

12.	I converse vigorously with team members.	1	2	3	4	5
13.	I clarify my role within the team.	1	2	3	4	5
14.	I demonstrate my concern for the happiness of others.	1	2	3	4	5
15.	I offer a plan to accomplish work.	1	2	3	4	5
16.	I am flexible in making decisions.	1	2	3	4	5
17.	I set the standards for the team.	1	2	3	4	5
18.	I reveal my views and feelings to team members.	1	2	3	4	5
19.	I inspire team members to do good work.	1	2	3	4	5
20.	I help team members get along by dispelling conflict.	1	2	3	4	5

Source: Adapted from Northouse (2016).

Step 2. You measure two major types of leadership behaviors: task and relationship. To articulate the score, you will first need to sum the responses on the odd-numbered items. Enter that total number below under task. Next, tally up the even-numbered items, and this will become the relationship score.

Totals: Task Score _______ and Relationship Score ______

45–50	Very high range
40–44	High range
35–39	Moderately broad range
30–34	Somewhat small range
25–29	Low range
10–24	Very low range

Step 3. Looking at the scoring interpretation above, conduct your assessment of self as follows: According to Northouse (2016), the task score refers to the degree to which you help others by defining their roles and letting them know what is expected of them. He also states that the score you receive for a relationship is a measure of the degree to which you try to make subordinates feel comfortable with themselves, each other, and the team itself. Through a compare and contrast analysis, you can have others feel this out about you. Overall, this will give you more analysis about self.

Chapter 6

- Leadership and Social Groups
- How Sociologists view Social Group Leadership?
- Social Group Phenomenon
- The Sociological Theory Connection

As You Read

- Define group interaction?
- What does leadership have to do with group formation?
- What is the difference between primary and secondary groups?
- What would sociologists think of social group leadership?

Sociology of Leadership

Thinking Critically!

1. Is it important to have groupthink?
2. Make a list of how you spend each hour of a typical day? How much time in the day is spent entirely by yourself or with a group?
3. Remembering that a group is two or more individuals who interact with one another and are together physically at the same location, and break your groups down to primary or secondary. Which group do you think is more effective? Explain your position.
4. On the basis of your interaction with the group, which ones involve conflict or competition?
5. Leaders must show that they can draw people and develop relationships around a common purpose. Why is this so important for leadership? Do you think that working as a group helps you more or leadership? Explain!

Chapter 6

Leadership and Social Groups

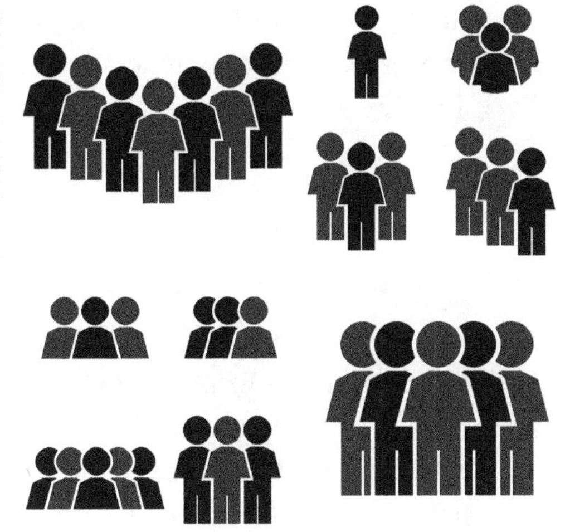
© Yafeto/Shutterstock.com

The key to successful leadership today is influence, not authority.

Kenneth Blanchard

If one who claims to be a leader looks behind him or herself and no one is following, then one cannot pretend to be a leader (Ross, 2012). From a micro-sociological perspective, there must be an interaction between a leader and a follower. The ability to influence one's behavior is mutual between the leader and the follower. In other words, leaders affect the behavior of followers and followers change the behavior of leaders. Looking at it another way, one can say that leadership is a two-way affair because you cannot have one without the other, and without followers, there can be no leader. Although we don't need to hit this too hard, leadership involves followers being willing to obey its leaders. Therefore, leadership is about member's cooperation and support. If a leader communicates a threat or attempts to use force, he or she will find himself or herself not being a leader for long. We will always place leadership with a particular task or situation.

Leadership is the ability to organize a group of people to achieve a common purpose. Two or more people interacting is considered a group with each other sharing similar characteristics, and collectively have a sense of unity. In other words, they perceive themselves as belonging to the group and can distinguish between members and nonmembers. Leaders suffer in isolation and the more they understand group structure, the better they can position themselves to lead the organization. For example, religious groups are an excellent example of social groups. They are often larger groups that all share a common identity. Although the members of a religious group share something in common (the religious organization), they also identify with each other as members of that group. As a member, one can expect to behave in a certain way, and it is the leader who may articulate what that behavior may be for the group. Humans associate with groups for several reasons. First, groups protect people from human and nonhuman dangers and second, groups can help people with resources, sharing responsibility for obtaining food, clothing, and shelter. When people associate with a group, this helps them to accomplish all tasks quickly and more efficiently.

Division of Labor

It is the groups that make the division of labor possible. In primitive societies, it was sex and age that made the division of labor possible. However, in modern societies, it is centered on one's specialization because, at this point, the division of labor is very complex. The family is one of the groups that individuals rely on for material and psychological support in modern societies. We already know that social isolation is linked to suicide, to the mental problems of the aged, and to schizophrenia. It was Emile Durkheim (1897), in his famous piece *Suicide*, who concluded that the main reason for attempting or committing suicide was a lack of involvement in groups.

Defining Social Groups

During conversations, we sometimes use the group to describe any collection of people ranging in size from three to several million, our families, our classes, members of our organization, or even to specify units in the military. However, sociologists use four different terms to make important distinctions among all of these. Sociologists distinguish among groups, aggregates, collectivities, and social categories. Again, a social group is two or more people who interact regularly and identify with one another (Mills, 1967). According to Merton (1957), when one belongs to a social group, the person is not only able to distinguish members from nonmembers, but one can also expect certain kinds of behavior from its members versus those who are outside the group. Simply put, as a result of this interaction, the members of the social group feel a shared or common sense of belonging. However, a group differs from an ***aggregate***, referred to a collection of people who just happen to be in the same location at the same time, such as passengers on a bus/train or a crowd on the street. In contrast, people in the aggregate do not interact to any significant degree and do not feel any shared sense of belonging. Aggregates are a potential ***collectivity*** in that it is a temporary collection of people who are interacting in response to a particular stimulus. An example would be people who gather because of a car accident. The people who gather around the scene of the crash would no longer be part of an aggregate but would be a collectivity. They would engage in conversation to ascertain what happens, share information and observations, and may help the injured or call the police and ambulance. Their interaction is centered on the immediate situation, and when everything has been completed in regards to the accident or ceases, the interaction stops. A group also differs from a ***category***. A category is some people who may never have met one another but who may share similar characteristics such as age, race, or sex. They can also be women, men, high-school students, teachers, musicians, and elderly. Social scientists often use categories in research when they want to see if there is any correlation between the correlation, income and political attitudes, mental health, and urban residence as an example. However, we need to understand that categories are just an idea in that the individuals involved do not necessarily interact with one another in any ongoing way, nor are they aware of belonging to a group. For example, blue-collar workers might complain about their ability to make ends meet, but feel that they may not necessarily have anything in common with teachers, who also earn relatively low wages, and they too cannot make ends meet. It is these categories that serve as a recruiting tool for groups. As with aggregates and collectivities, categories only become groups when individuals become aware of their likeness and start to interact on a regular basis. Again, this will only happen when people identify with or share a special interest, special characteristic, or a particular problem.

Social Group Formation

No one can live without some sense of belonging and identification with other people. Almost everyone in society participates in a social group, and the reason is that a human being is a social creature. In other words, people are social animals who live in and associate with social groups. Therefore, a social group is a collection of human beings who are involved in a social relationship with others for a shared goal under a respective set of codes. Sociologists posit that it is not surprising that we join in couples, families, military platoons, churches, businesses, sports clubs, political parties, and numerous large organizations. When formed, social groups are composed of individuals who share awareness of joint membership founded on shared experiences, loyalties, and interests. It is about "we" belonging to this particular group. One might argue in the broadest sense that everyone in society belongs to one large social group. For example, Americans have a social identity from Koreans. However, sociologists do not consider an entire community to be a social group, because most of its people do not know each other personally or interact with one another on a regular basis.

Leaders must show that they can draw people and develop relationships around a common purpose. As a student, you might want to form a social group to share notes to study for an exam and serve as the leader by recommending the time and place to make this event happen and take charge in other ways. It is important for leaders who are running social groups or organizations to provide structure, clarify norms, build cohesiveness, and promote standards of excellence (Northouse, 2014). One of the best ways to accomplish this is by having someone in charge who will lead the group and not only provide this structure but also establish rules and regulations that will accumulate into norms.

As a result of the interaction that takes place among members, a group develops an internal structure. There are boundaries associated with every group, and these may come in the form of norms, values, and interrelated statuses and roles, such as those of the leader, followers, and others who play a particular role in the group. However, in some groups, this structure is rigid and explicit, and members may hold official positions, and values and norms may be embodied in written objectives and rules. On the flip side, some groups may be much more flexible; values and norms may be vague and shifting, and statuses and roles may be subject to negotiations and change.

Primary Group

Charles Horton Cooley coined the term ***primary group*** do describe a small intimate group of people who relate to one another to direct, for example, family activities (Cooley, 1929). The primary group is the nucleus of all social groups. However, Cooley wanted to distinguish this group from what he called a secondary group, which we will discuss later. The core difference between the primary and the secondary group lies in the quality of relationships between members and the degree of personal involvement.

Cooley applied the term primary group to social groups because they were among the first group people experienced in life. We considered these people as having a primary relationship. They meet face-to-face with the overall goal of helping each other. They also meet for companionship in an attempt to work on mutually agreed upon goals. They have strong and personal loyalties to its members, spending lots of time together. Put simply, getting to know each other very well and showing genuine concern for one's welfare is the hallmark of a primary group. Primary groups are also central to our social identity, which is why members always think of themselves as "we." Moreover, the strength of primary relationships gives the personal a great comfort and security, which is clearly evident in individual performance.

Primary groups are small because scores of people are unable to relate to one another directly and personally. For example, two, four, or even six people can carry on a single conversation, but bigger than that direct interaction personally involving everyone becomes virtually impossible (Berelson & Steiner, 1967). The characteristics of a primary group are physical proximity, small size, personal relationship, continuity of relationship, the intensity of shared interest, the similarity of background, as well as the stability of the group.

Secondary Group

For the most part, a secondary group is typically large. However, it can also be small in some aspects. The group is goal-oriented and consists of some people who interact on a relatively temporary, anonymous, and impersonal basis. The members come together for a particular reason or practical purpose as a means to an end. Notably, this could be coworkers or some political organization, which has a limited face-to-face contact. Secondary relationship involved little personal knowledge and weak emotional ties. In some cases, some people may work in an office for decades with some coworkers, but a more typical example of the secondary relationship is the students in a college course who may not see one another after the semester ends. The bottom line is that the different characteristics that describe primary groups apply to secondary groups. The overall coordination of secondary groups tends to divert the focus of social interaction from personal matters to jointly beneficial cooperation.

How do Sociologists view Social Group Leadership?

To address this, we must first address the three main sociological theories and their view of leadership; functionalism, conflict, and social interactionist theory:

1. **Functionalism—**Emile Durkheim would say that leaders are measured by their ability to influence others in the group. From a functionalist perspective, it is recommended that one examines the group's values and behavior, particularly the group's leader to get an understanding of the leader's impact on the group. However, one must realize that successful groups often have successful leaders.
2. **Conflict**—Karl Marx would argue that bureaucracy was set up as a means to exploit workers and allow the bourgeoisie to continue to gain wealth. We can put forth an argument that democratic leadership styles will increase employee productivity. If a democratic environment is not implemented, then bureaucracy can end up stifling the employee and organization, which will lead to low productivity with the understanding that greater participation in leadership roles does not mean the organization will succeed.

3. **Symbolic Interactionism**—The great George Herbert Mead and Charles Horton Cooley posit that people are social products and those who have jobs would develop attitudes toward their jobs, which have an overall impact on productivity and job satisfaction. Along with leadership, the personal position has a huge effect on job performance and satisfaction. However, people have a tendency to feel good about themselves and their jobs when they feel some degree of control over their actions, and it is the liberal work environment that allows this to happen. In other words, this helps the worker to feel connected to their jobs.

One element that is always present in groups will be leadership. In other words, leadership is one of the vital components of group dynamics. Although social groups vary in the extent to which they designate one or more members as leaders, it is the responsibility of those members to elect someone to serve as their leader to direct their activities. For example, some friendship groups may never grant anyone the apparent status as a leader. However, within families, we can surmise that parents share leadership responsibilities, although husband and wife sometimes disagree about who is really in charge. We might also add that secondary groups, such as a business office, we might find that leadership is likely to involve formal status with clearly defined roles.

Sticking with the family for a moment, traditional cultural patterns confer leadership on the parents, though often on the male as head of household if two or more spouses are in the home. In other cases when forming friendship groups, one or more persons may slowly emerge as leaders, even though there is characteristically no formal process of selection. In larger secondary groups, leaders are frequently and officially chosen through election or recruitment.

There is no argument that leaders are people with unusual personal ability, but research has failed to produce consistent evidence that there is such a category as "natural born leaders." There are no set personal qualities that all leaders have in common, and this is the primary reason why leadership is so complex. Rather, virtually anyone may be recognized as a leader depending on the particular needs of a group (Northouse, 2016; Ridgeway, 1983).

A leader is someone who, to a large extent by certain personality characteristics, is consistently able to influence the behavior of others. Groups have leaders even if the leaders do not hold formal positions of authority and even if the group is determined not to have a leader. As group size increases, so do the problems of coordinating decisions and activities. A group leader can emerge in many ways and for a variety of reasons. However, this will depend on group needs, but again, and in all cases, a leader has the ability, the power, to influence the way people behave in the group. A leader can do this because of his or her ability bring people together, directing various types of communications (technology dependent), coordinating activities, settling disputes, and making decisions.

Although all groups and organizations have leaders, not all leaders have the same role and function with the group. The two scholars in small group leadership were Bales (1953), and Slater (1955) who uncovered two kinds of leaders who play different roles within the group. A leader performs two essential functions: directing activities and making group decisions (**instrumental leadership**), and creating harmony and ensuring that all members are rather happy (**expressive leadership**). In other words, the instrumental leader has the capability to organize the group in pursuit of its goals whereas the expressive leader creates coherence and solidarity among its members. Although group members look to instrumental leaders to get things done, it is the expressive leaders who provide the collective well-being of the group. Expressive leaders are less concerned with the performance goals of a group than they are with providing emotional support. However, these leaders do attempt to lessen tension and conflict among them. We should also note that one person cannot fill both of these roles (instrumental and expressive) at the same time. Making sure everyone performs his or her task may interfere with encouraging and creating harmonious relationships within the group. Heap (1977) posits that there are usually two or more leaders in a group to help facilitate this activity; again the instrumental and the expressive leader.

Although a successful group will need both of these leaders in the group, groups that have only instrumental leaders are likely to be overwhelmed in conflict and lose their corporate identity. The group members may also feel that their leaders are insensitive to their concerns and cease to cooperate or participate in the group endeavors. On the flip side, groups having only expressive leaders may get along well but never get anything done. Even various tasks are not accomplished, thus threatening the group's very existence. The bottom line is that a group needs both types of leadership to be efficient and rarely will you find both in one individual with one well-known exception (Franklin Roosevelt).

Franklin Roosevelt is sometimes cited as an example, because as an instrumental leader, he developed a plan relieve us of the Great Depression. He also got more legislation passed through Congress in first 100 days in office than any of his predecessors did. As an expressive leader, President Roosevelt soothed people with his fireside chats, assuring them that "The only thing we have to fear is fear itself." Most leaders are clearly one or the other. Ronald Reagan and Barack Obama were known as great communicators. However, President Reagan couldn't keep his facts straight and left important decisions to subordinates. President Obama was just the opposite in that according to the Gallup poll, he was always willing to make hard decisions and is characterized as a strong and decisive leader. Both were clearly expressive leaders. Jimmy Carter and Richard Nixon, who planned and analyzed just about everything and failed to inspire much besides public distrust and ridicule, were examples of instrumental leaders.

There is clear evidence that leaders tend to direct groups toward activities in which the leaders themselves excel, the way a leader leads a group's activities is often as important as what he or she influences the group to do. In studies with groups of boys, White and Lippitt (1960) found that groups with permissive or laissez-faire leaders could not seem to get organized. They go on to say that autocratic leaders were no more effective: their attempts to dominate the group created disruptive internal dissension. Furthermore, Democratic leaders, who involved all members in group decisions and activities, seemed best able to maintain harmony while directing the group toward their goals.

When it came to some characteristics of these group leaders, it appears they are taller than members of the group. Although there are certainly no hard and fast rules, it seems that leaders are more likely to be taller than the average group member, to be judged better looking than other colleagues, to have a higher IQ, and to be more sociable, talkative, determined, and self-confident (Bass, 1990; Crosbie, 1975).

Conformity and Leadership

Sociologists, we find, are interested in two forms of group behavior: ***conformity* and *leadership***. Overall, the pressure to conform can be rather convincing, particularly when it comes to small groups. There are lots of people who go along with the majority regardless of the consequences or their personal opinions. However, nothing makes this more apparent than Solomon Asch's classic experiments from the 1950s (Asch, 1955). Asch assembled various groups of student volunteers in what was described as a test of visual discrimination and then asked the subjects which of the three lines on a card was as long as the line on another card. To ensure objectivity, each of the student groups had only one actual issue; the others were Asch's unknown accomplices, whom he had instructed to provide what was clearly an incorrect answer. The experimenter found that almost one-third of the subjects changed their minds and accepted the majority's wrong answer. In a later conversation, those who conformed to the majority admitted later that they had no doubt about what the right answer was, but preferred to avoid the discomfort of being different from other people, even people they did not know. Apparently, many of us are prepared to compromise our judgment in the interests of group conformity.

If you are not a stranger, the pressure to conform is even stronger. During **groupthink**, members of a cohesive group endorse a single explanation or answer, usually at the expense of disregarding reality. Also, the group does not tolerate dissenting opinions because they see them as signs of unfaithfulness to the group. The point is that those who have doubts or other ideas won't speak out or contradict the leader of the group because one must be reminded that the leader may be strong-willed to the point he or she will not care for that behavior. Group-think decisions often prove tragic, as when President Kennedy and his top advisors authorized the CIA's decision to invade Cuba. The bottom line is that collective decisions tend to be more effective when members disagree while considering other possibilities.

Characteristics of Leaders in Social Groups

Leaders are special people who step up to the plate to not only get things done but also go the extra mile to do the right thing, at the right time, for the right reasons. Understand that this is the test for leadership. According to Drucker (2002), the only definition of a leader is the one who has followers. It is hard these days to predict who might become a leader. Sometimes, it is the one who steps up to the plate to a group into action. Other times, it is the group or organization that choose the individual to become their leader. Nevertheless, we selected a leader because he or she stands out among the rest. This person has some unique characteristics that allow him or her to stand out. Yukl (2012) posits that personality differences between people who become leaders and individuals who don't are minuscule. Leaders tend to be brilliant, very dominant, more extroverted, more psychologically balanced, very confident, and very liberal than other group members (Bass, 1990; Hare, Blumberg, Davies, & Kent, 1994; Northouse, 2016). Keyes (1982) supports comments made earlier in that leaders also tend to be taller and more physically attractive than people who are not leaders. Becoming a leader might be because the person is in the right place at the right time. It might also be because of one's ability to emerge as a leader because of the situation.

Leadership Styles

We associate leadership styles with the way in which a leader views leadership and performs it to accomplish their group or organizational goals. For leaders, understanding various styles and how one can develop or change their style and come closer to the ideal one aspire to become is critical to being a successful leader. Another definition that came forward argued leadership is the process of persuasion or example by which an individual (or leadership team) induces a group to pursue

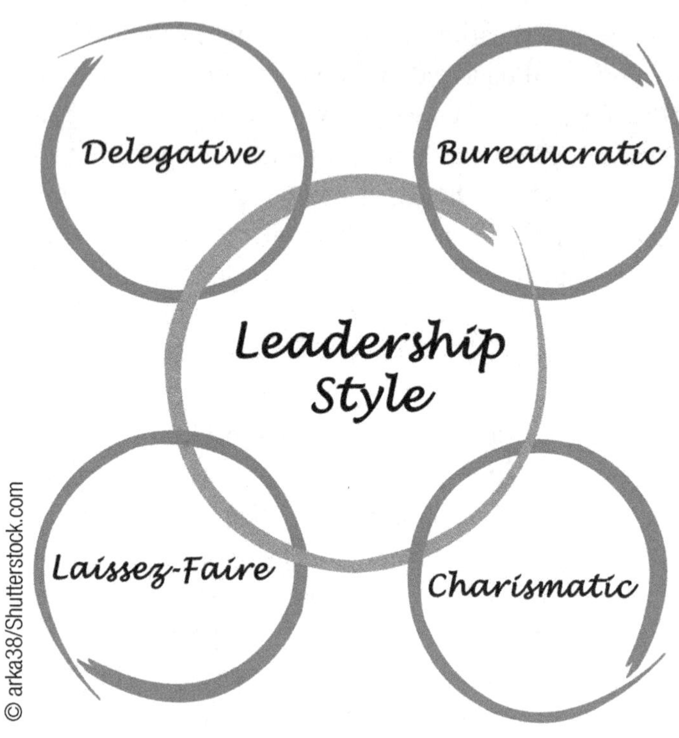

objectives held by the leader or shared by the leader and his or her followers (Gardner, 1993). Now, if we were to accept this meaning, leadership style is the process used to carry out leadership.

We can also surmise that a leader's styles encompass how one relates to others. The relationship is important whether inside or outside the organization but keep in mind that it's about the position and how successful the leader is in the organization. For example, we know that the leader must accomplish various tasks, so we need to understand how he or she gets it done by looking at their processes and procedures to make that happen. Also, lets not forget about emergencies in that when they come up, how does a leader handle it? The leader might also need to mobilize the organization to facilitate change. So again, what does he to do? All of this hinges on a leader's leadership style. The one reason why we provided so much information on various leadership theories and styles in Chapter 2 was for that purpose.

We must add that we can reveal a leader's style as it relates to the organization by looking at both the environment of that organization and its relationships within the community. For example, if a leader is suspicious and jealous of power, others in the organization are likely to behave likewise, not just in dealing with both colleagues and the community, but all involved parties as a whole. If we find that the leader is cooperative and open with others, then this behavior is more likely to encourage the same approaches. The style of the leader defines an organization.

Ross (2012) has argued never to flip the script in that a leader is supposed to serve others, not oneself. A leader who is concerned for just the bottom line undermines the mission of the organization. Therefore, the leader runs the risk of not being successful. For that reason alone, one must be mindful of both his or her leadership style and those of others you might hire as leaders. They can serve as a crucial part of helping you to facilitate the organization maintaining its competitive edge or keep it on the right track.

From a sociological perspective, we find that sociologists are concerned with three types of leadership styles: democratic, authoritarian, and laissez-faire. White and Lippit (1960) found that groups with permissive or ***laissez-faire*** leaders could not seem to get organized. This type of leadership tends to minimize their position and power, allowing group members to operate more or less on their own. ***Autocratic*** leaders were no more useful in that their attempts to dominate the group created disruptive internal dissension. They were also instrumental in their outlook, making decisions on their own and demanding strict compliance from subordinates. The understanding is that this style of leadership is likely to win a little or no personal affection from the group members. Believe me, it is less efficient in promoting the goals of the group. However, ***Democratic*** leaders involved all members of the group in decisions and activities, and this led to the group not only maintaining harmony but also directing the group to fulfill its goals were very successful. They have more artistic qualities but are less successful in crisis situations (when there is little time for discussion).

The Social Phenomenon

In an attempt to simplify a leader's role in a social group, we must address leadership as part of a social phenomenon. If we argue that a leader is necessary for the survival of a group, then we must also posit that leadership direction serves as the action to facilitate the success of the group. It is also evident that leadership can only occur if acted upon by the leader in relationship to other people in the group. Just the leader provides leadership for others to act and if carried out correctly, the group succeeds on their endeavors. The leader is part of the social phenomenon, because we have to recognize that no one can be a leader all by oneself, the leader needs the help of others. The relationships which the leader builds upon seek to establish the roles that each member will play. Rendering an active interaction, the leader expects the members of the group to complete their action by acting as he or she would by playing the leader's role. Mead (1934) called this role-taking in that it refers to social interaction in which people adopt and act out a particular social role.

The leader is part of the group structure, and as such he or she carries on shared relationship with other members of the social group. These relationships do define their overall role in the group. However, when we view leadership as a status in organizational structure or a function is defined by mutual relations with others in a particular group structure, it is easy to understand why there cannot just be a generalization of traits characteristic of leaders by some leadership theorists.

If we look at this from another angle, we might argue that role-taking is a process of anticipating and viewing behavior as motivated by an imputed social role (Michalec & Hafferty, 2015). For example, we could say from the child playing at being "a mother" to the adult playing at being "a medical doctor," role-taking is a universal feature of social life. From an empirical point of view, the definition suggests that this process is very complicated. For in Mead's view, we must consider role-taking as an elementary feature of social life, but it's not a simple process. We should also note that the leadership process is not divorced from the broader situational context. Furthermore, aspects of the group's mission, the authority system of the larger organization, and the social, economic, and cultural characteristics of the society in which the organization is embedded are critical influences on the nature of leadership (Kellerman, 1984).

The Sociological Theory Connection

Emile Durkheim would look at this from a functionalist perspective by examining a groups' values and behaviors and its association with the leader. He might say that successful groups might have a successful leader. Karl Marx, in his usual self, might argue that the although democratic leadership styles may increase a worker's productivity, the fact that a worker has to engage in bureaucracy to get and keep the job is an issue. Symbolic Interactionists theorists will attempt to define the interaction of between leadership and employee. They will use variables like an employee's job performance and satisfaction and connect that with leadership. They might also have as a controlling variable, the personal attitude to ascertain if it affects one's productivity at work. There is an understanding that democratic work environments do help people to fell connected to their jobs.

Chapter Summary

There is no argument that most individuals become socially attracted to groups. Group members will highly value a leader who possesses and displays behaviors that are likely to move the group toward its goal and achieves success. As considered above, we find that sociologists have done extensive studies on groups, breaking them down by primary, secondary, or ingroup and outgroup, as well as other aspects. Leadership theorists, for the most part, have done the same, looking at leadership from a group approach while tapping into the behavior of individuals directing group's activities toward specific group goals. Leadership seems to understand a leader's ability to influence a group's effectiveness. It would be several years later that the primary focus of leadership theorists would move into a broader spectrum of a group's organizational behavior. Leadership styles affect groups in various ways. Leadership is a social phenomenon, and that is why sociology of leadership works to go deeper into our understanding of this sensation.

References

Asch, S (1955). Opinions and social pressure. *Scientific American*, 195, 51-55.

Bales, R. F. (1953). The Equilibrium problems in small groups. In T. Parsons et al. (Eds.), *Working papers in the theory of action*, pp. 111–162. Glencoe, IL: Free Press.

Bass, B. M. (1990). *Bass & stogdill's handbook of leadership: Theory, research, & managerial applications.* (3rd ed.). New York, NY: Free Press.

Berelson, B., & Steiner, G. A. (1967). *Human behavior*. Santa Fe Springs, CA: Harcourt Bruce and World, Inc.

Cooley, C. H. (1929). *Social organization*. New York, NY: Scribner's

Crosbie, P. V. (ed.). (1975). *Interaction in small groups*. New York, NY: Macmillan.

Drucker, P. F. 2002. *The effective executive*. New York: HarperCollins Publishers.

Durkheim, E. (1897). *Suicide: A study in sociology*. John A Spaulding and George Simpson trans. New York Press.

Gardner, J. (1993). *On Leadership*. New York, NY: Free Press.

Hare, H., Blumberg, H. H., Davies, M. F., & Kent, M. V. (1994). *Small group research: A handbook.* Norwood, NJ: Ablex Publishing Corp.

Heap, K. (1977). *Group theory for social workers*. New York, NY: Pergamon Press.

Kellerman, B. (1984). *Leadership: Multidisciplinary perspectives*. Englewood Cliffs, NJ: Prentice-Hall, Inc.

Keyes, R. (1982). *The height of your life*. Boston, MA: Warner.

Mead, G. H. (1934). *Mind, self, and society*. Chicago, IL: The University of Chicago Press.

Merton, R. K. (1957). *Social theory and social structure*. Glencoe, IL: Free Press.

Michalec, B., & Hafferty, F. W. (2015). Role theory and the practice of interprofessional education: A critical appraisal and call to sociologists. *Social Theory & Health*, 13(2), 180–201.

Mills, T. M. (1967). *The sociology of small groups*. Englewood Cliffs, NJ: Prentice-Hall, Inc.

Northouse, P. G. (2016). *Leadership: Theory and practice*. (7th ed.). Thousand Oaks, CA: Sage Publications, Inc.

Northouse, P. G. (2014). *Introduction to leadership: Concepts and practice*. Thousand Oaks, CA: Sage Publications, Inc.

Ridgeway, C. L. (1983). *The dynamics of small groups*. New York, NY: St. Martin's Press.

Ross, L. F. (2008). *Leadership: So what makes you think you can lead*. Philadelphia, PA: Xlibris Publishers.

Ross, L. F. (2012). *Leadership: So what makes you think you can lead*. Philadelphia: Xlibris Publishers.

Slater, P. E. (1955). Role differentiation in small groups. In A. Paul Hare (Ed.), *Small groups: studies in social interaction*, pp. 498–515. New York, NY: Knopf.

White, R. K., & Lippitt, R. D. (1960). *Autocracy and democracy*. New York, NY: Harper & Row.

Yukl, G. (2012). *Leadership in organizations. 8th ed.)*. Upper Saddle River, NJ: Prentice Hall.

Chapter 6

Leadership Skill-Building Exercise

Personal Development Plan

Personal Developing Plan

Leaders must know their overall purpose in life. One of the key ways to understand this is to have Personal Development Plan. This plan is critical to your personal as well as professional development, and sets the beginning stages of pointing you in the right direction for success. Overall, this plan will also make you a productive member of society. Chapter 6 Leadership Skill-Building Exercise is designed to help you develop your plan so it may serve as a roadmap of action into the future. This plan not only acts as a decision-making tool but also provides standards by which to live. This plan is a living document, subject to change from time to time to help you proceed toward your goals. Some of the things that might be addressed in this plan are yourself, family, your involvement in community or school activities, and of course your job. Although it's nice to go out to 10 years to start off, at a minimum you should address goals that go out at least 5 years. You will use data from the other Leadership Skill-Building Exercises to fill in this plan. Your facilitator or instructor will let you know when to finalize this plan for review. To start off, you might want to discuss the story you wrote about self in Chapter 1, Leadership Skill-Building Exercise. You might also look at Chapter 2 Leadership Skill-Building Exercise, to see if the story you told there centers on you particularly. The first part of the plan is to conduct a personal SWOT analysis on self.

There is no doubt that you can succeed in life by using your God-given talent. Use the key SWOT questions below to help you get started. As with the other exercises, you should be honest with your overall assessment of self. The whole idea is to generate results that you can use in your leadership development. Using the example key SWOT questions and your overall story, make a list of items to cover each SWOT concept. In other words, complete a SWOT on yourself. Another example is that you might want to think about your strengths in relation to those who know you well in that what will they say about your strengths (teachers, family members, boss, etc.).

According to Ross (2008), the SWOT analysis is the most popular strategic analysis tool used today. He states that SWOT stands for Strength, Weakness, Opportunities, and Threats. Although many businesses use this tool to help them maintain the competitive advantage, you too will use it to help you capitalize on your strengths and minimize the effects of your weaknesses. You will

also make the most of any opportunities and use this tool to address and then reduce the impact of any threats to your overall success in your leadership walk or personal life. After this SWOT exercise, you will use what you have developed to start the process of formulating your Personal Development Plan.

Key SWOT Questions
STRENGTHS
What are your core values?
What do others describe as your strengths?
What are you good at doing?
Describe things that place you above the rest (skills, education, etc.)?
WEAKNESSES
Describe what others see as your weaknesses?
What tasks will you avoid due to lack of training?
Name areas you need to improve on?
What personality traits need to change because of obstacles to success?
OPPORTUNITIES
What new technology you might use to propel you forward?
What mistakes have you noticed by others that you can take advantage of in your personal life?
What are the biggest changes in society that you need to be in tune with so that you can maintain the competitive edge of self?
Is there a skill that you possess that allows you to take an advantage over others?
THREATS
What obstacles to you face in your life that hinders you from success?
Describe any skills or standards you are unable to meet?
Is there anyone competing against you in the role that you play on the job or in society?
What threats are there to your overall goals in life? Can weaknesses lead to threats?

Personal Development Plan

By John Doe

Personal Development Planning

As part of this exercise, you will need to put together a Personal Development Plan. The plan is designed to help get you on track to learning more about yourself. More importantly, you will use this plan to set courses of action that should be used to improve your success in all of your endeavors. You will design what is known as SMART goals. SMART stands for Specific, Measurable, Attainable, Relevant, and Timely. Although employees are responsible for creating and implementing their personal development plans, leaders play a vital and supportive role in the overall process.

Personal development plans can also take on a life of their own, changing from time to time to help one achieve the necessary skills for success. This plan can be very useful for your job, particularly if you need to identify skills that need to improve. Areas defined in the SWOT analysis must be addressed in this plan. The plan can be used to support your career change, business desires, and identify areas for professional development.

Personal Development Plan

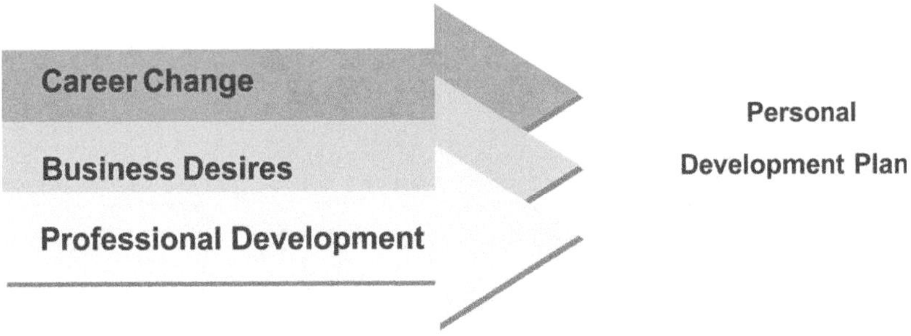

Step 1. Write your plan. Looking at your SWOT analysis and given guidance from your facilitator, you are now ready to create a Personal Development Plan for yourself. Again, this plan is designed to help you bring about change. The initial step is to identify requirements for the role you are playing in society (job, student, etc.). Identify your areas of strengths and the ways that might use them more effectively.

Step 2. Identify areas for development. Start by discussing the role you are currently playing in society, and this might be as a student, family member, or employee. You must understand that you are playing some role in society and that it must be addressed in the plan. If there are areas that need more development, address them here.

Step 3. Make sure your plan centers on SMART goals. The sole purpose of building a SMART plan is to establish clearly defined goals to bring about change for the better. In other words, make sure:

- Specific – Ensure your goal is clear and be very precise.
- Measurable – Identify the completion of the goal by using dates and times or anything that indicates completion of the goal.

- Attainable – Make sure the goal you have decided upon is achievable. In other words, your goals can not be unrealistic to the point that cannot be attainable.
- Relevant – Ensure that your development actions are related to the environment that you are operating in and test them to make sure of completion and the fact they are still relevant to your situation.
- Timely – All goals must be completed promptly. The bottom line here is to set a timetable for overall completion, reviewing them from time to time to ensure completion.

Summary/Recap

1. Develop your objectives.
2. Identify specific actions you plan to take.
3. Identify obstacles that may impede your process and how they might be alleviated.
4. Address any support that might need to facilitate progress.

Chapter 7

- Leadership from a Sociologist's Perspective
- Max Weber
- Authority and Power
- The Return to the Sociological Approach

Sociology of Leadership

Thinking Critically!

Observe the national evening news for one week, noting people featured who have some kind of authority. List each of them and note their area of influence. What form of authority would you say each represents: charismatic, traditionally, or rational-legal? How has the kind of authority that a person has reflected in his or her position in society (that is, race, class, gender, occupation, education, and so on) being displayed (Anderson & Taylor, 2010)?

As You Read

- Revisit your overall position on functional, conflict, and symbolic interactionist theories.
- What theory explains leadership from a sociological perspective better? Why?
- Does power give you the authority to act as a leader?

Chapter 7

Leadership from a Sociologist's Perspective

Max Weber (1864–1920)

One can argue that leadership is nothing more than power and authority over a person or group of individuals. The great sociologist Max Weber is in a better position than anyone else to discuss these two terms, especially when it comes to legitimate and illegitimate power and his various types of authority. However, before we get into this more deeply, let's first discuss just a little bit about the man. Weber pronounced "VAY-ber " was one of the founding figures in the field of sociology and is one of the most famous sociologists in history. Born in 1864, Weber grew up in Berlin Germany, and his family was wealthy. His father was a judge and later became a successful politician. This German scholar argued how the Industrial Revolution affected social actions, centered on the forces that motivate people to act in various circumstances. He was an individual who wanted to influence events through political leadership, because he did not like the direction of social change in industrial societies.

Weber took issue with Karl Marx, another famous sociologist because he did not believe that social change could trace variations in the economy as Marx had implied. He felt that factors such as religious ideas played a significant role. Although he felt that social equality was inevitable, he nevertheless did not like what was happening in society. Weber posits that these social changes would develop into an increase in the power of the state over individuals. In his attempt to expand sociological theory further, Weber offered a more general theory of authority that was less wedded to capitalism and ownership of the means of production (Witt, 2016).

Weberian Approach to Leadership

Max Weber's overall contributions to the field of leadership cannot be mistaken. He laid the foundations of modern political sociology and pointed out that the state is the only authority that can successfully claim a monopoly on the right to use force within a given territory. The state may also choose to delegate some of its powers to other agencies, such as local authorities, the military, or the police. However, the state can override all other institutions and is thus the central and most vital component of political order. We must understand that the "State" is not quite the thing as the "government." In this case, the state is an impersonal social authority, whereas the government is the collection of individuals who happen to be directing the power of the state at any given moment. Politics is about power and about one who gets it, how it is obtained, applied, and for the most part to what purposes it is placed. Weber (1947) defined power as the ability to control the behavior of others, even in the absence of their consent. Simply, power is the capacity to participate effectively in a decision-making process. Those who for one reason or another cannot affect the process are therefore powerless. We also need to understand that power may be exercised blatantly or subtly, legally or illegally, justly or unjustly. It may derive from any of some resources, such as wealth, prestige, numbers, or organizational efficiency. However, its ultimate basis is the capability to compel compliance, if necessary through the threat or use of force.

A leader influences people, and that is the bottom line. However, to claim that you are the head of an individual, group, or organization, one must show that you have power and authority to be in that position. Weber said it best when he argued that although social class and its associated control over material resources may determine who has power in most instances, these are not the only possible foundations for power (2016). For example, in American society, the upper class or elite class as some say, represent those in charge, heads of multinational corporations, foundations, universities, capitalist elite, owners of lands, stocks, and bonds and other assets. People become wealthy because of the assets they own. For the most part, one could make a convincing argument that these are the leaders in society. There are other sources to include social status, in which people defer to others out of respect for their social position or prestige, and organizational resources, in which members of a group gain power through their ability to organize to accomplish some specific goal by maximizing their available resources (2016). Finally, Weber argued that these social resources draw their power from people's willingness to obey the authority of someone else, which in turn is their perception of the legitimacy of that person's right to lead (2016).

Authority and Power

Max Weber said that power is the "probability that one actor within a social relationship will be in a position to carry out his will despite resistance, regardless of the basis on which this probability rest" (Weber, 1947). He went on to state that authority (*Herrschaft*), on the other hand, is the "probability that a command with a given content will be obeyed by a given group of persons" (1947). Weber goes on to say that the difference between power and authority rests on the fact that power is centered on the personal characteristics of individuals or groups, whereas authority is a person's social position or role. While Weber asserts power is a merely real relation, authority is a legal relation of domination and subjection. Weber distinguishes three types of authority. He argued that each is legitimate, because it rests on the implicit or explicit consent of the governed. A person who can successfully claim one of these types of authority is regarded as having the right to compel obedience, at least within socially specified limits. Many scholars have included comments like these to define leadership (Bass, 1990; Benton, 2003; Blanchard & Hodges, 2003; Covey, 1991; Abercrombie, Hill, & Turner, 1988; Northouse, 2016). According to Weber, there are three authority types: **Traditional authority**, **Rational-legal authority** and **Charismatic authority,** which he went on to call "ideal types" of authority relations.

Traditional Authority

Traditional authority is a form of authority in which ancient customs legitimate power. Leaders can do this if they fuse power with tradition. For example, chieftainships and monarchies have always used this power, and historically it has been the most common source of legitimation of power. This authority is associated with unwritten laws and has an almost sacred quality. The competence or policies of a particular rule are not really at issue in such a system, so long as he or she has a legitimate claim to the throne or another legendary ruling status.

Traditional authority is based on long-standing, established, and widely accepted customs and practices. One can also say it is because it has always been that way. Queen Elizabeth of the British Empire could serve as the best example of this authority. It is obtained at birth and passed on to offspring according to a long tradition that says authority rest in a royal family, with a set procedure for succession to the throne.

Weber stated that this power centers on establishing the belief that leaders have a traditional and legitimate right to exercise authority; particular, those in command. Weber said that one could do this because traditional authority is power legitimated by respect for long-established cultural patterns. For example, the ruling of Japan for generations in the middle of the 20th century is a case of a revered emperor whose absolute authority went largely unquestioned. Moreover, it has a connection to the past and justifies its legitimacy by claiming that they conform to precedents (Coleman, 2016). And, the rights and power of an individual or group are not challenged by the people. You see this is because of the way their society has traditionally remained governed, and there is overall respect for the old cultural principles and observances.

Although this power is passed down, traditional authority systems often are pass through heredity and will not change. This creates inequalities among the people, and this type of system helps to preserve the problem. A traditional authority system will persist unless it's opposed by the people in the society. Weber understood that detailed rules and regulations rarely constrained people exercising traditional authority. Their people are expected to obey them as a matter of personal loyalty to members of families whose power has become accepted as legitimate over many generations (Coleman, 2016; Weber, Gerth, & Mills, 2015; Witt, 2016). The problem with traditional authority is that it lacks any headway to facilitate social change because of its stand on maintaining the status quo.

Rational-legal Authority

Rational-legal authority is a type of authority in which power is legitimate by explicit rules and procedures that define the obligations of the rulers. The rules and procedures are typically found in a written constitution and set of laws that, at least in theory, have been socially agreed upon by the people. This form of authority is characteristic of the political systems of the most modern societies. Rational-legal authority stresses a government of laws, not of particular rules. The power of an official in a country such as the United States, Canada, or Russia derives from the office the person holds, not from personal characteristics such as birthright. For the United States, this authority comes from the U.S. Constitution. In other words, we know that the U.S. Constitution gives the Congress and the President the authority to make and enforce laws and policies of the United States. Officials can exercise power only within the legally defined limits that have been formally set in advance. Thus, the legitimacy of this power, established by statute, is a form of rational-legal authority. Put another way, rational-legal authority is a system in which an individual or governmental institution exerts power based on a system of rules. We should also note that this power extends beyond governments to include any organization and bureaucracies are the purest forms of rational-legal authority. Quite simple, it is the person who has the authority that is appointed or elected by a process. Once the person leaves the office or institution, their authority is gone. The authority will always remain with the office and not the individual (Weber, Gerth, & Mills, 2015; Witt, 2016).

Americans thus acknowledge the right of the president or even of a minor bureaucrat to exercise power, provided that person does not exceed the specific boundaries of authority that is attached to his or her respective office. When President Nixon did overstep these limits by using his position to persecute his opponents and to obstruct a criminal investigation of his aides' activities, his actions were considered illegitimate and abuse of power, and he was forced to resign. A similar or worse fate would doubtless await a new Russian leader who used power in ways considered illegitimate in that country.

Rational-legal authority embodies informal bureaucracy, the belief in the legality of official rules and hierarchies centered on efficiency. It is the logical fit between means and intended goals (2016). Those placed in leadership positions in the hierarchy have this authority and can issue commands. Social change has to be orderly and completed in an incremental manner. It also must also subscribe to the law and scientific calculation. This formal bureaucracy appears legitimate if the authority spreads among leaders based on their qualifications and capability and these leaders have a tendency to exercise control by knowledge. Weber feared that this modern form of authority might become an "iron cage," lacking spirit and radical possibility.

Guillen (2010) research indicates several key things under Weber's leadership perspective:

1. Leaders have personal authority in that founder or empire builders gain legitimacy by relying "on the ideas of personal gift, talent, exemplary character, demonstrated success, or even divine inspiration" (p. 225); They also "surround themselves with confidants, personal retainers, and disciples, with an inner circle of unconditional supporters and collaborators who further solidify the founder's grip on the company"; However, the limit of their authority is that their employees and customers "demand proof of gift and continued success" (p. 227).
2. Under traditional authority we find that heirs of founders or empire builders gain legitimacy by honoring family traditions, appearing to be modest and hard-working, behaving as an equal and being energetic more than taking liberties, ensuring "that the collaborators of the founder or empire builder do not undermine their plans and commands", representing all of their family's legacy, and managing any family conflict (pp. 227–228).
3. In regards to legal-rational authority, "professional managers build the legitimacy of their authority on the basis of their technical competence, academic qualifications, formal knowledge, or success in other managerial positions" (p. 228); market failures may undermine the authority, "or anti-bureaucratic or anti-technocratic reactions from employees or customers" (p. 228).
4. It was Vilfredo Pareto and Robert Michels who further developed these themes. Centering on what they called issues of elite (leadership) recruitment, homogeneity, interaction, value consensus, solidarity, and integration, Pareto developed the theory of the "circulation of elites"

in that elites (i.e. leaders) are "subject to a law of social decadence or entropy, whereby they find it difficult to reproduce themselves over time." Michels went a bit further in that he developed the "iron law of oligarchy." which is a model of how increasing bureaucratization, organizational complexity, and interorganizational interactions eventually generate vertical differentiation and a distancing between the leaders and the led (pp. 228–229).

5. Reinhard Bendix expanded on the Weberian three ideal types of authority in his *Work and Authority in Industry* (1956), which discusses how "the ruling classes of different societies deal with the breakdown of traditional patterns of subordination among the people in the wake of industrialization." There is a compare and contrast analysis that looks at England, the United States, Russia, and East Germany to examine how these different societies have transitioned from traditional to legal authority (pp. 229–230).
6. Michael Useem's *The Inner Circle* (1984) compares corporate government in the US and the UK (p. 231); He goes on to develops his "inner circle" theory by saying "corporations and their leaders often make decisions that are beneficial to all large companies as opposed to just their own." However, this approach is more similar to C. Wright Mills than Weber or Pareto (p. 231).

Charismatic Authority

© Andrii Kondiuk/Shutterstock.com

Max Weber introduces the term "charisma" to describe a person with exceptional leadership skills. Intrigued by charisma, Max Weber believed that an individual who has this extraordinary personal quality could turn an audience into followers. We bestow charismatic authority upon people because of their charm or strong personality, and unlike tradition or rational-legal authority, it does not emanate inherited or achieved social status. The charismatic leader is not obeyed because of a statute of law but due to their unique personal qualities and abilities to create obedience among the people. Although charisma has no link to an individual's position in society or may not even have any actual power; it is an element of individual personality. However, the result is the same as the other authority discussed above in that the power exercised by the charismatic leader is likely to be viewed, by some, as legitimate. Heroism, victories, and success for the community help to establish continued authority. We must also note that conventional cultural norms do not constrain charismatic authority. Leaders with this authority may make their rules as if they were drawing from a higher power.

Weber believed that this concept provided answers regarding the relationship of leadership to society and decision-making. Although it's hard for charismatic leaders to maintain long-term authority, once the leader loses charisma or dies, the authority tends to shift to traditional or legal-rational-based systems. However, the uniqueness of charismatic authority is that it lies within the person and not the position. The bottom line is that it differs from traditional and legal-rational authority in that it cannot be institutionalized.

On the basis of Jesus' divine powers, he serves as an excellent example of charismatic authority. Another example is the authority of Mahatma Gandhi of India in the first half of the 1900s. Although not a religious leader, Nazi leader Adolph Hitler used his charisma to thrust a troubled world in war. The bottom line is that all of these leaders demonstrated the unique qualities to create obedience and develop followers among people in their societies (Weber, Gerth, & Mills, 2015; Witt, 2016).

Weber (1947) defined charisma as a unique personality trait that enables this person to have exceptional powers to lead; reserved for a select few. McMahon (2010) states that the sociological literature stresses that charismatic leadership is born out of stressful situations. He goes on to say that such leaders express sentiments deeply held by followers. We can agree that this is very true in that these are the leaders who can rally a nation or excel in their ability to take social movements to a level that causes political leaders to act. An example would be Martin Luther King, Jr. in his capacity to lead the civil rights movement, which caused legislators to pass the Civil Rights Act of 1964. King had precisely the type of personality that Weber conceptualized as charismatic in that he and others viewed him as extraordinary. King was not only competent at his tasks but many people identified with his vision of a "beloved community" devoid of racism, and he had the talent to articulate this view forcefully through powerful oratory (Barker, Johnson, & Lavalette, 2001). We can teach leadership and King is a good example. King's charisma, in part, is the result of training that he received from his preacher father and also from institutions such as Crozier College, where he took courses in preaching as well as public speaking (2001). Clearly, he had a great personality that he used to win over the masses that he directed his attention too. Therefore, charismatic authority derives from an individual's personal characteristics. Charismatic have authority because they excite and inspire people. Another example is that President Barack Obama had charisma and this propelled him to the Presidency of the United States in 2008. He had the ability to gain a large political following in part because many people liked not only what he had to say, but also the manner in which he stated it. Weber believed that this type of authority is an individual who has exceptional blessedness, heroism, or exemplary character of an individual. These leaders are legitimate in times of crisis, called upon by followers to facilitate change because they have unusual gifts. This type of leader can break with authority based on traditions by an appeal to a higher power (some genius or God), and the follower does not think they have a choice but to obey her command (Witt, 2016).

The Return to the Sociological Approach

The Institutional Approach: Leadership and Social Integration

According to Guillen (2010), the institutional approach to leadership is focused on the mutual dependence between the leader and the follower. He further states that in the tradition of Émile Durkheim, institutionalists see leadership as an essential feature of a modern, differentiated society, one that fosters social integration, in a mostly Parsonsian fashion. On the basis of this understanding, leaders exist because the organization or institution needs order and integration and with them, there will be chaos or anomie. It is leadership that is shaped by taken-for-granted symbolic, normative, and cognitive institutions (2010). Other key points:

- A leader spends their day organizing the followers for a common purpose;
- Leadership is about functions of the organization, helping that institution maintain its objective, taking action, not only to complete its mission but to resolve conflict as it moves forward by balancing the internal and external requirements of the institution; and
- It is followers who look to their leaders for meaning and purpose (2010).

The Neo-Marxist Take on Leadership

The Neo-Marxist take on leadership centers on authority and power which are determined on the relationship between leadership and social classes in a capitalist market. "As a result, ideas, ideologies, symbols, myths, cognition, and the like are assumed to reflect more fundamental class dynamics and are unceremoniously dismissed as epiphenomenal. Unlike Vilfredo Pareto, the neo-Marxists see the elite transformation as the result of political change and not of psychology" (2010, p. 233). We can put forth an argument here that Karl Marx would posit that this is about the haves and the have-nots. Nevertheless, the connection between elite recruitment and social class takes precedence because of the three-way interaction between business, government, and military elites in the United States. As the famous C. Wright Mills would say, the power elites control the higher circles within society. Mills was the first social scientist "to call attention to the interlocking role that elite members play by their positions in various types of organizations (business, government, military, universities, and nonprofit (2010)). Moreover, the pattern of interlocking elite membership has been documented for virtually every country in the world, including not only capitalist but also communist societies (2010). This is more about the relative position of the social classes in various societies in that one might find that those in the upper classes are more likely to be in powerful positions within society. It should also be noted that recent work "argues and demonstrates that business leaders act in unison only to the extent that they are structurally positioned in ways that generate similarity in behavior, including geographic proximity, common industry membership, cross-shareholdings, and interlocking directorates" (2010, pp. 233–234).

Symbolic Interaction and Leadership

As one might have learned in an introductory course in sociology, symbolic interaction theory emphasizes the importance of symbolic communication, gestures, and language in the development of the individual, group, and society. Our ability to use symbolic communication is what makes us human. At a micro level of analysis, sociologists use this theory to focus in on the social interaction happening in small groups. When we observe a social setting, one can surmise that the communication process is at work supplying meaning to something and it is the people's actions that reflect the interpretation of that meaning. Leaders and their overall effectiveness continue to be part of the ongoing sociological inquiry of the problem-solving activities of groups. However, we know that Max Weber saw the social world as a human construct which is both a consequence and a contributor to dominant meaning systems (Kellerman, 1984). Charles Cooley being concerned with the structure and function of social action believed that inherent human tendency was the primary cause of social change. Although individual differences provide the avenues for change in society, it can only become effective in the context of group structure or interaction because it is the group that facilitates and encourages the appropriate expression of individual qualities. For Cooley, he "believed that all the phenomena of life and therefore the data of the social sciences were grounded in the imaginative properties of the mind, and that behavior was influenced not so much by internal (psychological) and external (sociological) forces but by what lay between, a reflective and socially derived interpretation of inner and outer events as they are experienced at the time" (1984, pp. 164–165). As a result, leadership for Cooley is about the images and thoughts it provokes in people minds and this case; it is the leader who must appeal to the imaginations of the likely members of the group who would later follow him or her to success. Between the leader and group members, it is the positive feelings demonstrated through the patterns of social interaction that constitutes leadership which produced in the right way, gives the leader an appealing display of power. In Cooley's later writings, he asserts that a combination of biological and romantic notions of leadership link between those being led and the behavior of the leader (1984).

Herbert Mead enhances this position in his argument about the personal attributes of a leader. For him, a leader must be a consequence of the internalization of the "generalized other" to leadership positions. In other words "the qualities expected of a leader are, therefore, a function of the prevailing symbols and meaning systems extant within the group: A person will be perceived as a leader to demonstrate in a satisfactory manner those actions and characteristics which exemplify the normative ideals of leadership within a particular universe of discourse" (Kellerman, 1984, p. 167). Overall, the symbolic interaction paradigm association with leadership is very complex. However, Cooley and Mead's breakdown of how leadership is tied to the ongoing social interaction in specific settings based on symbolic communications, images, and in particular language is clear. Leaders can lead effectively because they appeal to the imaginations of the members they are leading. A leader's interpretation of those meanings enhances one's ability to provoke positive feelings through various interactions, which result in successful leadership.

Social Networks and Leadership

The social networks look at leadership "not regarding the relationship between the leader and the led, but more pointedly as the intervention of a third party, the potential leader, in a given system of relationships." (Guillen, 2010, p. 234). Another sociologist by the name of Georg Simmel compared to power and influence in dyadic and triadic relationships. More specifically, he theorized about the intervention of a third party in a preexisting relationship between two parties. In his analysis, a third party enjoys influence, or can exercise leadership, in four different ways:

1. either two sides are hostile toward one another and therefore compete for the favor of a third element;
2. they compete for the support of the third part and therefore are hostile toward one another;
3. the nonpartisan arbiter balances or seeks accord between the two parties in the preexisting relationship; and
4. the divider-and-ruler intentionally produces the conflict [between the two sides in the preexisting relationship] to gain a dominant position. (p. 234).

Another argument is that third party may not have a huge amount of influence or leadership. However, it can pass power to one of the other parties to give that party superiority over others. Social relationships are also critical in this approach. You probably heard of the slogan, "Knowledge is power;" well, in this case, it is true. There is an advantage of those possessing vital information, which leads them to take the initiative, get ahead, and exercise leadership (pp. 234–235). In the process of establishing relationships with others, an individual acquires a brokerage advantage to the extent that he or she connects persons or clusters of individuals not otherwise attached to each other. The broker benefits from his or her ability to bring together separate groups from opposite sides of the so-called structural holes in the network (p. 235). Accordingly, a broker can use these holes to their advantage by "regulating flows and shaping how activities spanning the gap are to take place" (p. 235). So the bottom line here is that having essential information, generated from a network provides an advantage for the leader. The more diverse the information, the better. Moreover, "empirical research has found that individuals with access to various information perform better than others. Empirical studies have also shown, however, that people of different gender and race obtain unequal returns to their network resources as they attempt to advance their careers" (p. 135).

So, What is Leadership, Sociologically Speaking?

According to the research conducted by Guillen (2010) and based on the overlapping of perspectives, leadership is a relationship, not a characteristic of one person (Weberian, institutional, network) (p. 235). This author supports the conclusion put forth here. We do need to center on leadership being a relational concept, looking at it from a multidimensional approach to explaining its patterns. The key players here are the leaders and followers and how they relate to each other. For example, it is true that neo-Marxists and Weberians see the world as a structure of domination; institutional. Therefore, there is a need to introduce a hierarchical dimension to leadership to make social integration possible, understanding that the network approach is less concerned with hierarchy (p. 236). A leader must respond to various situations but is unable to do so without those that follow him or her. This is just one of the reasons why leaders cannot assume the position of authority without first understanding who they are, from their social identity, the power they hold, how they were socialized to be who they are in relationship to self and others in society.

Critical Thinking

Observe the national evening news for one week, noting people featured who have some kind of authority. List each of them and note their area of influence. What form of authority would you say each reperesents: charismatic, traditionally, or rational-legal? How has the kind of authority that a person has reflected in his or her position in society (that is, race, class, gender, occupation, education, and so on) being displayed (Anderson and Taylor, 2010)?

Chapter Summary

As you can clearly see, some significant contributors to sociology understood leadership from a sociological perceptive, especially Max Weber. This book supports the sociology and leadership link in many ways, and you have seen some of those connections already. However, there is more, and I ask you to continue through the others chapters; I hope that you see this link.

Glossary

Symbolic Interaction Theory Emphasizes the importance of symbolic communication, gestures, and generally language in the development of the individual, group, and society.

References

Abercrombie, N., Hill, S., & Turner, B. S. (1988). *The penguin dictionary of sociology*. New York, NY: Penguin Books.

Anderson, M. L., & Taylor, H. F. (2010). *Sociology: The essentials* (6th Ed.). Belmont, CA: Wadsworth.

Barker, C., Johnson A. A., & Lavalette M. (Eds.). (2001). *Leadership and social movements*. New York, NY: Manchester University Press.

Bass, B. M. (1990). *Bass & Stogdill's handbook of leadership: Theory, research, and managerial applications*. (3rd ed.). New York, NY: The Free Press.

Benton, D. A. (2003). *Executive charisma*. New York, NY: McGraw-Hill.

Blanchard, K., & Hodges, P. (2003). *The servant leader:Transforming your heart, head, hands & habits*. Nashville, TN: J. Countryman.

Coleman, J. A. (2016). Authority, power, leadership: Sociological understandings. Retrieved from http://newtheologyreview.com/index.php/ntr/article/viewFile/563/746

Covey, S. R. (1991). *Principle-Centered leadership*. New York, NY: Simon & Schuster.

Guillen, M. F. (2010). Classical sociological approaches to the study of leadership. In N. Nohria, & R. Khurana (Eds.). *Handbook of leadership theory and practice: A Harvard business school centennial colloquium*, pp. 223–305. Boston, MA: Harvard Business Press.

Kellerman, B. (1984). *Leadership: Multidisciplinary perspectives*. Englewood Cliffs, NJ: Prentice-Hall, Inc.

McMahon, J. T. (2010). *Leadership classics*. Long Grove, IL: Waveland Press, Inc.

Northouse, P. G. (2016). *Leadership: Theory and practice*. (7th ed.). Thousand Oaks, CA: Sage Publications, Inc.

Weber, M. (1947). *The theory of social and economic organizations* (T. Parsons, Trans.). New York, NY: Free Press.

Weber, M., Gerth, H. H., & Mills, C. W. (2015). *From Max Weber: Essays in sociology*. Rochester, NY: Scholar's Choice.

Witt, J. (2016). *SOC*. (4th ed.). New York, NY: McGraw-Hill Education.

Chapter 7

Leadership Skill-Building Exercise

The Impact of Diversity

The Impact of Diversity

By the year 2050, the majority will not only be Hispanic heritage but more people of color than ever before. In fact, the U.S. Census reported that in the year 2011, more children of color were born than whites (Henslin, 2017). I have learned in my leadership walk that diversity allows for a wide range of views to be introduced in various settings. Diversity has a way of challenging the status quo, and it can be used as a vehicle for change in any organization. According to Frey (2015) and Sonnensechein (1997), both argue that diversity can stimulate social, economic, intellectual, and emotional growth. Diversity also helps one to define his or her place in the global community. So you want to be a leader? Think about how you will value diversity in your group, team, or organization. Think about what tools you need to learn to solve conflicts and negotiate courses of action for the benefit of all involved parties.

Chapter 7: Leadership Skill-building Exercise allows for the facilitator to come up with his or her diversity training program lasting no more than an hour or less. You will find a host of exercises online to administer to students, clubs, or organization for learning purposes. I like to use a valuing diversity self-assessment worksheet and then follow-up with a diversity statistics quiz, both of which you can find online to use free to assess individuals. Then, this tends to lead to fascinating discussions.

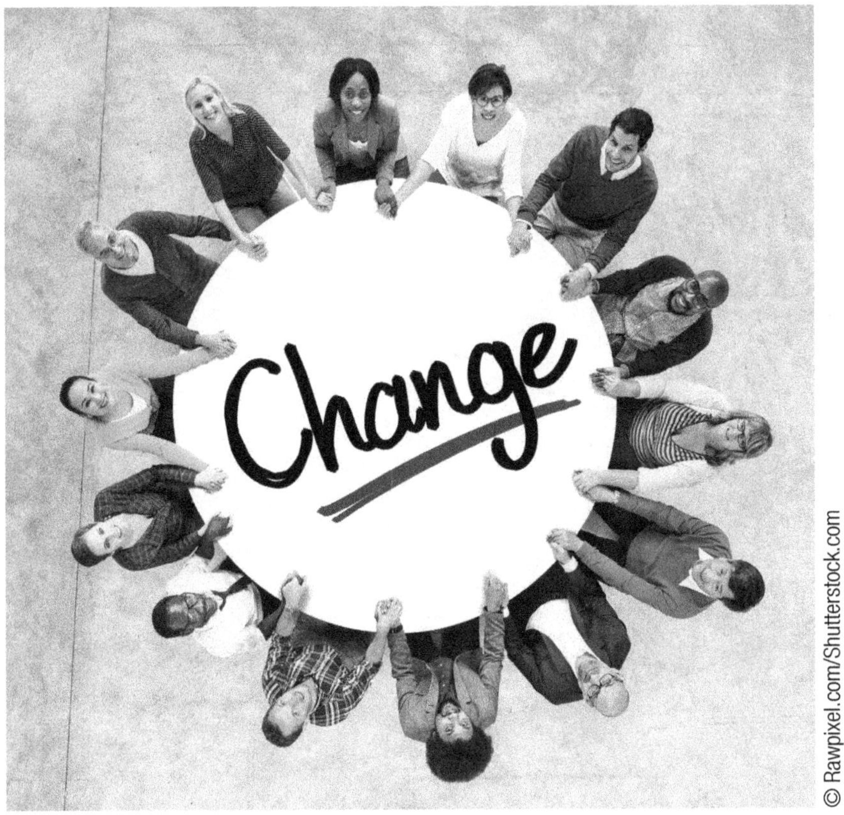

© Rawpixel.com/Shutterstock.com

Sociology of Leadership

Thinking Critically!

1. How can transformational leadership be used to facilitate the development of personal qualities to affect positive change in society? Does these personal qualities support groups interactions so that they can function as a team for positive change?
2. When something drastically happens, people advocate for change. What leadership trait do you find most important?
3. What does leadership have to do with it and why is it needed to facilitate change as a whole?
4. Finish this statement: Social change is for the betterment of society and this may be the biggest reason leadership is needed to facilitate that change. However, here are some more reasons . . .

Chapter 8

- Leadership and Social Change
- Collective Behavior and Leadership
- Theories of Social Change
- Leadership and Social Movements

As You Read

- Is leadership connected to social change in society? What about social movements?
- What generates social change in society?
- What social movement rallied a nation to change and who was its leader?

Chapter 8

Leadership and Social Change

© Forty3Zero/Shutterstock.com

Education is the most powerful weapon we can use to change the world.

Nelson Mandela

Like the concept leadership, there is also a problem with defining social change. From a macrosociological perspective, sociologists use the term ***social change*** to address changes in behavior patterns, social relationships, organizations, and social structure. Put another way, we can surmise that social change refers to change in the structure and organization of social relationships of society. Therefore, we should understand that change is always present and revealed by shifts in people's social relationships. The bottom line is that no society is free from change. Throughout history, we have seen different aspects of social change in many societies, some rapid and some minor. Nevertheless, these changes have an impact on people. As a result, social change may bring many difficulties and problems, whereas some may not bring about difficulties at all. ***Macrosociology*** is areas concerned with large-scale patterns operating at the group level of society. One of the things that we should remind ourselves of is that society is a network of social relationships. Leadership is critical to the social transformation of society. Social psychology theorists use leadership in the analysis of small groups whereas sociologists present leadership as the application of influence or power in social collectivities. However and more recently, sociologists have wrestled with the concept of leadership and centered on the idea of power being particularly concerned with the structural conditions that allow some to exercise power over others. Some sociologists have questioned the Weberian assumption that subordinates must legitimate leadership roles. Max Weber's argument still stands to some degree, due in part because those who are in power hold legitimate leadership positions, particularly in organizations and institutions. As rapid social change continues to come to societies, leadership plays an important role because of a leader's ability to provide guidance on the planning and implantation of this change.

Collective Behavior and Leadership

Collective behavior concerns the actions of large groups of people who do not conform to establish social norms for one reason or another. Sometimes called crowd behavior, this group of individuals seems subordinate to a collective mentality. However, in contemporary sociology, there is less interest in the topic of crowd behavior. In 1895, Le Bon (2011) published his famous work call *The Crowd: Study of the Popular Mind.* He stated that in periods of social decline and disintegration, society is vulnerable to the rule of crowds. We had seen these events when crowds gathered to protest the allege killing of black men; *Michael Brown, Jr.*, Ferguson, Missouri; *Walter Scott*, North Charleston, South Carolina; and *Freddie Gray*, Baltimore Maryland, are just a few examples that led to a social decline in society. These events showed what sociologists called a collective behavior on the part of residents in those areas, the mobilization of a large group of people in an attempt to change the structure of society. These events could be secular movements of social protests (i.e. the ***Black Lives Matter***) and religious efforts to change society through generalized beliefs and values that direct the social movement in periods of rapid change and political disruption. Overall, the gathering of crowds in a collective behavior manner can lead to a departure from usual standards of social conduct. However, those participating collective behavior activities are there because they believe in a uniform action to expedite social change. This is one of the main reasons why leadership is necessary at that point.

A leader must understand and approach collective behavior with care and diligence. We find that those collective groups tend to emerge when interactions between individuals endorse opposing views when responding to their reality. In other words, the groups exhibit behavior patterns that support their line of thinking as to what is right or wrong in society. To help address these concerns, a leader is chosen or steps up to reveal his or her leadership role. Those involved in leadership at the group or organization levels provide a unique theoretical framing of developing collective behavior in organizational settings. However, we might need a new methodology for analyzing relationships between those evolving behavioral patterns and the interaction norms underlying them, and a useful means for finding leadership opportunities within the structure of the organization or group.

Theories of Social Change

Social change occurs for a variety of reasons. However, five general theories will help us understand why social change happens: (1) Evolutionary Theory, (2) Cyclical Theory, (3) Functional Theory of Social Change, (4) Conflict Theory of Social Change, and (5) Technological Theory.

1. **Evolutionary Theory**—This theory is sometimes called the Darwinian Theory of biological evolution where society and culture meet. There is a host of social theorists who support that conclusion that cultures and societies progress upward. In other words, instead of regular cycles, these scholars have identified distinct stages of development, from simple to more complex forms. The argument here is that society and culture were subject to the same universal laws of biological and organism growth. These theorists tend to associate evolution with the increased development of society and continued to project into the future improved social and cultural customs. All of this is from the famous work of Charles Darwin (2010), a British biologist who stated species of organisms evolved from simpler organisms to more

complex organisms through what he called the processes of variations and natural selection. Continuing on the efforts put forth by Darwin, Herbert Spencer (2009) argued that sociology is the study of evolution in its most complex form. He believed in social evolution and stated that society could be explored scientifically. Encouraged by Darwin, Spencer began to survey the other sciences, particularly the fields of sociology, psychology, biology, and ethics from an evolutionary idea. The founder of sociology, Auguste Comte (1798–1857), is considered an evolutionary theorist of change in society. Comte saw human societies as moving forward in their thinking, from mythology to the scientific method. Emile Durkheim (1893–1933) agreed with Comte's position in that he felt that society progressed from simple to more complex forms of social organization. Present-day sociologists tend to reject this theory because it's too uncritically applied by an earlier generation of sociologists. However, it has a very prominent place in interpreting social change. It does help to bring about a growing interest in historical and comparative studies of social change. This theory also adds to the body of knowledge for sociobiologists to continue on their quest to examine behavioral links between humans and other animals (Maryanski, 2004).

2. **Cyclical Theories**—These theories address the rise of entire societies. Like Darwin and Spencer, Oswald Spengler also believed that societies were like biological organisms, passed through stages of birth, youth, come to maturity, begin to decay as one reaches old age, and later death. His argument was that "cultures are biological organisms, and world history is their collective biography . . . Every culture passes through the age-phases of the individual man" (Spengler, 1964, pp. 21–22). Spengler went on to conduct extensive research on the life span of societies. He estimates the average lifespan for most societies at about 1,000 years. Nevertheless, the cycle does exist, and one can provide a connection to leadership to display its results. Many of the nations have risen to power and later declined to insignificance (Roman Empire, Greece, and Egypt). There is an argument put forth that every society faces challenges to its existence. However, it is the group responsibility to work out these solutions for society to survive. For example, using leadership is the ruling elite (society's leaders) that must attempt to control the masses (multitudes) by use of charm or force. The use of force may hold society together for years, that is, hundreds of years, but society is doomed at some point in its life cycle. Moreover, Toynbee (1946) provided a good example as he stated that even society's use of force might not result in its downfall. Although no society lives forever in that show is one born, it must also decay and die.
3. **Functional Theory of Social Change**—Functional theorists posit that social change must contribute to the overall stability of society. Therefore, from time to time, there must be minor adjustments to maintain equilibrium and order in society. Talcott Parsons (1902–1979), one of America's most famous functional theorists, provides an excellent example of this change through his equilibrium model. According to Parsons, as changes occur in one part of society, adjustments have to be made to the other parts. A failure to do so will create what he calls strains in a society which upsets society's equilibrium. The functionalist argument is evident in that social institutions were established to contribute to society's stability. If we make drastic changes to these social institutions, it will, therefore, threaten societal equilibrium. However, some critics state that this approach virtually neglects the use of force by the powerful to continue the illusion of a stable, well-integrated society (Gouldner, 1960).

We find that the functionalist's premise of social change is based on different generations of sociologists. Research indicates still another connection to Charles Darwin in that each of them compared changes in society to change in biological organisms (simple forms to more complex structures). However, when societies are straightforward and small, there are limited roles for people to perform. Therefore, everyone can complete any tasks associated with their roles. As societies grow, mature, and develop, we find that many people may not have the time or talent to perform every role mandated to support society's equilibrium. At this point, people began to specialize their roles in what Emile Durkheim calls a ***division of labor*** (Durkheim, 1984). The argument that the division of labor is important to the maturity of society stands because it allows people to specialize in specific roles. These specialized roles can include leadership roles to help not only societies but also social institutions move forward. Leadership also may act as a buffer to help facilitate social change when those in specialized roles are resistant to this change.

4. **Conflict Theory of Social Change**—Although functionalist's theorists tend to minimize the importance of change in society, the argument from conflict theorists (notably Karl Marx) is that social change is inevitable because of social conflict between groups seeking power and resources. Therefore, social change is needed to correct social injustices and inequalities to help maintain society's equilibrium. Simply, *Karl Marx* did not necessarily disagree with the evolutionary argument, because he believed that societies did develop along a particular path. However, the key to his argument is that he did not view various changes in society as an improvement over the previous change, because the bourgeoisie still owned and controlled the means of production. Marx associated modern society with capitalism in that he saw the Industrial Revolution as capitalist revolution (Collins & Makowsky, 1993). Therefore, history, according to Marx, proceeds through various stages, each of which exploits a class of people, particularly the proletariat or working class. As a result, he claims that through a socialist revolution led by the proletariat, society will move to the final stage of development: a classless community society or a community of free individuals (Holt, 2015; Marx, 2013). For Marx, we must have changed to not only root out the social injustice that causes social conflict but also rid the world of social classes and harness, what he calls, the marvels of technology to improve people lives. Marx also believed that leaders who worked in the industry were nothing but pure capitalists. He argued "it is not because he is a leader of an industry that a man is a capitalist; on the contrary, he is a leader of industry because he is a capitalist. The leadership of industry is an attribute of capital, just as in feudal times the functions of general and judge were attributes of landed property" (Marx, p. 7966). Since a leader is classified as a capitalist, one may surmise that he or she has an interest in keeping the status quo by controlling the state of the working class in society.
5. **Technological Theory**—Like the other theories discussed above in the chapter, we find that there is also the host of technology theories attempting to address technology. The greatest of these arguments tends to address the association between technology and society. The social sciences, known as the soft sciences compared with the hard sciences like biology, physics, geology, astronomy, and chemistry, tend to center on how technology changes society over a period. And, when people think categorically about changes brought about by science, their first response is always technology. ***Technology*** is another form of culture that allows people to procure goods and services based on their wants quickly and needs to change their natural environment. According to Schaefer and Lamm (1992), technology refers to the application of knowledge to the making of tools and the utilization of natural resources.

It is technology that helps to facilitate change in society. For example, in the post-industrial society, it was technology playing center stage to lead to an information age. Still today, technology is playing a pivotal role fueling us through the age of globalization. Globalization is the growing integration of nations due in part to capitalism and its association with cultures, social movements, commercial markets, and the exchange of designs to feed the processes. As a leader, one looks at the unique challenges presented by the advancement in technology that has materialized as a result of rapid globalization. It is these multinational organizations which grew and continue to grow outside national boundaries that drive the power of social change in and outside these borders. The bottom line is that there are no boundaries and many organizations through the advent of advanced technology can operate anywhere in the world, becoming stronger and more powerful as they proceed. Karl Marx understood this well in that if an organization can grow stronger, this serves as another way for the bourgeoisie or what C. Wright Mills calls the power elite, to control the working class. Moreover, it is Mills (1956) who reminds us of the interwoven power of leaders associated with the military, corporate, and political elements of society and suggests that the ordinary citizen is a relatively powerless subject of manipulation by those entities.

Leadership and Social Movements

There is no doubt that when one starts to address a social movement, one concept that always comes up is leadership. Who is in charge of the movement? The concept of leadership is just another applied use to study sociology and its connection to society. Bates (1967) said it in that from time to time; we must "consider an old and sometimes vexing question in sociology: What is and ought to be the relationship between fundamental sociological knowledge and the practical affairs of society" (p. 69)? The connection of leadership and its connection to social movements are worthy of sociological inquiry. The linkage between leadership and social movements gives us a sense of enlightenment that may act as a powerful tool for relieving human suffering and guiding humanity on its way to a healthier future. Leadership does matter. However, as Barker, Johnson, and Lavalette (2001) note, why has there been little attention as to what leaders do? They go on to identify five reasons for this problem:

1. There is a sympathetic necessity to avoid the historic great man theories and give proper theoretical weight to both the circumstances in which social movements develop and the part played by members of the group. The many leadership theories may lead to why these changes exist in the first place.

2. Few, if any, academics want to revive traditional agitator theories which imply that there would be no strikes, no militant movement activity, were it not for the malign troublemakers who caused them. The general idea is to pay particular attention to the real grievances motivating movements as a whole and avoid treating group members as though they do not matter.
3. Academic theory is affected by activist's ideologies. Therefore, social movement leadership used to be dominated by old movements associated with permanent presences, bureaucratic structures, and centralized leaderships. However, nowadays we find decentralized networks of activists and leaders without strong abilities.
4. Over the years, theorists have associated leadership with particular forms of organization. In result, activists tended to reject leadership altogether which led to unresolved paradoxes, to say we don't need leaders, yet offer to lead. The bottom line is that undigested ideas of independence can invoke real problems of leadership in social movements out of existence, generating barriers to real-world and theoretical advance.
5. We must recognize that the underlying patterns of social movement theorizing have a tendency to divert attention from issues to do with leadership. Although the collective behavior tradition stressing movement irrationalism could never explore leadership questions satisfactorily, it was addressed by resource mobilization, and political process approaches leadership. (pp. 1–2)

The study of leadership specifically adds to the body of knowledge of not just sociology but leadership in general. We can even go a bit further in that sociology of leadership as a whole will give us a better understanding of the social sciences and the business world as we know it today. Discovering leadership in social movements gives us just another tool to facilitate this understanding. Nevertheless, the need to study leadership has been a relentless catchphrase as suggested by McCarthy and Zald (1987) who wrote:

> Leadership phenomena are an even more crucial aspect of the study of a MO (movement organization) than of other large-scale organizations. Because the situation of the MO is unstable, because the organization has few material incentives under its control, and because of the non-routinized nature of its tasks, the success or failure of the MO can be highly dependent on the qualities and commitment of the leadership cadre and the tactics they use (p. 135).

As far as a social movement is a concern, the purpose of leadership is to respond to those members associated with the movement and guide them to the objective. And, one can define a ***social movement*** as a large group of people acting together on behalf of some key goal or idea to change a particular part of society. In some aspect, this social movement may promote or oppose a social or cultural change in society. Although social movements provide a vehicle for social change within society, there is no doubt that social movements would never take place without leaders. Snow, Soule, and Kriesi (2007) posit that numerous scholars have noted that leadership in social movements has yet to theorize adequately. They also assert that a focus on great leaders risks the neglect of structural opportunities and obstacles to collect action, while this will fail to address the human agency involvement. Moreover, any approach to leadership in social movements must examine the actions of leaders within the structural contexts and recognize the multiple levels of leadership and roles of participants. From a strategic point of view, we wholeheartedly agree.

A failure to address the overall structure from a leader-participant point of view is wrong. We can define a social movement as a large group of people acting in concert on behalf of some objective or idea. We should recognize the Civil Rights Movement as a great example. This goal or idea either promotes or opposes a social or cultural change. Leadership is critical and social movements are more organized and more focused than collective behavior. Witt (2016) agrees that leadership is necessary, because he states "leadership is a central factor in the mobilization of the discontented into social movements" (p. 371). However, Marx and Engles (1978) argued that outside leaders (intellectuals) were required for revolutionary movements because the masses were incapable of developing a theoretical understanding of revolutionary struggle.

Leadership is about the relationship with others, and those who participate in social movements makes this even more important. As we discussed in Chapter 7, one of the major sociological traditions in which leadership interactions have flowed from Weber's argument of the three types of authority (Kalberg, 2017). Like Weber; Barker, Johnson, and Lavalette (2001) support this position when they posit that a leader's authority is about domination and one's ability to get people to obey commands when direct force is not applied. Hence, the establishment of a relationship. However, they go on to say that what is missing from the Weberian position when centering on movement leadership is any sense of people following others out of rational conviction in the correctness of their views. In other words, Democratic leadership does not exist. *Democratic leadership* style gives everyone an open seat at the table, encouraging the group or team to generate ideas without any conviction freely.

Barker, Johnson, and Lavalette (2001) suggest a dialogical approach which offers a way of generating insights into the relations of leader to movements. They alleged that it points to us considering leadership in movements as part of a process of ongoing dialogs in which words and answers contribute to the development of practices and ideas. Naturally, it demands that we study not only the ways that people lead others by persuasive speech and action but also how groups or followers respond. Those who conduct research on leadership general find information addressing the importance of a leader's communications. Even a savvy leader fully understands that his or her success centers on their ability to communicate and they must master that ability to win in their endeavors. The golden thread tying all functions of leadership together is clear communications. And, those functions of leadership are as follows:

- **Always form a community**—If leadership expects to succeed in a social movement of any kind, it must build and maintain a close-knit community. Societies are forever rapidly changing and continue to provide a shift in relationships. According to Witt (2016), sociology arose as a discipline to better understand and direct the transition from traditional to modern society. To (or "intending to") doing this, early sociologists sought to develop models that described the fundamental differences between the two. The whole idea is to understand better how traditional societies operate so that we might actually identify the underlying factors that shape core concerns in modern society, such as social order, inequality, and interaction (2016). The changes in society deal with social structure as a whole. This is why sociologists are always speaking about what holds society together? Two good answers are addressed by Ferdinand Tönnies and Emile Durkheim. To support the idea of close-net community, we must turn our attention to Ferdinand Tönnies (1855–1936). In his study of industrialized cities, particularly Germany where he grew up, he analyzes what he called a fundamental shift in community relationships. He defined these changes as Gemeinschaft (Guh-MINE-shoft) or private community to Gesellschaft (Guh-ZELL-shoft) or impersonal association (1988). Gemeinschaft is a type of society (rural) in which life appears to be close-knit or intimate with a strong consensus on values that unite members of the group. On the other hand, Gesellschaft is a type of society (urban) that dominates impersonal relationships with little connection to the group or consensus on values. We find that members are more concerned about individual accomplishments and self-interest. Emile Durkheim (1858–1917) introduces us to the terms mechanical and organic solidarity. He goes on to state that it is in these terms that social integration takes place and as societies got larger, they develop what he called a specialized division of labor. In other words, the social structure depends on the division of labor in society. For example, goods and services can be carried out by one individual or can be divided among many people. The social integration is the process of being united by shared values and bonds which are similar to Tönnies' argument. When it came to smaller groups, Durkheim (1984) termed this process as *mechanical solidarity*, those united (a shared consciousness) in which people feel a result of performing the same or similar tasks. Naturally, it implies that all individuals are performing the same tasks and as such, they developed a shared consciousness. However, there is no need to ask people what they do because they all do the same thing. On the flip side, it is a society that becomes more complicated because people are not doing the same thing. There are more different types of things to do in society, and now dependence on others becomes essential for group survival. As a result, mechanical solidarity is then replaced by what Durkheim's calls *organic solidarity*; a collective consciousness is resting on the need society's members have for one another in a highly specialized division of labor. Again to put it simply, members of the group depend on one another for the specific work that each person must perform to contribute to the whole group and this work has become more specialized and complex. The bottom line is that Durkheim chose the term organic solidarity because, at this point, individuals become dependent in much the same way as organs of the human body: connected, specialized, and in some cases interdependent but designed to help make the body function as a whole.

- **Develop and communicate a clear vision** —It's not easy for leaders to create and communicate a vision without having that big idea that will resonate with others in the community. Leaders must get people excited about what is going on, but first, he or she must create a process for identifying and communicating the vision. Centered on what the group could and should be doing to facilitate change, a famous big idea, illustrated by the remarks of President John F. Kennedy for a charge to NASA when he said "We choose to go the moon in this decade and do the other things, not because they are easy, but because they are hard" (Gort, 1962). Great leaders dream big ideas and communicate them effectively, charging members to go and carry out the mission in a manner that will make all proud. It is leaders who motivate us to go places we would not otherwise go, and this is the example for which inspired NASA to go forth and do great things for humanity, and they did and are still doing this today.
- **Support the people's needs**—We need to understand that regardless of any movement (e.g. social or political), leaders must support members' needs to the point they are willing to go the extra mile for the group. As a leader, you charge them to do something, now take care of them when they do. Leaders must be accountable to others because it is the right

thing to do and its part of leading by example. Supporting members' needs is the prelude to building and sustaining relationships with the group. One of the reasons why people follow leaders is that their needs will be taken care of without hesitation. Erik Erikson once said that leadership depends on the interaction between leadership and followers (Kellerman, 1984). I couldn't agree more in that part of the interaction phase is knowing that members will be taken care of as they pursue the goals of the group. "The powerful interaction that particularly interests Erikson often takes place with within sociopolitical movements rather than in political systems operating routinely through established institutions" (1984, pp. 74–75). The bottom line is that the overall success of leadership not only depends on the relationship between the group and the leader but also the significance of the leader's ability to take care of the needs of the group.

- **Overcome setbacks and adversity**—A leader is obligated to take responsibility for his or her actions. Although not all leaders have the ability to handle adversity, those who can clearly have the advantage are the winners. You heard the saying "when the going gets tough, the tough gets going." Get tough and get going. Leaders of social movements must overcome setbacks and adversity, move the obstacles, and get back on track.
- **Always move forward**—Through great skill, leaders push and move forward, making big wins and not getting sidetracked. A leader's action and words are vital to this forward push. One great example is the conversation that General George S. Patton had with another general. But first, Paton once said that wars might be fought with weapons, but men win them. Frankly, it is the spirit of men who follow and the man who leads that gains the victory. Speaking to another general, Patton was asked: "I thought you would want to fall back and rest." Patton replies by saying "Not me. I don't like to pay for the same real estate twice." Leaders are charged with the authority to move forward and never look back: go for the prize. The only way a leader of a social movement can be successful is always rapidly progress toward the goal.

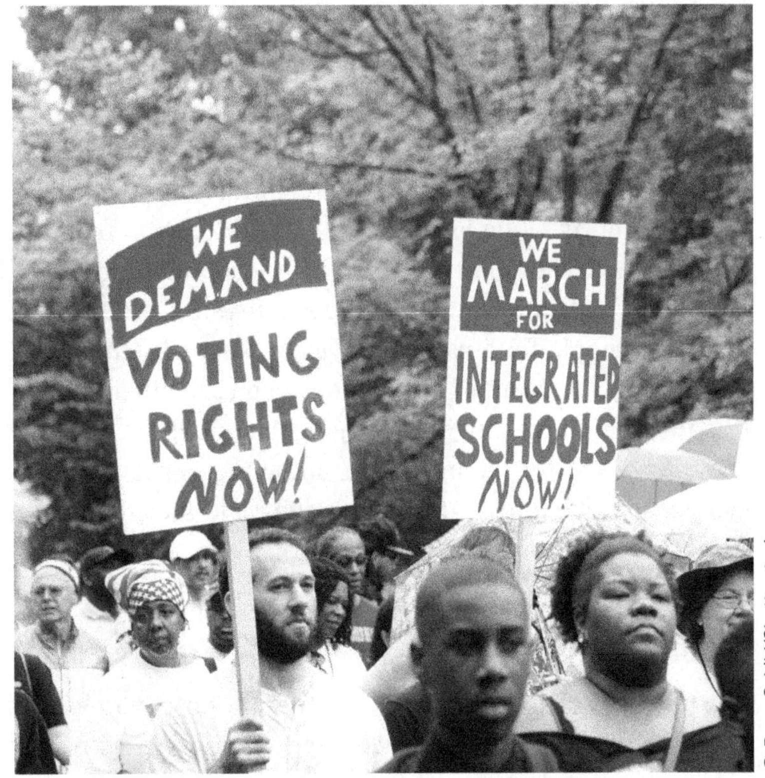

© Rena Schild/Shutterstock.com

When we examine the great sociologist Max Weber in this discussion of social movements, we can't help but notice his theory of charismatic leadership. Weber (1978) elaborates on what he calls the movement forms associated with charismatic leadership, including the emotional character of the community and the appointment of officials based on loyalty to the charismatic leader. Although he spent a lot of his time focusing on the interactional nature of leadership, the notion of charisma is commonly used to refer to a personality type, and Weber's insight into the effects of leadership on movement characteristics, for the most part, has been neglected (Snow, Soule, & Kriesi, 2007). However, it is more than just having the charisma that pushes a person to lead a social movement. There is an assortment of individuals who lead social movements, and this includes men and women. They tend to come from the middle class and are highly educated, but we must understand why this nonrepresentative quality of movement leaders seem to the rule rather than the exception and what implications the social composition of leadership has for social movements (2007).

There is an inequality when it comes to social movements as far as gender is a concern. Robnett (1997) posits that women often function in the role of "bridge leader," which she defines as "an intermediate layer of leadership, whose task includes bridging potential constituents and adherents, as well as potential formal leaders to the movement" (p. 191). In a supporting argument, Jones (1993) maintains that women usually engage in leadership activities that establish networks and formal cement ties because of their skills associated with family life and family-like symbols (p. 119). Even today, we still find women struggling to secure top leadership positions in various organizations. Women are going to college and getting an education in record numbers far more than men. We must include women in the top posts or run the risk of them being excluded from a considerable amount of power wielded by top movement leaders (Snow, Soule, & Kriesi, 2007). From a strategic leadership point of view, it is important to have diversity in these leadership positions because leaders with different backgrounds and experiences make different strategic choices, which have a tendency to influence the movement success. We can point to the Civil Rights Movement as an example in that there was a host of diversity that helps led the movement to its success.

Challenges of Mobilization

The early stages of a social movement always have had its problems of mobilization. As theorists Snow, Soule, and Kriesi (2007) state, to understand how leadership affects mobilization, we must examine the interactive relationships among various types of leaders and movement participants. There will always be challenges to mobilize people for a cause. However, one thing is for sure in that you can execute the task if you can communicate efficiently and rally the people. If you want to unite a nation, you better be a great orator. Some great speakers of our time are surely Martin Luther King, Jr., John F. Kennedy, Ronald Reagan, Bill Clinton, and Barack Obama.

Being a great orator plays well for leadership. In 1953, Dr. Karl W. Deutsch wrote this book called *Nationalism and Social Communication*. Deutsch (1953) asserts that the key to rallying a nation of people for a particular cause, especially those discontent, centers on one's communications skills. I don't think that anyone can argue that point at all. However, Dr. Deutsch states that it is the communication that creates a national consciousness that is reinforced by race, culture, geography and for the most part, a common enemy. Communication is based on the transfer of symbols, which allows individuals to create meaning and as these communication standards are steadfast (Hackman & Johnson, 2013).

Charismatic Leadership and Social Change

The power to change society is easier with those who have charisma. As you learned in Chapter 2, this is because of the excellent leader relationship with supporters. We must consider charismatic leaders powerful agents of social change. There are various theories of charismatic leadership emphasizing these personality and behavior patterns and their effects on followers, organizations, and society. Although this emphasis fails to address why and how the charismatic leader/follower interaction can generate social change, some theorists suggest that it is the way charismatic leaders communicate with their supporters (Northouse, 2016).

Transformational Leadership and Social Change

Transformational leadership style makes social change look easy. The transformational leader can appeal to a follower's higher moral values and follow-up with a system of rewards that they are more likely to be successfully in their endeavors. The whole idea is to enact what transformational leadership theory argues a vision centered on followers looking beyond their self-interest for the good of the group.

Servant Leadership and Social Change

To be considered a great leader, one must be a servant leader. There is no doubt that to facilitate change in society, it's best to serve others. Jesus once said to his disciple's James and John that true greatness comes in helping others (Ross, 2008). If in my view everyone is a leader, then we all are in a position to effect social change in society. Servant leadership style is the best way to show others that you are serious about social change because you illustrate above all else that you are there to serve. Maxwell (2005) said it best when he described leadership in that it is:

> People more than projects; movement more than maintenance; art more than science; intuition more than formula; vision more than procedure; risk more than caution; action more than reaction; relationships more than rules; who you are more than what you do (p. 113).

I wholeheartedly agree with this position in that at the end of the day, leadership to me is one's ability to develop relationships with people in the form of art, using your intuition to take risks, setting a vision to articulate the movement of the organization well into the future so that it can maintain its competitive advantage. However, you will not be able to do any of these things if the organization is trying to find out who you are or what you stand for as a person. Servant leadership helps to facilitate this process. So you want to effect positive social change in society than act as a servant leader. As Robert Greenleaf reminds us for sure, a servant leader is a servant first.

Critical Thinking

How can transformational leadership be used to facilitate the development of personal qualities to affect positive change? Does these personal qualities support group interactions so that they can function as a team to push for positive social change?

Chapter Summary

Leadership is critical and social movements are more organized and more focused than collective behavior. However, you must emulate servant leadership style to be more efficient in your cause. I like to think that a leader is unique not only because he has charisma but also a great orator. It always helps to communicate, interact, and once again communicate so that people understand clearly where you are coming from in your endeavors. Like many aspects of society, there is also an inequality when it comes to social movements. Technology rules in that you can mobilize quicker in this era of globalization, and we can thank the advancements in technology that have to lead the way.

Glossary

Black Lives Matter (BLM) An international movement which originated in the African-American community to bring awareness of violence and systemic racism toward black people.

Collective Behavior The actions of large groups of people that do not conform to establish social norms.

Democratic Leadership A leadership style that gives everyone an open seat at the table, encouraging the group or team to generate ideas without any conviction freely.

Division of Labor As a social division of labor, people specialize in various roles within society as a whole.

Gemeinschaft A type of society (rural) in which life appears to be close-knit or intimate, with a strong consensus on values that unite members of the group.

Gesellschaft A type of society (urban) that is dominated by an impersonal relationship with little connection to the group or consensus on values.

Globalization The increasing integration of nations due in part to capitalism and its association with cultures, social movements, commercial markets, and the exchange of designs to feed the processes.

Macrosociology The areas concerned with large-scale patterns operating at the group level of society.

Mechanical Solidarity Those united (a shared consciousness) in which people feel a result of performing the same or similar tasks.

Organic Solidarity A collective consciousness sleeping on the need society's members have for one another in a highly specialized division of labor.

Social change The change of behavior patterns, social relationships, organizations, and social structures over a period.

Social Movement A large group of people acting together on behalf of some key objective or idea to change a particular part of society.

Technology Another form of culture that allows people to procure goods and services based on their wants quickly and needs to modify their natural environment.

References

Barker, C., A. A. Johnson, & M. Lavalette. (Eds.). 2001. *Leadership and social movements*. New York: Manchester University Press.

Bates, A. P. (1967). *The sociological enterprise*. Boston, MA: Houghton Mifflin Company.

Collins, R., & Makowsky, M. (1993). *The discovery of society*. (5th ed.). New York, NY: McGraw-Hill, Inc.

Darwin, C. (2010). *The works of Charles Darwin, volume 15: On the origin of species, 1859*. New York, NY: New York University Press.

Deutsch, K. W. (1953). *Nationalism and social communication: An inquiry into the foundations of nationality*. Cambridge, MA: MIT Press.

Durkheim, E. (1984). *The division of labor in society* (Trans. Karen E. Fields). New York, NY: Free Press.

Gouldner, A. (1960). The norm of reciprocity. *American Sociology Review*, 25, 161–177.

Gort, T. E. (1962). President Kennedy's speech at Rice University. Retrieved from http://customers.hbci.com/~tgort/jfk_rice.htm

Hackman, M. Z., & Johnson, C. E. (2013). *Leadership: A communicative perspective.* (6th ed.). Long Grove, IL: Waveland Press, Inc.

Holt, J. P. (2015). *The social thought of Karl Marx (Social Thinkers Series).* Thousand Oaks, CA: Sage Publications, Inc.

Jones, K. B. (1993). *Compassionate authority: Democracy and the representation of women.* New York, NY: Routledge.

Kalberg, S. (2017). *The social thought of Max Weber (Social Thinkers Series).* Los Angeles, CA: Sage Publication, Inc.

Kellerman, B. (1984). *Leadership: Multidisciplinary perspectives.* Englewood Cliffs, NJ: Prentice-Hall, Inc.

Le Bon, G. (2011). *The crowd: Study of the popular mind.* Amazon Digital Services, LLC.

Maryanski, A. R. (2004). Evaluation theory. In G. Ritzer (Ed.), *Encyclopedia of social theory*, (pp. 257–263). Thousand Oaks, CA: Sage.

Marx, K. (2013). *Complete works of Karl Marx Kindle edition.* Minerva Classics.

Marx, K., & Engels, F. (1978). *The Marx-Engles reader.* (2nd ed.). R. C. Tucker (Ed.). New York: W. W. Norton & Company.

Maxwell, J. C. (2005). *The 360-degree leader: Developing your influences from anywhere in the organization.* Nashville, TN: Thomas Nelson, Inc.

McCarthy, J. D., & Zald, M. N. (1987). Resource mobilization and social movements: A partial theory. *In Social Movements: Perspectives and Issues.* Eds. Buechler, S. M. and Cylke, F. K. (1997). Mountain View, CA: Mayfield Publishing Company.

Mills, C. Wright. (1956). *The power elite.* New York, NY: Oxford University Press.

Northouse, P. G. (2016). *Leadership: Theory and practice.* (7th ed.). Thousand Oaks, CA: Sage Publications, Inc.

Robnett, B. (1997). *How long? African-American women in the struggle for civil rights.* New York, NY: Oxford University Press.

Ross, L. F. 2008. *So you want to be a strategic leader: Here are the essentials to get you started.* Philadelphia, PA: Xlibris Publishers.

Schaefer, R. T., & Lamm, R. P. (1992). *Sociology.* (4th ed.). New York, NY: McGraw-Hill, Inc.

Snow, D. A., Soule, S. A., & Kriesi, H. (2007). *The Blackwell companion to social movements.* Malden, MA: Blackwell Publishing.

Spencer, H. (2009). *Principles of biology (V.2).* New York, NY: Cornell University Library.

Spengler, O. (1964). The life cycle of cultures. In Amitai & Eva Etzioni (Eds.) *Social changes: Sources, patterns, and consequences*, pp. 21–23. New York, NY: Basic Books.

Toynbee, A.J. (1946). *A study of history: Abridgement of volumes I-VI (Royal Institute of International Affairs).* D. C. Somervell (Ed.). New York, NY: Oxford University Press.

Weber, M. (1978). *Economy and society: An outline of interpreative sociology.* (2 vols)., Guenther, R., & Wittich, C. (eds.). Berkely, CA: University of California Press.

Witt, J. (2016). *SOC.* (4th ed.) New York, NY: McGraw-Hill Education.

Chapter 8

Leadership Skill-Building Exercise

My Personal Identity

Who Am I?

There has always been an argument put forth by leadership theorists that for organizations to make effective leaders, they must first identify potential employees who are perceived to have leadership potential. After this identification, they must move them through a pipeline for leadership development. According to Carter, Ulrich, and Goldsmith (2005), organizations must train those in various leadership pipelines. One of the basic training techniques is to put individuals through a process call deliberate practice whereby these potential leaders learn how to lead effectively.

There are also many skill development programs that can assess an individual's leadership potential by determining his or her personality, values, and behavior. Organizations use socialization techniques to direct potential leaders toward the vision, mission, and core values of the organization. One critical process which organizations use to facilitate the socialization process is through action learning. Action learning is used to build self-awareness through the team or individual learning techniques. Organizational observers may employ applications to accurately review one's overall competence, development, experience, skills, creativity, and communication.

It is best for one to find out who they are as a person before trying to become a leader to lead others. The overall impact of who you are has tended to affect how one thinks, feels, and act around others. In most cases, your overall function in life depends on knowing who you are as a person. Knowing who you are is a long process, and it begins with the socialization process and continues through life. One should develop a sense of self-awareness to learn more about self. Therefore, this next skill-building exercise is about writing a story about who you are and what you stand for as a person. At this point, you should have gathered a host of information about self during the previous exercises. Now look at the figure and think about the concept of personality identity. Your personal identity is about the development of self over the course of your

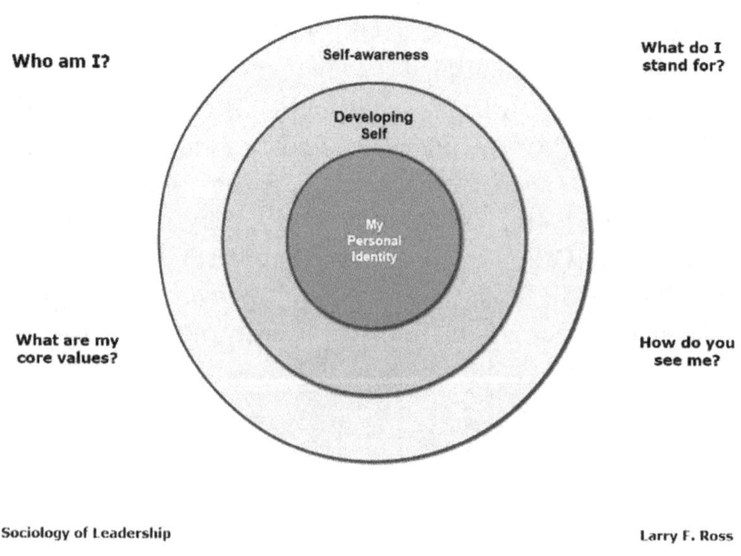

life, and as stated before, it began when you were first socialized. Think of it as your self-image, the way you and others see yourself.

Ask yourself these questions and address these statements in an article about self:

- What makes you different from others?
- What are your core values?
- How do you look to others (your body image or attractiveness)?
- What are your personal goals?
- Describe your personality and character?
- Generalize what you stand for in life and how this relates to others.
- What is your job regarding what you do only?
- Describe your strengths and weaknesses and there overall impact on your personal identity?
- Know thyself before you act!
- Your personal identity requires you to examine your beliefs and values so that you live life accordingly.

Now we want you to put something on paper by writing a story of what you learned and share with others. Write your article and this one should be very different from other stories you have written about self.

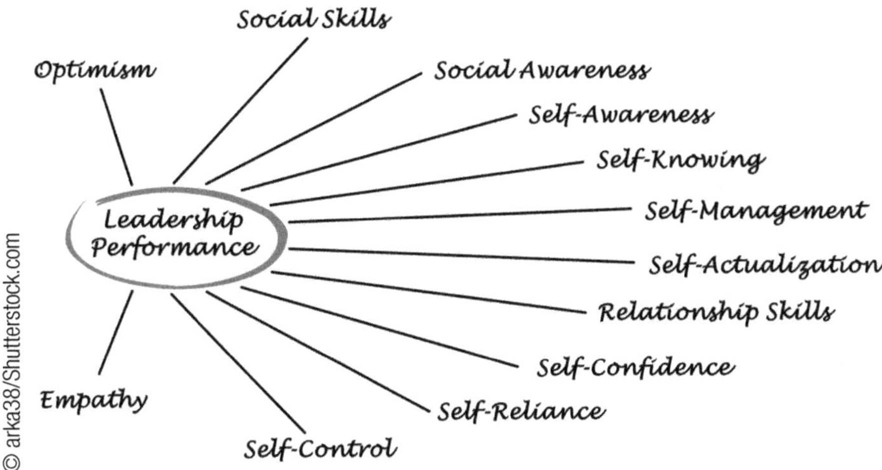

Chapter 9

- Self-Leadership Development
- The would be Leader
- The Eight Cognitive Processes and the Myers-Briggs
- What is your personality type?

Sociology of Leadership

Thinking Critically!

1. How do you think that President Kennedy, acting as an agent of political socialization, made such an impact on Bill Clinton?
2. Thinking about your field or major area of study, does your personality type indicate a successful endeavor?
3. For centuries, great leaders made decisions that had an impact on United States of America's society. Since you are a member of society and want to contribute to it in a successful manner, what decisions will you make for the betterment of self? Provide details and share with others.
4. When does leadership of self matter?

It's all about you this time!!

As You Read

- What does leadership have to do with one's personality?
- Who is better at leadership; an extrovert or introvert?
- What impact has one made in your life and how have you responded to this drive?

Chapter 9

Self-Leadership Development

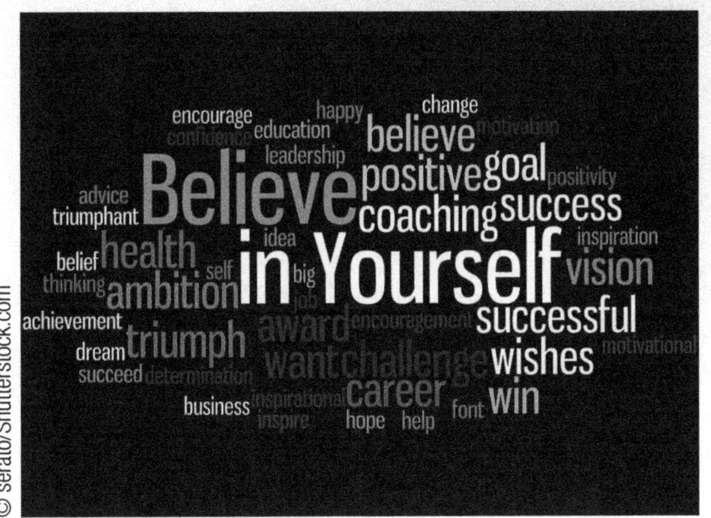

Leadership has a significant role in creating the state of mind that is the society. They can serve as symbols of the moral unity of the society. They can express the values that hold the society together. Most important, they can conceive and articulate goals that lift people out of their petty preoccupations, carry them above the conflicts that tear a society apart, and unite them in the pursuit of objectives worthy of their efforts.

John W. Gardner

The above capture should get you to thinking about who you are, why you are here, and at some point come you will ask where you go from here. The bigger question is how do you fit in society? We have all seen the power of society to shape individual choices. When you were first born, your parents took care of you, they put your clothes on, and they fed you and also put a roof over your head, and you developed relationships as you got older. Getting old, you began to extend the development of your independence. Now you are older, and it appears you need to make decisions for yourself. In other words, you see individuality first hand in the social context. As many great sociologists have suggested, it is the society that shapes our choices and even where we live has a bearing on our lives. However, the era of globalization makes for the gradually interconnected world. So thinking globally may be a good way to learn more about self.

We all have problems at some time or another that we have to deal with in our lifetime. The problems are that we just want it to go away without ever taking charge of it for ourselves. Self-leadership development may be the most underutilized tool in leadership development. Mostly, it is understanding yourself and knowing what to do to lead yourself. Regularly, we spend time analyzing and discussing others' leadership successes and failures, but we fail to address the self-leadership failures on both sides. As a leader of self, you are charged to attack your problems head-on because you were socialized to do so. I realized sometimes this might be hard to do. However, in the end, you will thank yourself.

The would be Leader

Think about this question, what did this person do to become President of the United States or what the person's life was like when growing up and becoming the leader of the free world? I like to tell this story to my class, and many are not aware of this fact. It concerns the former President of the United States, William (Bill), Jefferson Clinton. The date was July 24, 1963, approximately 54 years ago, Bill Clinton who at the time was 16 years old, attended an event for the American Legion Boys Nation at the White House. Clinton shook hands with President John F. Kennedy, and he later stated that the handshake inspired him to a life of public service. A Rhodes Scholar and 30 years later, Bill Clinton became the 42nd President of the United States. What a powerful socialization event.

Babies are born without any culture, and they must be transformed by their parents, teachers, and others who play a significant role in developing them into cultural and socially adaptable Homo sapiens. As you already know at this point, the overall process of obtaining culture is referred to as socialization. We must further remind ourselves here that it is through this process we acquire the language of a culture born into and the role we will play in life. We also learned early on that norms are origins of appropriate as well as expected behavior. However, as far as leadership is concerned, we need to bring to your attention a deeper aspect of the socialization process, which is personality formation. Most of our human character comes from the genes of our parents, but it is the socialization process that has the tendency to mold it in a particular direction through specific beliefs, attitudes, and experiences (Albrecht, Chadwick, & Jacobson, 1987; Kosslyn & Rosenberg, 2001; Myers, 2011).

Critically Thinking

How do you think that President Kennedy, acting as an agent of political Socialization, made such an impact on Bill Clinton?

The Eight Cognitive Processes and the Myers-Briggs

One of the essential elements of self-leadership development is that we break the cognitive code by understanding our ability to gather information and make decisions. As Nardi (2005) asserts, the general idea may be that we actively make decisions based on personal values, which involve talking with others and acting on our values, not just thinking about them. Or it could be we like engaging the world around us directly through the five senses, trusting our gut instinct. Simply, we use the eight cognitive processes actively to get from one moment to the next within the larger systems of life, our environment, our use of tools, our relationships with other people, and our culture (2005). According to Berens and Nardi (2013), the eight cognitive processes are extraverted Sensing, introverted Sensing, extraverted iNtuiting, introverted iNtuiting, extraverted Thinking, introverted Thinking, extraverted Feeling, and introverted Feeling, which is broken down by information-assessing processes and organizing–evaluating processes. For a detailed description of these processes, review Figures 9.1a and 9.1b.

Figure 9.1a Information-Accessing Processes—Perception

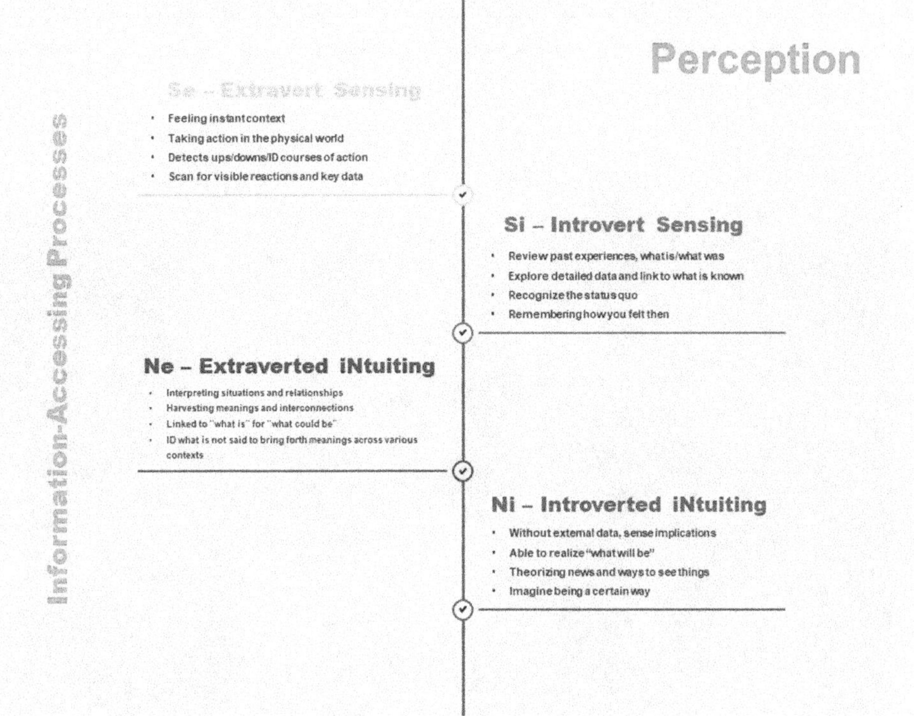

Source: Adapted from Berens and Nardi (2013). (Used with permission).

Figure 9.1b Organizing–Evaluating Processes—Judgment

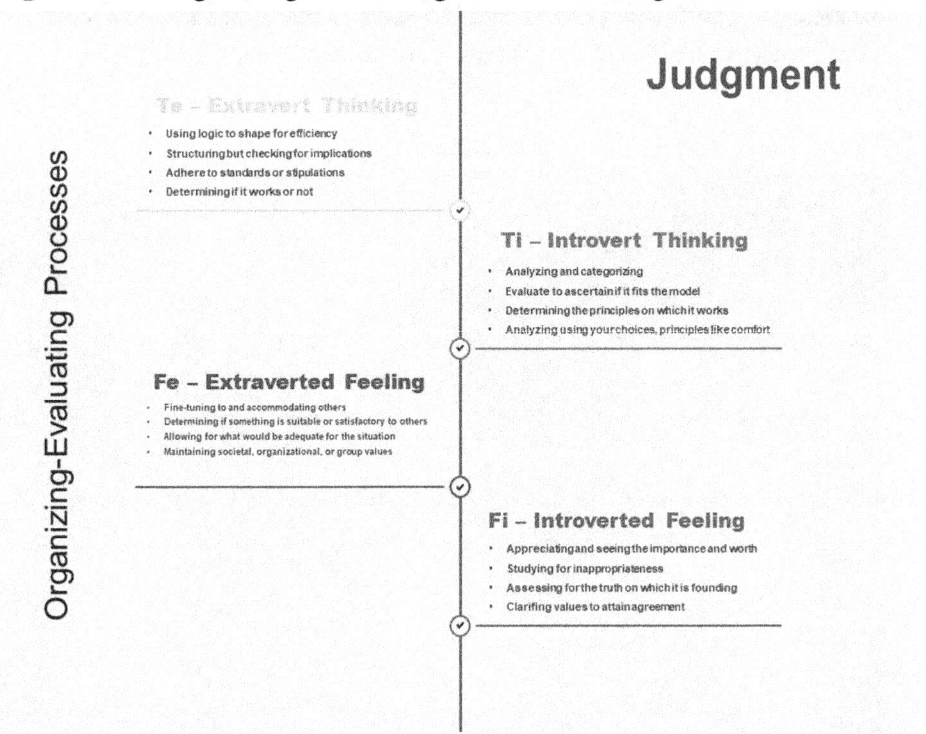

Source: Adapted from Berens and Nardi (2013). (Used with permission).

Your personality type is just another piece of your overall leadership persona. Now do yourself a favor and review Figures 9.2a through 9.2h. You will need to refer back to these figures when completing the Leadership Skill-Building Exercise for Chapter 9 at the end of the book. At the end of reviewing the figures, you will find some thoughts by the author.

Figure 9.2a The Distinction between Inner and Outer Experience

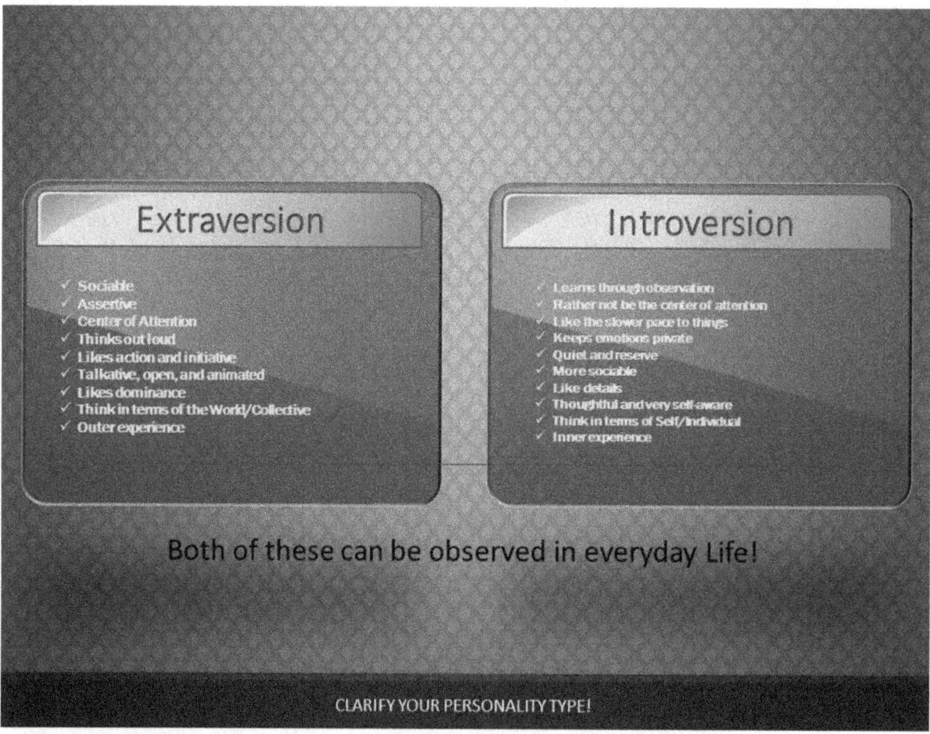

Source: Adapted from Quenk (2009), Myres (1995), and Drenth (2014b).

Figure 9.2b The Processing of Data

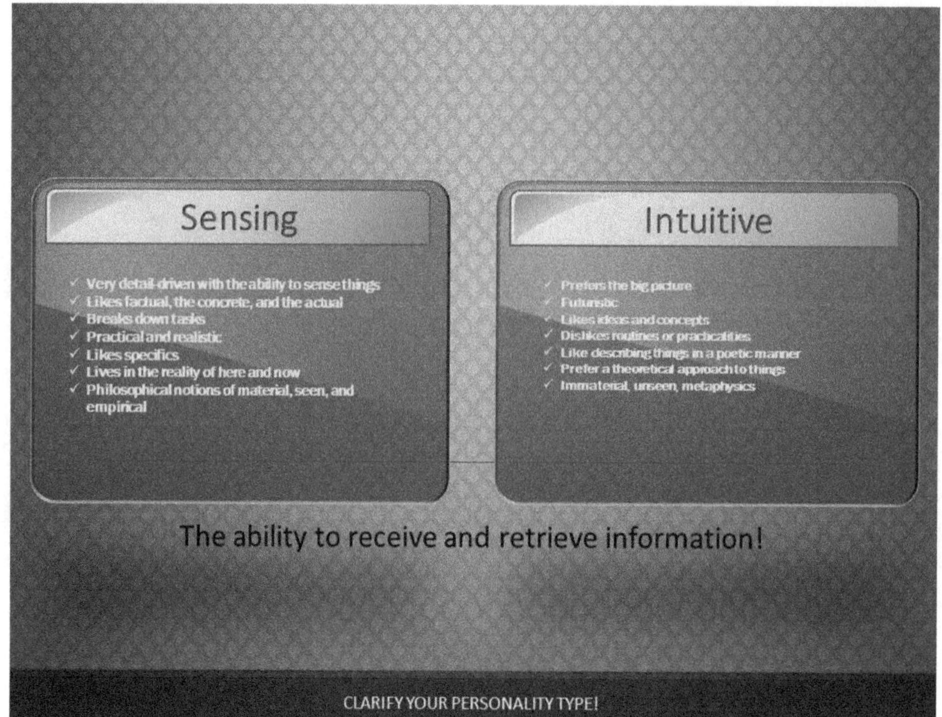

Source: Adapted from Quenk (2009), Myres (1995), and Drenth (2014b).

Figure 9.2c How Do You Make Decisions?

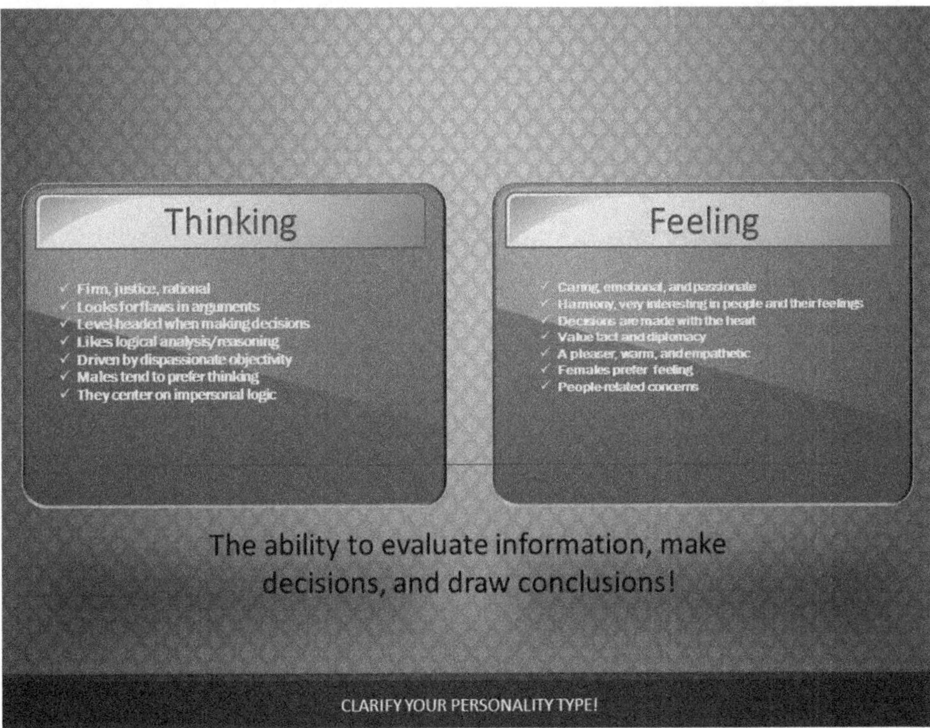

Source: Adapted from Quenk (2009), Myres (1995), and Drenth (2014b).

Figure 9.2d How do You Prefer to Live Your Life

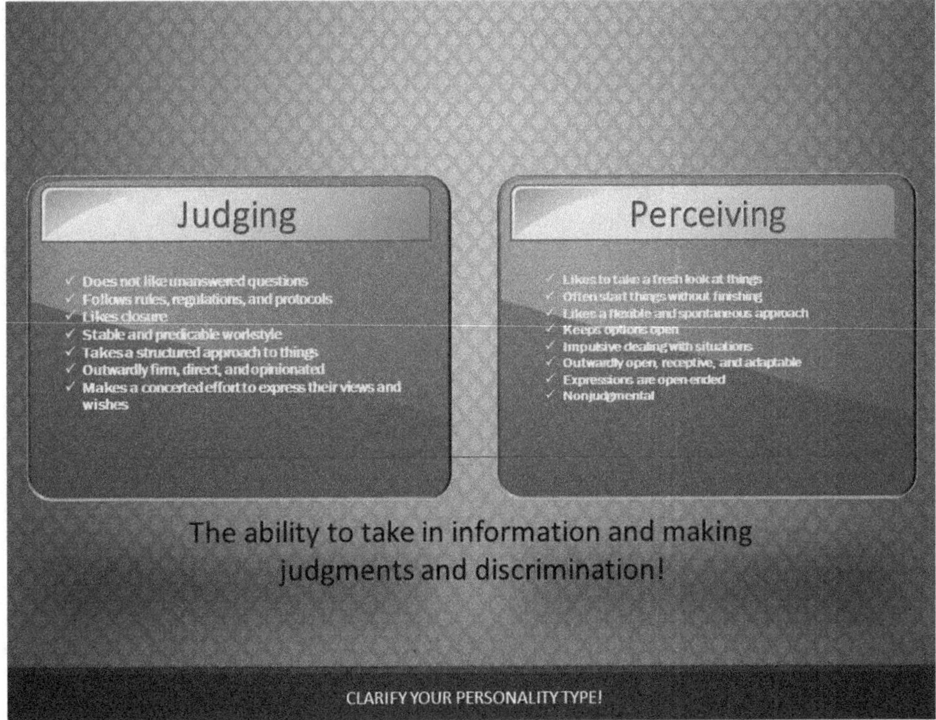

Source: Adapted from Quenk (2009), Myres (1995), and Drenth (2014b)

Figure 9.2e Myers Briggs Personality Type Indicator

ISTJ

This person is honest and direct and can be resolute and obedient at times. He or she is very accountable, composed, and practical, but has a tendency to create and enforce order in organizations.

This person is stubborn at times and can be insensitive to the needs of others. Often unreasonable, he or she tends to blame themselves for inaction. By the book and judgmental is this person's calling card. A leader cannot be judgmental.

ISFJ

This person is dependable and patient. He or she is compessionate to others, and often keeps a sharp eye on things. One thing that stands out is that he or she is loyal and hard-working which is a plus.

This person is known to take things personally, and at times repress their feelings when there are problems. There is some indication that he or she is unwilling to change in that the status quo is okay. Leaders must be change agents.

INFJ

Known to be obsessive, creative, and astute, this person is determined in their interactions or objectives. Other attributes include being pivotal and inspirational for a cause.

This person is a perfectionist who also appears extremely reserved and sensitive at times. He or she burns out easily. They will not act unless there is a cause. It might be hard at times for the leader to maintain the competitive advantage under these conditions.

INTJ

This person is imaginative with a strategic mind. He or she is independent and hardworking and determined. There are indications that he or she is also very self-confident and is a jack-of-all-trades. A leader would embrace these traits for sure.

Some call this person arrogant and overly analytical. He or she is clueless in the romance area and likes structure. There are those who do not like arrogant leaders.

CLARIFY YOUR PERSONALITY TYPE!

Source: Adapted from Quenk (2009), Myres (1995), and Drenth (2014b).

Figure 9.2f Myers Briggs Personality Type Indicator

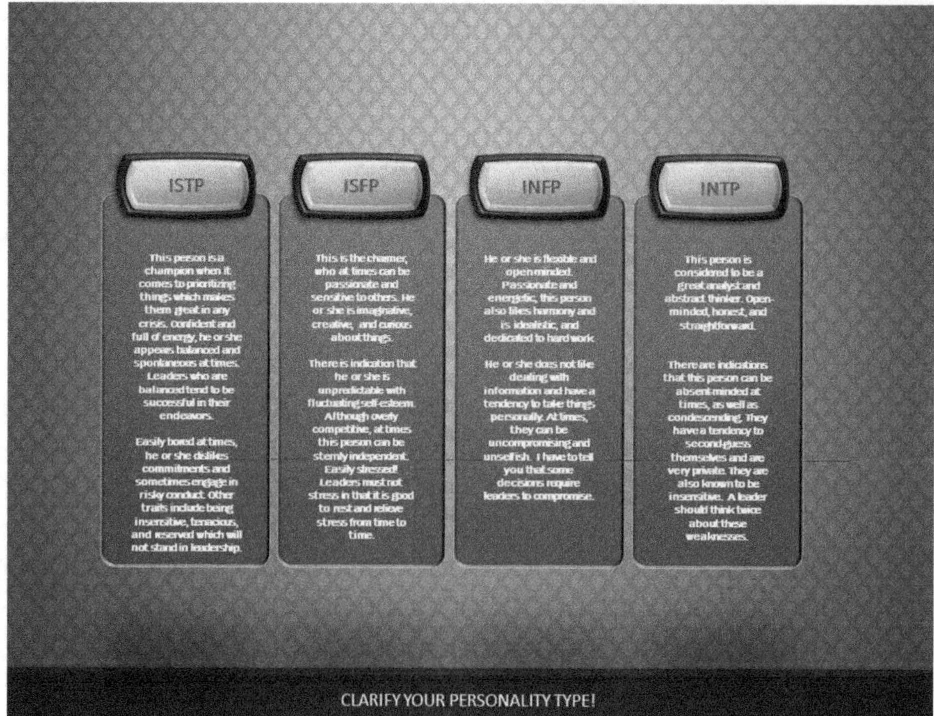

Source: Adapted from Quenk (2009), Myres (1995), and Drenth (2014b).

Figure 9.2g Myers Briggs Personality Type Indicator

ESTP

This person likes to motivate others to drive action toward the ultimate goal of the organization. The genuine salesperson, he or she understands people well and will use rules and regulations to guide their behavior. All of this can be great for leadership.

From a macrosociological point of view, he or she may miss the big picture. They also appear unstructured, unresponsive, annoyed, and can be defiant at times.

ESFP

They like people, new ideas, and new gadgets which are good leadership traits. Very talkative, this person like to tell stories about things. They have the people skills to get things done and will use their values to make decisions. Values are important in leadership. He or she will learn as they interact with others.

However, they are easily bored and sensitive at times. They are poor in the long-term planning arena because they tend to get unfocused for various reasons.

ENFP

One thing is clear about this person in that they are very observant and always curious about things around them. However, one must not become a micro-manager. Besides being popular and friendly, they are excellent communicators which are good leadership traits.

Although they lack focus and tend to over think things, they have poor practical skills which may end up being a significant problem in leadership. One more thing is that they stress easily and are highly emotional at times.

ENTP

They are quick thinkers and very knowledgeable. He or she are excellent barnstormers and energetic when they want to be in organizations.

They are very argumentative and insensitive which can be very bad for leadership. They dislike practical matters and they have problems focusing. Being intolerant is a problem.

CLARIFY YOUR PERSONALITY TYPE!

Source: Adapted from Quenk (2009), Myres (1995), and Drenth (2014b).

Figure 9.2h Myers Briggs Personality Type Indicator

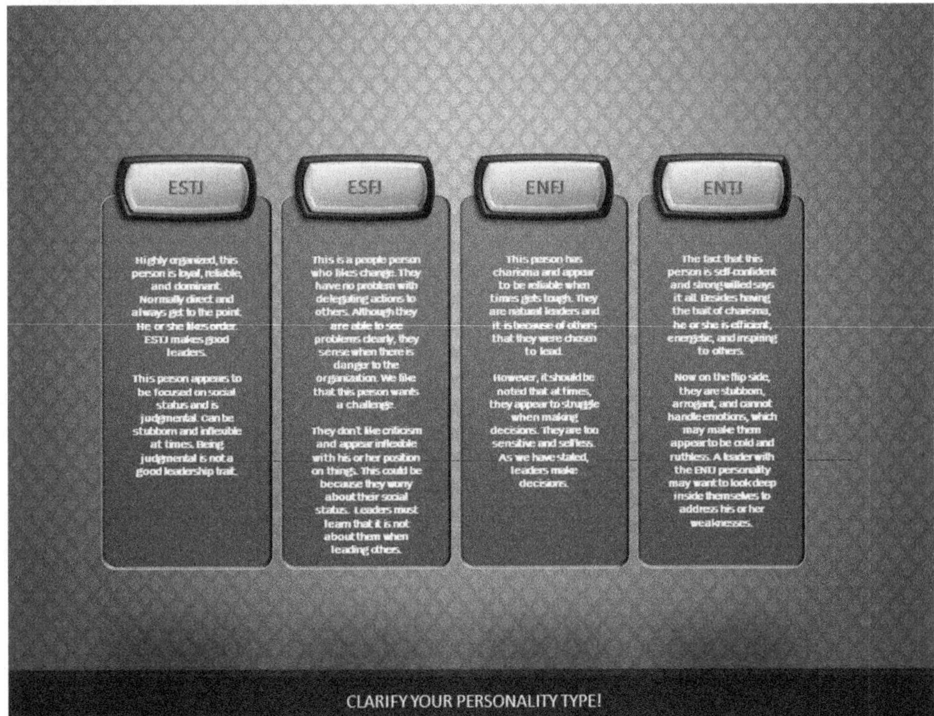

Source: Adapted from Quenk (2009), Myres (1995), and Drenth (2014b).

I began my leadership walk by serving in the U.S. Army and went on to finish my second career with the Federal government at U.S. Department of Defense, Defense Contract Management Agency. During my leadership walk, I have come across many individuals, and I can honestly say that some were good and some bad. I also can say that I have been in leadership roles my entire adult life before becoming a professor. I have been leading others for so long that I find myself placed in a position that I must learn how not to lead others. However, I learned early on that if I wanted to lead others, I must first lead myself. So while in the U.S. Army, I totally believed in the slogan "Be all that You Can Be."

One does not set out to take charge of others because, for the most part, leaders are chosen. If by chance that you get into a situation and are selected, you must first make a decision if you want to lead others. As you ponder which way to go, you begin to think about how far you can go in the leadership position. While you are still thinking about what action to take, you also discuss with yourself and others, who are close to you, if you have what it takes to lead others. In other words, you might think about your overall ability to motivate, inspire, direct, and delegate. You might even go deeper and ask yourself, can you be loyal to the organization and enforce the rules. You begin to wonder if you have what it takes to see those problems clearly enough to be a successful leader. Some say that it's hard to be a leader because you are the person who must understand people's attitudes and become a change agent to get things done.

As you continue to think about the decision you will make regarding accepting or not accepting the position of leader, another hard question comes up about your leadership style, in that just what kind of style will you adopt or try to emulate to be successful in your organization? What about your personal persona? Can you interact with others to the point of being called a people person? Can you plan effectively to get the job done? You may also recall in Chapter 2 that there are many styles to choose. However, there are some styles in which you must adapt oneself as the situation changes. Therefore, the next question to address is that are you able to change if the situation requires?

Then there are those emotions that Daniel Goldman speaks so passionately about and the role that they play in your leadership walk. Are you easily stressed to the point that you burn out and cause conflict in the organization or tend to overthink things, which affects your leadership walks? Can you communicate effectively to get the job done and do you have the charisma that Max Weber describes to move individuals to success? It is not enough to be popular and friendly in the eyes of a team. The bottom line is that you must know what you are doing, and this can be a technical nightmare. So your practical skills must be above reproach.

One cannot be insensitive, intolerant, impatient, cold, condescending, inefficient, impractical, ruthless, stubborn, reserved, and unreasonable to the point that it leads to conflict in the organization. We lead by example and by that way, it is okay to follow the golden rule regarding treating others like you want to be treated. Be optimistic and energetic about leadership. Learn how to prioritize and assert your authority with care. Put on the charm and be sensitive to the needs of others while inspiring and convening them that hard work pays off. Being honest and straightforward wins every time because people will learn to trust you. Now learn to trust them and lead.

The MBTI

Over a period of years, millions of people have taken the Myers-Briggs Test (MBTI). Scholars have even tested the validity of the MBTI using a variety of techniques. In one study that I found particularly attractive to the environment for which you are in concerns students at the undergraduate level. Published in the Journal of Psychological Type, DiRienzo, Das, Synn, Kitts, and McGrath (2010) did a study on the relationship between MBTI and academic performance across academic disciplines at Elon University which covered 6,260 students and here is a brief description as to what they found:

- **Communication**—A statically greater percentage of ENFPs were found in the communication discipline compared to the Elon student body.
- **Business**—A significantly higher percentage of ETSJs and ESTPs and a significantly lower proportion of ENFPs were found in the business area. However, in academic performance, ESTJs had a significantly higher average GPA, but ESTPs had a significantly lower GPA. It should be noted that the GPA of the ENFPs did not differ significantly from the average. Interesting was the fact that all four of the SJ types had statistically higher average GPAs, and all of the Thinking and Perceiving types had a lower average GPA, three of the four to a statistically significant degree.
- **Education**—The percentage of ESFJs was significantly higher in education, and this type had a statistically higher average GPA. Additionally, all Feeling and Judging types had a significantly greater average GPA, with five out of eight Perceiving types having a significantly lower average.
- **Fine Arts**—A significantly higher percentage of ENFPs and INFPs were found in Fine Arts, but neither model performed significantly differently from the mean GPA. Noted was the fact that all four of the Feeling and Judging types had a higher average.
- **Social Sciences and Hard Sciences**—In the Hard Sciences and Social Sciences, no dominant types were found, which seems fascinating. However, two Sensing, Feeling, and Judging types had statistically higher average GPAs. On the other hand, the Social Sciences had four Feeling and Judging types that had significantly higher average GPAs and all Thinking and Perceiving types had lower average GPAs, two of which were statistically lower.

The data from the school as a whole suggested that all four Introverted and Judging Types and all four Feeling and Judging types had statistically higher average GPAs. Moreover, six of the eight Perceiving types had significantly lower average GPAs, and Extraverted and Perceiving types had significantly lower average GPAs. So the finding at the school level was similar to the results at the academic level.

Another study which I found fascinating was the *Relationships between the Myers-Briggs Type Indicator Personality Profiling, Academic Performance and Student Satisfaction in Nursing Students.* Interesting enough, this study indicated that nursing students who were extroverts were more likely to be satisfied in the nursing program compared to those who were introverts (Kim & Han, 2014). Extroverts focus their attention on people and objects, thinking out loud, they orient themselves to the outer world and read and understand people in various social situations. Like most personality test, the MBTI has critics.

The MBTI has its critics and what is so interesting is the fact that most of these are psychologists who have reservations as to its reliability and validity. Although very popular with the business community, schools, churches, community, management and leadership workshops, as well as counseling centers, many see it as an invaluable tool for understanding their behaviors as well the behavior of others (Pittenger, 1993). Nevertheless, this author does not necessary agree with this assertion having used this tool throughout his career for that very purpose above. According to CAPT (2017), the MBTI was developed by Isabel Briggs Myers along with her mother, Katherine Briggs. However, it was Katherine Briggs who led the way after she became interested in type theory. However, this was after she reviewed Carl Jung's book on Psychological Type. Isabel Briggs Myers went on to develop a keen interest in the type theory and began to create the MBTI in the early 1940s as a test designed to be used for personnel selection. Myers believed that various occupations favored different personality types or orientations and that Jung's theory was the key to understanding the link between one's personality and job performance (Center for Applications of Psychological Type, 2012). The MBTI is very popular because of its use with licensed psychologists and counselors, as well as college instructors, and individuals who are certified to administer and interpret the MBTI.

Self-Leadership Journey

Several years ago, I read something about the fact that there is a difference between knowing who you are as a person. As we discussed earlier, great philosophers like Socrates and his dialogue Plato elaborated on the concept "Know Thyself." Socrates first introduces this concept in an attempt to tell one that if you want to enter the sacred temple, to know your place. In other words, an admonition

to those entering the holy temple to remember or be aware of their place. What is more intriguing is that "Socrates says, but I have no leisure for them at all; and the reason, my friend, is this: I am not yet able, as the Delphic inscription has it, to know myself; so it seems to me ridiculous, when I do not yet know that, to investigate irrelevant things." The irony here is that one must partake in a personal discovery of self before going into an organization and leading. Use your sociological imagination processes that you might have learned in your introduction to sociology course to help you facilitate this process.

As a leader, you must know how you are perceived. Although we have discussed this already, I want to entertain the notion here again for the simple reason that knowing who you are is critical at this stage. You need to strip away all personalities and get to the core of your essence. In other words, dismiss your false self-images and move on to better things in your life and center on the ones that make you great in the eyes of others. This chapter is designed to help you to accomplish this most important leadership task, which is leading self. As stated in Chapter 2, if you cannot lead self, how might you lead others? Bryant and Kazan (2013) suggest that we try these six things that will help to lead oneself:

1. Observe yourself.
2. Consider and reconsider the beliefs that are running you.
3. Practice imagination.
4. Correct and reward yourself.
5. Surround yourself with your likes.
6. Be prepared to make this decision, of being responsible for your life, every day (pp. 196–197).

Realizing that you are just one human being in this never-ending society we call the United States, get to know oneself. As you walk through your life journey, remember that we all have perfections and imperfections. At some point, you will make improvements, and that is okay which means you are on keeping yourself on track, moving toward your ultimate goal of success.

What used to be true may no longer fit your beliefs anymore, but remember you are required to guide your actions and behaviors. Nevertheless, if there is a problem with self, make a concerted effort to commit to change. However, always realize that you may not be the same person or the person you are now or want to be later.

Talk to yourself, reverse bad behaviors if need be. In other words, practice self-talk and speak to yourself as if you were talking to your best friend. Make sure that you instill a sense of pride and courage about your purpose in this life so go forth and make yourself proud of who you are and what you have become, always remembering that your priority in life is to lead self.

There is nothing wrong with celebrating your accomplished life journey goals, and as you travel various routes, you may come to a fork in the road, but remember leaders make decisions as to which way to go. Therefore, self-leadership also requires one to make decisions, and at the end of the day, it is you who recognizes just how effective and noneffective you might be in this life. You and only you have this power.

There is something to be said for being an eagle as opposed to a crow in that, like the eagle, you are charged to defend your territory. Study and learn new skills that help you to survive this complex society of ours. Don't hang around crows and remember that the things that may happen to you are your responsibility. In other words, it's about you now, and you cannot blame others for your mishaps.

Out of all of the above, number six seems to be the most important because it means making tough decisions about self. Life is a challenge, but it does not have to be if you face it head-on and with a sense of responsibility. Always push the slogan that "the best is yet to come."

With all of the problems in society, maybe it is time for people to become social entrepreneurs so that they may use self-leadership techniques to make better decisions as one attempt to solve problems and not depend on others to do it for them. Adam Smith once said that the "greatest improvement in the productive power of society" came from the "division of labor" in society (Bornstein & Davis, 2010). He argued that if one worker were to specialize on a narrow aspect of production, then all employees could later combine their efforts to produce many items at once. Smith's keen insight provided the theoretical framework for the industrial revolution. However, this assertion ignited fuel when in the early part of the 20th century, Smith's overall idea became widely applied in industry after Frederick Winslow Taylor published *The Principles of Scientific Management* which demanded factories maximized their production efficiency through narrow task allocation and enforced standardization of methods (Taylor, 1998). The division of labor influenced more than factory lines, and over time Taylor's principle took hold across society. The sense is that as specialization and atomization became the norm, people in different industries, professions, and sectors move farther apart, and even today, the bridges that link businesses, social organizations, and government agencies remain narrow and undertraveled (Bornstein & Davis, 2010). Various classes (upper, middle, and poor) are becoming further apart, and it is at this point for survival, one must take the responsibility to lead self. By becoming a social entrepreneur, a self-leader places himself or herself at the forefront of survival in society. Social entrepreneurs are creative combiners, capable of carving out spaces in a society that fosters complete solutions and if they specialize in anything it will be to bring people together who wouldn't merge naturally (2010). The overall purpose to bring people together is so that everyone will get to know each other better and each will make a concerted effort to help one another. This will ignite a social movement like never before, the social movement of self-leadership. The connection to self-leadership contributes to energize a social movement designed to solve social problems for self and others in society. There are great examples from the action-oriented Clinton Global Initiative which brings together not only business leaders, philanthropists, policy makers, and social innovators and gives the latter groups a prominent role, but also to the creation of President Obama's Office of Social Innovation in the White House, which is aimed at integrating the insights of social entrepreneurs into high-level policy making. This goes a long way toward solving a host of social problems in society through the integration of labor. Although social entrepreneurs work to shift mindsets about what is possible at the individual level, those who engage in the process of self-leadership make the task easier, and this is the primary reason why leadership centers first on leading self. However, it's not just becoming a social entrepreneur that will get you ahead; you must also understand the mechanics of making better decisions for self. Self-leadership is the ability of one to make good, solid decisions so that your self-leadership journey will be easier. As Bryant and Kazan (2013) asserts, self-leadership works whether you are an employee, manager, teacher, parent, or even someone who currently doesn't want to be defined by what you do, but it works because it is the foundation for being an effective human being living in a contemporary world. We do understand that leadership means to some extent taking charge of other people. However, self-leadership is taking charge of a cause and being in control of our actions, and this may mean calling others to action and doing the right thing and doing it well (Kresl, 2015).

Leaders make Decisions

During the earlier part of socialization, your parents are in charge, and at that time, they made the overall decisions in your life. When one gets older, he or she begins to take charge of their affairs or life and as an independent person made decisions. We all know that parents want their children to be better than them, and to facilitate that process, they tend to socialize toward that goal. This is not saying that they stop doing this when you grow-up and leave. Quite the contrary, they are always going to attempt to guide you in the right direction, but the question might be if you are willing to listen.

Decisions can be simple or complex. However, you must make decisions in this complex world. Understanding this is also part of the self-leadership process; you finally grew up and began to make those decisions, right or wrong, they are your decisions. Leaders make decisions, and this includes ones who decided to lead self. A decision is a result of choosing, and it's a choice made after considering a various course of action in a situation of uncertainty. According to Pellosniemi (2014), we make many decisions during our life, and most of them have few or long-lasting effects. The bottom line, drifting through life without actively taking charge of distinct situations isn't deciding. In my view, self-leadership is about making decisions that help you to be a productive member of society. Nevertheless, how can one be better about making decisions about self? Just like in a business enterprise, we are expected to make quick decisions, sometimes with enough information, to multitask and stay focused, to continuously learn and develop, to innovate and create, to be confident and motivated, and above all else, do this without any stress (2014). However, we also understand that with real information, we are more likely to make better decisions with better outcomes to guide our actions. In one aspect, you would be better off becoming a social entrepreneur and push decisions that center around a better course of action for your life.

> "What is important is seldom urgent and what is urgent is seldom important."
>
> *Dwight D. Eisenhower*

We have a tendency to wait for others or for some government action to solve the matter for us. Thereby, relieving us of the overall responsibility. This is not self-leadership. We are all decision-makers, both at work and in life, but it starts with us because right decision-making is fundamental to our success in life. However, we must address why decisions fail, and they do because of:

1. Built in human laziness
2. Differences of opinion are unwelcome or not accepted by others
3. Decision-making roles are unclear as to who has the power to decide and implement
4. We passively forget about the decision that we made, and it falls by the waste side
5. You failed to make a commitment to implement the decision

For a person who wants to excel in self-leadership attributes, the above cannot happen. Self-leadership is also being able to collaborate effectively with others. Collaboration is social interaction with others who might provide you with various input to not only solve the problem but may also give you information for you to make better decisions. Some may even call this social decision-making, which entails using information and knowledge in a social context to make better decisions about self. We must understand that it is self-leadership that guides these processes and this is critical. Dwight D. Eisenhower said it best in that "what is important is seldom urgent and what is urgent is seldom important." However, decision-making can help the self-leader find the essential and focus on what is most important. Hence, your wildly important goals and your wildly important decisions. Social decisions lead to the well-being of self, and you need to create a culture to help you in your endeavors while asking hard and uncomfortable questions, actually listening to others and respecting the diversity of opinions and insights received. So here is a big social decision that you can make right now and that decision center around you deciding to enhance your social skills.

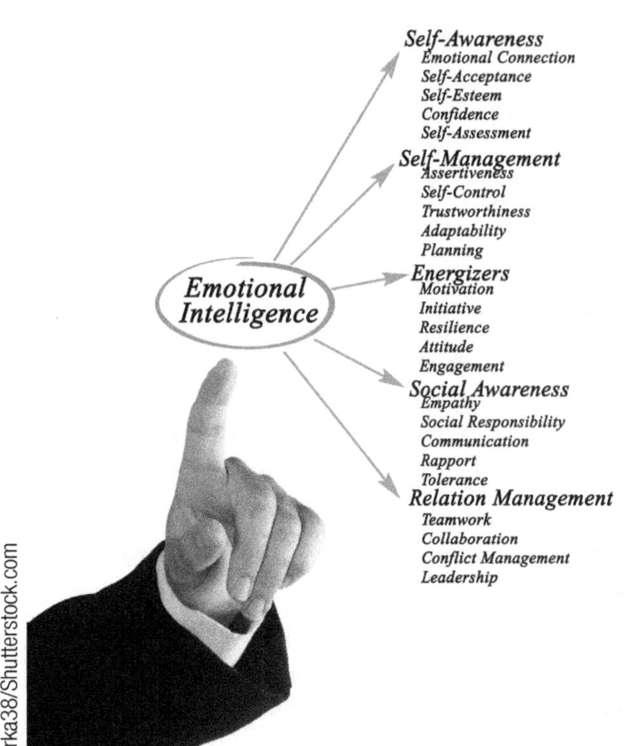

Social Skill

This part of self-leadership is critical. I met the great scholar Daniel Goleman doing his visit to the U.S. Department of Education in Washington, D.C. During that time, I was serving as the Director of Equal Employment Opportunity Services for the agency. I became intrigued about his explanation about the power of emotional intelligence and how this is more important than someone's IQ. He went on to speak about the responsibility of teachers to students and the ways in which they could help them to harvest this emotional intelligence and use it to the best of their ability. However, he also spoke about leadership's ability to do the same in that one must develop his or her social skills to support building their relationships with others. When I found out that he would be the speaker, I bought and read his book, and to my amazement, it seemed to resonate with me as I searched to understand more about my leadership skills and ability. You see during that time, I was working on my doctorate in strategic leadership, and as I began to get deeper into my studies, I wanted to review other's understanding as to what make leaders great. I like to think that I get it and one of the things that I get is that a leader will need to have excellent social skills if he or she is going to be active in leadership.

Not sounding corny here, but leaders are members of society who were socialized just like everyone else. However, for a leader to be successful, my argument is simple in that one must understand and use their social skills. A social skill concerns a leader's ability to manage relationships with others. Developing relationships is the key. Daniel Goleman identifies this power as a component of emotional intelligence and claims it is not a simple task to grasp. So exactly what is a social skill? Goleman (2004) tells us that it is:

1. Friendliness with a purpose, which is the ability to move people in the direction you desire.
2. Having a wide circle of acquaintances, finding common ground with people of all kinds for the express purpose of building rapport.
3. The culmination of the other dimensions of emotional intelligence (self-awareness, self-regulation, motivation, and empathy).

4. Adapting to managing teams and putting their empathy to work.
5. An expert persuader, a manifestation of self-awareness, self-regulation, and empathy combined.

Goleman (2004) goes on to say that at some point a socially skilled person may at times appear not to be working while at work, idly schmoozing, chatting in the hallways with colleagues, or joking around with individuals who may not connect to their real jobs. Not limiting the scope of their relationships, a socially skilled person will make a concerted effort to build ties with others with the understanding that he or she may need that connection later on down the road. As far as leadership is concerned, being socially skilled is crucial to most companies. For example, a leader who cannot express empathy may not have it all because social skills allow leaders to put their emotional intelligence to work (2004).

Chapter Summary

The concept self-leadership is just what it implies in that one must lead self to be successful in life. Believe it or not, you learned this as part of your socialization process which began with your parents. And it was during that period, your parents did all of the things for you. However, when you got older, you started to take on more responsibility for yourself, and this is all part of the socialization process. One of the essential elements of self-leadership development is that we break the cognitive code by understanding our ability to gather information and make decisions. Breaking the cognitive code helps in our quest to lead self. Although decisions can be simple or complex, don't be afraid to get it wrong. In other words, make decisions because it's your job to do so as a leader of self. Being a leader means that you must understand and use your emotional intelligence, particularly your social skills. If you have not already done so, review all the figures before completing the Leadership Skill-Building Exercise for Chapter 9.

Web Resources

16 Personalities

https://www.16personalities.com/

Celebrity Types

http://www.celebritytypes.com/personality-tests.php

References

Albrecht, S. L., Chadwick, B. A., & Jacobson, C. K. (1987). *Social psychology.* (2nd ed.). Englewood Cliffs, NJ: Prentice-hall, Inc.

Berens, V. L., & Nardi, D. (2013). Understanding yourself and others: An introduction to the personality type code. Retrieved from http://www.cognitiveprocesses.com/

Bornstein, D., & Davis, S. (2010). *Social entrepreneurship: What everyone needs to know?* New York, NY: Oxford Press.

Bryant, A., & Kazan, A. (2013). *Self-leadership: How to become a more successful, efficient, and effective leaders from the inside out.* New York, NY: McGraw-Hill.

Center for Applications of Psychological Type. (2017). The story of Isabel Briggs Myers. Retrieved from https://www.capt.org/mbti-assessment/isabel-myers.htm?bhcp=1

Center for Applications of Psychological Type. (2012). The story of Isabel Briggs Myers. Retrieved from http://.capt.org/mbti-assessment/isabel-myers.htm

DiRienzo, C., Das, J., Synn, W., Kitts, J., & McGrath, K. (2010). The relationship between MBTI and academic performance: A study across academic disciplines. *Journal of Psychological Type*, 70(5), 53–67.

Drenth, A. J. (2014b). *The 16 personality types: Profiles, theory, & type development (kindle edition).* Inquire Books.

Goleman, D. (2004). What makes a leader? *Harvard Business Review*, 1, 1–12.

Huetteman, L. (2012). *The value of core values: Five keys to success through values-centered leadership.* Valrico, FL: Fidelis SDG, LLC.

Kim, M., & Han, S. (2014). Relationships between the Myers-Briggs Type Indicator personality profiling, academic performance and student satisfaction in nursing students. International Journal of Bio-Science and Bio-Technology, 6(6), pp.1–12.

Kresl, E. (2015). *Self-leadership: The art & science of control.* Create Space Independent Publishing Platform.

Kosslyn, S. M., & Rossenberg, R. S. (2001). *Psychology: The brain, the person, the world.* Boston, MA: Allyn & Bacon.

Myers, D. G. (2011). *Psychology*. (10th ed.). Holland, MI: Worth Publishers.

Myers, I. B. (1995). *Gifts differing: Understanding personality type*. Mountain View, CA: CPP, Inc.

Nardi, D. (2005). *8 keys to self-leadership: From awareness to action.* Huntington Beach, CA: Unite Business Press.

Pellosniemi, J. (2014). *Social decision-making: The introduction*. Helsinki, Finland: Libris Oly.

Pittenger, D. J. (1993), Measuring the MBTI . . . and coming up short. *Journal of Career Planning & Employment,* 54(1), 48–52.

Quenk, N. L. (2009). *Essentials of Myers-Briggs type indicator assessment (essentials of psychology assessment.* (2nd ed.). New York, NY: John Wiley & Sons, Inc.

Taylor, F. W. (1998). *The principles of scientific management.* Mineola, NY: Dover Publications, Inc.

Chapter 9

Leadership Skill-Building Exercise

Values Audit

At some point during your leadership walk, someone or somebody is going to say what do you stand for and you will need to address this question with confidence. You might even ask yourself that question as situations arise in your life. You sincerely begin to think about values and which ones are more important. Although various groups and organization have core values, people also have the same core values, especially leaders and when they enter an organization to take charge, they may conduct something similar to a values audit to ascertain which values are going to set the tone for the organization. The primary reason we are doing this leadership exercise is so that you have a general idea of what values are and the role they might play in making you, not only a leader but also an overall better person in society. Always ask yourself, what you stand for when confronted with situations that challenge you to do things that have an impact on you and others under your control.

Remember that it is those core values that centers on how one must behave in society or the workplace. Core values don't change in that it shows where you stand as a person. We can associate core values with culture, the genuineness and passion people perceived when they talk about you as an individual or even a leader. The object of this exercise does not teach you specific values that you may adopt; the values audit is designed to help make you aware of your personally held values and attempt to compare then with others, as well as groups in society. I hope that as you increase your awareness of these commonly held values, you might come to modify poorly held values.
Student Handouts: Value Audit Activity Cards

Teacher/Student Instructions

Instructions

There are several ways the facilitator can accomplish this exercise. However, we will address only two that will center on a long and short version. First, let's talk a little bit about values. Values are critical, and it is clear that people need them more than ever before. Huettman (2012) states "our society these days seems to devote much less attention to the subject of character than it did in years past" (p. 64). She goes on to say as I do that it is a shame because it may be one of the causes why we are undergoing so many unfortunate lapses in business, government, sports, and other areas. However, I would explicitly add members of society to this debate. People in society need to have a set of positive core values that they can pass on to other generations. As far as business is concerned, many leaders do not know how to incorporate values into their daily procedures, and this too creates a big problem. I have to say that this is one of the main reasons why they have to bring in a consultant because of so much conflict, disorganization, and lack of effective communications in the workplace. What happens to us that many seem not to know what is right and wrong anymore? Our children are dying in the streets from killings or drug overdose and the question is why? Why can't we regulate self to the point that we emulate good core values or is it that they were never introduced by those who know? If you haven't heard, children are the future of society and if we don't get it straight now, we never will as we continue to move forward in society. We need to get back to the basics and the quicker we do this, the better. Here is another chance. So clarify your values so that we can do what we do best in that pass it on to individuals who would come after you; your children. Finally, as you participate in this exercise just remember that not all values are relative within the social context and therefore, we must combine positive values that we have learned from our family and the community as a whole and above all society in which the individual operates.

Long Version

Step 1. Give each participant five (5×7) cards and also tell them to take out a plain sheet of paper. Tell each member to review the list of values from the table below. From the list, tell then to write their ten (10) most important values or come up with other values and place no more than 10 on paper. As the facilitator, it is up to you if one can use other values that are not part of the original values in the table. Make sure you remind them that the definitions are subjective and somewhat arbitrary. Make sure that you tell them that they are not required to accept the value explanation. The value cards were adapted from **http://casaa.unm.edu/inst/Personal%20Values%20Card%20Sort.pdf.**

You may also go to the above site ahead of time and pull down those values and use them in the exercise. However, you will need to let the facilitator know that you have completed that action.

Step 2. Have each participant study the ten (10) cards they have chosen which they wrote on the paper. Using the five (5×7) cards, tell them to identify their top five values only and write one value on each card. The list of five values should be the ones that best represent the participant. Remember to tell them that it is okay to use values that are not part of the table. However, it is still up to you, the facilitator, to allow this action.

Step 3. Once everyone has identified their five values, you will ask them if they have a problem with sharing their values with other members of the group. If agreed, have them get up and begin discussions with their peers as to why they choose their particular values. If someone is uncomfortable with this action, have them sit this one out until everyone has had time to accomplish the task. However, it is important that all participate in that everyone should have something to say about his or her values.

Step 4. Everyone should have had a chance to take part in Step 3 and now with them back in their seats, have them separate their five (5) value cards into ethical and non-ethical values. They should have two piles. As the facilitator, be prepared just in case someone asks what the difference between ethical and non-ethical values is and have that ready.

Step 5. Next have each participant identify the value that needs the most work, In other words, identify the one that they do not mind sharing next to the person he or she is sitting in the room.

Step 6. Now narrow it down to just one clear value that you are willing to address as your core value. If all agree, hold that one core value up so that all can see as you walk around the room. If someone is uncomfortable completing this action, let them pass on this step.

When all questions are answered and actions completed, the activity should end. You may want to ask each participant that based on their core values, do they walk the talk as directed by their values? Please give us examples. See if others have identified similar values and ask them to discuss some examples that may demonstrate their value. Ask them to match their value up with members of society or leadership with examples. What if anything should change in your view?

Short Version

Step 1. Give each participant three (5×7) cards. Tell each member to review the list of values from the table below and only place one value on each card that represents their core value. Do not allow them to come up with values not displayed in the table.

Step 2. Once everyone has identified their three values, you will ask them if they have a problem with sharing their values with other members of the group. If agreed, have them get up and begin discussions. After this action, ask them to identify the one value that is most important to them. In other words, ask them to identify that one value that they care about the most.

Step 3. Have each share in the room what would happen if he or she were to give up that particular value. What would their life be like with values?

When all questions are answered and actions completed, the activity should end. You may want to ask each participant that based on their core values, do they walk the talk as directed by their chosen values? Please give us examples. See if others have identified similar values and ask them to discuss some examples that may demonstrate their value. Ask them to match their value up with members of society or leadership with examples. What if anything should change in your view?

Value	Definition
Acceptance	To be admitted to a group or organization; approval
Accountability	Being obliged to answer for one's own actions
Ambition	Eagerness or strong desire to achieve something
Authenticity	Quality of being genuine or real in the eyes of others
Challenge	To engage in competition; a test of one's ability
Conformity	Matching attitudes, beliefs, and behaviors to group norms or compliance with rules
Control	The authority or ability to manage; direct actions in your charge; regulate
Creativity	Being creative; various forms of originality; innovation
Dedication	The act of dedicating; making a commitment; promise or pledge
Diversity	Respecting and wanting difference and variety; multiformity
Empathy	The ability to understand, respect the experiences or motivation of others
Expertness	Displays a high degree of skill or knowledge in a particular field
Fairness	Being in accordance with the rules or just to all parties

Faith	Belief in God or religious doctrines; unshakeable/strong belief without proof/evidence
Flexibility	Responsive to change or susceptible to influence or persuasion
Freedom	The power to act, speak, or think without interference of others
Friendship	A friendly relation or intimacy; friends
Hardworking	Diligent in carrying out tasks, industrious, untiring or tireless
Harmony	Establishing relationships in which various components exist together without destroying others
Health	Overall soundness of body and mind or physical and mental well-being
Helpfulness	The ability to provide support, assistance, cooperation to others; lending an advantage
Honesty	Sincerity, truthfulness, a sense of integrity
Independence	The state of being independent; freedom from control or influences of another or others
Integrity	Character above reproach; adherence to moral/ethical standards; honesty
Justice	A sense of decency and moral rightness; fair treatment and just to others; conformity
Knowledge	According to Herbert Spencer, science is organized knowledge; awareness/understanding
Leadership	The ability to lead, provide guidance, and direction
Loyalty	The feeling or attitude of being devoted to a person, group, or organization
Morality	One who adheres to good standards of conduct; high ethical standards of what is right or wrong
Patience	The ability to handle inconvenience or endure hardship; tolerant and even-tempered
Power	The ability to act or do something effectively; exert one's authority; exercise control; political
Responsibility	Being accountable to a person, group, or organization
Risk-Taker	Enjoys taking risks; may result in loss or injury to yourself or the organization
Self-Respect	Due respect for oneself and one's character and conduct
Spirituality	Letting God be your CEO; believing in something higher than yourself

Value	Definition
Sociability	The ability to be sociable
Tradition	The handing down from generation to generation of the same customs or beliefs
Trustworthiness	Known for doing the right thing always; being answerable to someone for something
Wealth	To have plenty of money or desire monetary income
Wisdom	Ability to apply knowledge, experience, understanding, and use common sense/insight
Additional Values	

Leadership Skill-Building Exercise

FAIRNESS Being in accordance with the rules or just to all parties 1	**ACCOUNTABILITY** Being obliged to answer for one's own actions 2
FLEXIBILITY Responsive to change or susceptible to influence or persuasion 3	**SELF-RESPECT** Due respect for oneself and one's character and conduct 4
CONFORMITY Matching attitudes, beliefs, and behaviors to group norms or compliance with rules, standards, regulations, or laws 5	**HONESTY** Sincerity, truthfulness, a sense of integrity 6
HARDWORKING Diligent in carrying out tasks, industrious, untiring or tireless 7	**RISK-TAKER** Enjoys taking risks; May result in loss or injury to yourself or the organization 8
TRUSTWORTHINESS Known for doing the right thing always; being answerable to someone for something; responsible for one's conduct 9	**LEADERSHIP** The ability to lead, provide guidance and direction 10
FRIENDSHIP A friendly relation or intimacy; friends 11	**SOCIABILITY** The ability to be sociable 12
LOYALTY The feeling or attitude of being devoted to a person, group, or organization 13	**INTEGRITY** Character above reproach; adherence to moral/ethical standards; honesty 14
CREATIVITY Being creative; various forms of originality; innovation 15	**RESONSIBILITY** Being accountable to a person, group or organization 16

EXPERTNESS	EMPATHY
Displays a high degree of skill or knowledge in a particular field 17	The ability to understand, respect the experiences or motivation of others; recognize the emotional feelings of others 18
MORALITY/ETHICS One who adheres to good standards of conduct; high ethical standards of what is right or wrong; moral principles/character 19	**CONTROL** The authority or ability to manage; direct actions in your charge; regulate 20
SPIRITUALITY Letting God be your CEO; believing in something higher than yourself; having a constant awareness of the spiritual dimension of nature 21	**HARMONY** Establishing relationships in which various components exist together without destroying one another; structured relationship with all on one accord 22
JUSTICE A sense of decency and moral rightness; fair treatment and just to others; conformity to truth 23	**POWER** The ability to act or do something effectively; exert one's authority; exercise control; political, social, or economic control 24
KNOWLEDGE According to Herbert Spencer, science is organized knowledge; awareness/understanding gained through experience or study; the ability to know; facts or feelings 25	**FAITH** Belief in God or religious doctrines; unshakeable/strong belief without proof or evidence; trust in God 26
INDEPENDENCE The state of being independent; freedom from control or influence of another or others, self-sufficient to sustain oneself or family 27	**WISDOM** The ability to apply knowledge, experience, understanding, and use common sense and insight; to discern or judge what is true or right; articulate a wise course of action 28
HELPFULNESS The ability to provide support, assistance, cooperation to others; lending an advantage; a sense of concern for other's needs; outreach 29	**HEALTH** Overall soundness of body or mind or physical and mental well-being; freedom from disease or abnormality 30

CHALLENGE To engage in competition; a test of one's ability 31	TRADITION The handing down from generation to generation of the same customs or beliefs; specific practices of long standing 32
FREEDOM The power to act, speak, or think without interference of others 33	DEDICATION The act of dedicating; making a commitment; promise or pledge 34
SUCCESS Attainment of professional position; achieving goals or successful outcome of your endeavors 35	PATIENCE The ability to handle inconvenience or endure hardship; tolerant and even-tempered 36
ACCEPTANCE To be admitted to a group or organization; approval 37	AMBITION A strong desire to make things happen; eagerness for success, achievement, or distinction 38
AUTHENTICITY Quality of being genuine or real in the eyes of others 39	DIVERSITY Respecting and wanting difference and variety; multiformity 40

Value Audit Activity Cards Adapted from http://casaa.unm.edu/inst/Personal%20Values%20Card%20Sort.pdf

OTHER VALUE 41	OTHER VALUE 42
OTHER VALUE 43	OTHER VALUE 44
OTHER VALUE 45	OTHER VALUE 46
OTHER VALUE 47	OTHER VALUE 48

Sociology of Leadership

Chapter 10

- Leadership in Social Institutions
- The Sociological Perspectives
- The Institutions
- Does Strategic Leadership Matter?

As You Read

- Pay particular attention to the sociological perspectives associated with each institution.
- What is the impact of those who control the wealth of society and do you consider it as a perpetrator of social inequality?

Thinking Critically!

1. In your view, what are the major contributors to inequality in the United States and around the world?
2. To what extent should leadership be shared?
3. What is your view that the family maintains the economic system for the capitalists?
4. On the basis of your knowledge about society, do you believe that the insitution of family still serves as the leader for social and economic stability.

Chapter 10

Leadership in Social Institutions

Nothing in the world is more dangerous than a sincere ignorance and conscientious stupidity.

Martin Luther King, Jr.

In our examination of leadership in social institutions, we will use our sociological imagination to address the core social institutions, which are family, government (political), economy, education, and religion, because these seem to have the most effect on people in society. A social institution is very bureaucratic and complicated. However, one thing that connects these institutions from a sociological point of view is that they all have an integrated set of social norms and values. From a sociologist perspective, ***social institutions*** are systems and structures within society designed to shape the activities of groups and individuals. According to C. Wright Mills' sociological imagination, we can place a mental image in our mind to give us an understanding of the link between private and social concerns. We can do this by looking at what he called patterns or events of our own and that of society (Robertson, 1987). I also have to tell you that leadership has an impact on everything and this includes the social institutions of society. However, when it comes to national policy, strategic leaders can affect how society operates as a whole.

The Sociological Perspectives

The ***structural factionalism perspective*** would argue that social institutions provide critical functions for the needs of society and this helps to maintain order and unity. For example, a functionalist's theorist will say that the family contributes to the social stability of society by performing essential functions such as reproduction, socialization, and social status. Functionalists look at society from a macrosociological level. ***Conflict theory*** will state that social institution, to include education, religion, and politics, represents the interests of those in authority and thus creates and maintains inequalities in society. In other words, by controlling the means of production, these social institutions help to keep those who have the overall power, property, and privilege in place. Like the structural-functionalism perspective, conflict theory also looks at society from a macrosociological level. When it comes to ***symbolic interactionism***, social institutions are created through individual participation that gives meaning to and is part of the everyday experience of members. For example, symbolic interactionist theorists would focus on meanings that people give their religious experiences, especially how they use symbols as a means to conduct rituals or shared beliefs designed to forge a community of like-minded people. Symbolic interactionism sees society from a microsociological level.

The Institutions

Institution of Family

The family is a typical social group in society that consists of one or more parents and children. According to sociologists, a family is one whose members are related by blood, marriage, or adoption (Ferris & Stein, 2014; Henslin, 2017; Macions, 2005). The family is a sort of kinship which provides for the needs of the group. They also share goals and make long-term commitments to one another by caring and sharing a familiar history that is passed on from various generations. However, it is the parents that socialize their children and provide emotional support. The parents also provide other needs to facilitate the well-being of the family.

Structural-Functionalism

Simply, the family is a social structure designed to support member's needs. Ancestors pass traditions down, and these carry over from generation to generation. Overall, the family helps to bring about stability in society. Therefore, the family structure is good.

Conflict Theory

This perspective has a lot to say about the family because as Karl Marx would say that economics is the primary cause of conflict within the family. This battle ensues because of different interests between groups (for example, wealthy and poor). Korgen and White (2015) suggest that relations among family members and even the average size of families are influenced by changes in the economic system. They go on to say that it is the family that maintains the economic system of capitalists. Of course, this is Marx argument because he feels that with the "owners" in control of the means of production, the "workers" have to work hard to secure resources and this causes conflict between the two. You might recall in Chapter 2, Marx would say that the owners are the leaders in these corporations for which the poor work. This does n't mean that there is no conflict between husband and wife. There is conflict, and the reason is that the traditional patriarchal family structure also worked to perpetuate the capitalist economic system because it allowed men to devote themselves to making money while wives took care of them, their children, and their home, for no pay (2015).

Symbolic Interactionism

For the most part, we can argue that gender inequality is exposed here, because as far as the family is a concern, duties and responsibilities were instilled with the family structure through socialization.

Moreover, although conflict theorists use a macrolevel approach to see the connections between families and economic system for that matter, symbolic interactionists use a microlevel analysis to focus on how institutions influence the roles men and women play and the status they assume in the family (Korgen & White, 2015). Families have changed and continue to change. For example, people are not getting married, and those that tend to have fewer children. In another twist for the family structure, same-sex marriages are taking place as a result of a ruling by the Supreme Court. Same-sex marriages will no doubt have a long-lasting effect on the family structure. By the way, more women are now working outside the home like never before, and this is because you will find that single family moms are running the household without what had come to be known as a home with both parents. In regards to intimate relationships, Schaefer (2009) suggests that sociologists look at the microlevel of family and other intimate relationships and how these individuals interact with one another, whether they are cohabiting partners or longtime married couples. I agree, because basically we are looking to examine all types of relationships that make up a family. Moreover, we should understand that based on family structures today, they might not involve any relationship by blood, marriage, or adoption.

The Leadership Connection

Every institution needs leadership, and the family system is no different. Of all social institutions, the family is the most important. The family leadership sets the example for their children and provides the emotional support needed for productive members of society. Galbraith and Schvaneveldt (2005) suggest that real leadership is not only required in organizational settings, but it is also necessary to families. They also assert that although families are in need of a well-functioning executive subsystem, once in place, families hold the key link for establishing an emotional environment and a family culture favorable to growth for the person and the family as a whole. If the family is not saddled with real leadership, then there is a risk of no connection to the community as a whole. As a result, it is the family well-being that will be in jeopardy. However, there is also other data that signals the importance of the role leadership plays in the family.

In a cross-sectional study, the researcher used transformational leadership style to address parenting within families for assessing adolescent health-enhancing behaviors. The overall goal was to examine the cross-sectional relationships between parents' transformational leadership style and adolescent dietary and activity behaviors. Morton, Wilson, Perlmutter, and Beauchamp (2012) found that family transformational parenting behaviors were positively associated with both healthy dietary intake and leisure-time physical activity levels among adolescents. They further state that family leadership procedures may be necessary reasons for adolescent health-enhancing behaviors, and offers support for the utility of transformational leadership theory as a viable framework for understanding the role of parents. I agree in that this is just another example of just how important leadership is in society. I must also note that two separate hierarchical regression analyses were performed on the entire data (n=822 for dietary behaviors and n=798 for physical activity behaviors) (2012). The use of transformational leadership style in the family institution brings some creditability as to the importance of sociology of leadership.

Political Institution

This institution is called government, but for our purposes, we will say politics or political. The institution of politics sets norms in a means to bring order to society. These norms are regulated by those who have power and authority in society with the understanding that Federal government has three branches: Executive, Legislature, and Judicial. This institution takes the lead in enforcing the laws, establishing new legislation, and interpreting the laws of society. Norms are laws that are there to protect members of society. This is the institution that governs society by executing formal authority over us all.

Sociological Perspectives

Functionalists will state that the political institution is there to provide another piece of the pie for a stable society. As such, it is charged to protect members of society from external threats or enemies. They will argue that defining goals and establishing norms is part of a normal process of this institution. Just one part of the puzzle so to speak is to maintain society's equilibrium. As you may already know and understand, conflict theory takes another view of the political institution, which is that the laws or policies that are enacted invite inequality. Those in charge of this establishment have the power and are clearly associated with those who control the means of production which is used to hold the workers down who has less power. Spearheaded by Karl Marx thinking, you may recall he hates capitalism. Now here comes symbolic interactionism position on the political institution. Using Weberian analysis, we might say that the political establishment has the legitimate authority to use force to stabilize society when it feels something is out of control.

The Leadership Connection

The leadership connection is simple in that using an analogy from above, we might state that the President, who is the leader of the free world, has the legal authority to deploy assets to regulate society. Leaders of Congress also have the power to enact laws to help society as a whole. In other words, it is through their leadership that public policies are enacted from legislative laws.

Institution of Economics

This institution is used to set norms regarding commerce. In other words, the economic institution regulates the production of goods and services. As a result of globalization, significant changes in this system continues to evolve. The institution allows members of society to consume products and services through various control mechanisms. It has a well-established division of labor. Society is suffering from what I will call economic insecurity, and this may be more evident in the urban areas. Cohen and Kennedy (2000) add that we are living in a time of social exclusion and economic marginality and this may be perpetrated by the fact that many people around the world, not just the United States, are engaging in multiple and fluctuating forms of low-paid employment, community or family support, and semi-criminal activities. This might be a good description for solving the problems that are going on in the great city of Chicago, which in 2010, took over as the murder capital of the United States.

In 2013, CNBC reported that the top 1% controls 39% of the world's wealth and in their view, this is not going to change anytime soon in that it will get worst. In other words, the rich just keeps on getting richer. Can this be a major contributor to inequality around the world? Korgen and White (2015) suggest that inequality among nations is related to what each contributes to and takes from the global economy. They also assert that Global North nations (most postindustrial countries such as the United States, Western European nations, and Japan) mainly contribute service work in the knowledge economy, with high-skilled workers, whereas those in the Global South nations (e.g., most Latin American, Africa, Middle Eastern, and Asians nations) tend to produce raw materials or provide cheap labor to produce the goods consumed in Global North countries. I want to say that they hit the "nail on the head" therein that I wholeheartedly support this conclusion, and it is the one reason why the jobs are going South, and many working class people in the United States are suffering. Let me be clear in that as suggested by Korgen and White (2015), growing levels of economic inequality can be seen within Global North nations. However, in the United States as a whole, inequality has increased steadily for the past 20 years, as middle and lowers classes have lost jobs and income and the very wealthy have gained greater income. The bottom line is that sociologists think of the economy as the distribution of goods and services for the benefit of society.

Sociological Perspectives

The functionalist perspective would concentrate on the roles people play in various economic institutions and claim that it is the roles that are necessary for the economic establishment to operate correctly. It is the economy that helps to make society possible. Karl Marx would state that the economic institution is designed to regulate those who have not or the poor so that others will continue to get rich through their capitalist ways. He calls it the haves (bourgeoisie) or in some aspects the economic elite versus the haves nots (proletariat), whereas the haves use their wealth and power to influence and exploit the have-nots in society. According to Marx, those that own the means of production will continue to control the major economic features of society for the benefit of the wealthy. Symbolic interactionists profess that the economic institution is just another workplace to be interpreted, designed to address the meaning of their work.

The Leadership Connection

When most people think of economics, they tend to focus in on financial institutions and the role they play with members of society. For example, families depend on this institution to help them finance big ticket items (house, car, etc.), but they also expect them to guard their money when they save for retirement. The link to society is evident. People trust, for the most part, those leaders who are in charge of banking institutions to do right for them. Lately, this has not been the case. There are some financial institutions' leaders who have purposely tried to defraud consumers. There are other examples of the car industry whom leaders knew in advance that parts of the car were unsafe.

Still they chose to allow those vehicles to leave the assembly plant dangerous because of greed. And, let's not forget the leaders associated with the housing crisis. A sure sign of bad leadership is when those that are willing to charge minority groups more for the purchase of their homes compared to others or letting people who buy houses for which they could not afford, all for the greed of money. For the most part, this has placed a stain on leadership at these organizations. Leadership guides all of this and thus creates a problem for many in society.

Richard Rawlinson wrote this remarkable article for Booz & Company called *Leadership Lessons and the Economic Crisis: Where We've Come From and Where We're Headed.* What caught my eye is that he presents an argument for a change in the character of leadership and advocates that this change must complement structural and process change in the rebuilding of our companies and our economy. He states that leadership and management practices of financial institutions have been discredited. The norms and values of these organizations must change if society is going to get back on track of "doing the right thing, at the right time, for the right moment" (Ross, 2008). I also like the fact that he feels more diversity among the ranks is a good thing, and an approach may also be needed to recognize the power of the collective social environment to strengthen some social and public virtues as a counterweight to the inevitable human bias toward self-interest. The self-interests or selfishness of greed is what got many leaders in trouble in the first place.

Institution of Education

The educational institutions provide for the needs of members of society through formal and informal education. The official way to acquire knowledge or skills, this institution helps to facilitate our socialization process by transmitting culture and values so we might function in society with a sense of responsibility. The overall purpose of education is social integration, social placement, social and cultural innovation, and of course, facilitates the socialization process. The institution also prepares us for professional roles in society and evaluates student's success.

Sociological Perspectives

The functionalist perspective feels that education serves to fulfill society's various needs as discussed previously. The education institution uses formal processes to help us to subscribe to a set of beliefs and cultural values that in most cases are mandated by society. Although conflict theorists suggest that these formal processes promote social inequality, they also feel that various funding levels throughout society differ and this causes another ripple effect that reinforces inequality. Well, in the end, those who are rich or bourgeoisie will have no problem going to the elite schools, and this will facilitate them getting the best jobs as a result of their education and once again triggering what conflict theorist's state is an inequality in society. However, one thing that must be noted is the fact that there are some who are poor that receive their education at the elite or Ivy League universities based on their merit in various high schools across society. The symbolic interactionism perspective concentrates on social interactions in the schools, which, according to them, have an impact on the development of gender roles. Overall, this is about a teacher's expectations designed to address educational problems that may come up in the school. The theorists from this perspective tend to address his or her concerns by observing or discussing the interaction between the teacher and the student.

The Leadership Connection

Leadership is designed to influence others, and as far as the institution of education is concerned, there is no difference. However, every time a new administration takes over the Federal government, they appoint a new leader; the Secretary of Education who implements the new policies of President of the United States. These new policies have a direct impact on society as a whole. For example, during the George W. Bush administration we had "No Child Left Behind," and for Barack Obama, the policy was "Common Core." These national educational systems were designed to promote best practices under national leadership policy.

Institution of Religion

This institution helps to move us closer to the supernatural and sacredness to the point that we are unable to explain. In other words, it provides an explanation for the unexplained natural phenomena. Because it provides for the normative structure of society, this helps to control the natural world. Although not associated with regular laws, many churches expect its members to adhere to religious codes, rituals, and the sacredness of God and the church. You may recall the argument between Karl Marx and Max Weber as to what holds society together. For Marx, it was economics whereas, for Weber, it was religion. Moreover, in Weber's famous work *The Protestant Ethic and the Spirit of Capitalism,* his argument is clear in that it is a religion that broke tradition and brought about capitalism. Marx likened religion to drugs in that he called it opium of the people because if taken, it helps one to forget their misery. A uniformed set of beliefs, it is a religion that promotes norms associated with how one should live in society.

Sociological Perspectives

Piggybacking on what Emile Durkheim once said, it is a religion that promotes social solidarity, and this provides what he called a sense of meaning for our lives. Overall, it is through religion that creates a social bond for us, reinforcing social norms, and giving us social unity and stability. This helps to motive members of society so that they will work toward positive change. Anything less signifies dysfunction in society. Just like the other social institutions, for conflict theorists, religion promotes and reinforces inequality. It is religious differences in society that promote social conflict. I have to tell you that we can see this all over the world, the hostility and violence that continues to sacrifice many in the Middle East and elsewhere. The interpretation of one's religion experiences belongs with the symbolic interactionalism theorists. They suggest that our religious experiences are not holy or sacred unless we say so because of the meanings we place on them. There must be some special significance that gives rise to the various religious meanings in people's lives.

The Leadership Connection

The argument continues in that as with all social institutions, there has to be leadership. The church is no different. The person in charge of the church is there for a reason, and that is to guide members to belief in something higher than themselves for the betterment of not just the church, but in many cases for society as a whole.

Does Strategic Leadership Matter?

There was a remarkable study on national leadership since World War II that asked the question do leaders matter? What was so interesting about the study is that it talked about some of the institutions we are discussing in this chapter. We must understand that when one speaks about national leadership, we talk about leadership at the strategic level. In others words, strategic leadership. So let's flip the script a bit and not say do leaders matter, but ask does strategic leadership matter? According to Lussier and Achua (2001), ***Strategic Leadership*** is the process of providing the direction and inspirations necessary to create and implement a vision, mission, and strategies to achieve and sustain organizational objectives. However, Ross (2008) adds that it is also individuals and teams enacting strategic leadership when they think, act, and influence others. We need to recognize that this goes a long way to promote and sustain the competitive advantage of an organization. A strategic leader will not last long if he or she is not able to forecast the future. Therefore, one of the most significant tasks of a strategic leader is direction setting, creating a future for the organization, and this cannot be done if he or she is not able to accurately forecast or anticipate the future (2001).

As far as leadership is concerned, there was a significant study designed to look at several countries to understand their economic growth across decades. The study addressed just how effective these strategic leaders were at the national level and saw if changes in those societies were specifically the result of growth. For example, one result indicated that in the United States, incumbents were much more likely to be reelected during economic booms than during recessions (Jones & Olken, 2005). Good point in that Presidents Bill Clinton and Barack Obama were reelected handily do in part to the economy being on the right track. Both of them served two terms (8 years) in the White House. There is another indication when it comes to the amount of power that a leader has nationally. Specifically, the research indicates that a leader's effects appear more pronounced when they have fewer constraints on their power (2005). There are also indications that policies might change when changing or the death of a national leader. The formation and articulation of strategic policy at the national level are the responsibility of a strategic leader. Although the study found substantial effects of leaders on monetary policy, changes in other areas like fiscal and trade policy were unclear. Overall, the report indicates:

1. On average, leaders have detectable, causative impacts on national growth.
2. Leaders do have an effect on monetary policy.
3. There are mixed results on trade and fiscal policies.
4. There are no effects on security policy.

On the basis of this study, there is evidence to support that there is a substantial causative influence on the economic outcomes of national leaders and there are unyielding effects when one is an autocratic institution compared to a democratic institution (2001).

In a related study that was conducted in 2011, it looked at the impact of educated leaders after reviewing data on approximately 1,000 political leaders between the years 1875 and 2004. During this study, researchers specifically investigated whether having more education as a leader affects the rate of economic growth. According to Besley, Montalvo, and Reynal-Querol (2011), it is considered one of the most robust findings in empirical research on leader education and economic outcomes. Their research does indicate that not only is leadership necessary for economic growth, but those leaders who are educated generate higher growth for their economies. The bottom line is that a leaders' characteristics seem to be important in explaining outcomes in society, particularly economic outcomes. In the end, strategic leaders do matter, particularly at the national level where they are in a position to have an impact on economic growth. However, you also must remember they have an impact in other organizations. Sometimes called the CEO or Chief Executive Officer, you may recall that they control the institutions charged to do good, yet in some aspects did wrong to consumers.

Chapter Summary

The social institutions provide for the basic needs of its members, socializing us as to the proper norms and values of society. They are used to promote social values, engage in the process of socialization, and establish patterns of social behavior and institute social control measures to facilitate social order. One sole responsibility is that these institutions help to provide roles in society. Social institutions also talk to one another in an attempt to help members of society advance in their everyday life. Therefore, your family makeup, the laws you are required to obey, your career and schooling, and even believing in a higher power are all based on these social institutions that are run by society. However, one must understand that none of the above happens without, in this case, strategic leadership.

Glossary

Social Institutions Systems and structures within society designed to shape the activities of groups and individuals.

Strategic Leadership The process of providing the direction and inspirations necessary to create and implement a vision, mission, and strategies to achieve and sustain organizational objectives

References

Besley, T., Montalvo, J. G., & Reynal-Querol, M. (2011). *The Economic Journal*, 121(554), 205–227.

Cohen, R., & Kennedy, P. (2000). *Global Sociology*. New York, NY: New York University Press.

Ferris, K., & Stein, J. (2014). *The real world: An introduction to sociology*. (4th ed.) New York, NY: W. W. Norton.

Galbraith, K. A., & Schvaneveldt, J. D. (2005). Family leadership styles and family well-being. *Family and Consumer Sciences Research Journal*, 33(3), 220–239.

Henslin, J. M. (2017). Essentials of Sociology: A down-to-earth approach. (12th ed.). Boston, MA: Pearson.

Jones, B. F., & Olken, B. A. (2005). Do leaders matter? National leadership and growth since World War II. *The Quarterly Journal of Economics*, 120(3), 835–864.

Korgen, K. O., & White, J. M. (2015). *The engaged sociologist: Connecting the classroom to the community.* (5th ed.). Thousand Oaks, CA: Sage Publications, Inc.

Lussier, R. N., & Achua, C. F. (2001). *Leadership: Theory, application, skill development.* Australia: South-Western College Publishing.

Macions, J. J. (2005). *Sociology.* (10th ed.). Upper Saddle River, NJ: Prentice Hall.

Morton, K. L., Wilson, A. H., Perlmutter, L. S., & Beauchamp, M. R. (2012). Family leadership styles and adolescent dietary and physical activity behaviors: A cross-sectional study. *International Journal of Behaviors Nutrition and Physical Activity*, 1–9.

Robertson, I. (1987). *Sociology.* (3rd ed.). New York, NY: Worth Publishers.

Ross, L. F. (2008). *So you want to be a strategic leader: Here are the essentials to get you started.* Philadelphia, PA: Xlibris Publishers.

Schaefer, R.T. (2009). *Sociology: A brief introduction.* (8th ed.). New York, NY: McGraw-Hill.

Chapter 10

Leadership Skill-Building Exercise

Servant Leadership

Servant Leadership Exercise 1

Robert K. Greenleaf is considered the father of servant leadership. His central premise is that a leader must be a servant first in order to lead others. He went on to describe 10 unique characteristics of servant leadership, which we have discussed briefly in Chapter 2. These features include listening, empathy, healing, awareness, persuasion, conceptualization, foresight, stewardship, commitment to the growth of people, and building community. Jesus expresses the greatest example of servant leadership. He stated very clearly that if one wants to be in charge, they must first be a servant to all. The Bible teaches us for even the Son of man did not come for someone to serve Him, but to serve, and offer up His life as a ransom for many.

Practicing servant leadership is the key to being a great leader. If we begin to exhibit the characteristics of servant leadership, we are well on our way to becoming great. The next series of exercises are designed to help you become aware of the roles servant leadership plays in society, organizations, and elsewhere in the world with the hope that you too may lead by this excellent example.

Who Makes a Difference?

Step 1. On an index card or piece of paper, participants will write information to address the following:

1. Name five most influential people in history.
2. Name the last five NBA championship winners.
3. Name the first five Presidents of the United States.
4. Name five US representatives.

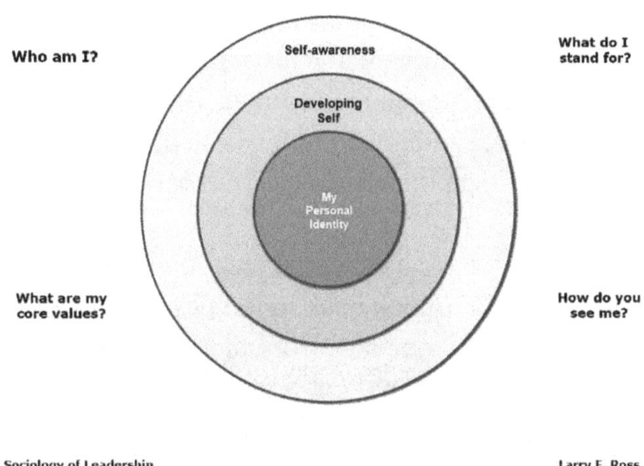

Step 2. Discuss how each participant did in exercise.

Step 3. On another piece of paper, participants will write information to address the following:

1. List two teachers who had an impact on you in school.
2. Name two friends who helped you during a tough time.
3. Name three people who have taught you something worthwhile.
4. Identify someone who made you feel special.
5. Give us a sense of who you like to spend time with and this can be family, friends, or others?
6. Who inspires you to be successful? Name your heroes!

Step 4. Discuss which one was easier for the participants.

> **Note:** There are lots of people who have made a difference in your life. Some were not rich or had the most credentials or awards. They were there when you needed them to be there, and that is important. At the end of the day, they cared enough to help you be successful in your endeavors.

Always say thank you!

Source: Adapted from Http://www.pittsburgareachamber.com/Portals/0Session%206%20-%20Service %20%Servant%20Leadership.pdf

Servant Leadership Exercise 2

Becoming a Servant Leader

Step 1. Using what you learned in Chapter 2 on servant leadership, this task is to identify servant leadership skills in others. Therefore, for as long as your instructor assigns you to this task, go to various establishments (Home, school, Target, Wal-Mart, CVS, etc.) and see if you can identify the ten characteristics of servant leadership skills in others. Write what you have found on index cards of paper and be prepared to present to other participants what you learned.

Step 2. Remember the following when engaged in this activity in that servant leaders:

- Listen with great care and concern for others.
- They will choose to walk in other people's shoes and will not reject them for who they are in society. Strives to understand and empathize with others.
- Makes an effort to help or heal others and make them whole, to include self.
- Awareness of ethics and values as integrated into a holistic position.
- They rely on persuasion rather than the positional authority that may coerce someone into compliance.
- To dream great things, one must have a conceptualization of day-to-day realities.
- A servant leader has the foresight to look back in the past to move forward toward the future.
- Having enough stewardship to serve the needs of others. Openness and persuasion are the keys to success for servant leaders and not one's ability to control others.
- They make a concerted effort to commit to the growth of people in society or their institution.

- A facilitator of human lives, the servant leader seeks to identify areas that help to build a community and then set out to show the way.

Step 3. After attempting to identify these characteristics in others, write them down for later use with others. Remember, putting other's first must be a way of life for servant leaders.

Step 4. At some period after that, the instructor of this event will hold an initial discussion on the results of both exercises.

Source: Adapted from Http://www.pittsburgareachamber.com/Portals/0Session%206%20-%20Service%20%Servant%20Leadership.pdf

© Ollyy/Shutterstock.com

Chapter 11

- Leadership in Diversity
- Dealing with Differences and the Generation Gap
- The Value of Diversity
- Leadership Connection

As You Read

- Remember the Golden Rule!
- What would you do to enhance diversity?
- What can dominant groups do to foster diversity? Again, think about what can you do?

Sociology of Leadership

Thinking Critically!

1. We must learn how to manage diversity and engage in diplomacy.
2. What is the relationship between compliance with legislative acts and valuing diversity? Explain.
3. Describe someone you know who has been discriminated against which violates EEO laws. Without details, let's discussed without divulging any names.
4. Why, in your view, is it important to value diversity?
5. In your view, how can recommendations for employment equity for people with disabilities be helpful in ensuring equity for other non-dominant group members?

Chapter 11

Leadership in Diversity

© Rawpixel.com/Shutterstock.com

You must admit that over the past few chapters, we have seen leadership being addressed in many ways. Scholars and practitioners have defined and approached this concept from many angles and now it is the time to entertain the relationship of leadership and its connection to diversity. In the preceding chapters, I made a concerted effort to review leadership from a micro level to a macro level, centering on various diverse theories and paradigms and in a sense emotional aspects of leadership through the lens of intelligence. These leadership paradigms can also be used to address another challenge in society, the stereotypical views of leadership. People with diverse backgrounds understand leadership in different ways. I don't think that I have to tell you this, but I will in that if we are able to bring some light to where people with diverse backgrounds are coming from with this debate, others just might open their eyes to change instead of dismissing diversity all together as if it does not exist. Just like the massive information leaders require to being successful, understanding the ins and outs of diversity is no different.

London and Wueste (1992) posit that leaders need to understand the many things they can do to manage diversity and support women and people of color. Although we are sitting at the beginning of the 21st Century, we still have problems with inequality and discrimination not only in society, but in organizations as well. Any suggestions or actions taken by leadership to address these serious problems will go a long way toward success in a leader's endeavors. The U.S. population continues to become increasingly diverse. Yet, women and people of color remain underrepresented in leadership positions across this country. Having served and retired from Federal service, leader representation of women and people of color at the Federal level is lacking. In an article published by *The New Republic*, it reports that every level of government is suffering from a serious woman problem. Vinik (2014) addresses this issue in his article by saying that men make up 80% of the Senate and 81% of the house with two black and four Hispanic senators. Although he claims that the lower chamber of congress is no better, his report goes deeper in that it's suggested that this discrepancy is prevalent across all levels of government. This supports and may go a long way to enhance Karl Marx's old argument. Simply, he would claim that the most leaders in society are white males, capitalists, and members of the bourgeoisie (example congress), and those who are poor or the proletariat are under the control of them. Arguments from both sides create conflict and perpetrate inequality in society because of the bourgeoisie owning or controlling the means of production. Although most poor people in America are white, what does this do to Marx's argument; you be the judge. Use your sociological imagination and think about this matter clearly. Looking at the data outlined in the research from this reporting indicates that white male dominates elected office from the Federal down to the county level in this country (2014).

In a somewhat related, according to the report by Creamer (2012), asking why are women underrepresented in corporate America four decades after the feminist revolution. She looks at America's leadership in the biggest corporations (Fortune 500). The survey, conducted in late September 2011 by Catalyst, indicates that there is one woman for every six men and this basic ratio hasn't changed in six years (2012). This report also taps into the equal pay for equal work argument generated by women. The argument put forth here is that men hold power and the United States remains a male-dominated society (2012). In my view, more diversity might go a long way to solve some of these problems and remember that we all have the ability to bring something to the table. Diversity enhances an organization to be successful. However, more than that, it helps the organization to maintain its competitive advantage and easily positions the organization for the future. No matter how you put it, diversity is a strength that needs to be used by an organization to succeed. Therefore, society as a whole must begin to have serious discussions not only on race and culture, but also on diversity and inclusion. When we speak of diversity, remind yourself that it's more than just race or gender in that it is also about differences between the generations. There are problems brewing in this area as well.

Dealing with Difference and the Generation Gap

Traditionalists (Born before 1940)	**Baby Boomers (Born 1940–1960)**	**Generation X (Born 1960–1980)**	**Millennials (Born 1980–2000)**	**2020 Generation (Born after 2000)**

We have marshaled in a new era with the introduction of the 21st Century and this has brought about changes in society. However, alone with that came the millennials into the workplace. A new generation seems determined to do things their way and people are asking why? Ross (2008) states that "generational diversity is the latest focus on diversity and this seems to be a new and growing problem for leaders" (p. 87). Currently, there is four generations operating in the workplace. However, as you can see from the table above, soon to debate is the 2020 generation. Just like the problems associated with the generations in the workplace now, what can we expect with the 2020 generation once they arrive on the scene and take over various different occupational roles in the workplace? So who are the generations?

The traditionalists, sometimes called the silent generation were born before 1940. Apart from the "Great Depression" and the World War II heroes, they were part of an era that respected authority and appreciated things. This generation regarded interpersonal communications as a key to success, and they believed in personal sacrifices to be successful in life. They are about civic duty and understand that one must go up the chain for decisions and they call this hierarchy leadership. The baby boomers came on the scene during 1940–1960. They are driven when it comes to one's work ethic and appear to be more optimistic about the world around them. Their view of authority lies in the love and hate spectrum. They believe in consensus when dealing with others and require all to act as part of a team. Leadership for them is a consensus. On the other hand, we have generation X who appeared during the years of 1960–1980. When they arrived and started to appear in the workplace, they were skeptical and in some cases distrustful about the future. Somewhat reluctant to commit to a relationship, this is the generation who center on self and has a tendency to leave others out of the equation. However, they view leadership as being competent to accomplish the mission of the organization. Millennials made their appearance during the period 1980–2000 and like the traditionalists feel that one must have a sense of civic duty in order to accomplish things in life. I like the fact that they are ambitious and think of authority as polite. Unlike some members of the older generations, they have an appreciation for diversity and inclusion and are considered, for the most part, tech savvy. On the basis of the Millennials overall socialization, they are considered the most educated generation to ever come into the workplace. Leadership for them is about achieving the goals of the organization as set out by the leaders and one must be loyal in their relationships in order to make that happen. Now, here comes the 2020 generation, sometimes called generation C or Z, born after 2000. Like the millennials, they will be more advanced in technology. However, one thing is for sure in that they will also be socially well connected and can operate in a fast-paced environment with ease. Friedrich, Peterson, Koster, and Blum (2010) call these individuals "digital natives" and claim that they will transform the world as we know it and they may have a point. What is so striking about their comments is the claim that their interests will help to drive massive change in how people around the world socialize, work, and live their lives, using information and communication tools to do so. I would be the first to say that the things that are on the street today will quickly become obsolete just as before when we ushered in a new century.

As the younger generation moves into leadership positions, there will be arguments and conflicts, because it is the older generations who will resent those moves. The question for organizations is how do they recruit and maintain an effective leadership cadre that is loyal and dedicated to the mission of the organization? Knowledge is power and for the most part, prior wisdom is king. Nevertheless, organizations need change and these companies must look like the members they serve and this is where diversity and generational understanding comes into play here. Therefore, the need for cross-generational leadership may be the answer. In other words, organizations must find unique ways to recruit, train, and retain talent. It is the future talent of the organization that will position themselves for leadership positions.

The Value of Diversity

Founded on the central beliefs of justice, equality, and inclusion, this nation, continues to strive for full participation and equality for all citizens. America is a multicultural society devoted to inclusive participation in our democracy, laws, and social policies that have developed over time to reflect this commitment. We hear from time to time that we must value other people's difference in society. We must do the same when it comes to those working in organizations. Organizations draw its leadership from members, not only in society, but also from within the company. For years now, demographic trends have indicated that minorities and women are the fastest growing segments of the workforce (Chin & Trimble, 2015; Connerley & Pedersen, 2005; Williams, 2013). We also note that organizations that draw their leadership from within usually send those members to informal and formal training. Although organizations understand the importance of diversity, focusing on the laws that protect race, ethnicity, sex, race, religion, nationality, and social orientation, many only play lip service to these requirements. We need to recognize that diversity training works twofold: (1) to encourage what I call a diversity of thought; and (2) training to enhance the culture so that members will understand that leadership places a high value on the importance of diversity in the organization.

A diversity of thought helps the organization develop new ideas and approaches for the sole purpose of positioning the organization for positive change. This overall transformation is specifically designed to facilitate an organization's social change. You see an organization that must feel a sense of responsibility to change the way it thinks toward diversity. Social change has the ability to modify the organization's behavior and attitude. Social change also helps to articulate the values of inclusions and fairness so that members know where the organization stands on diversity. Perception is something else and that is why people intuitively assess the culture of the organization just to see if it values diversity or play lip service to it as I stated above. In other words, let's not just tolerate diversity, we need to recognize it for what it is worth which brings value to the organization as well as to the people it serves. Having served as the diversity chief for several Federal government agencies, I understand well that this might be hard for some organizations, but understand that there are legal ramifications for not obeying Civil Right Laws. Facilitating small-group interactions is just one example that an organization can use to create a positive environment. Let's be clearer in that diversity is very important for the organization and a failure to support it will affect the organization's performance in at least three ways:

1. If an organization does not value diversity, then it may overlook the most competent people for the positions with the organization.
2. Given the demographics in most countries, especially in the United States, the population for consumers and industrial buyers is increasingly represented by people from protected categories. Simply having people from groups similar to these diverse consumers and buyers in important organizational positions may provide a competitive advantage.
3. If employees from protected categories feel that they are not valued, this perception will likely affect morale, leading to diminished productivity (McLean, 2006, p. 264).

Consider the questions in Table 11.1 and discuss with your instructor.

United States is considered the most diverse country in the world and this is what makes America great. Organizations that understand and manage diversity effectively are able to achieve outstanding performance in their quest to be a leader in their field.

Table 11.1

Generations Interview
1. What generation do you consider yourself a member of?
2. What do you like about your generation?
3. What do you wish other generations knew or understood about your generation?
4. Do you feel all your work-related talents and skills are used on the job?
5. What challenges do you face at work that may have to do with your generation?

*Source:*Adapted from Raines (2003).

Theoretical Perspectives

There continues to be patterns of inequality in society. Stratification is the unequal distribution of goods and services and in its basic form continues to divide society by social classes because of the resources each demands. Karl Marx, the political, economic, and social philosopher continues his argument that the source of inequality in society is the system of economic production run by the capitalists. The bourgeoisie- and proletariat-associated problems (class struggle and social conflict) as suggested by Marx still stand here. Max Weber, as you recall, disagreed with Marx, because he felt it was more centered on one's wealth, property, and income. In addition, if one had prestige and the power to influence others, he or she has an impact on the decision-making process of society. This gives a person the ability to protect one's self-interest and achieve his or her goals. You can get this source of power by being active in a political organization. For example, we discussed earlier that white males seem to control this process by holding most elected offices in congress. However, this power can also come from labor unions or other pressure groups that lobby state and Federal legislatures. I also should not have to tell you that with great wealth, one may use their riches to promote their causes. For example, many powerful rich person's formed Political Action Groups to collect funds to help their candidates for the recent election that just passed (2016). Some groups were effective while others were not. Now, there is Gerhard Lenski, a contemporary sociologist, who followed Weber's idea of property, prestige, and power. The short story is that this is the nature of inequality, the degree of inequality or the specific criteria affecting a group's position, and it is closely related to subsistence technology, the means by which the society satisfies basic needs such as hunger and thirsts (Healey, 2012).

Leadership Connection

In regards to diversity, we find that there are many challenges for leaders practically when it comes to organizations. Leaders in organizations must figure out how to embrace diversity so that they can maintain a competitive edge. Therefore, the leadership connection is clear in that leaders are responsible for addressing the problems associated with diversity. Leaders must understand the complex structural barriers that give advantage to some and hinder others. Leaders are the gatekeepers who must bring equity to the organization. We use diversity to empower people and this makes the organization effective by accepting, respecting, and using the differences in every person associated with the group. By using a synergy effect, the leader is able to create a competitive advantage over those organizations that are using persons acting alone.

The Challenge

When we were born, we began to learn our environment and this created a certain bias or prejudice. As we got older, environments grew to include not just family, but also friends, peers, teachers, idols, and various reading materials, designed to influence us on what is right or wrong in society. Deeply rooted within us, these things tend to shape our perceptions about how we view things in society as well as how we respond. As new information comes forward, out biases serve as a filtering lens as to what makes sense in a world that is so complex. Simply, diversity is not just black, white, male, female, gay, straight, Jewish, Christian, young or old, extrovert, introvert, fast or slow learner, controlling or people type, and conservative and liberal. Organizations do not need people fighting and disbelieving other members, because it's the right thing to do for all, up and down the ranks. Although attitudes are hard to change, organizations can turn to those soft skill training events that are designed to address our feelings or emotions that influences our actions. The great thing to take from these training events is that we can change a person's attitude. Two social psychologists, Wells and Petty (1980), conducted an experiment and proved such a point. They were able to do this with an experiment using students to address what would be fair to raise tuition rates. In the end, the research revealed that motor responses (nodding or shaking) of their head tended to signal agreement or disagreement with the rising of tuition. Sometimes, the challenge will be to change the attitudes of members, but this is the responsibility of leadership, and how he or she does it makes all the difference in the world.

Chapter Summary

Founded on the central beliefs of justice, equality, and inclusion, this nation continues to strive for full participation and equality for all citizens. America is a multicultural society devoted to inclusive participation in our democracy, laws, and social policies have developed over time to reflect this commitment. The overall partaking of people of color and the infusion of diverse expressions and involvements into decision-making practices ensure a sense of cultural competency and efficiency within policy-based results to social issues. Leaders are charged to ensure that all people participate in decisions that surround social issues, especially ones that have an impact on society as a whole. Managing and leveraging diversity gives leaders an edge so that he or she will be successful in all their endeavors.

References

Chin, J. L., & Trimble, J. E. (2015). *Diversity and leadership*. Thousand Oak, CA: Sage Publishing, Inc.

Connerley, M. L., & Pedersen, P. B. (2005). *Leadership in a diverse and multicultural environment: Developing awareness, knowledge, and skills*. Thousand Oaks, CA: Sage Publications, Inc.

Creamer, B. (2012). 14 percent: Why are women under represented in the C-Suites corporate America? *Hawaiibuiness*, 1–2.

Friedrich, R., Peterson, M., Koster, & Blum, S. (2010). The rise of generation C: Implications for the world of 2020. Strategy&: PwC, 1–24, Retrieved from http://www.strategyand.pwc.com/media/file/Strategyand_Rise-of-Generation-C.pdf.pdf

Healey, J. F. (2012). *Diversity and society: Race, ethnicity, and gender*. (3rd ed.). Thousand Oaks, CA: Pine Forge Press.

London, M., & Wueste, R. A. (1992). *Human resource development in changing organizations*. Westport, CT: Quorum.

McLean, G. N. (2006). *Organization development: Principles, process, performance*. San Francisco, CA: Berrett-Koehler Publishers, Inc.

Ross, L. F. (2008). *So you want to be a strategic leader: Here are the essentials to get you started.* Philadelphia, PA: Xlibris Publishers.

Vinik, D. (2014). Report: Every level of government is suffering from a serious woman problem. *The new Republic*, 1–2.

Wells, G. L., & Petty, R. E. (1980). The effects of overt head movements on persuasion: Compatibility and incompatibility of responses. *Basic and Applied Social Psychology*, 1, 219–230.

Williams, D. A. (2013). *Strategic diversity leadership: Activating change and transformation in higher education.* Sterling, VA: Stylus Publishing, LLC.

Chapter 11

Leadership Skill-Building Exercise

Authentic Leadership Skill-set

Authentic Leadership Skill-Set

I can't think of anything better than appearing to be real and authentic to others. As Ross (2008) asserts, no one can look into the mirror and claim to be authentic on their own in that others have to see you that way. George (2003) states that leadership is authenticity, not style, and this person must lead a balanced life to appear to be real and genuine with others. Karl Marx would quickly say that it is the leaders who are the capitalists and they own and control the means of production, while the proletariats are held in place by low wages. What if we could flip the script? The question would be if those leaders are willing to do the right thing and if so, I don't think that Marx would have a problem with supporting the need for those leaders being held in high regard. However, for leaders held in high esteem, they should lead with a purpose, exhibit good core values, integrity, and be good stewards for not just the organizations but also the workers they serve. The workers might see them as being authentic, real, and genuine. I just don't think that this is hard for a leader to accomplish even with the complexities of the twenty-first- 21st cCentury organizations.

Step 1. The Leadership Skill-Building Exercise is designed to assess your authentic leadership potential regarding the four components of self-awareness, internalized moral perspective, balanced processing, and relational transparency. There are no right or wrong answers. The questionnaire below contains statements about Authentic Leadership potential. Using the scoring system below, you are asked to place a checkmark in the box that represents how you feel about each statement:

- Totally Disagree (1)
- Mostly Disagree (2)
- Neutral (3)
- Mostly Agree (4)
- Totally Agree (5)

As with previous exercises, you will want, to be honest in that this tool is only as good as the quality of your answers. You do not have to be in a leadership position to complete this exercise. You may still be able to relate these questions to something similar in your environment.

	Authentic Leadership Skill-Set	TD	MD	N	MA	TA
1.	I am prepared to list and share my three greatest flaws.	1	2	3	4	5
2.	My activities reveal my core values.	1	2	3	4	5
3.	I seek out others' views in advance before making decisions.	1	2	3	4	5
4.	I willingly share my emotional state with others.	1	2	3	4	5
5.	I am prepared to list and share my three greatest gifts.	1	2	3	4	5
6.	I do not permit team stress to dominate me.	1	2	3	4	5
7.	I employ active listening skills to monitor the ideas of those who think differently from me.	1	2	3	4	5
8.	I expose myself to others so they distinguish who I truthfully am as an individual.	1	2	3	4	5
9.	I welcome criticism as a way of accepting who I am as an individual.	1	2	3	4	5
10.	Individuals know where I stand on contentious matters.	1	2	3	4	5
11.	I never highlight my own viewpoint at the expense of others.	1	2	3	4	5
12.	I seldom present an "untrue" position to others.	1	2	3	4	5
13.	I take responsibility for my own state of mind.	1	2	3	4	5

Author Index

Subject Index

NOTE: Page references in *italics* refer to figures

About the Author

Larry F. Ross, DSL, is a sociology professor, currently serving at South Louisiana Community College in the Division of Liberal Arts and Humanities. He is the author of two books: *So You Want to Be a Strategic Leader: Here are the Essentials to get you Started* and *Leadership: So What Makes You Think You Can Lead*, as well as several articles. Retired U.S. Army officer, he has held leadership positions for over 36 years, which include several Director Positions in the Federal government. His various interests include leadership and sociology. However, he also has an active interest in diversity management and criminology. He holds a doctorate in strategic leadership from Regent University, Master's from Southern Illinois University—Edwardsville in sociology, and a Bachelor's degree from the University of the State of New York in liberal arts.

CPSIA information can be obtained
at www.ICGtesting.com
Printed in the USA
LVHW062227100720
660271LV00001B/6